Richard Henry Clarke

Lives of the Deceased Bishops of the Catholic Church in the United States

Volume 2

Richard Henry Clarke

Lives of the Deceased Bishops of the Catholic Church in the United States
Volume 2

ISBN/EAN: 9783741114472

Manufactured in Europe, USA, Canada, Australia, Japa

Cover: Foto ©Lupo / pixelio.de

Manufactured and distributed by brebook publishing software (www.brebook.com)

Richard Henry Clarke

Lives of the Deceased Bishops of the Catholic Church in the United States

LIVES

OF THE

DECEASED BISHOPS

OF THE

Catholic Church

IN THE UNITED STATES,

WITH AN APPENDIX AND AN ANALYTICAL INDEX.

BY RICHARD H. CLARKE, LL. D.

Author's Revised, Enlarged and Corrected Edition.

VOL. II.

NEW YORK:
RICHARD H. CLARKE, Nos. 49 & 51 CHAMBERS STREET.

1888.

TO

Our Holy Father,

PIUS IX.,

WHO DEFINED THE DOGMA OF
THE IMMACULATE CONCEPTION OF THE VIRGIN MOTHER;

WHO CONVENED THE ŒCUMENICAL COUNCIL
OF THE VATICAN, AND DEFINED THE DOGMA OF
PAPAL INFALLIBILITY;

WHOSE PROLONGED PONTIFICATE HAS BEEN
A TRIUMPHAL PROCESSION
FROM CROSS TO CROSS, AND FROM CROWN TO CROWN;

WHOM HISTORY WILL CALL PIUS THE GREAT·

THESE VOLUMES ARE REVERENTLY DEDICATED BY HIS
DEVOTED SON IN CHRIST,

The Author.

CONTENTS OF VOL. II.

A.D.*		PAGE
1834.	Right Rev. Simon Gabriel Bruté, First Bishop of Vincennes....	7
1835.	Right Rev. William Clancy, Coadjutor Bishop of Charleston, afterwards Bishop of Guiana.............................	44
1835.	Most Rev. Anthony Blanc, Fifth Bishop and First Archbishop of New Orleans..	58
1837.	Most Rev. John Hughes, Fourth Bishop and First Archbishop of New York...	73
1837.	Right Rev. Mathias Loras, First Bishop of Dubuque...........	126
1838.	Right Rev. Richard Pius Miles, First Bishop of Nashville......	147
1840.	Right Rev. Francis Garcia Diego y Moreno, First Bishop of California...	157
1841.	Right Rev. John Mary Joseph Chanche, First Bishop of Natchez.	166
1841.	Right Rev. Peter Paul Lefevre, Coadjutor Bishop of Detroit....	191
1842.	Most Rev. John Mary Odin, First Bishop of Galveston, Sixth Bishop and Second Archbishop of New Orleans.............	203
1844.	Right Rev. William Quarter, First Bishop of Chicago..........	240
1844.	Right Rev. Andrew Byrne, First Bishop of Little Rock.........	264
1844.	Right Rev. William Tyler, First Bishop of Hartford...........	272
1844.	Right Rev. Ignatius Aloysius Reynolds, Second Bishop of Charleston...	291
1844.	Right Rev. John Bernard Fitzpatrick, Third Bishop of Boston...	310
1847.	Right Rev. John Timon, First Bishop of Buffalo...............	337
1847.	Right Rev. John S. Bazin, Third Bishop of Vincennes.........	370
1848.	Right Rev. James Oliver Van de Velde, Second Bishop of Chicago and Second Bishop of Natchez.......................	372
1850.	Right Rev. Bernard O'Reilley, Second Bishop of Hartford.....	391
1850.	Right Rev. Francis Xavier Gartland, First Bishop of Savannah..	408

* The dates given in the Table of Contents refer to the years in which the Bishops were consecrated.

Contents.

A.D.		PAGE
1851.	Right Rev. Joseph Cretin, First Bishop of St. Paul............	415
1852.	Right Rev. John Nepomucene Neumann, Fourth Bishop of Philadelphia...	431
1853.	Right Rev. Frederic Baraga, First Bishop of Marquette and Saut St. Mary...	468
1853.	Right Rev. George Aloysius Carrell, First Bishop of Covington..	505
1854.	Right Rev. Josue Maria Young, Second Bishop of Erie.........	514
1857.	Right Rev. Henry Damian Juncker, First Bishop of Alton......	529
1857.	Right Rev. Clement Smyth, Second Bishop of Dubuque........	536
1857.	Right Rev. John Barry, Second Bishop of Savannah............	551
1858.	Right Rev. John Henry Luers, First Bishop of Fort Wayne.....	555
1865.	Right Rev. Peter Joseph Lavialle, Third Bishop of Louisville...	586

APPENDIX : I. Right Rev. Edward Barron, Vicar-Apostolic of Liberia 595

II. Right Rev. Charles Augustus Mary Joseph de Faubin-Janson, Bishop of Nancy, France................. 601

III. Cardinal Cagetan Bedini, Archbishop of Thebes, Papal Nuncio... 605

ANALYTICAL INDEX 613

THE LIVES

OF THE

Deceased Bishops of the Catholic Church

IN THE UNITED STATES.

RIGHT REV. SIMON GABRIEL BRUTÉ, D.D.,

*First Bishop of Vincennes, A.D. 1834.**

THE admirable character and invaluable services of Bishop Bruté present to us a rare history in actual life. While his virtues and sentiments flowed from the purest and sweetest fountains of heavenly inspiration, his life and actions were in the most perfect sympathy with his fellow-men. With learning the most varied and profound, he united the most child-like simplicity and humility. In the midst of the most active and laborious duties he always could find time for study, and was never too much engaged to do an act of charity, to assist others in their laudable efforts, or to render a service to his neighbor. As a minister of religion, as a professor, as a friend, as a ruler in the Church, his example is a model for imitation. As a priest and Bishop, he tenderly loved his

---

* Authorities: *Memoirs of Bishop Bruté*, by Rt. Rev. Bishop Bayley; *Funeral Oration of Dr. Bruté*, by Rev. John McCaffrey; *Life of Mrs. Seton*, by Rev. C. I. White; *Life of Bishop Flaget*, by Archbishop Spalding; etc., etc.

flock, and spent himself for their good; deeming his time well applied that was devoted to the promotion of their happiness and eternal salvation, or to the assuaging of their griefs and relieving their necessities. The humblest child or beggar shared in his unbounded kindness, equally with the more favored and honored members of his flock. To all he was a true pastor and father.

Simon Gabriel Bruté de Remur was born March 20, 1779, at Rennes, the capital of Brittany, in France. According to the pious custom of Catholic countries, no time was lost in bringing him to the regenerating waters of baptism; he was baptized early on the following morning at the parish church of St. Germain. His parents were in affluent circumstances, his father being Superintendent of the royal domains in Brittany, with a promise of the succession to the first brevet of Farmer-General of the Revenues at Paris. The prospects of the family were, however, blasted by the untimely death of Mr. Bruté, who left his affairs in an embarrassed condition, by reason of his kindness and indulgence to others. He allowed persons to become indebted to him to more than a million of francs. Advised by friends and lawyers to renounce the succession to his estate, Madame Bruté, following her own energetic views, and preferring an honorable name to wealth, assumed the management of it, even at the sacrifice of her own property; and succeeded, by close application to the task, in greatly reducing the losses, and in paying her husband's debts.

Guided by the home instructions and example of such a mother, and directed by such a spiritual father as the celebrated Abbé Carron, his heart became deeply imbued with religious impressions from his earliest years. The vivid and grateful memory with which he cherished these impressions, the recollection of his first confession, his studies of Christian doctrine, his first prayer-book, which he sacredly preserved for many years, the sacred pictures he received, and especially his first communion, were evidences, throughout a long life, of the good and lasting effects of early Catholic education. In after-life, when writing his " Remembrances" of these early incidents, he closes an account of his first communion by exclaiming: " I thank thee, O my God, for the state of innocence and piety I was in the day I performed this most important act;" and again, "My heart is full when I think of that day—thanks! thanks! O my God!"

At school he was, though very young, an attentive student; earnest in his studies, conscientious in his conduct, cheerful and generous in his nature, frank and gentlemanly in his deportment, winning the friendship of his preceptors and companions. With a memory that enabled him, through life and amidst the most engrossing cares, to relate minutely all that he had ever seen or heard; with a lively imagination that enabled him to perceive and enhance the beauties of both the spiritual and the external worlds; and with a close application that enabled him to overcome all difficulties, he became a ripe and accomplished scholar. Commencing with the primary school, and progressing through the intermediate classes up to the college of his native town, he was in each of them a thorough student. He became familiar with the Latin and Greek languages; in the former he recited from memory whole chapters from the classics, and in the latter he pursued the study of the Fathers of the Church. He was well versed in literature, and recited even in his old age, and with ease, all the fables of

Lafontaine, and entire scenes from Racine and Corneille. Music and drawing were judiciously interspersed with his severer studies, and in the latter he acquired a proficiency which he used in after years in delineating the scenes and incidents of the French Revolution, and in illustrating his descriptions of his early life. He also received, as a preparation for the French Polytechnic School, which he once thought of entering, a thorough course of mathematics. When the French Revolution destroyed the Catholic schools at Rennes, he followed up his studies assiduously at home.

It was at this period of his life that young Bruté witnessed, in his own native city, scenes that made an indelible impression upon his heart, and tended, in a great measure, to form and ripen in him those splendid traits of character which were the ornaments of his life: scenes which we cannot read of at this distant day without sickening with horror at their atrocity. He was a spectator of the worst enactments of the French Revolution, and, thanks to the teachings and example of a good mother, and the directions and counsels of holy priests, his young heart passed through the fiery and bloody ordeal of the "Reign of Terror" unscathed and unsullied. Twenty-five years afterwards he described the scenes he witnessed when a boy, and illustrated them with drawings from his pen, with such minuteness and accuracy, as to show how keenly alive he was to the sympathies and endearments of the occasion. He witnessed the defection of friends, schoolmates, neighbors, and even ecclesiastics, from the line of duty; and he saw some, whom he had known and respected, carried away by the prevailing passion and becoming the willing and cruel, but, as he charitably thought, the deluded instruments of the revolution in the persecution, banishment, and murder of their former friends. His gentle heart, instead of becoming callous from familiarity with human woe, sufferings, and death, became doubly sensitive to the impressions of sympathy, generosity, and love, and so practised in acts of human and Christian benevolence and tender charity, that these became through life his daily habit and study, and were the ornaments and charm of his noble character. His mother's house was frequently the refuge of holy priests hunted down by the demons of the revolution, when to harbor them was punished with death; and young Gabriel has himself described the pleasure it gave him to serve them, and the happiness he felt in their society. It was his habit to visit, relieve, and comfort them in their secret asylums and prisons; and oh! with what fervor would he kneel at their feet and make his confession, and receive absolution from those who, perhaps on the morrow, received the scarlet robes and jewelled diadems of martyrdom in heaven! Drawn by his sympathy and protected by his youth, he was a constant attendant at the trial of saintly priests and religious before the revolutionary tribunals at Rennes, and on his return home could repeat every word to his mother, so deeply did the harsh words of the revolutionary judges and the gentle but courageous words of the victims sink in his heart. There he saw condemned his preceptors, his relatives, and his pastors, and was the gentle messenger that conveyed the news of their fate to absent friends and relatives, who dared not be seen in the dread tribunals. There he saw the victims, forgetful of their own danger, fervently defending the innocence and pleading for the safety of their fellow-victims. Following an aged priest, and the three noble sisters who had harbored him, as they passed beneath his window, amidst the cries of the mob, "*à la guillotine!*" he stood, during their trial, leaning on the back of the venerable martyr's chair, and almost touching his snowy locks with his hands. How touchingly he describes the scene: "During the whole time," he writes of this case in his *Notes*, "Mr. Raoul was engaged in prayer. Methinks I can still hear the sounds, and low, little swellings of his prayer—some of the Psalms, it seemed like the Latin final or syllable, rising, from time to time, in a half-suppressed murmur—whilst the jailer or executioner (for he was always present) was putting on the handcuffs, and securing them so tight that I remember the priest gave signs of uneasiness, and looked at the man as if entreating him not to screw them so tight." On another occasion, while seated at his studies at home, he heard in the distance the notes of the "*Libera me Domine*," from the burial service of the Church, a chant which had long ceased to be heard, as of yore, in the streets of Rennes; the sounds grew more distinct and were mingled with the rapid tramp of feet, as the soldiers hurried on their victim. "I understood it all," he writes, "and ran to the door to go out and follow them, agitated and partially frightened with the usual terror which rested on my heart, but at the same time animated by the song of death, for it was the priest who was thus singing his own *Libera*." Many were the scenes like these he witnessed. The prisoners were usually guillotined within twenty-four hours after their arrest; and finally the soldiers, in the rural districts, used to pursue and shoot them on the spot, without trial or condemnation. He saw the sacred shrines at which he worshipped from his tenderest years, and where the God of love reposed, desecrated; all Christian traditions and customs abolished; and the Lord's day obliterated, and in its stead the heathen festivals of reason and of love substituted.

The reverses of his family's fortunes had compelled his mother to open and conduct a printing-office, a business with which she was probably well acquainted, as she was, at the time of her marriage to Mr. Bruté, the widow of Francis Vatar, who had been "Printer to the King and Parliament at Rennes." In the height of "the Terror" his mother made him work in her printing-office, to save him from being enrolled in a regiment of children fourteen, fifteen, and sixteen years of age, called "The Hope of the Country;" and he says that he thus became a pretty good compositor. The schools, such as it was proper for him to attend, were closed; but this did not prevent him from zealously pursuing his studies at his mother's house, any more than the closing of the churches and the slaughter of the priests prevented him from attending to his daily exercises of devotion in the secrecy of that chapel-home, or from the practice of every virtue in the limited and persecuted society in which he moved. Dr. McCaffrey, in his admirable *Funeral Oration*, thus eloquently describes this portion of young Bruté's life:—

"But what is most important, and especially for the young to observe, is this: that while he zealously devoted himself to the pursuit of knowledge, he was equally and still more zealous in the pursuit of virtue; while he prepared himself by laborious study to render service to his fellow-men, he never forgot that higher service which he owed to God. His virtuous parents, and especially his mother,—a woman of admirable character, a parent equally enlightened and affectionate,—had inspired his heart in childhood with sentiments of tender piety. She laid all her hopes of his usefulness and happiness on the only sure foundation of religion. She had taught him in times which tried the souls of Christians, to be always ready to lay down his life for the faith, to shed his blood, if necessary, for the love of God. France was then, by her own terrific example, teaching the world a great moral and religious lesson. Her revolutionary rulers had proscribed Christianity, and made infidelity and impiety the law of the land. History has told us the horrors that ensued. While this unhappy country was deluged with the blood of her best and noblest sons; while the cross was torn from its elevation and trampled in the dust; while churches were pillaged and desecrated, and the faithful obliged, as the primitive martyrs, to meet in silence and darkness, at the risk of their lives, for the celebration of the divine mysteries; while the priests who had not been exiled or guillotined were hunted as wild beasts, shot down in the fields, hung to the lamp-posts, or reserved for the slow tortures and solemn mockeries of judicial murder; the prisons were everywhere crowded with those who were too noble-minded to conceal or abjure their faith; and these heroic sufferers were refused the consolations of religion, or could receive them only from such as were willing to stake their lives upon the charitable mission. Simon Gabriel Bruté, then but a boy of tender years, with a full knowledge of the risk he ran, and with his fond mother's hearty consent, was employed to convey the Blessed Sacrament to the prisoners in his native town of Rennes. In the disguise of a baker's boy, protected only by his innocence and premature discretion, or rather by his good angel, who fondly bore him company on such errands,—he supplied the victims of persecution not only with that bread which nourishes the body, but with the bread of angels, the food which gives life to the soul. He made his first communion in the parish church of St. Germain in 1791, and the scenes of horrible impiety and bloody persecution which he witnessed soon afterwards, but confirmed his faith and animated his piety. He saw and shared the apprehension, the alarm, the secrecy and danger, with which God was worshipped and his mysteries dispensed to the faithful: he saw, and as we have mentioned, he sympathized with heroic confessors imprisoned and exposed to death for their attachment to religion; he saw the sanctity of the cloister sacrilegiously invaded, and helpless nuns, who had hoped to spend their days in retirement and prayer, cast out upon a heartless world by ferocious monsters, who professed to be the friends of liberty and humanity; he saw the procession of venerable priests, and heard them chanting in solemn harmony the '*Miserere*' and '*De Profundis*,' as they marched, a noble band of martyrs, from the tribunal of injustice to the place of execution; he saw numbers of innocent victims of every class led as lambs to the slaughter, because of their unwavering allegiance to the faith 'once delivered to the saints.' Thus familiar in his early years with the elevating spectacle of religion triumphant over suffering and death, his soul was nerved for heroic deeds of virtue, and he understood and felt in its full force the exclamation of St. Paul: 'Who shall separate us from the love of Christ? shall tribulation? or distress? or famine? or nakedness? or danger? or persecution? or the sword? . . . . In all these things we overcome, because of Him that hath loved us.'"

The benevolent leanings of Mr. Bruté's nature, and his habitual desire to serve his fellow-men, directed his choice of a vocation in life. The great preponderance of religious ideas and tastes in his character and education would most certainly have led him to embrace the holy ministry, with its devotions, sacrifices, deeds of charity, and sublime ends, above all others. But that career was closed to him and others in France at that time, and he selected that profession in which it seemed to him he could most benefit humanity. With these views he entered the Medical College of Dr. Duval, an eminent surgeon of Rennes, February 10, 1796. After two years well spent with Dr. Duval, in laying the solid foundation for the noble profession he had chosen, he went to Paris in 1799. "Though trained to piety betimes," says Dr. McCaffrey, "and accustomed to regard religion as a pearl above all price; though even in the very morning of life he had girded himself for mortal conflict, with a courage not unworthy of the martyr's crown, yet had he need of all the deep impressions graven on his soul, and of no ordinary strength of mind, and of a fortitude which heaven only could bestow, to pass with principles unshaken and piety unimpaired through the medical schools of the French capital." While the professors were violent disciples of the prevailing infidel philosophy, the students were steeped in licentiousness. Atheism and Materialism were peculiarly prevalent among the medical schools; man was made the strict and mere material subject of science—God, his Creator, was excluded from all recognition: death was regarded as his annihilation, and neither hope nor fear was conceded to him beyond the grave. The pride of the human heart is but too apt to lead those engaged in the study of the physical sciences, to see only the material before them, with whose admirable structure and properties they become enamored, forgetful of the omnipotent and omniscient hand that created and formed it. This pride is but too apt to cause such intellects to arrogate to themselves the credit of science and penetration, which they received only from God, and of which He can at any time deprive them. The excited partisan zeal of the times added energy and bitterness to this spirit, and the professor's chair at Paris became the pulpit of infidelity and of the grossest materialism. Religion, the great enemy of these errors, was consequently assailed, calumniated, sneered at, and ridiculed. Thus, while Mr. Bruté enjoyed the advantage of listening to the skilful, scientific, and learned lectures of such professors as La Mark, Fourcroy, Esquirol, Pinel, and Bichât, he was compelled to endure the annoyance of this unfair and dishonorable warfare upon all he cherished in life or death; for these eminent professors, while conveying the mysteries of science, did not scruple to endeavor to insinuate the infidel poison into the minds of their pupils. In this crisis of his life, the solid religious education he received from his pious mother and good parish priest at Rennes, proved an invincible armor and shield to his soul. He took particular pains to practice his duties and profess his religion, thereby combating error with example. Not content with this, he entered into a combination with a number of his fellow-students, particularly with those from his native province, noble spirits like himself, to oppose boldly these pernicious teachings; and the means they adopted for this purpose were to select such subjects in natural theology, for their theses before their class, as would enable them to advocate the truths of Christianity and avow their belief in them. The good effects of fearlessly practising and defending religion were seen in this instance; the attention of the government was called to the matter, and the First Consul, who was then endeavoring to restore religion in France, caused an intimation to be given out, in the columns of an official journal, unfavorable to the pernicious attempts and practices of the infidel professors, and they, taking a timely hint, desisted from their wicked work. Young Bruté graduated in medicine in 1803, with the highest honors; out of eleven hundred students—one hundred and twenty were selected by "concursus" as the best, —and after undergoing a second examination, Mr. Bruté won the first prize among these chosen students.* He was immediately appointed Physician to the First Dispensary in Paris, a position which he declined; because now, all obstacles being removed, his natural desire to do good, and the inward grace which he received from above, led him to a more perfect vocation. He did not abandon the profession of medicine, says Dr. McCaffrey, "from any feelings of disgust. He always honored it as one of the noblest to which a highly gifted and philanthropic man can devote himself. Delightful as his conversation was to all, and to men of science in particular, it was peculiarly so to the student, or to the practitioner or professor of medicine. They often expressed their astonishment that, after a lapse of twenty or thirty

---

* He presented his prize to Dr. Duval, his first preceptor in medicine, "in recognition of his kindness."

years, engrossed by pursuits of a very different order, he retained so perfect and minute a knowledge of all that he had studied in his youth under the great masters of the French capital." *

He entered the Seminary of St. Sulpice, at Paris, in November, 1803, and commenced the study of theology with ardor far surpassing that of any of his previous studies. Theology was truly to him the mistress and the mother of sciences. His mind was peculiarly fitted for it, and he resolved to explore it to its fountain source. Theology in all its branches, the ancient Fathers, the Canon Law, and Church history, he studied with the most ardent application. He seemed now to have found his proper element, and he availed himself of every possible means of storing his mind with learning, and enriching his soul with graces. The ardent and sincere piety of his earlier years now ripened into the solid and active devotion of the true man of God. He became a model to all in the Seminary. Amongst his professors were many of the most eminent theologians of that age, and amongst his fellow-students many, like himself, afterwards became distinguished members of the Hierarchy. It was at this period of his life that he commenced collecting a library; books were his delight—a taste which he never abandoned. Now, as in his previous pursuits, he made copious notes and memoranda of his studies, as a means of assisting the memory, and of giving outward form and expression to his ideas and acquirements. He was a good illustration of the remark that "the Frenchman is born

---

* The only occasion, on which we have heard of his attempting the practice, was at Mt. St. Mary's College, when one of the students broke his arm, and the regular physician could not be had at once; Mr. Bruté set the arm so skilfully as to leave nothing for the doctor to do when he came.

with a pen in his hand." This industrious habit, without interfering with, but rather promoting, the labors of a long and useful life, has secured for us many interesting and valuable materials, and some of the most touching and affecting incidents of one of the most remarkable eras in the history of the world. His notes on theology are evidences of his thorough application to that noble science. It has well been said, "that the four years he spent in the Seminary of St. Sulpice were what the Scripture calls 'full years.'" He was ordained in the priesthood, in the parish church of St. Sulpice, by Monseigneur André, the retired Bishop of Quimper, on the Saturday before Trinity Sunday, 1808.

His great learning and exemplary traits of character peculiarly fitted him to guide the studies of young candidates for the priesthood. His own desires led him to prefer this service in the Church. He accordingly refused the offers of the Bishop of Nantes, the position of assistant chaplain to the Emperor Napoleon, and a canonicate in the Cathedral at Rennes. He became, in preference, a member of the Sulpitian Order, was appointed professor of theology in the Sulpitian Seminary at his native city of Rennes, and for two years was not only their professor, but, still more, a model of excellence to the young levites of that diocese. He had at times during his ecclesiastical studies thought of devoting himself to the foreign missions, as the most serviceable, laborious, and self-sacrificing service in the ministry. The presence of the excellent Bishop Flaget, of Kentucky, in France in 1809 and 1810, probably recalled his attention to this field. To be separated from his good mother, his friends, country, his library, and his young levites, to all of whom he was greatly attached, was a severe trial; but he was equal to sacrifices for God and his neighbor. His superior, the illustrious Mr. Emery, approved his choice, and he accordingly joined Bishop Flaget at Bordeaux, and sailed with him for America, arriving at Baltimore August 10, 1810. We may form some appreciation of the acquisition to the Church in America, gained in Mr. Bruté, from the following passages in Dr. McCaffrey's *Funeral Oration.* " His mind was too rich in treasures of classic lore, too amply furnished from the armories of science, for him to have been a dull or careless student. Whether he conversed with a friend, or lectured to a class, or heralded the message of salvation from the pulpit, the evidence of profound knowledge, as well as of remarkable genius, incessantly flashed before you." "We have regarded him as an example for youthful students in the world: from this moment he becomes the model of those who belong to the sanctuary. If he has been pious and edifying in the lively and dangerous scenes through which he has passed, he is much more zealous for the sublime virtues of his holy vocation in the retirement to which God has called him. If he sought with ardor and unremitting toil for secular knowledge, while he destined himself to a secular profession, with still greater ardor and unremitting toil, even with a holy enthusiasm and in the true spirit of a patient, self-denying labor, does he pursue that knowledge which ought to adorn the ecclesiastical profession. It is thus only he could have acquired those immense stores of erudition, which for so many years caused him to be consulted by men of letters, by learned ecclesiastics, even by the highest dignitaries of the Church in the United States, as a sort of oracle or living library of sacred erudition. Besides those treasures of knowledge which he brought away from his earlier studies, as the children of Israel carried the spoils of Egypt into the Holy Land, he became intimately conversant (more so perhaps than any other man this country has ever seen) with the writings of the Fathers of the Church and the primitive sources of ecclesiastical history. He turned his attention to the Hebrew language, in consequence of its importance in religion to the Sacred Scriptures, which were now his constant study. Scholastic theology he acquired thoroughly, and he grew familiar with all the great defenders and ornaments of religion in every age. Hence there were few subjects indeed on which he was not able, when consulted, to throw a strong light, no matter what depth of research or extent of reading the understanding of them required."

He was, on his arrival at Baltimore, made professor of philosophy in St. Mary's, a position in which for two years he rendered invaluable services in elevating the reputation of the institution, and in training young men in learning and piety. In his vacations, when wearied nature needed relaxation, he spent his time in missionary labors where the services of priests were much needed and difficult to obtain. In 1812, while thus engaged on the mission at St. Joseph's, on the eastern shore of Maryland, he received letters calling him to Emmittsburg, to assist Mr. Dubois in his arduous labors in that region. Here he seems to have set to work to do as much good as human efforts could accomplish, yet with such humility that he seemed unconscious of his great achievements. His learning, his piety, his charities, his ministry among the people, seemed to throw a sacred halo about his path. "He could never have hoped," says Bishop Bayley, "to have done as much good amongst the inhabitants of India or China, by the exertion of the highest apostolic zeal, as he was permitted to do in this country. It is no disparagement of those holy and eminent men, who have adorned the annals of the Catholic Church in this country—of a Carroll, a Cheverus, a Dubois, and a Flaget, to say that no one has ever exerted a more beneficial influence in favor of the Catholic religion than Bishop Bruté." At Emmittsburg, he became the spiritual attendant to the Sisters of Charity, and his counsels and assistance did much towards building up this then young and struggling institution. "In Mother Seton," writes the author of her Life,* "he found a soul who could follow him in his lofty and beautiful flights on the wings of faith, who could catch the fire of his thoughts and commune with him in the enjoyment of their elevating power. From him, in a great measure, did she learn how to preserve her soul in peace, amid the trials of her position, and, abandoning herself to the will of God in all things, to look forward with hope and joy to the term of all earthly suffering and vicissitude." He was not only confessor to the institution of the Sisters of Charity for nearly twenty years, but its untiring friend, devoting his time, talents, and labors to its development and prosperity. Having sustained her courage and animated her heart in life, he was constantly beside the death-bed of Mother Seton in her last illness, cheering the noble and departing soul, "suggesting the most perfect sentiments of resignation, penance, love, confidence, and union with Jesus Christ."

In 1815 he went to France to interest the clergy and people of that country in favor of the American missions, and also for the purpose of bringing over his

---

* *Life of Mrs. Seton*, by Rev. C. I. White, D.D.

library, which consisted of nearly five thousand volumes of valuable and choice works, which he placed at the service of St. Mary's College. Returning in November of the same year, he was appointed President of St. Mary's College, Baltimore, a position which he filled with his accustomed usefulness, ability, and energy for about two years. On the death of Rev. Mr. Duhamel he resigned the Presidency of St. Mary's, and returned to Emmittsburg, where his virtues, his labors, his learning, his charities, and his teachings, spread blessings on all sides. This portion of his life, up to his appointment to the Episcopal office, is described in so masterly a manner by Dr. McCaffrey, that we cannot refrain from inserting it here:—

" His duties here were multiplied and various, and required to discharge them no ordinary share of zeal, industry, and versatility of powers. He was confessor to the Sisters of Charity, and for many years pastor of the congregation at Emmittsburg, while he frequently exercised in this congregation some of the most arduous functions of the holy ministry. In the Ecclesiastical Seminary he lectured on Sacred Scripture, and was Professor of Theology and Moral Philosophy. In the college he taught, at different times, natural philosophy and various other branches. True greatness dignifies whatever sphere it moves in. His genius and learning were conspicuous, when they expatiated through the palace-halls of the queen of sciences, Divinity; they were not less admirable, when they descended to the humble task of teaching youth geography, or explaining the little catechism to children. As Paul planted and Apollo watered, but God gave the increase,* so having

---
* 1 Cor. iii. 6.

the immediate direction of the ecclesiastical students and the chief care of instructing them, he nurtured with pious solicitude and zeal the growing seminary, which the venerable Mr. Dubois had devoted all his energies to plant and rear; and the labors of both were rewarded by heaven with abundant fruits. His cheerful piety, amiable manners, and lively interest in the welfare of his pupils, were sure to win their hearts; his eminent holiness of life secured not only respect, but veneration. His exhortations to virtue and piety could scarcely fail of effect, because he recommended only what he practised himself. No standard of Christian or priestly excellence to which he pointed could appear too high, since he was himself a living instance of its attainment. If, forgetful of this earth, he always pointed and allured to heaven, he also led the way. His piety was most tender and affectionate, and he showed clearly by his example what it is to love God with one's whole heart and whole soul, and with all the powers of one's mind. In all things he was a model to those subject to his direction. His hours of sleep were few, and long before the morning's dawn he arose to converse with his God, and to give to Him the first-fruits of the day. During these early meditations his soul, absorbed in heavenly contemplation and intimate union with its Creator, was largely visited with the refreshing dues of divine grace; and when he approached the altar and offered up the Holy Sacrifice, his heart, already full to overflowing, was always overpowered by mingled emotions of reverential awe and gratitude and love, and often found relief in copious tears. He descended to the discharge of his ordinary duties; but, like Moses, he bore the marks of converse with his God, and, as words of heavenly wisdom fell from his tongue, you could readily fancy that his lips, like those of Isaias, had been touched by the seraph with living coals of fire from the altar. His time was all divided between prayer and labor. He loved so well 'the beauty of the house of the Lord, and the place where his glory dwelleth,' * that he spent whole hours kneeling before the Blessed Sacrament; and eventually he made it a rule, whenever it was practicable, to recite the divine office in His holy presence. Thither he would repair on returning from a long journey during the rigors of winter, and, until he had satisfied his devotion, no persuasions could induce him to attend to his personal comfort; at other times, unless he was en gaged in active duties, you would find him in the midst of his splendid library, surrounded by the writings of the Fathers and Doctors of the Church, and whatever besides is most rare and valuable in science and literature, pursuing his devoted studies with intense application and wonderful activity of mind, or committing to paper, for the benefit of others, the results of his profound investigations. His recreation was but variety of labor. When his wearied mind demanded its turn of relaxation, the most arduous bodily toil succeeded; and this round of exertions, bodily and corporeal, was kept up with an elasticity of spirits and activity of mind truly surprising. After a journey of fifty miles, performed on foot in a single day, book in hand, praying and reading by turns, and scarcely stopping to take the simple refection that nature required, he would meet his friends in the evening with a freshness of spirits and gaiety of conversation which could not be surpassed.

---

* Pslam xxv.

If, as a pastor, he had made an appointment, no obstacle could hinder him from keeping it. The mountain torrent, swollen with wintry rains and overflowing its banks, could not stop him. If other means of crossing it were not at hand, he plunged into its freezing tide, and, amid masses of floating ice, swam to the opposite shore. No sacrifice of comfort, or necessary repose, neither hunger nor thirst, nor summer's heats nor winter's colds, could check his enthusiastic zeal, or cause him to fail in punctuality to his engagement. But his charity towards the poor was perhaps the most edifying trait in his character. It did not consist in merely pitying their miseries and exhorting others to relieve them. He was in the habit of visiting them in person, and in his own hands he bore the assistance which they needed and he was able to procure them, thus literally 'feeding the hungry and clothing the naked.' His benevolence was ingenious in obtaining means for its exercise. Many a time he stripped himself of garments necessary to his own comfort, to bestow them on some shivering victim of poverty. But he seemed to delight in suffering himself, that he might alleviate the sufferings of others. Ingratitude on their part but inflamed his charity the more. The bigot who drove him from his door by day, could not prevent him from bringing clothes and provisions to his needy family by night. However careful he might be to conceal his extraordinary good works, the general spirit and tenor of his conduct could not be hidden from the young ecclesiastics whom he taught by word and example.

"As a Professor of Theology, he excelled chiefly in two things: a vast erudition, which left nothing unexplored, and a singular power of generalizing, which enabled him to grasp his whole subject and handle it with ease, by bringing all its details under a few grand principles. In exhibiting and supporting these principles he put forth all his strength. After adducing the evidence which his extensive reading readily furnished, elucidating it by his luminous explanations, and applying the logical tests with cautious judgment and impartial rigor, his excursive mind brought in a rich and almost gorgeous profusion of analogies and illustrations from every part of the wide domains of human knowledge. Thus qualified for the task of directing and instructing ecclesiastics, he was able to render immense services to religion. There is scarcely a diocese in this country which is not indebted (some of them very largely indebted) to his zeal, piety, and learning, and his great success in communicating his own spirit and knowledge to those whose ecclesiastical education he directed. If many worthy and highly useful missionaries have gone forth from Mount St. Mary's to bear the blessings of religion to those who had them not before, or were but ill provided with them, it is under God owing in a great degree to Mr. Bruté. If the bold assailants of our faith have been made to repent their temerity by its able defenders, no small proportion of these issued from the school, and were armed for the defence by the learned Bishop Bruté.

"In other spheres he labored with equal devotion and similar success. He was for many years the spiritual director of the Sisters of Charity at St. Joseph's, and the main auxiliary of Mr. Dubois, under whose Superiorship the Sisterhood arose from the humblest beginnings to a state of prosperous maturity. It was Mr. Bruté's arduous and responsible task to strengthen the vocation, foster the piety, enlighten and confirm the virtue, and fan into a burning flame the charity both of the novices and professed sisters." . . . .

"The pious congregation of Emmittsburg will tell how fruitful were the labors of their beloved pastor. The whole neighborhood around will attest the happy effects of his missionary toils, his instructions, his prayers, his unquenchable charity. Where is the poor man's cottage that he has not entered as a messenger of peace and mercy? Who was sick, and he did not visit and comfort him? Who was in want, and he did not afford him, poor though he was himself and always wished to be, some charitable relief? What road was there so rough, what weather so inclement, what night so dark, that he would not fly on foot and alone to minister the sweet consolations of religion? Did scandals arise? How his soul burned within him until the scandal was extinguished and the evil remedied! Were neighbors at enmity? He was seen cowering under the fury of a winter's storm, and pelted with driving sleet and snow, as he returned a considerable distance from the blessed work of reconciliation. It was the anniversary of that day on which our Saviour died to make our peace with God. But who can recount the innumerable instances of his disinterested zeal, his burning charity, his heroic self-denial? How many of his virtuous deeds, how many acts of benevolence—now known to none but God —will be brought to light before the assembled universe on the great day when every one will receive his proper retribution!

"His extraordinary piety was obvious to all; manifesting itself at the altar, where he offered the spotless Lamb, as in the pulpit, where he proclaimed the truths of the Gospel. Even those who could not understand him, because of his imperfect pronounciation of our language, often went away deeply moved and edified; although they could not account for this effect, nor explain it otherwise than by saying that he appeared to them not as a man, but as an angel, speaking to their souls in the name and by the authority of God. But for those who did understand him well, what a rich spiritual repast was afforded by his eloquence, for he was eloquent in spite of his defects of idiom and pronunciation. How pleased were they to hang upon his accents! How did they love to follow the eagle flights of his genius! How soon did their faith shake off its heavy slumbers, as conscience, from the deep abyss of the heart, responded to his bold appeals, and the smallest spark of charity rose into a consuming flame, and hope grew strong within them and began to fix a steady look on heaven! And how much more eloquent in the cause of virtue than eloquence itself, was the powerful pleading of his example!"

From his daily memoranda, which were headed with these remarkable words: "*One day of a Priest—Eternity!*" we learn that on a single day, besides Mass, preaching, and his other duties, he spoke to sixty-two different persons on religious matters; to some about their Easter duty, to others about circulating evil reports, to others about their scandals, and so on. On another occasion, learning that Rev. Mr. Hickey was to be recalled from the Mountain, he arose next morning at his usual early hour, offered up the holy sacrifice, and started on foot for Baltimore, in order to secure the retention of Father Hickey at Emmittsburg; reached Taneytown in time for breakfast; at Winchester he found he had not a cent in his pocket with which to purchase dinner, and had to get it on credit; he arrived the same evening at Baltimore, a distance of fifty-two miles, having read on the way three hundred and eighty-eight pages in D'Anquètil's History of France, fourteen pages in Cicero de Officiis, three chapters in the New Testament, recited his Office, and said the Rosary three times. He started on his return the following morning, in· a raging storm, from which he was frequently compelled to take shelter, reading and praying as usual on the way. In one of his journeyings on foot, he is said to have reached Frederick City some time after the retiring hour of the pastor; rather than disturb the rest of any one, though the night was cold and stormy, he wrapt himself up in his cloak and slept soundly in the vestibule of the church, where he was found the next morning by the pastor as he was going into the church to say Mass. Yet this humble priest was an oracle of learning to the clergy and Bishops of the country, was consulted on the most abstruse points from all quarters, attended councils of the Prelates as theologian, and rendered invaluable services in their deliberations; indeed, from his secluded home in the mountain, his influence was felt throughout the entire Church of America.

The . Prelates assembled in the Second Provincial Council of Baltimore, in October, 1833, by their first act requested the Holy Father to erect a new Episcopal See at Vincennes, embracing Indiana and the greater part of Illinois. They also nominated as its Bishop the Rev. Mr. Bruté, concurring thus with the recommendation of Bishops Flaget and Rosati, who, the previous year, while at Vincennes, agreed to propose his name. The Bishop-elect was giving a retreat to the Sisters of Charity at St. Joseph's when the appointment arrived, and he opened and read the documents on his knees. His humility was very much disturbed by an event so unexpected by him, and he immediately started for Baltimore, in order to make a spiritual retreat and seek the light of Heaven as to the course he should pursue. No one ever considered and weighed a question of duty and conscience more earnestly and carefully than he pondered over this. He finally, with his accustomed delicacy, left it to Bishops Flaget and Chabrât, from whose jurisdiction the new See had just been separated, to decide whether he should accept or not. These Prelates were most earnest in recommending him to accept, and he yielded with characteristic modesty and diffidence. It required no small amount of courage to assume such a burden, for the field to which he was called was a wild, uncultivated, and laborious one.

Indiana was first visited by Catholic missionaries during the period that the French were exploring and colonizing the valley of the Mississippi. Vincennes received its name from a gallant French officer, who was murdered by the Indians in 1736, in the same massacre and side by side with the martyred Father Senat. Bishop Bruté believed that the celebrated dialogue on religion, in which Father Mermet, in 1712, confounded the medicine man of the Mascoutens, took place at or near the present site of Vincennes. The church records of Vincennes commenced in 1749; the Jesuits then had the mission, and it appears that Father Meurin was not only their pastor, but also discharged the functions of the civil court. There are two other stations in the territory of Indiana which were also attended by Jesuit Fathers. The Jesuits were finally suppressed, and the mission closed. In 1770 M. Gibault, Vicar-General of the Bishop of Quebec, visited Vincennes, and continued his missionary visits for several years, performing great labors, and keeping alive the faith in that remote region. In 1778 he spent two weeks at Vincennes; by his influence he induced the French inhabitants to declare in favor of the United States against Great Britain, and the oath of allegiance to the American Government was administered by him in the church with great solemnity. In 1779 Vincennes was captured by the British; and when Col. George Rogers Clark assembled his troops to recapture the town, Father Gibault made a patriotic address to them, and bestowed his blessing upon "the heroic little band." His exertions are said to have greatly facilitated our conquest of the great North-western Territory now teeming with States and Catholic dioceses. In 1785 he became resident pastor at Vincennes, and was accompanied by another priest. On his recall, in 1789, he appointed a layman, Pierre Mallet, "guardian of the church;" a guardianship which continued until the Abbé Flaget arrived there in 1792. The mission was continued by Bishop Carroll, and afterwards by Bishop Flaget, with their limited resources; and when the new Bishop went to take possession, such was the scattered condition of the flock, with scarcely priests or churches, that he exclaimed: "Poor diocese of Vincennes!" But, immediately rallying his noble courage, he continued, "Let us, however, put trust in God, and what a change can a few years, through His blessing and the perseverance of zealous souls, effect!"

Bishop Bruté made immediate preparations for his journey to Vincennes. His poverty was so great that he received from the Sisters of Charity a present of two hundred dollars to enable him to establish himself in his

See. He was received by those zealous Prelates of the West, Bishops Flaget, Rosati, and Purcell, with the most affectionate attention. At Bardstown he made a second spiritual retreat, as a preparation for his consecration; on October 26, 1834, he assisted at the consecration of the Cathedral at St. Louis by those venerable Prelates; and on the 28th he received his episcopal consecration in the same temple, at the hands of Bishop Flaget, assisted by Bishops Rosati and Purcell. On November 5th he approached his episcopal city, was met on the way by the Rev. Mr. Lalumière, accompanied by a number of citizens, Catholic and Protestant, who escorted him into the city; and on the same afternoon he was installed by Bishop Flaget, assisted by Bishops Rosati and Purcell, and Rev. Messrs. Lalumière, Hitzelberger, and Abell, and Father Petit. His whole diocese possessed but three priests, and one of those belonged to the diocese of St. Louis, but was permitted to assist him for one year. His Cathedral consisted of four brick walls and a roof, unplastered and unwhitewashed, without sanctuary, or place for sacred vessels and vestments. The altar was of plain wood, but was surmounted with a neatly gilded tabernacle, a cross and six handsome candlesticks, a present from France, which strangely contrasted with all else around. His episcopal palace consisted of a single small room and closet twenty-five by twelve feet, without cellar below or garret above. The pew-rents of the Cathedral amounted for the year to one hundred dollars, and the support of the pastor was a subscription list of two hundred and fifty dollars. There was neither seminary, college, religious establishment, nor school. There had been a school at Vincennes, kept by four Sisters of Charity from Nazareth, in Kentucky; but even these had been withdrawn. His first care was to secure their return to Vincennes, and the reopening of the school. His next step was the visitation of his extensive diocese, in order to ascertain its condition and wants. Before setting out on this arduous journey, he began his ministry at Vincennes by preaching, confessions, confirmation, and first communion. He then visited the congregations within thirty miles of Vincennes, awakening all to a sense of their past neglect, their necessity of conversion and repentance, and recalling all to the Catholic traditions and practices of their ancestors. He found the people, who were mostly French, forgetful and negligent of their religion, and given to many bad practices; but they were amiable and impressible, and welcomed their Bishop with sincere joy. He addressed to his flock a Pastoral Letter, full of love, charity, zeal, and apostolical instruction and winning appeals; addressing therein also the Protestants in affectionate terms, and endeavoring by his sweet and gentle words to attract all to the Church of God.

It would extend this memoir beyond our limits, interesting and edifying as are the details, to follow this saintly and laborious apostle through his visitation of the diocese. He traveled without comfort or convenience from village to village, and even from family to family, instructing the ignorant, reproving the negligent and wicked; summoning all to God and their duty; baptizing, confessing, and confirming; he broke the bread of life to many who had not received it for years, and received converts into the Church; he started the people in various localities to building temples for the worship of God, and schools for the education of their children; the

Indian and European shared equally his paternal solicitude; his sleep was short, his labors long, his meals scant, and his bed was a bench and a little straw, with his cloak for a covering, or the naked floor; he traveled on horseback, and though over fifty years of age, he seemed incapable of fatigue or discouragement. He saw much to console and comfort him in the good dispositions of the people, but still more to sadden his heart at the necessitous and impoverished condition of his diocese. So patient, so cheerful was he under his fatigues and hardships, that no word of complaint, impatience, or even allusions to them ever escaped his lips or pen. To labor and to endure for others was, on the contrary, his highest delight and happiness.

He was chiefly struck during his journey with the great want of clergymen throughout his diocese, and with the want of means for the erection of churches and houses of education. He resolved to do all in his power to supply these wants, and turned his attention to his own loved France, as the place from which he hoped to secure both priests and money for his diocese. He crossed the ocean for this purpose, and was received with every demonstration of kindness and veneration by all classes of people in various countries. King and people, prince and peasant, showed him every mark of respect and honor, and aided him generously in his noble cause. His simplicity of character and humility of soul were somewhat disturbed by his contact with courts, princes, and nobles; but he bore this, as he bore everything, with cheerfulness, for the love of God and his Church. He did not return without visiting the shrines of the Apostles, and obtaining the blessing of the Holy Father upon himself and his diocese.

His return to his diocese was hailed with joy by all, Catholics and Protestants, for all had witnessed his deeds and admired his virtues. He resumed at once the arduous duties of his office, though then for the first time experiencing the decline of his strength with his increasing years; but he labored on with the unceasing vigor and the unsparing application of a young man, till the frail body, unequal to the undying zeal and love of the soul, yielded to inevitable dissolution. He expended the means collected in his European tour with the judicious effort of making it accomplish the greatest possible amount of good, in establishing a Diocesan Seminary at Vincennes, an Orphan Asylum, and a Free school. He had a surplus left for the completion of his Cathedral, and the erection of small churches in localities where they were most needed. He brought with him from France twenty priests and seminarians, whom he distributed through his diocese with great foresight and judgment; and yet, with this increase in his colaborers, his own labors seemed only to increase. While not engaged in the arduous work of visiting his diocese, he was, while at Vincennes, both Bishop and pastor, attending to confessions, sick calls, and every detail; and at the same time he was professor of theology for his Seminary, and teacher in one of his academies. While on his visitations, which were frequent, there was no office of ministry, religion, or charity that he did not perform; and the immensity of these may be judged from the fact that great numbers of Catholic immigrants were then working on the public improvements of Indiana and Illinois, who, besides the usual labor it costs the priesthood to attend such missions, were then suffering severely from cholera and malarious fevers. For them he celebrated the Holy Sacrifice in their miserable cabins, heard their confessions, administered the other sacraments, and smoothed the way for the sick and dying to their long home. In the midst of all his labors, he wrote for the Catholic press, and kept up the most excellent custom of writing twice a month to each of his priests on the interests of their respective missions, and for the guidance of their labors and stimulation of their zeal. It has already been related that, when he entered his diocese, he had but three priests, and one of these was a loan from Bishop Rosati; when, after his brief episcopate, he left it forever, he bequeathed to the Church of Indiana twenty-four priests, twenty-three churches, besides six church buildings and twenty-eight stations occasionally visited, two religious communities, one theological seminary, one college for young men, one female academy, and two free schools. With such achievements the reader will be surprised to learn that he was opposed to going in debt, and never would sign a mortgage on church property. "Difficulties that would have disheartened almost any one else only served to increase his zeal and charity. Having commenced a journey of four hundred miles in such a state of bodily suffering that he could not sit upright on his horse, he nevertheless completed it without the intermission of a single day. Shortly before his death he left Vincennes to visit a distant mission, which he had already visited thrice within the year; and though so weak that he could scarcely support his tottering frame, in the absence of the pastor, he attended to three distant sick calls on the same day, and, almost dying, administered the consolations of religion to those who appeared no nearer dissolution than himself."* His

---

* Dr. McCaffrey's *Funeral Oration.*

benignity, kindness to all, and angelic charity, even when himself the greatest of sufferers, were the crowning virtues of his character. He loved poverty for himself, while his delight was to bestow upon others. The only value he could see in money and worldly goods was in the good they could accomplish for religion and the poor. Father Hickey said of him, that "if he had five dollars in his pocket, it went to the first person who asked for it." His food and clothes were of the plainest kind, for he gave away frequently all except what he wore upon his person, and even these were not safe, for he was known frequently to take off his linen and underclothes to bestow them upon the poor negroes whom he visited and solaced. He crossed the ocean nine times, a voyager of the Church and of Heaven; and his conduct on these occasions was admirable, indeed inspiring. His attentions to the sick on ship-board, his tenderness to the timid and distressed, his noble calmness when storm and danger made all others fear, and his careful and affectionate nursing even of the poor deck-passengers, made him appear more like an angel than a man; and amidst all these attentions to others he found time for prayer, meditation, and labor. He was as unruffled on the ocean as in his own loved library; and on one of his voyages, which experienced thirty days of storm, he performed the above works of mercy for his fellow-passengers, accomplished a great amount of writing, prepared immense materials for his European correspondence, and delighted and instructed all by his cheerful and learned conversations on every subject.

In 1837 he caught a severe cold while riding on the outside of a coach in Ohio, on his way to the Council at Baltimore; this grew into confirmed consumption, and hastened the dissolution of a noble frame already spent with labors and services of the most exalted kind. Let the eloquent words of one who knew and loved him well, and who received the details from an eye-witness, narrate the last and most impressive scenes in the drama of this truly Christian life: "Death, which could be no unwelcome visitor to one whose thoughts, hopes, and affections all centred in a better world, found him full-handed of good works, and longing only to be dissolved, and to be with Christ. Invincibly patient and resigned under the severest suffering; full of tender piety; calm, collected, and brightly exhibiting his characteristic virtues to the last, he set a beautiful example of the manner in which a Christian should prepare himself to run his final race, and to win the crown of a glorious immortality. As his strength diminished, his devotion increased. He sought no alleviation of his sufferings; on the contrary, he was eager still to labor and endure, in the twofold view of doing good to others and resembling more his crucified Saviour. When unable to walk or stand, he would at least sit up and write to any one whom he could hope to benefit by his correspondence; and to those around him he would speak on pious subjects, such as the love of God, conformity to His holy will, or devotion to the Blessed Virgin, with the unction of a Saint and the ardor of a Seraph. But six hours before his death he wrote with his own hand, and not without much difficulty and pain, several moving letters to persons who had unfortunately abandoned the practice of their faith, and to whom he wished to make this dying appeal in behalf of their souls, while the portals of eternity were closing upon him. These last precious days of his life were taken up in works of charity, in instructing, edifying, and consoling those who were with him, and in intimate and affectionate communion with his God, whom he hoped soon to see face to face, and to love and enjoy forever. He preferred often to be left alone, that he might the more freely indulge his pious feelings; and for this end he would allow no one to watch by him at night until his mortal agony had begun. When his friends affectionately sought to know what they could do to relieve his sufferings, he would answer them by pointing out some passage of Sacred Scripture, or chapter of the following of Christ, which he desired them to read to him, or by asking them to say some prayers for his happy death. No agonies of pain could extort from him a single expression of distress. 'The will of God be done,' was the constant language of his lips, as it was the abiding sentiment of his heart. When preparing to receive the holy *Viaticum*, he wrote to us in the true spirit of saintly humility, requesting the prayers of our Seminary and of the Sisterhood, and begging pardon for whatever offences or bad example he had ever given to any one at either institution. A few days before his dissolution, the strength of his naturally vigorous constitution rallied for a time, and his physician promised him at least a temporary recovery; he told the physician he was mistaken, and whether he knew it supernaturally or otherwise, he named the exact time of his approaching departure. He gave himself the orders for preparing his grave, and as calmly directed the modes of sepulture, and proper rites to be observed, as if he was discharging an ordinary duty. On the morning of the day before his death he remarked to the clergyman who attended him with unwearied solicitude and affection: 'My dear child, I have the whole day yet to stay with you, to-morrow with God!' To another pious friend he used these simple but expressive words: 'I am going home.' Heaven was indeed his home: he had always so regarded it; there was his treasure; his heart was there; he had ever longed to be with God, and 'see Him as He is;' and now the door of the Father's house was opening to him, and angels were on the wing to receive his departing spirit, and conduct it to its place of rest. He was happy, therefore, amid the pangs and terrors of death; for he trusted that he was but going home. After having received the last Sacrament he directed the departing prayers to be recited, which he answered devoutly and fervently until the last, and then on the morning of the 26th of June (1839), at half-past one o'clock, he calmly and sweetly surrendered his soul into the hands of his Creator.

"His death was deplored as a general calamity. He was especially lamented by the poor, the widow, and orphan. The people of Vincennes felt that they had lost a public benefactor, and his own flock, both clergy and laity, bewailed, as well they might, the death of such a pastor. All, with one accord, mourned for the scholar, the philanthropist, and saint. Crowds of persons, of every rank and of all denominations, visited his corpse, and assisted at the ceremonies of his burial. The Mayor and civil authorities, and learned societies of Vincennes, passed resolutions to attend his funeral. The whole population poured forth to accompany, in solemn silence, his honored remains to their last resting-place on earth." *

His remains were interred under his Cathedral sanc-

---

* *Funeral Oration* by Rev. Dr. McCaffrey.

tuary; his name is engraved upon many a heart; his memory and virtues are the common heritage of the Catholic Church, than which no other could have produced such a man, priest, Prelate, Christian.

RIGHT REV. WILLIAM CLANCY, D.D.,

*Coadjutor Bishop of Charleston, A.D. 1835.**

THE Right Rev. William Clancy was a native of Cork, Ireland. At an early age he embraced the ecclesiastical state, and at the College of Carlow enjoyed the benefit of Dr. England's instruction in theology, as well as his friendship and esteem. He was afterwards, and for six years, curate of Carlow College. In 1829 he was offered, and accepted, the chair of theology in the same institution, and discharged the duties of this position with distinguished ability for the six years preceding his elevation to the Episcopal dignity. He was greatly respected and esteemed by the illustrious Bishop Doyle, and by the venerable Dr. Fitzgerald, his predecessor as President of Carlow. He also performed missionary duties, in the mean time, in his native city and county of Cork. Dr. Clancy was noted for his charity and kindness of heart, no less than for his learning and ability.

In 1835, when it was decided to appoint a Coadjutor Bishop to assist Bishop England of Charleston, whose labors extended over a vast diocese, and who was occasionally absent on the duties of a legation with which he was charged by the Holy See, Dr. Clancy was selected for the position, under the title of Bishop of Oriense. He was consecrated in the Cathedral of Carlow, on Sunday, February 1, 1835, by the Right Rev. Dr. Nolan, assisted

---

* Authorities: *The Catholic Diary*, vols. 3, 4, and 5; *Freeman's Journal*, 1842; *Catholic Magazine*, 1847, &c., &c.

by the Most Rev. Dr. Slattery, of Cashel and Emly, and the Right Rev. Dr. Kinsella, of Kilkenny, in the presence of a large number of Prelates and clergy, amongst whom were the Very Rev. Dr. Fitzgerald, Rev. Dr. Cullen, and other distinguished ecclesiastics. The three consecrating Prelates were all former professors of divinity and philosophy in the same College of Carlow in which Dr. Clancy had been a professor. The latter wore the mitre in which Bishop Doyle was consecrated in 1819, a present from the successor of that honored Prelate. The consecration sermon was preached by Rev. Mr. O'Sullivan, of Bantry, the first pupil who was ordained priest out of Dr. Clancy's class of moral theology.

After his consecration he was afflicted with a severe illness, which prostrated his health and greatly impeded his preparations for departure. On recovering, he visited his friends and family at Cork. In the mean time he exerted himself successfully in securing ecclesiastical students for the diocese of Charleston, some of whom sailed before him and others followed. In October, 1835, between sixty and seventy of the clergy of Cork and Cloyne united in extending to Dr. Clancy an invitation to attend a complimentary and farewell banquet. He returned to Carlow College to pay his friends there a last visit, when the students gave him a most affectionate welcome and presented an address. On both of these occasions he delivered responses characterized by fervid eloquence and generous friendship and gratitude. He shortly afterwards sailed for New York, where he arrived November 2; and after a short visit to Philadelphia, sailed from New York and arrived at Charleston on Sunday morning, November 21, 1835. He was received by Bishop England and the assembled clergy of the Diocese at the Seminary, with a most hearty welcome. Shortly afterwards the clergy and lay delegates of the Diocese of Charleston presented an address to Bishop Clancy, which was responded to by him in his usual happy and eloquent style. For two years he performed the functions of Coadjutor Bishop, and assisted Bishop England in his arduous duties, spread over an immense diocese, as they were, and extended to a widely scattered flock. He also sat among the Fathers of the Provincial Council of Baltimore, which assembled in that city in May, 1837. In the summer of 1837 he was translated to the See of Demarara, in British Guiana, and although the climate to which he was thus sent was almost certain death to any European, he seems to have cheerfully obeyed the voice of the Sovereign Pontiff, and lost no time in preparing to join his new flock.

A circumstance occurred about the time of his translation, which is well worthy of recording. Bishop Clancy had his attention called, by a lady of South Carolina, to one of the works of Washington Irving containing the narrative of a supposed historical occurrence, which was calculated to draw reproach and disgrace upon the Catholic Church. The culpably careless, sometimes malicious manner, in which Protestant writers, not contented with expressing their individual opinions, profess to give historical facts and quote historical monuments and documents falsely or erroneously to the prejudice of the Church, has always been a grievance with Catholics. English literature teems with such instances, and the works of Sir Walter Scott have well been said to have proved powerful auxiliaries for creating and cherishing prejudice against the Church. In the case to which allusion is now made, the fact that so just a man and unprejudiced a Protestant as Washington Irving should have fallen into so gross an error, should warn Protestant writers against the too common habit of their class, in launching against Catholics every weapon with which ignorance, bigotry, or malice may supply them, without considering whether such weapons are to be tolerated in honorable warfare; and should warn the public, since the very hideousness and absurdity of such attacks are not sufficient, against believing stories too obviously untrue for the credulity even of a child. It is due, however, to the memory of Mr. Irving, to state that when his attention was called to the matter he promptly aided the investigation into the truth, and promised to correct in future editions the misrepresentation complained of, and avowed his entire freedom from all prejudice against the Catholic Church. The correspondence between Bishop Clancy and Mr. Irving is very interesting, and is transcribed herein both as a curious literary incident, and as an example to encourage Catholics to defend themselves and their Church against similar attacks, so common in our literature.

No. 1.

The Right Rev. Dr. Clancy to Washington Irving, Esq.

"CHARLESTON, December 28, 1836.

"DEAR SIR—Number 2 of the *Crayon Miscellany*, containing 'Abbotsford' and ' Newstead Abbey,' printed in 1835 by Carey and Lea, of Philadelphia, was put into my hands by a respectable and pure-minded Carolinian lady, who blushingly told me that even Washington

Irving recorded a disgraceful historical fact against Catholicity, regarding an indulgence said to be granted to the Augustinian friars in the reign of one of the English kings.

"Though a Presbyterian by birth, she said she could never believe that a number of the Christian priesthood of any country or age were so notoriously depraved as this portion of your book represents them to have been. She asked me whether as a Catholic Bishop I knew of its truth from ecclesiastical history, or whether I believed the circumstance as stated. After reading pages 98 and 181 of 'Newstead Abbey,' which run thus:— 'This order (Augustinian) was originally simple and abstemious in its mode of living, and exemplary in its conduct; but it would seem that it gradually lapsed into those abuses which disgraced too many of the wealthy monastic establishments, for there are documents amongst its archives, which intimate the prevalence of gross misrule and dissolute sensuality among its members. One of the parchment scrolls (found in the eagle of molten brass) throws rather an awkward light upon the kind of life led by the friars of Newstead. It is an indulgence granted to them for a certain number of months, in which plenary pardon is assured in advance *for all kinds of crime*, among which several of the most gross and sensual are specifically mentioned,' I did not hesitate to assure her on the faith of a Christian Bishop, that the statement appeared to me not only false but impossible, and wholly irreconcilable with the principles or practice of Roman Catholic theology, which I had taught in one of the first colleges in Europe, and which I learned in my youth under some of the most eminent French and Irish professors.

"The reading of your 'Sketch Book' impressed my mind favorably towards you, not only as a polished scholar, but as a fair writer, as far as a fair exercise of the imaginative faculties, which poets, novelists and painters so freely, and sometimes so usefully adopt, is compatible with historical details. But on this occasion you have left the region of amusing fiction, and called your book an *historical notice;* consequently, I have a right to ask, as a man of honor, whether you have seen the documents, and satisfied yourself as to their authenticity, integrity, and veracity, according to the laws of sound criticism and the rules of written testimony. If this abominable story issued from the press of the clerical pandemonium of New York, which disgraces the dignity of a few individual American ministers, whose death-warrant has been already signed and sealed by Col. Stone and other enlightened Protestant citizens, I would not dwell upon the loathsome fable for a moment; but the mental gems of 'Geoffrey Crayon,'

'Like orient pearls at random strung,'

find homes and hearts ready to enshrine them in the schools of youthful innocence, and on the shelves of philosophers and Christians of all denominations and countries. It is, therefore, not only as a guardian of public morals, but as a fearless friend to historical truth, that I raise my voice and am so sensibly slow in the belief of this infamous extract. May I hope for your fame that it was an unintentional error of fact, or a hasty view of some forged parchment, like the famed letter of Pope Gregory XVI. by that foolish fanatic McGhee, was palmed upon an aristocratic audience at Exeter Hall, and believed for a few days in London and elsewhere. You

know, from history, how easy the execution of such a record could have been at former periods of British history. May I then, respectfully, but firmly, as a British subject, and a Roman Catholic Bishop, ask an explanation for what I conceive to be a libel on the faith and morality of millions, and a slander upon one of the ancient religious institutions of a portion of my country?
"Yours faithfully in Christ,
"✠ WILLIAM CLANCY, Bishop, &c.
"WASHINGTON IRVING, Esq."

No. 2.
Mr. Irving's Answer.
"GREENBURG, April 29, 1837.
"DEAR SIR—I must apologize to you for not having replied to your letter at an earlier date; but it was received in a hurried moment, during a hasty visit to town, and mislaid among my papers, so that it has but just been found. I feel sincere and deep regret that anything in my writings should have given you the concern you express, and I am made conscious by it, that in the matter in question I have written without sufficient circumspection. As to the passages cited by you from 'Newstead Abbey,' they were taken from a memorandum noted down after inspecting the document to which they relate. That document was found in the way I have stated, among the deeds and grants of the Abbey, and was considered genuine. I did not examine it particularly; the part to which I have alluded was pointed out to me by Colonel Wildman. As it is very possible there might have been some error or misapprehension in this matter, I will write to Colonel Wildman on the subject, and if I find I labor under a mistake, will make a point of acknowledging and correcting it in a future edition

"I can only add that I have not been influenced in this matter by any feeling of hostility to the Roman Catholic Church, being perfectly free from anything of the kind, and regarding with sincere indignation and disgust the assaults made upon that church by various bigots of the Protestant sects in this country. I have the honor to remain, very respectfully, your much obliged servant,

WASHINGTON IRVING.

"Right Rev. WM. CLANCY,
 "Bishop of Oriense, Coadjutor of Charleston Diocese."

No. 3.

Bishop Clancy to Washington Irving, Esq.

"CHARLESTON, May 26, 1837.

"DEAR SIR—On my return from the Provincial Council of Baltimore, I found your letter, dated Greenburg, April 29, 1837, on my table. I regret that circumstances prevented you from answering my inquiries at an earlier period, as it would be grateful to the assembled hierarchy and clergy of the United States, even by a private communication, to learn that so enlightened and influential a writer 'regards with sincerest indignation and disgust the assaults made upon the Catholic Church by various bigots of the Protestant sects in this country.' The object of my letter is partially obtained by your candid and honorable declaration that you 'did not examine the document particularly,' and the promise of a correction in another edition if you have misstated the meaning of the original. You will, in all probability, get no additional evidence from Colonel Wildman, if he be the same individual who directed your attention to it. As it is, I presume, a Latin parchment scroll, in the peculiar style and lettering of the supposed age of Leo

X. (*clarum et venerabile nomen*), I shall write to Dr. Lingard, the celebrated English historian, and also to Counsellor D'Alton, of Dublin, not less celebrated as an antiquarian, and ask either or both of these gentlemen to investigate its authenticity and its exact meaning. So anxious am I to satisfy myself fully on the matter, that I should not hesitate, if my professional avocations should ever call me to Europe, to visit that part of England specifically for the purpose of ocular inspection. It would be a strange contradiction, if the same Pope who so sternly and justly refused a dispensation to the Eighth Henry, who has been strongly but truly called a royal monster, would grant an *indulgence in advance, for all kinds of crime*, to a religious order who were bound by vows of chastity, poverty, and obedience. As this word indulgence is strangely misunderstood by Protestants, you will not refuse to learn what the Catholic Church understands by it. It is merely a remission or mitigation of those temporal punishments which the sinner still owes to the Eternal Justice, even after the forgiveness of the guilt of his offences; just like the act of St. Paul to the incestuous Corinthian, whom he excommunicated (1 Cor. v.); and in the second chapter of his second epistle, having been informed of the sorrow and repentance of the criminal, he tells the Corinthians, 'to whom ye forgive anything, I forgive also; for if I forgave anything, to whom I forgave it for your sakes forgave I it, in the person of Christ.' In like manner, in the early ages, the Bishops granted, at the request of the martyrs, a remission of the canonical penance to those individuals whose repentance was marked by peculiar fervor; this relaxation was exactly our indulgence; so that it was not an encouragement or permission to sin; on the contrary, it implies and presupposes a sincere conversion from sin; a real detestation of iniquity, and a fixed determination to avoid it for the time to come. Again, the only doctrine which the Council of Trent proposes as an article of faith regarding them is, 'That Jesus Christ has imparted to his Church the power of granting indulgences, and that the use of them is beneficial.' I am very far from denying that indulgences have been abused by individuals—so has every spiritual and material gift of God to man.

"You will find a similarly true explanation in any of our standard works on this or any other of the misunderstood or misrepresented tenets of Catholicity. (See Bossuet, Doyle, Milner, O'Leary, etc., etc.) After this short sermon on the occasion of the supposed reformation, permit me to ask of you an indulgence in the proper sense of the term, namely, to publish your letter. It may tend to give the public mind a proper direction and feeling, not merely on this particular subject, but on the general interests of fair and full religious investigations. It may, perhaps, excite a love for charity and truth, which are and ever will be the great foundations of practical Christianity.

"Yours faithfully in Christ,
"✠ WILLIAM CLANCY.

"WASHINGTON IRVING, Esq."

No. 4.
The same to the same.

"NEW YORK, July 20, 1837.

"DEAR SIR—I have been unexpectedly translated to Demarara, and am on my way through England to my new destination. I should feel obliged by a letter of introduction to Colonel Wildman, as I consider a personal inspection of the documents at Newstead Abbey a matter of curiosity and importance.

"Yours faithfully in Christ,
"✠ WILLIAM CLANCY.

"WASHINGTON IRVING, Esq."

No. 5.
Washington Irving, Esq., to Bishop Clancy.

"GREENBURG, August 2, 1837.

"DEAR SIR—Enclosed I send you the required letter of introduction to Colonel Wildman, which you would have received sooner had I not been from home. I can only repeat my sincere disposition to correct any erroneous statement I may have made through misapprehension of the purport of the Newstead documents, and my deep regret at having by any ill-judged exercise of my pen caused you so much chagrin. Very respectfully, dear sir, your most obedient servant,

"WASHINGTON IRVING.

"The Right Rev. WM. CLANCY,
"Bishop of Demarara."

No. 6.
Washington Irving, Esq., to Colonel Wildman.

"GREENBURG, BANKS OF THE HUDSON,
"August 2, 1837.

"MY DEAR SIR—At the request of the Right Rev. Wm. Clancy, Catholic Bishop of Demarara, I give him this letter of introduction to procure for him the inspection of the ancient documents of the Abbey, found in the brazen eagle at Newstead; particularly an indulgence, the tenor of which he affirms I must have greatly misstated, provided it be a genuine document. If I have, by any misapprehension of the document in question, been led into error, I shall be most happy to have the error corrected; and I am sure you will take a pleasure in submitting the ancient archives of the Abbey to the inspection of the Bishop. With kindest remembrances to Mrs. Wildman, I remain ever, my dear sir, yours most faithfully,

"WASHINGTON IRVING.

"Colonel THOMAS WILDMAN."

No. 7.
Note by Bishop Clancy.

"I went from Nottingham on Wednesday, the 24th of October, accompanied by the Rev. William Wilson, the Catholic pastor of the district, to Newstead Abbey, after sending the letter of Washington Irving to Colonel Wildman. This truly respectable English gentleman promptly showed the original, and afforded every facility for deciphering it. As we were not able to take a perfect copy on that day, the Colonel most hospitably invited me and my rev. companion to spend the following Friday at the Abbey. In the meantime I procured a work called *Court Hand Restored*, in order to take a full and fair copy. The following is the result of my researches: The most inexperienced person will perceive that so far from its being an indulgence to friars from a Pope, Bishop, or any ecclesiastical authority, that it is a pardon for civil offences, which an English King thought proper to impart to real or imaginary offenders against the forest laws in Sherwood, County of Nottingham. As I am about to sail in a few days for the distant and unhealthy shores of British Guiana, I deemed it expedient, in order to set the matter at rest, to consign th publication of these papers to the Rev. W. Wilson, to be transmitted by him to the editors of the *Catholic Magazine*, and orthodox journals in London. After their publication, I wish to have a copy of them transmitted to Washington Irving, Esq., in order that he may fulfil his promise of 'correcting in a future edition,' an error which, if true, would exhibit Catholicity in the most vicious, degraded, and damnable aspect, in which her worst enemies in England and the United States ever depicted the 'milk white hind' of eighteen centuries."

"✠ WILLIAM CLANCY, Bishop of Orierse,
"Vicar Apostolic of British Guiana."

We are not able to ascertain whether the foregoing note of Bishop Clancy, giving the result of his inspection of the documents at Newstead Abbey, ever reached the eye of Washington Irving : the foregoing correspondence, accompanied by the Bishop's note, was published at length in the *London Catholic Magazine* and in the *New York Freeman's Journal*, in 1842. It is to be presumed that he never saw them, and yet it would seem strange, after the expression he gave to the just sentiments he addressed to Bishop Clancy, that he would have permitted another edition of Newstead Abbey to be issued without fully investigating the subject, to which his attention had thus been so earnestly called. However this may be, it is strangely true that, after the publication of Dr. Clancy's researches at the Abbey, and the result of them, editions of Newstead Abbey, revised by the author, were published, with the obnoxious passages retained, and they are still retained in every edition of Irving's Works to the present time. Hence the necessity for reproducing the refutation of them.

Bishop Clancy discharged the duties of Vicar Apostolic in British Guiana for about ten years. Among the conversions to the faith effected in that country through his instrumentality, was that of Mr. Justice Firebrace, a Judge of the Colony, at Georgetown, in Demarara. The Judge's brother soon followed his example. He returned, however, to his native country in 1847, in bad health, and with a constitution completely shattered by his labors and the poisoning influences of that unhealthy climate. He died in Ireland in the summer of 1847, greatly lamented by numerous friends both among the clergy and laity.

MOST REV. ANTHONY BLANC, D.D.,

Fifth Bishop and First Archbishop of New Orleans, A.D. 1835.*

ARCHBISHOP BLANC was born at Sury, a town neai Lyons, in France, October 11, 1792. The condition of religion in his native country, during his tender years, was not favorable to the moral training of youth; but in the bosom of a pious family he imbibed early lessons in religion and acquired a good education. After the restoration of the Church in France, he was among the first to embrace the ecclesiastical state, and received ordination in the holy priesthood about the year 1816. He was ordained by dispensation one or two years before the canonical age, which saved him from military conscription. The banner of the cross was his standard, and under it he enlisted for life. He came to the United States shortly after his ordination, and was one of that noble band of young missionaries who volunteered under Bishop Dubourg, of New Orleans, and left his native country in company with that distinguished Prelate for the arduous mission of the Southwestern States, then attached to the diocese of New Orleans.

He embarked from Bordeaux July 1, 1817, and landed at Annapolis, Maryland, in September, having made the voyage in a sailing-vessel. While Bishop Dubourg proceeded to Baltimore with a portion of his colony, Father Blanc remained at Annapolis at the head of the others,

---

* Authorities: *New Orleans Delta*, June 23, 1860; *Life of Bishop Flaget*, by Most Rev. Dr. Spalding; *Life of Bishop Timon*, by Deuther; *Life of Father De Andreis*; *Catholic Almanac*, 1861; *Catholic Magazines*, and *Metropolitans*; *Freeman's Journal*, and other periodical publications; etc., etc.

who consisted chiefly of young candidates for the ministry. They were received with characteristic hospitality and entertained at the mansion of Charles Carroll of Carrollton, where they remained until the end of October. Then Father Blanc joined the Bishop at Baltimore, and the whole company started on their westward journey in two divisions, the Bishop and Father Blanc being with the last division. For two days they traveled in a stage, but this was so frequently upset on the way, and proved so dangerous, that Father Blanc made the rest of the journey to Pittsburgh on foot with the Bishop, which took them five days more. From Pittsburgh to Louisville they traveled on a flat-boat, arrived at Louisville November 30, and at St. Thomas', Bardstown, on the 2d of December.

From this time he spent nearly fifteen years of arduous missionary life in the wide field then presented to his zeal, commencing with the mission at Vincennes, to which he was appointed April 25, 1818, together with Father Jeanjean, the former to take charge of the mission, the latter to found a college. A misunderstanding with a faction of the people defeated the plans of Father Jeanjean, who was soon recalled, and Father Blanc was left alone in that vast and scattered mission for several months. He was then joined by Father Ferrari, a Lazarist. During his stay at Vincennes, Father Blanc succeeded in building two log chapels, rude but pioneer shrines of the West; one in Davis County, seven miles from Liverpool, now Washington; and the other on the Illinois side of the Wabash, twelve miles from Vincennes, in a French settlement. His zealous and active attention to the mission in that region relieved the mind of Bishop Flaget very much, to whose diocese his services were generously given for the time by Bishop Dubourg, and enabled the former to give his care to other suffering portions of his flock. In February, 1820, Father Blanc was recalled, and stationed at New Orleans. Subsequently to this he was stationed successively at Natchez, Point Coupé, and Baton Rouge, in all of which places he labored with devotion and zeal for the good of souls.

Bishop De Neckere called him to New Orleans, and appointed him Associate Vicar-General with the aged Father Richard in December, 1831. That saintly Prelate was desirous of resigning the Episcopal office, and without consulting Father Blanc, procured from Rome his appointment as Coadjutor of New Orleans, and had, in fact, applied for his appointment as his successor. Father Blanc received the Bulls appointing him coadjutor in 1832, but he was only willing to accept the appointment on condition that Bishop De Neckere would abandon his intention of resigning;· but as the latter would not consent to do this, he returned the Bulls to Rome. On the death of Bishop De Neckere, in 1833, and the refusal of Father Jeanjean to accept the succession, Father Blanc was appointed Administrator of the diocese of New Orleans, and in October, 1835, he received the Bulls from Rome appointing him Bishop of New Orleans. On his acceptance the clergy and people of the diocese openly expressed their joy at receiving "a Bishop of such estimable virtues."

Bishop Blanc was consecrated at the Cathedral of New Orleans, on Sunday, November 22, 1835, by Bishop Rosati, assisted by Bishops Purcell and Portier, the latter of whom preached the consecration sermon both in English and French. The consecration was described as "one of the most august ceremonies ever witnessed in the Cathedral of New Orleans," accustomed as it was to be the scene of the most solemn pageants of the Church.

The diocese of New Orleans presented a laborious field to the new Bishop. The Catholic population, composed probably to the extent of one-half of French Creoles, and the remainder of Catholics from other States and from foreign countries, was numerous, and needed the active exertions of Bishop and priests. The Episcopal visitations formed a prominent feature in the administration of Bishop Blanc. The numbers of persons who received confirmation at his hands were very great, embracing many converts. Spiritual retreats were frequently given to the people at New Orleans and other places, and some idea may be formed of the increase of faith and devotion amongst them, from the fact that in 1820 there were scarcely twenty pascal communions in the city of New Orleans, and by the exertions of Bishops Dubourg and Blanc, and their zealous clergy, the number was increased in 1838 to ten thousand in that city. The diocese of New Orleans embraced the States of Louisiana and Mississippi. In 1838 Texas was added to the jurisdiction of Bishop Blanc, and his promptness in taking measures to remedy the evils under which the Church was laboring there deserves all praise. He secured the services of the Lazarists at the Barrens, in Missouri, despatched thither Fathers Timon and Odin, and subsequently promoted the erection of that country into a Vicariate Apostolic, and still later into an Episcopal See, with Dr. Odin as its ecclesiastical ruler. It was also under his administration that Mississippi was erected into a separate diocese from Louisiana, with its Episcopal See at Natchez.

To provide his large diocese with faithful clergymen was one of Bishop Blanc's earliest and most earnest efforts. His clergy were greatly recruited from abroad for some time, and the zealous priests, whom he cordially received from foreign countries, were especially commended by him to the respect and support of his people; because, as he so justly remarked in one of his pastorals, the Church knows neither clime nor nationality, and recognizes no party in her ministry, and that the term *foreign* could not be applied to Catholic clergymen coming from abroad to Louisiana to labor for the salvation of souls. At the same time he recognized the importance of rearing up, from among the youths of the South, a body of native clergy, to co-operate in the great work of extending the Church and her institutions. Thus, in 1838, the Diocesan Seminary was established under his auspices in the parish of Assumption, and confided to the Lazarist Fathers, whom he extensively introduced into his diocese, and who, on their part, achieved important results for the cause of religion. After the destruction of the Seminary, February 28, 1855, another was erected by the Lazarists at Jefferson City, and, in 1858, the present Ecclesiastical Seminary was erected in the city of New Orleans. In 1842, he welcomed at New Orleans nineteen Lazarists, a colony composed of priests, students, and brothers, brought over from Europe by Father Timon for the missions of the Southwest. The Bishop distributed them amongst the different houses of the city, to enable them to study English, and prepare for the missions.

The Society of Jesus was another powerful and invaluable means of encouraging the cause of education and religion, which Bishop Blanc promoted in his diocese

At the time of his death, the Jesuit Fathers had charge of the College of St. Charles at Grand Coteau, of the College of the Immaculate Conception in the city of New Orleans, and of several parishes in the diocese.

It was also during Bishop Blanc's administration that the invaluable services of the Redemptorists were procured. Not only in the District of Lafayette, which was specially confided to them, but also in New Orleans, where their principal convent was established before the Prelate's death, have they worked with apostolic zeal and accomplished most gratifying results in the work of salvation.

Gratifying and encouraging as was the progress of the faith in his diocese, Bishop Blanc's administration was not free from those evils which, in his own as well as in other dioceses, flowed inevitably from the vicious system of lay trusteeships as a mode for the tenure of church property. His manner of dealing with this hydra-headed monster of that day in the American church did equal honor to his well-known mildness, to the charity of his character, and to his firmness and vigor in vindicating the laws of the Church and the prerogatives of his own office. On the death of the Rev. Aloysius Moni, rector of the Cathedral or Church of St. Louis at New Orleans, Bishop Blanc appointed the worthy Father Etienne Rousselon to succeed him as rector of that church. The lay trustees refused to allow the duly appointed pastor to officiate in the temple consecrated to the service of God, and at a meeting of their body passed resolutions declaring the appointment by the Bishop null and void, forbidding the priests attached to the Cathedral to obey Father Rousselon's directions under pain of forfeiture of salary and dismissal, and forfeiting the salary and place of any of said priests who should decline to perform any function under the usurped authority of the lay trustees. It seems incredible that persons claiming to be Catholics could have entered into such proceedings, or used such language, repugnant as they are to the very idea of a church of God, and to the name of Catholic. Bishop Blanc mildly addressed them on the subject, and they published an insulting reply. His charity still restrained him from proceeding to extremities, without first consulting his clergy. He accordingly summoned together the several pastors of the city, and in accordance with their unanimous advice he issued a pastoral address, in which he ably vindicated his right to nominate to the vacant office, proved that he, and not the Trustees, was responsible to God for the spiritual welfare of the flock, over which the Holy Ghost had appointed him Bishop, and finally, that he acted in accordance with the express declarations of the Council of Trent. He then proceeded to forbid any clergyman, but the one appointed by him, to officiate in the Cathedral, and warned the laity against the evil of schism, to which the conduct of the Trustees, if persevered in, would inevitably lead. All his mild measures having failed, he resorted to sterner means, and interdicted the church. An election of Trustees was held, at which the well-disposed members of the congregation determined to contest the matter with the refractory Trustees. But as the constitution of the church allowed, or was construed to allow, all who chose to attend the church the right to vote, without regard to their religious views, it was easy for the malcontents to muster their one thousand and fifty votes, given by persons of every form of religious belief and unbelief, while the true Catholic vote of the congregation was cast against the Trustees by five hundred and fifty legitimate voters. A controversy of over a year's duration ensued. On one occasion, as the priest appointed by the Bishop was about to ascend the sacred desk, he was stopped by two young men of the congregation and prevented from preaching. Litigation in the courts, between the Trustees and the Bishop, and appeals to the Legislature, ensued, all of which were decided ultimately in favor of Bishop Blanc. Throughout this controversy, which now forms a part of the history of the Church, and is here recorded not in the spirit of uncharitableness, but rather as the instructive lesson of the past, the Bishop did not claim to destroy the legal and vested title of the Trustees to hold the temporalities under their charter: his object was to limit them to that title and restrain them from encroachments on the spiritual and ecclesiastical authority. His conduct through those trying times was ever marked by the mildness so characteristic of his nature, which, blended as it was with firmness, assisted greatly in promoting an amicable result. The controversy was happily adjusted by Bishop Blanc, with the co-operation and counsel of Bishop Portier, of Mobile, in the latter part of the year 1844, and the Abbé Maenhaut was appointed by the Bishop rector of St. Louis, an event which, to the credit of the Trustees and the congregation, has been followed by peace and harmony to the present day.

In a few years after his consecration Bishop Blanc had doubled the number of the churches of New Orleans, and it was he that built the chapel of St. Mary, adjoining the episcopal residence, and to supply the place of old St. Mary's of the Ursulines, the corner-stone of which he laid February 16, 1845. It has continued ever since to be the private chapel of the Bishop, while affording parochial accommodations at the same time to a Catholic congregation in the neighborhood.

The Seventh Council of Baltimore, which assembled May 6, 1849, recommended the increase of metropolitan sees in the United States, and accordingly, by apostolic briefs, dated July 19, 1850, New Orleans was erected into an Archdiocese, with the dioceses of Mobile, Natchez, Little Rock, and Galveston as suffragans, and Bishop Blanc was raised to the dignity of Archbishop. His wisdom, learning, and all-prevailing mildness, blended with great force of character, had made him an influential and useful member of the Catholic Hierarchy in the United States. He attended the First Provincial Council of Baltimore, in 1829, as theologian to Bishop Fenwick, of Boston. He also attended as a Prelate the Third, Fourth, Fifth, Sixth, and Seventh Provincial Councils of Baltimore, and the First Plenary Council in 1852. He also summoned together, and presided over, as metropolitan, the First Provincial Council of New Orleans, held in the Cathedral, and commencing January 20, 1856; an event most auspicious for the church in the Southwest. The Council was attended by the Archbishop, four suffragan Bishops, with their theologians, and five superiors of religious congregations. The pastoral letter of the Archbishop and his suffragans, addressed to the Catholics of the dioceses of that province, was spoken of by cotemporory publications as "replete with paternal admonitions and salutary counsels to Catholics, especially at this period of our country's history." In 1855, Archbishop Blanc, on the invitation of our Holy Father Pius IX., repaired to Rome to attend that august assembly of Cardinals, Archbishops, and Bishops, who, on the ever-memorable 8th of December, received from the lips of the Vicar of Christ and Infallible Teacher of the Church, the solemn definition of the dogma of the Immaculate Conception of the Blessed Virgin Mary. Devoted client of the Immaculate Mother as he was, Archbishop Blanc fervently rejoiced in this glorious and auspicious event, in which he was a zealous actor; and no one of the venerable Prelates assembled in the basilica of St. Peter on that happy occasion more cordially sympathized with the event than Archbishop Blanc, or more truly realized in his heart the beauty and truth of those exquisite lines of the late Rev. Dr. Faber:—

> "O purest of creatures! sweet mother! sweet maid!
> The one spotless womb wherein Jesus was laid!
> Dark night hath come down on us, Mother! and we
> Look out for thy shining, sweet Star of the Sea!
>
> "Deep night hath come down on this rough-spoken world,
> And the banners of darkness are boldly unfurled;
> And the tempest-tost church—all her eyes are on thee,
> They look to thy shining, sweet Star of the Sea!
>
> "The Church doth what God hath first taught her to do;
> He looked o'er the world to find hearts that were true;
> Through the ages He looked, and He found none but thee,
> And He loved thy clear shining, sweet Star of the Sea!"

His elevation to the Archiepiscopal dignity, while it increased the influence for good which Archbishop Blanc had always exerted in the Church, also added to his labors and solicitudes. Yet he continued as before to give minute and detailed interest and attention to every part of his varied and increasing duties. He had the consolation of consecrating Bishop Quinlan, of Mobile, in the Cathedral of New Orleans, on Sunday, December 4, 1859. The ceremony was a most imposing one, and was attended by the following Prelates besides Archbishop Blanc:—Archbishop Purcell, Bishops Elder, Wood, Odin, Juncker, and Lynch. Archbishops Blanc and Purcell, and Bishop Wood, accompanied the newly consecrated Bishop to his see and assisted at his solemn installation on the following Sunday.

His visitations never lost in their extent or their good results. It was during one of these missions for the Church, or for her suffering children, during a season afflicted with yellow-fever, that he incautiously met with a serious accident, which proved painful during life, and was perhaps to some extent connected with his death. On landing from a steamer on the dock at New Orleans, his foot descended into a hole in the dock, by which he was thrown, and both bones of the leg above the ankle were broken. His labors for his flock continued as energetic as ever; neither the infirmities of health, nor the feebleness of advancing years, checked the energy and zeal of his efforts. New churches and institutions sprang up in various parts of his diocese, and he was deeply interested in every step thus taken in providing the means of education and salvation for his people. Thus he was frequently engaged in laying the cornerstones of new churches or institutions, and in dedicating and inaugurating them, and in bringing back into the Church large numbers of careless Catholics, and many converts. Mention has already been made of the introduction and success of the three great religious orders, Lazarists, Redemptorists, and Jesuits. Besides these may be mentioned the Christian Brothers, with their numerous schools; the Sisters of Charity, with their numerous asylums and other noble works; the Sisters of Notre Dame, having charge of the female schools of St. Alphonsus' Church; the Sisters of the Good Shepherd; the Congregation of our Lady of Mount Carmel; the Congregation of the Holy Cross. That the number of Catholic churches was increased from twenty-six to seventy-three in the diocese during his administration, not including the increase in Texas and Mississippi, before their separation; the number of the clergy from twenty-seven to ninety-two; the number of colleges established were two, besides the Ecclesiastical Seminary; eight academies for young ladies; nine free schools; thirteen orphan asylums, and three convents, are facts which will attest his zeal and labors. The following article, published in the *New Orleans Picayune*, shortly before his death in 1860, gives an account of the progress of Catholicity during his administration:—

"In our notices of religious movements in this city, we should overlook an important feature did we neglect to allude to the active agencies used by the Catholic Church. It is now that it does not, as in the early history of New Orleans (before the influx of the non-Catholic elements), exert a predominating influence throughout the entire city. But the contact with Protestant churches has aroused the Catholic Church to vigilance and activity. It is not now content with keeping open the Cathedral and a few chapels for worship; but in the suburbs, and wherever the field is contested, it piles up large masses of brick and mortar, dedicates the edifices reared without parade or appeals to public contributions, to the service of God, and lights the fire upon the altar which is never permitted to go out. It manages to increase its number of orphan asylums and houses of industry as the wants of the helpless demand succor. It multiplies its schools as the public schools grow in public favor. It institutes popular lectures to teach the Catholic faith to those who through curiosity may be induced to visit the lecture-room, but would not be found in the Church. Its female missionaries—the Sisters of Charity—are made nurses in our public hospitals, and have even a private hospital of their own. To counteract the teaching of Protestant tracts, it now issues in a cheap and attractive form tracts on the history, growth, progress, and claims of the Catholic Church, which are distributed without cost to all who will read.

"In family ministrations, by visiting the family fireside, counseling youth in the highways, and instilling the principles of its faith into the minds of the young students in its schools, its priests' equal the most active of their Protestant neighbors.

"Many of the most striking buildings of our city are institutions, charitable or religious, of the Catholic Church. In Jefferson City it has founded a theological school, which promises to become one of considerable importance. At present the institution is a large four-story edifice, but a whole square is in the future to be occupied by the buildings appertaining to the accommodation of the young acolytes.

"It cannot be denied that in many cases the families of the Catholic population, especially the females, are more constant and devout in their attendance upon religious services than those who profess Protestantism. Mass is performed every morning, and the houses of worship are always well thronged. A constant succession of worshippers, from early dawn to ten o'clock, are to be seen entering or leaving the Catholic churches. In this they set an example worthy of imitation.

"Abstracting the mind from the secular concerns, and looking at the religious movements of this city, it seems to be a great battle-field between Catholicity and Protestantism. There is action everywhere. All the agencies for operating upon the human mind, invented in this active age, are employed by both of the opposing forces. Perhaps in system and persistence of effort the Catholics have the advantage. Each is aided by immigration; the one by immigrants from the Old World, the other by additions to our population of native-born American citizens.

"It is doubtful whether the Catholic clergy in any city, by their mode of action, or by their personal influence, are less subject to the criticism of their opponents than in this; and nowhere are their energy and devotion more calculated to infuse vitality, zeal, and liberality in the hearts of their opponents."

Archbishop Blanc after a life of many years of usefulness, labor, charity, and benediction to his flock, died suddenly at his residence in New Orleans, on Wednesday, June 20, 1860, aged about sixty-eight years. For some years past his health had not been as good as usual, but there was nothing to cause alarm or even uneasiness, and he continued as before to discharge with activity the arduous duties of his office. On the Sunday before his death he confirmed one hundred and twelve persons at Thibodeauxville, and returned to New Orleans on Monday in his usual good health, except that he complained of weakness in the leg that had been broken about two years before. He had an appointment to administer confirmation at the Chapel of St. Mary.

adjoining his residence, on the following Thursday, the day which followed that of his death. On Wednesday he arose as usual, said Mass, breakfasted with his priests, and addressed himself to his work for the day. A half-hour before his death a clergyman, who was in his room on business, left him in his usual health and spirits. Fifteen minutes later he accompanied some friends, who called on him, from his room to the head of the stairs. Returning to his room, he was engaged in opening his letters, which had just been brought from the post-office, when suddenly feeling himself struck with regurgitation of blood to the heart, he called aloud, rang his bell, and threw himself on the bed. A servant, who immediately answered the bell, found him lying on the bed, and evidently in a dying condition. Father Rousselon, his long and faithful friend and Vicar-General, was called, and found him speechless and probably unconscious; he had barely time to administer to his dying friend and Archbishop extreme unction and the last absolution, when he expired; it was about one o'clock in the day. He was solemnly interred on the 24th. Thus passed to his long and just reward the good and eminent Archbishop Blanc, "whose venerated memory is embalmed in the hearts of both priests and people."

MOST REV. JOHN HUGHES, D.D.,

Fourth Bishop and First Archbishop of New York, A.D. 1837.*

ARCHBISHOP HUGHES occupied a pre-eminent position in the Hierarchy of the Catholic Church in the United States. His life is a study worthy of the most careful consideration of Prelate, priest, and layman. His struggles in early life to overcome the impediments which fortune threw in his way, and to attain admission into the holy ministry, and the success with which, apparently by his own efforts and perseverance, he emerged from the life of manual labor to the field of the highest and most brilliant intellectual and moral usefulness and triumphs, present an example worthy of emulation. His varied and gigantic services to religion, and his bold, able, and successful championship of the faith in the United States, at a time when such services were most needed, seem to mark him out as a man raised by Providence for great purposes, as the man for the times and country in which his lot was cast, and as one whose influence is destined long to survive him.

John Hughes was born at Annaloghan, in the County Tyrone, Ireland, June 24, 1797. His parents were Patrick Hughes and Margaret McKenna, who were plain but comfortably well off, and respected for their virtues. Their sons aided the father in cultivating the farm of which he was tenant, and the daughters assisted the mother in her household duties. The father was better educated than most men of his class, and was a

---

* Hassard's *Life of Archbishop Hughes*; *Works of Archbishop Hughes*; *Catholic Magazine*; *Biographical Notices*; *Eulogies, Sermons*, etc., etc.

peaceable and prudent citizen amidst the factious and often lawless proceedings and excitements of his day. The mother was remarkable for a refinement of character beyond her opportunities and position. They were both truly pious and conscientious parents, whose chief study was to bring up their children in the fear of God, in truthfulness, in virtue, and in devotion to the faith and Church of their forefathers. John discovered from his earliest years a leaning towards the sanctuary, which greatly pleased his good parents. He went first to a day-school at Augher, with his elder brothers, and afterwards to a grammar-school at Auchnacloy. He was always a good student, a favorite with his teachers, and popular with his companions. His well-balanced character was even then manifested; for he was at the same time a leader in the class-room and a joyous and merry companion in recreation. He was well grounded in the English branches; but had not the advantage of the classics. Had his father's fortune continued prosperous, John no doubt would have been educated for the priesthood; but adversity compelled his father to withdraw him from school and set him at work with his brothers, on one of the farms, of which he conducted two. But he was not required to lay aside his books entirely, for the family as well as himself still cherished the hope of some day seeing him at the altar. In the midst of his labors he meditated earnestly on his true vocation, and he said to a friend in after-years: "Many a time have I thrown down my rake in the meadow, and, kneeling behind a hay-rick, begged of God and the Blessed Virgin to let me become a priest." Though he discharged his duties faithfully, it was evident that John's vocation was not to be a farmer. He was subsequently placed with a horticulturist, where he had opportunities of study, which he increased by reviewing at night all that he had learned at school. The persecutions under which Catholics then suffered in Ireland were keenly felt by Mr. Hughes and his family, and by none more than by John, who was open in his expressions of disgust and indignation. So no one more warmly seconded his father's inclination to emigrate and settle in America than did John; for he saw in the new and developing prospect before him in the New World a hope of accomplishing the darling project of his heart. He was nineteen years old when his father came on a visit of inquiry and observation to the United States, in 1816, at which time he returned to the farm and united with his brothers in its cultivation. His father settled at Chambersburg, and John came out and joined him there in 1817, leaving his mother, with one son and two daughters still in Ireland. After a short visit to his father at Chambersburg, he returned to Baltimore, and obtained a situation with a gardener or nurseryman on the eastern shore of Maryland. Just as he was laying his plans for resuming his studies in the intervals of labor, he lost his situation and returned to his father, where his mother and the rest of the family joined them in August, 1818. John worked for a year or more with his father, working in stone quarries, mending roads, and applying himself to any honest labor that presented itself. But it was not long before he became aware of his providential proximity to the College and Theological Seminary of Mount St. Mary, at Emmittsburg, Maryland; nor was he long in applying, though unknown and unintroduced, for admission to its classes, upon the condition, usual in such cases, of his rendering a return by teaching the youngest scholars, and by such other services as he could perform. But there was no vacancy at the time. Disappointment did not discourage him; but he went from time to time to the College to seek admission, and was told each time there was no vacancy. Far from becoming disheartened, he became only the more vigilant in watching his opportunity; and for this purpose he removed to Emmittsburg, and obtained work there, in order to be at hand when the long-sought vacancy should occur. He worked as a day-laborer on a little stone bridge over a small stream on the road from Emmittsburg to Taneytown. His deportment and associations gained for him a consideration not usually accorded to laborers. Here he made the acquaintance of Rev. Mr. Cooper, the benefactor of Mother Seton, who was then pastor at Emmittsburg. So anxious was he to enter the sacred enclosure of the Mountain, that he begged Mr. Dubois, the President, to receive him in any capacity until a vacancy occurred. He was not embarrassed when told that the only situation vacant was one in the garden. He joyously accepted this position as one step towards the priesthood. In return for his superintendence of the garden he was to receive board, lodging, and private instruction. There seems to have been a chain of providential circumstances leading the way to Mount St. Mary's. His duties were faithfully discharged in the garden, and his hours for study were availed of to the best advantage. His Latin Grammar was frequently his *vade mecum* in the garden, and the observation of this fact by the President led to his being relieved mostly of the garden, and introduced as a regular student in the College in 1820.

He was now twenty-three years of age. His application was untiring; and though he exercised some inspec-

tion over the garden, and occasionally left his class to
give directions to the workmen, or to adjust the sashes
of the hot-beds, his chief occupation was study. In
time he passed through the routine of being teacher of
Latin and mathematics, and of being prefect over the
students. He bore the many annoyances of this well-
known ordeal with great prudence, good temper, and
judgment. He acquired Latin, Greek, and mathematics
as the means to an end, and though he became proficient in them, they were not his favorite studies. It
was only when he became a theological student, and
entered the congenial realm of dogma, logic, and philosophy, that his soul seemed to expand to his work.
The close application to study which now characterized
him, and which he practised in order to repair the time
lost at out-door labor, would have impaired a less robust
frame; but those labors in the field and quarries had well
fitted the frame to sustain the studies and endure the intellectual exertions that were to follow. During this
period his future character began to develop; his presence of mind and coolness on several trying occasions,
and his first controversy in answering a Fourth of July
oration, in which the Catholic Church was reflected upon,
were indications of his future greatness and capacity.
In his theological studies he enjoyed the inestimable
privilege and advantage of being under the guidance
and instruction of the saintly and learned Bruté, between
whom and himself the warmest friendship ever afterwards
subsisted. He occasionally preached, and sometimes
gave wings to his muse to beguile a moment of relaxation. His first sermon, however, gave much brighter
promise of a future divine, than his maiden verses gave
of a future poet. In 1825, having already received eccle-

siastical tonsure and subdeaconship, he was made a deacon. He resolved to attach himself to the diocese of Philadelphia, and Rev. Michael Hurley, a distinguished Augustinian, of Philadelphia, was selected as his director for some time after he should have left the Seminary. This gentleman, in his correspondence with Mr. Hughes, gave him much wholesome and practical advice, and confirmed his taste for scholastic divinity by recommending him to make himself master of *The End of Controversy*. Bishop Conwell, while on a visitation of his diocese, met Mr. Hughes at Chambersburg; he requested the young Levite to preach, a duty which he performed so well upon a short notice, that the venerable prelate insisted upon his performing the whole visitation with him. In 1826 he answered, with remarkable ability, a tract entitled *Protestantism and Popery*, though his answer did not appear before 1827, when it was published in the *United States Catholic Miscellany*, of Charleston, and afterwards in pamphlet form at Chambersburg. His theological studies being finished, he was ordained a priest by Bishop Conwell, at St. Joseph's Church, Philadelphia, October 15, 1826.

The first few weeks of his priesthood were spent with his preceptor, the Rev. Dr. Hurley, at St. Augustine's, during which time he took his share in the confessions, sermons, and other parochial duties. His brief period of practical lessons in the holy ministry under this eminent divine, who taught him how to apply the precepts he had learned from the books, and from the Rev. Messrs. Dubois and Bruté, was of great service to the young priest. At this early period of his career, Dr. Hurley predicted for him a distinguished future. He was sent to Bedford by Bishop Conwell, who had summoned the Rev. Mr. Heyden of that place to Philadelphia. The labors and hardships of a country mission were well suited to his vigorous health and active temperament. His occupations here were incessant, and he was never so well pleased as when he had abundance of work. By his short residence at Bedford he made many friends, and left behind him many admirers. In January, 1827, Bishop Conwell recalled him to Philadelphia, at the request of Mr. Heyden, and stationed him at St. Joseph's, heretofore a part of St. Mary's parish, but now erected by the Bishop into a separate parish. The unhappy differences between the trustees of St. Mary's and Bishop Conwell were then at their height, and it required all the good judgment and prudent foresight of Mr. Hughes to steer his course safely through such embarrassing complications. That he succeeded in doing so is owing to his own clear and discriminating judgment and firmness, and to the prudent counsel of his friends, Messrs. Heyden, Hurley, Bruté, and Egan—the last of whom had succeeded Bishop Dubois in the Presidency of Mt. St. Mary's College. Seeing as he did, from the earliest period of his ministry, the evil effects of trusteeism, he became ever afterwards its bitter opponent. It was in this school that he learned those lessons which enabled him to deal so effectually and successfully with the trustee system in New York. He took no part in controversies, the result of which he could not control, and by keeping aloof he did not impair his usefulness amongst his people. He devoted himself most earnestly to his priestly duties, such as confessions, visiting the sick, preaching, and instructing the children. His sermons were carefully written and studied, and his efforts in the pulpit were so successful that he ranked among the eminent preachers, of whom there were several in Philadelphia. The pulpits of the eloquent orators, Dr. Hurley and Father Harold, were deserted by hundreds, who went to hear Mr. Hughes. Bishop Conwell was delighted with him, and would frequently say, "We'll make him a bishop some day." After the suspension of Rev. Mr. Harold, then pastor of St. Mary's, in April, 1827, Mr. Hughes was appointed pastor of the refractory congregation of St. Mary's, a position which he only accepted on the positive command of his superior. His position here was extremely embarrassing; though the trustees made no special opposition to his appointment, they refused to pay him any salary. His prudent course seemed even to have lulled their passions for a brief season. He and his assistant, however, before very long withdrew from the church, with the approval of the Bishop, leaving it to the trustees without a pastor. He returned to St. Joseph's and resumed his former active parochial duties there, abstaining wholly from the stormy proceedings through which the church of Philadelphia afterwards passed. He was during this period a close student, principally of controversial and doctrinal works. He had a brief controversy, in 1827, with Rev. Dr. Bedell, rector of St. Andrew's Protestant Episcopal Church in Philadelphia, in which he wrote under the *nom de plume* of "Friend of Truth and Justice." He also projected a Catholic Tract Society, as a means of combating current prejudices and constant attacks against Catholics; he wrote the first book for the Society, entitled *Andrew Dunn*, a controversy skilfully interwoven with the career of a hero. *Andrew Dunn* was quite a success, but it was the first and last publication of the Society. His sermons at St. Joseph's were well attended by Protestants, and he was thus instrumental in working the conversion of a large number of intelligent and devout Protestants. He was a constant correspondent of the learned and devout Mr. Bruté, to whom he submitted his controversial sermons, and whom he consulted on all occasions. His wise and good Mentor took the deepest interest in his young friend, to whom he was ever ready to impart his frank, earnest, and sincere advice. Fearing lest the eminence to which the young priest had attained, and the adulations of his admirers might engender and nurse sentiments of pride in his heart, he warned him repeatedly of these dangers, and advised him "to make in all things *positive good, simple, obscure duty* his principal joy and crown."

In 1829, Mr. Hughes, observing the destitute condition of a number of orphan children, for whom there was no admission into St. Joseph's Asylum, which was already full, established St. John's Orphan Asylum, into which they and others were received. For some time there seemed to be a rivalry between the two asylums, which he did all in his power to remove by accommodation; but for some time there was no arrangement, until all the parties realizing the spirit of those divine words, "Charity envieth not," so accommodated their differences as to assign all the boys to St. John's, all the girls to St. Joseph's, and St. Vincent's was abolished.

The passage of the Irish Emancipation Act, April 13, 1829, was hailed by the friends of Ireland in this country with great exultation and joy, and by no one more so than by Mr. Hughes, who was through life devotedly attached to his native country, whose wrongs he saw and felt in his youth; and he was an enthusiastic admirer of Daniel O'Connell. On the 31st of May a solemn thanksgiving Mass was celebrated at St. Augustine's Church, by Dr. Hurley, and Mr. Hughes preached the thanksgiving sermon, a production of great eloquence and power, which was afterwards issued in pamphlet form. The *Church Register*, the Protestant Episcopal organ, could not allow this exultation of patriots in the deliverance of a down-trodden country to pass without publishing a violent article on the subject, in which "the trumperies and delusions of popery" were discussed with the usual want of fairness and Christian charity. This was the occasion of a public controversy between Mr. Hughes, whose articles appeared in the *United States Gazette*, and the Rev. Dr. Delancey, whose organ was the *Church Register*. This controversy, which lasted several months, resulted in teaching Protestants that the time was past when they could abuse and vilify the Catholic Church with impunity, and that in Mr. Hughes that Church had a champion always ready and able to meet their assaults. In October of the same year Mr. Hughes attended the First Provincial Council of Baltimore, as theologian to the Very Rev. William Matthews, administrator of the Diocese of Philadelphia. Bishop Conwell returned about this time from Rome, where he had proposed the name of Mr. Hughes as the coadjutor Bishop of that see. The choice of the Council fell upon Bishop Kenrick, and Mr. Hughes was reserved for another field more suited to his ability and character. In June, 1830, Bishop Kenrick became Coadjutor-bishop and Administrator of Philadelphia, and Mr. Hughes hailed his arrival in that city as that of a worthy spirit to manage the schismatics of St. Mary's, and a man after his own heart. He sustained with his characteristic energy the measures of the new Bishop to heal the wounds of the Church.

In 1830 Mr. Hughes attended Bishop Kenrick on a visitation of the diocese, preaching, and aiding in his arduous duties that excellent Prelate, who was then in feeble health. He was now appointed the Bishop's secretary, was also agent for Mt. St. Mary's College, and performed many services not within his parochial duties. He delivered a series of lectures on the Evidences of the Christian Religion, which were attended by large numbers of Protestants, and found time also to continue his theological and controversial studies, and occasionally to exercise his pen in the interests of the Church. One of his measures in aid of the Bishop's efforts to put down trusteeism in Philadelphia was the erection of a new church without lay corporators, and rendering its altar and pulpit so attractive as to draw off all the desirable Catholics from St. Mary's. The cornerstone of this new temple was laid by Bishop Kenrick in May, 1831; Mr. Hughes canvassed most untiringly and successfully for contributions; a legacy of five thousand dollars, given to him for any religious or charitable object he might think proper, was applied to this purpose; and such was his success that the new church, then perhaps the finest in the country, though not so imposing as the Cathedral at Baltimore, was dedicated on the first Sunday of April, 1832. He succeeded not only in raising a beautiful temple to the honor and service of God, apparently without resources, and in spite of opposition from the schismatical trustees of St. Mary's, but also in giving essential aid to the death-blow of that long protracted scandal.

At the Diocesan Synod assembled at Philadelphia in May, 1832, he preached the opening sermon on the constitution of the Church and the order of church-govern ment; was appointed promoter of the Synod, and designated as one of three divines to deliberate concerning the establishment of a Diocesan Seminary, a subject on which he made a most earnest and eloquent appeal to the Synod, and, at its close, was chosen to make a complimentary address to Bishop Kenrick in the name of his brother clergymen.

In 1832, the Rev. John Breckinridge, the ablest champion of the Presbyterian Church in this country, commenced through the columns of *The Christian Advocate* a series of attacks against the Catholic Church and Catholics, and sent forth a challenge to Catholics, whether priests or Bishops, to meet him "on the whole field of controversy between Roman Catholics and Protestants." For some time the Presbyterians were exulting over the non-appearance of any champion of the Catholic cause to accept the challenge, and Catholics were sometimes tauntingly asked, "Why, if these things are untrue, does not your great Mr. Hughes reply to them." One of Mr. Hughes' congregation, when thus pressed, promised that the gauntlet should be taken up, and that too by his own pastor, to whom he went immediately with a copy of Mr. Breckinridge's letter in *The Christian Advocate*, and related to him what had occurred. Mr. Hughes' reply was, "Since you rely upon me I will not fail you." The celebrated Hughes and Breckinridge controversy, both the written and the oral discussions, grew out of this circumstance. *The Catholic Herald* was established by Mr. Hughes in order to supply the necessity for an organ to publish the Catholic side of the first or written controversy, and he was its editor at first, and a long time afterwards one of its contributors. Both sides of this oral discussion have been published together, forming a complete collection of what can be said for and against Catholicity and Protestantism, and especially on the subjects connected with the question as to whether either, and which of these, is opposed in its principles or doctrines to civil and religious liberty. These two public controversies established the fame of Mr. Hughes as the foremost among the champions of the Catholic Church in America. In every subsequent effort of his life he sustained his pre-eminent reputation. But in this, as in all his other controversies, he was acting on the defensive, and was drawn into these contests by the unprovoked attacks it was too much the custom of the anti-Catholic bigots of that day to make against the Church. When once embarked in the discussion, however, he did not remain on the defensive, but, like a good general, availed himself of every weakness of his adversaries, and of every advantage he gained over them, to carry the war into the enemy's country. That these unchristian and wicked assaults upon Catholicity have, in a great measure, ceased in our day, is chiefly owing to the resistance, and the triumphs, of those two illustrious defenders of the faith, Bishops England and Hughes.

Though engaged in these hard-fought contests with Protestants, no Catholic clergyman visited more in, or was received more cordially by, the best and most cultivated Protestant society than Mr. Hughes. He considered this as one of the means of removing prejudice, and of smoothing down asperities. As an evidence of this it may be stated, that after the Breckinridge discussion he was elected a member of the Wistar Club of Philadelphia, an association mostly of Protestant gentlemen for social purposes, into which none but persons of distinction were admitted, and to whose circles he contributed much by his varied attainments and fine social qualities. He was at the same time a model of the conscientious and hard-working priest. Though engaged in such heavy and exacting controversies, he never neglected his confessional, his sick, his children, and his inquirers for truth, and his converts. He commenced the collection of a theological and general library, which before his death grew into a valuable collection. The debts of St. John's Church now became so onerous, and all his efforts to arouse the people to make extraordinary efforts to liquidate them had so failed, that he resolved to visit Mexico to collect money for this purpose. After six months' application he thoroughly acquired the Spanish language. He announced his intended expedition and its object to his congregation one Sunday, whereupon the pewholders, aroused by the stirring appeal made to them by the Rev. Mr. Gartland, his assistant at St. John's, generously came forward and relieved him from the necessity of going to Mexico.

In 1836 it was proposed to divide the diocese of Philadelphia into two dioceses, Pittsburg to be the new see. Dr. Kenrick was spoken of either as coadjutor to Bishop Dubois of New York, or for translation to the new see of Pittsburg. Mr. Hughes was nominated for both Philadelphia and Pittsburg. All these arrangements were, however, abandoned for the time. On the appointment of a successor to Bishop Fenwick, of Cincinnati, Mr. Hughes was nominated on the same list with Dr. Purcell for that position, and so equal were the claims of those two eminent divines, that the Sacred Congregation were at a loss to whom to send the appointment. Bishop England was at Rome while these nominations were under consideration, and was asked by the Cardinal Prefect of the Propaganda if he could mention any particular, however trifling, to turn the scales in favor of one or the other nominee. Bishop England, after a moment's hesitation, replied: "There's one point, your Eminence, which may deserve to be considered. Mr. Hughes is emphatically a self-made man, and perhaps he would be on that account more acceptable to the people of a western diocese than Mr. Purcell." "Ah!" said the Cardinal, "I think that will do." The next day he met Bishop England again, and said, with an air of satisfaction, "Well, Bishop, the question is settled. As soon as I told the Cardinals what you said about *Mr. Purcell's* being a self-made man they agreed upon him unanimously, and the nomination will be at once presented to his Holiness for approval." Bishop England afterwards said to a friend in this country, "I was about to explain the mistake, but I reflected that it was no doubt the work of the Spirit of God, and was silent." The plans of Providence were not long after this made manifest and accomplished. The Council that met at Baltimore, April 16, 1837, nominated Mr. Hughes on the list with two other priests for the position of Coadjutor Bishop to Bishop Dubois, of New York. The choice fell upon Mr. Hughes, and the notification thereof arrived in the following November. He was consecrated with the title of Bishop of Basileopolis *in partibus infidelium*, on Sunday, November 26, at the Cathedral of St. Patrick, by Bishop Dubois, assisted by Bishops Kenrick and Fenwick. "I remember," said Archbishop McCloskey, "how all eyes were fixed, how all eyes were strained to get a glimpse at their newly consecrated Bishop; and as they saw that dignified and manly countenance, as they beheld those features beaming with the light of intellect, bearing upon them the impress of that force of character which peculiarly marked him throughout his life, that firmness of resolution, that unalterable and unbending will, and yet blending at the same time that great benignity and suavity of expression—when they marked the quiet composure and self-possession of every look and every gesture of his whole gait and demeanor—all hearts were drawn and warmed towards him. Every pulse within that vast assembly, both of clergy and laity, was quickened with a higher sense of courage and of hope. Every breast was filled with joy, and, as it were, with a new and younger might." *

About two weeks after the consecration of Bishop Hughes, Bishop Dubois was stricken with paralysis, and though he partially recovered, he never afterwards took a very active part in the affairs of the diocese. Bishop Hughes commenced immediately the arduous work imposed upon him. He visited the churches in and about New York, studied the condition of the diocese, and the qualifications of the clergy, preached frequently, and continued his daily missionary duties of the confessional and other works, and joined in the recitation of the daily office with Bishop Dubois and his clergy, as was their regular custom. Education was among the earliest subjects that engaged his attention, and the college at Lafargeville was founded by him to meet this great necessity.†

It was not long after his arrival in New York that an opportunity presented itself for Bishop Hughes to show of what material he was made, and how admirably he was suited to the position to which he had just been

---
* *Funeral Discourse*, 1864.   † See *Life of Bishop Dubois*, ante.

raised. The old dispute between the lay trustees of St. Patrick's and Bishop Dubois was now at its height, and the trustees had gone so far as to eject from the Sunday-school a teacher sent there by the Bishop, and to employ a constable to attend at the school to enforce their wishes. He adopted the bold plan of appealing from the trustees to the congregation. The pastoral letter Bishop Hughes addressed to the assembled congregations, supported by the name and signature of Bishop Dubois, completely won over the congregation to his side, and among the resolutions passed at one of the meetings of the congregation was the following:

"*Resolved*, That we know no difference between the authority of the Holy Church and that authority with which she has invested the Bishops for carrying on her mission for our spiritual good; and that we hold it as unworthy of our profession as Roman Catholics to oppose ourselves, or to suffer any one in our names, to oppose any let, obstacle, or hindrance—no matter how legal such act may be—which would hinder or prevent our Bishop from the full, free, and entire exercise of the rights, powers, and duties which God has appointed as inherent in his office, and the Church has authorized him to preserve, exercise, and fulfil."

The trustees were requested to enter the resolutions on the records of the Cathedral, and to adopt them as the fundamental rule of action for themselves and their successors; and those who were unwilling to do this were requested to resign. Some resigned, others adhered to the Bishop, and the regular election, which soon followed, resulted in the election of trustees who accepted the above views and supported the authority of the Church. The Bishop was unanimously requested to deliver a course of lectures in the Cathedral on the evils and dangers to religion of lay-trusteeism, a task which he performed with marked ability and with great research and ecclesiastical learning, and at the same time in the spirit of Christian charity.

This was an essential reorganization of the trustee system in the diocese of New York; for although the trustees who then held the title of church property, continued to do so, their subordination to the Bishop became a fixed principle, and they became in fact only the legal holders of the title. On Bishop Hughes' consecration as Coadjutor to Bishop Dubois, the temporalities of the diocese were at once placed in his charge, and although he could scarcely be regarded as a financier, his great energy and enlightened enterprise enabled him to accomplish much for the churches of the city of New York in particular, most of which were greatly embarrassed with debt. In 1841 the Bishop made an effort to relieve the oppressive burden of the indebtedness of the churches, by the formation of a "Church Debt Association." The whole indebtedness of the churches of the city amounted to about $300,000, and it required about $20,000 each year to pay the interest. His plan proposed a union of all the congregations in the raising of funds for equal annual distribution in payment of the debts of all, until every church should be out of debt. During the first year the sum of $17,000 was realized, and great unanimity prevailed on the subject. Time, however, and the occasional absences of the Bishop, and his inability to accomplish all by his own individual exertions, gradually led to a discontinuance of the "Association." In the same year he convoked the first Diocesan Synod of the diocese, in which, after suitable regulations were adopted in relation to the administration of the sacraments, marriage, and secret societies, the most stringent rules were adopted in relation to the temporalities of the churches and the boards of lay trustees. By these regulations all the employés of the church were placed under the control of the pastor; all moneys necessary for the support of the pastor and the maintenance of divine worship were to be supplied, and should never be withdrawn; the churches were never to be used for any meeting of a lay or even ecclesiastical purpose without the consent of the pastor; the pastor and Bishop were to have a voice in all church expenditures; and no pastor was to be given to any church, the trustees of which refused to abide by these regulations. He issued a pastoral letter embodying these regulations in detail, and reviewing the whole trustee system. There was a general acquiescence on the part of congregations and trustees; but St. Louis' Church, at Buffalo, was in the hands of a board of trustees who refused compliance, and carried their opposition to the extent of seeing their church deprived of a pastor, and of making an effort to appeal to Rome; but they were finally glad to yield to the Bishop, and to publish a card acknowledging and retracting their errors. The Bishop's next effort to relieve the temporalities of his churches consisted in his plan of raising a church loan abroad, for which purpose he visited Belgium in 1843, and proposed to the capitalists of that country his "*Emprunt Catholique de New York.*" But it did not meet with much encouragement. He succeeded, however, in securing the services of several missionaries for his diocese. In 1852 he again made an energetic effort to release the church debts, by consolidating the various congregations in one great movement for this end. His project for the erection of a new Cathedral was postponed in favor of this measure, and for the erection of several smaller churches in different parts of the city to accommodate the increasing Catholic population. For these purposes he organized the "Auxiliary Church Building Association," which was well received by the people, but was as short-lived as its predecessor, the "Church Debt Association." His efforts, however, and those of the pastors of the several churches separately, brought the affairs of those churches into a much better condition. St. Peter's Church was the one that caused him the greatest trouble and labor; its indebtedness at one time amounted to $140,000; the trustees were bankrupt and made an assignment, and after the case was for five years litigated in courts, and agitated between the lay trustees and the Bishop, the church was sold under the Sheriff's hammer, and thus passed into the hands of the Bishop. He discharged its liabilities, however, though not by law obliged to do so, and December 26, 1852, a solemn thanksgiving service was held in the church in commemoration of its extrication from such great and protracted difficulties; the Bishop preached on this joyous occasion, and the *Te Deum* was sung to express the thanks of the pastors and the people to the Almighty. So in other cases the trustees either resigned or passed the churches and church property into the hands of assignees, who sold or conveyed to the Bishop, he satisfying most scrupulously the claims of creditors, though not bound to do so by the law. St. Patrick's Cathedral and the Church of St. Nicholas were the only churches then remaining in the hands of lay trustees.

This system of trusteeism had grown up under the

law of 1813,* which authorized the male members of full age of any congregation, other than Episcopal and Reformed Protestant Dutch congregations, to elect from three to nine trustees, to hold the title and manage the church property. This law did not prohibit ecclesiastics owning, as individuals, property used for divine service. But during the ascendency of Know-Nothingism, a law was passed by the Legislature of New York, by which it was provided that all property held by any person in any ecclesiastical office or orders should, on his death, vest in the occupants or congregation using it, if they were incorporated or would incorporate, and in default, in the people of the State; and no deed of property to be used for divine worship was allowed to have any legal force or validity unless made to a corporation.† The Catholics of New York are indebted chiefly to Archbishop Hughes and to his Most Rev. successor, then Bishop of Albany, for the more just and reasonable provisions of the present law, which, in providing for the incorporation of Catholic churches, constitutes the Bishop, Vicar-General, pastor, and two laymen selected by them, as the trustees of the church property.‡

In 1839 the Holy See, in consequence of the increased infirmities of Bishop Dubois, relieved him of the administration of the diocese and appointed Bishop Hughes Administrator. In August of that year, while the latter was absent on the visitation of the diocese, Archbishop Eccleston arrived in New York with instructions to carry this arrangement into effect. Bishop Hughes' visitation, which was particularly productive of conversions and other happy fruits, being ended, he hurried back to New

---

* 2. *Revised Statutes of New York*, 606.   † 3. Ibid. 19.   ‡ 4. Ibid. 507.

York, to assume the heavy weight of care, labor, and responsibility now devolved upon him. During his previous career as priest and Bishop, he always found in the pious and learned Bishop Bruté a counselor and friend, whose profound wisdom, great learning, and tender suggestions had ever proved of invaluable service. But his good friend and adviser had now passed from the scenes of labor to those of reward, and the young Prelate had now to rely upon his own resources, guided by light and grace from the Holy Ghost. One of his first steps was the establishment of St. John's College, near Fordham, for which purpose he purchased the beautiful estate called Rose Hill, remarkable for its natural and cultivated beauties, and venerable in its historical associations with the War of Independence. The estate cost $30,000, and the expense of fitting up the buildings for the reception of students was $10,000. These amounts were raised by voluntary contributions, by collections in Europe, and by the loan of small sums at five per cent. interest. On the 14th of October, 1839, he addressed a pastoral letter to his diocese, recommending earnestly the new institution to the liberality of the people, and on the 16th of the same month he sailed for Europe, with the purpose of obtaining the aid of men and money for his diocese. This was his first visit to Europe; he was received by Pope, king, and people, in the various countries he visited, with every mark of respect and kindness. He was delighted with Rome, where he spent three months, and received valuable presents from the Holy Father. He also went to Vienna, to solicit aid from the Leopoldine Society, from which he obtained a liberal donation in aid of his College and Seminary. From Vienna he went to Munich, and thence to Paris, and in the latter city secured the services of a community of the Ladies of the Sacred Heart, to found a school in New York City. He visited his native country, where he formed the acquaintance of Daniel O'Connell, whom he greatly admired. In his native island he saw again and sympathized with his oppressed countrymen and the friends of his boyhood. He spoke publicly on several occasions while abroad, chiefly in the interest of the American Church, and after a successful mission, teeming with fruits, he returned to his episcopal city in July, 1840.

It was during the absence of Bishop Hughes in Europe, and without any correspondence with him, that the controversy on the public school question was commenced. In the early part of the present century, and for nearly twenty years, the public school funds in the State of New York were raised chiefly by taxation; and while in the State generally the schools were managed and the expenditures regulated by commissioners, inspectors, and trustees, and conformity to the school system left somewhat optional with the counties; in the city, on the contrary, the system was enforced, the taxes higher, and the school funds were distributed among certain schools and societies named by the Legislature, and such incorporated religious societies as then supported or might thereafter establish charity schools. This system was essentially defective in the inequality of the distribution, the absence of inspection and accountability, and the consequent liability to abuse. Gross abuses and frauds were brought to light, and prominent among them was the case of the Bethel Baptist Church. In 1824 the Legislature changed the law so as to provide for the naming, once in every three years, by the Common Council, of such schools and institutions as should be entitled to receive the school moneys, the corporation being responsible to the State for the faithful application of the funds. The disbursement of the greater part of the funds was entrusted to the Public School Society, incorporated for the purpose; it received the public moneys and added to them by a contribution of ten dollars from each life member and other contributions; and its annual expenditures amounted to about $130,000. Up to 1840 the Public School Society had established about one hundred schools, in which, according to theory, if not practice, a purely secular education was imparted, or at least only such general principles of religion and morality as were supposed to be common to all Christian denominations. Although it was a disputed point between the Society and the Catholics as to whether the law cut off all allowances to congregational or religious schools, still several Catholic schools or institutions had received portions of the school funds from time to time. The sums thus received were very inconsiderable, compared with their numbers and their proportion of the taxes paid; and the Catholics, while regarding education as a solemn duty and a prime necessity, yet, entertaining conscientious objections to schools for their children in which religion was ignored or taught in form or substance un-Catholic, if not anti-Catholic, were practically cut off from participation in the benefits of a public fund which they contributed their full share to raise. Their earnestness in these convictions is clearly demonstrated by the fact, that while they uncomplainingly paid all their taxes, they voluntarily taxed themselves again to establish and support their own separate schools. The opinion that the education of children, like other moral duties, pertains to the sphere of the family and not that of the State, was and is entertained as the only correct view by Catholics, and also by many persons out of the Catholic Church; and many enlightened persons of every shade of religious conviction have maintained, that if the State will intervene in this matter and impose taxes for educational purposes, the schools should be provided and the funds distributed in such a manner, as to secure to each denomination an education conformable to its creed and reconcilable with conscience. Thus the State could enforce the education of children as a public duty without violating the rights of conscience, or infringing upon the personal rights and equality of the citizens. The school controversy has never been fairly understood by the friends of the State system; the question involved is not one of opposition to education or to schools, for Catholics yield to none in their advocacy of both; the real question is as to the best and most just mode of promoting or managing this great interest; it is a question of means, not of purpose. And it may be stated that long after Catholics discovered in New York that the Public School Society, untrue to their professions and promises, actually introduced, or allowed the introduction of, sectarianism into the common schools, continued still to pay their taxes and to support their own schools besides. Their right to oppose this, as well as any other public measure, by appeals to reason, the sense of fair play, to the ballot-box, and by every other legal means of resistance or reform, cannot be questioned; and yet whenever they have done this, their opponents, ignoring the institutions of the country, and the universal right of citizens to be heard, raised the anti-popery hue and cry, and drowned the appeals to the right of the matter by clamors of conspiracy and other anti-Catholic battle-cries. The fact that Catholics only demand for themselves what they propose to concede to every other denomination, has never satisfied these mistaken opponents of a fair school system.

As a matter of history, however, the school controversy in New York did not originate with Catholics, but with fair-minded and enlightened Protestants, who were willing to view the question upon its merits, and, in viewing it, to elevate themselves above all partisan and sectarian prejudices and passions. Dr. Nott, the President of Union College, was open in the expression of his advocacy of the denominational school system, by which each denomination would share, in due proportion to its subjects or pupils in schools, in the common school fund. He even advocated the providing of schools for children of different nationalities. The denominational system is followed in several European countries of different religions, and possesses the great merit of bringing education to the very homes and altars of the people, leaving no one an excuse for not embracing its advantages; whereas our present school system drives fully one-third of the population, from conscientious motives, from the public schools. Dr. Nott had been the tutor, and was the life-long friend and adviser of Gov. Seward, and frequently expressed his views on the school question to that statesman during his occupancy of the gubernatorial chair of the State of New York. Gov. Seward, on one occasion, requested Dr. Nott to reduce his views to writing, promising to embody them in his message to the Legislature, and recommend their adoption. This he did in 1839, and the Governor, in his message to the Legislature on the 1st of January, 1840, presented the subject in the following remarkable passages:—

"Although our system of public education is well endowed, and has been eminently successful, there is yet occasion for the benevolent and enlightened action of the Legislature. The advantages of education ought to be secured to many, especially in our large cities, whom orphanage, the depravity of parents, or some form of accident or misfortune seems to have doomed to hopeless poverty and ignorance. Their intellects are as susceptible of expansion, of improvement, of refinement, of elevation, and of direction, as those minds which, through the favor of Providence, are permitted to develop themselves under the influence of better fortunes; they inherit the common lot to struggle against temptations, necessities, and vices; they are to assume the same domestic, social, and political relations; and they are born to the same ultimate destiny.

"The children of foreigners, found in great numbers in our populous cities and towns, and in the vicinity of our public works, are too often deprived of the advantages of our system of public education, in consequence of prejudices arising from difference of language *or religion*. It ought never to be forgotten that the public welfare is as deeply concerned in their education as in that of our own children. I do not hesitate, therefore, to recommend the establishment of schools, in which they may be instructed by teachers speaking the same language with themselves, *and professing the same faith*. There would be no inequality in such a measure, since it happens from the force of circumstances, if not from choice, that the responsibilities of education are in most instances confided by us to na tive citizens, and occasions seldom offer a trial of our magnanimity by committing that trust to persons differing from ourselves in language or religion. Since we have opened our country and all its fulness to the oppressed of every nation, we should evince wisdom equal to such generosity, by qualifying their children for the high responsibilities of citizenship." *

Although these enlightened and statesmanlike views do not present the strictly Catholic view of the school question, yet they are sufficiently broad to cover much of what Catholics contend for; for, although our claim is based upon the rights of conscience and the equal rights of citizens, yet the same schools that would be provided for Catholics in the case alluded to by Governor Seward, would be equally open to all Catholics, and the provision of such schools would probably be made equal to the demand or necessity for them.

Father Schneller, then pastor at Albany, who was acquainted with Governor Seward, and with several members of the Legislature, had conversations with those officials in reference to the recommendations of the Governor, and he wrote to the Very Rev. Dr. Power, then administering the concerns of the diocese in the absence of Bishop Hughes, expressing the opinions entertained at Albany, that if petitions were presented, praying for the participation of Catholic schools in the school fund, the measure could be carried. Dr. Power called a meeting of the trustees of the several Catholic churches and laid the subject before them; by their advice he visited Albany in person, and learned, from personal interviews and observation, the probability of

---

* *Assembly Documents*, 1840; vol. i. p. 5.

success. On his return to New York, a Catholic Association was formed, in order to secure uniformity and concert of action, weekly meetings were held, and a petition for a share of the school fund was presented to the Board of Assistant Aldermen. The Catholics were not alone in the movement, for their petition was followed by those of other religious denominations. These petitions were denied by the Board, but the meetings and the agitation continued. Had unanimity, moderation, and order prevailed throughout these meetings, something might have been accomplished. But this was not the case. *The Truth-Teller*, a Catholic newspaper, openly charged some of the leaders with political designs. This proved not only a firebrand thrown into the already excited meetings, but a powerful weapon in the hands of the opposition.

Such was the condition of the school question on the return of Bishop Hughes from Europe, in July, 1840. He saw that designing politicians had attempted to use the movement for their own selfish purposes, and that the interests of those most concerned in the movement were lost sight of. He at once began to attend and address the meetings, in order to bring them back to their legitimate object; and, as he said, "the first thing he did was to take measures that all politics should be excluded." From this time he assumed the control, attended all the meetings, and addressed them in the most forcible and stirring strains of eloquence and argument. The agitation had commenced, the appeal to public justice had been made, the cause was just, and what more appropriate or able leader could the Catholics have had than their own chief pastor? He prepared a petition to the Board of Aldermen, whose presentation was followed by remonstrances from the Public School Society, and the pastors of the Methodist Episcopal Churches of New York City. The latter adopted the mistaken course of foregoing a participation in the school fund themselves, rather than allow Catholics to participate therein, or rather, they preferred for their children schools of a general or non-religious character to those in which they could be taught their own creed. They preferred that Methodist children should attend schools in which Methodism was not taught, rather than have Catholic children attend schools in which Catholicity was taught.

Arrangements were made for a hearing of both sides before the Boards of Aldermen and Assistant Aldermen; the Bishop was the champion on these occasions of his Church and people, and was opposed by the Counsel for the Public School Society; by Rev. Drs. Bond, Bangs, and Reese, for the Methodists; by the Rev. Dr. Spring, for the Presbyterians; and by the Rev. Dr. Knox, for the Dutch Reformed Church. The Bishop's efforts before the Boards were among his ablest productions.* Pending the decision, negotiations for a compromise were interchanged, in which the Catholics offered to appoint no teachers, except such as the Public School Society, upon an examination, should find fully qualified; to afford every facility of visitation and inspection to the duly appointed agents of the State; to guard against abuses, and render their schools in every respect free from objection: but no arrangement was effected. The Bishop did not expect success before the City Councils; he regarded the appeal to them as a step in his progress to the Legislature. The petition was rejected January 12,

---

* See the *Works of Archbishop Hughes*.

1841, and the Catholics, headed by their Bishop, appealed by memorial to the Legislature. The memorial was referred by the Senate to the Hon. John C. Spencer, Secretary of State, and *ex-officio* Superintendent of Public Schools. The report of this official proposed an entire change in the system, by which a Commissioner of Public Schools was to be elected in each ward in the city; to these Commissioners the functions of the Public School Society were to be transferred, and the general school laws of the State were to be extended to the city. The Commissioners were to receive and supply the public moneys to the support of the public schools, which were now to be placed under their management. Seeing that it was impossible to carry their measure for a participation in the public school fund, the Catholics advocated Mr. Spencer's measure, on the ground that it was the least objectionable system they could get, and at least possessed the merit of excluding sectarianism from the schools. That such a measure should have elicited opposition from Protestants, would seem strange, were it not for the inconsistent course they pursued throughout the whole agitation. The Catholics favored the measure, therefore the Protestants should oppose it. The fact that it gave Protestants all they could desire for themselves was not enough; the system proposed to abstain from interfering with the religion of Catholic children attending the schools, and this, with the additional fact that Catholics favored it as the best measure they could get, was sufficient to elicit the most violent and unfair opposition. Not content with opposing the measure on its intrinsic merits, the controversy turned into the usual channel of abuse of Catholics. All the prejudices of the sects against the Catholic Church were appealed to, and

Bishop Hughes, as the great Catholic champion of the occasion, had his hands full of controversies, which he conducted with matchless argument, bold defiance, and unruffled courage. Some idea may now be formed of this excited controversy from the fact that such a respectable paper as the *Journal of Commerce* aspired to be esteemed, published in its columns an article teeming with the threadbare and exploded calumnies against Catholics, a sample of which was the disgraceful "*bull of excommunication*" from *Tristram Shandy*. This dishonorable appeal to the prejudices and ignorance of sectarianism appeared the day before the debate was appointed to take place on Mr. Spencer's School Bill in the Legislature. On the day itself on which the question was expected to be taken up, the agent of the Public School Society in Albany placed on the desk of each senator a copy of this paper, thus clearly exposing the unmanly mode of warfare adopted. The Catholic side of this question was conducted with acknowledged fairness, candor, and dignity, and won the sympathy of many enlightened and just Protestants, including men of eminence and intellect.

The question was postponed by the Senate from May, 1841, to January, 1842, in order that the intervening election might determine the controversy by an appeal to the people. In that election the opposing parties were the Whigs and "Locofocos," both of whom were equally hostile to the school reform. The Bishop and his friends could not support either of these parties, since to do so would have been to vote against their convictions, their interests, and their rights. They could not stand aloof, because the school question was one of the issues involved in the election. Under these circumstances they availed themselves of the common privileges of citizens in a Republic where the ballot-box is the legitimate mode of testing all popular questions, and presented candidates of their own, upon whom they bestowed their votes. It is not unlikely, had the whole election turned upon the school question, without reference to any of the old party issues, and the candidates had been nominated with reference to this question only, that the measure would have been carried; but while large numbers of the " Locofocos " were, as Catholics, favorable to the school reform, the candidate for Governor on the Whig ticket was Mr. Seward, the avowed advocate of that measure ; and the legislative candidates on both sides, in order not to embarrass their election, kept aloof from the school question. The election took place in the first week of November, 1841, and the candidates nominated by the friends of a free and equal school system received two thousand two hundred votes, enough to convince the two leading parties of their power to withhold their votes, and, in case of emergency, to hold, perhaps, the balance of power. Governor Seward, with whom Bishop Hughes became acquainted in one of his visitations of his diocese, was a firm friend of fair play on the school question, and from this common bond of sympathy sprang up a mutual regard and friendship. The Governor was almost as much abused for his advocacy of Catholic rights as Bishop Hughes himself, and narrowly escaped defeat in the election of 1841 on this account. Having promised the Bishop not to lose sight of the school question in the approaching Legislature, the Governor, in his Message of January 4, 1842, again presented the subject of the schools and school fund to the consideration of the Legislature, in the following paragraphs, which are well worthy of perpetuation:—

"It was among my earliest duties to bring to the notice of the Legislature the neglected condition of many thousand children, including a very large proportion of those of immigrant parentage, in our great commercial city; a misfortune then supposed to result from groundless prejudices and omissions of parental duty. Especially desirous at the same time not to disturb in any manner the public schools, which seemed to be efficiently conducted, although so many for whom they were established were unwilling to receive their instructions, I suggested, as I thought, in a spirit not inharmonious with our civil and religious institutions, that if necessary it might be expedient to bring those so excluded from such privileges into schools rendered especially attractive by the sympathies of those to whom the task of instruction should be confided. It has since been discovered that the magnitude of the evil was not fully known, and that its causes were very imperfectly understood. It will be shown in the proper report that twenty thousand children in the city of New York, of suitable age, are not at all instructed in any of the public schools, while the whole number of the residue of the State, not taught in common schools, does not exceed nine thousand. What had been regarded as individual, occasional, and accidental prejudices, have proved to be opinions pervading a large mass, including at least one religious communion equally with all others entitled to civil tolerance —opinions cherished through a period of sixteen years, and ripened into a permanent conscientious distrust of the impartiality of the education given in the public schools. This distrust has been rendered still deeper and more alienating by a subversion of precious civil rights of those whose consciences are thus offended.

"Happily, in this, as in other instances, the evil is discovered to have had its origin no deeper than in a departure from the equality of general laws." The message then proceeded to review the school system as then existing, and recommended the abolition of the Public School Society, and the creation of a board of commissioners to be elected by the people, whose duty it should be " to apportion the school moneys among all the schools, including those now existing, which shall be organized and conducted in conformity to its general regulations and the laws of the State, in the proportion of the number of pupils instructed.

"This proposition to gather the young from the streets and wharves into the nurseries which the State, solicitous for her security against ignorance, has prepared for them, has sometimes been treated as a device to appropriate the school fund to the endowment of seminaries for teaching languages and faiths, and thus to perpetuate the prejudices it seeks to remove; sometimes as a scheme for dividing that precious fund among a thousand jarring sects, and thus increasing the religious animosities it strives to heal; sometimes as a plan to subvert the prevailing religion and introduce one repugnant to the consciences of our fellow-citizens; while in truth it simply proposes, by enlightening equally the minds of all, to enable them to detect error wherever it may exist, and to reduce uncongenial masses into one intelligent, virtuous, harmonious, and happy people. Being now relieved from all such misconceptions, it presents the questions whether it is wise and more humane to educate the offspring of the poor than to leave them to grow up in ignorance and vice; whether juvenile vice is more easily eradicated by the Court of Sessions than by common schools; whether parents have a right to be heard concerning the instruction and instructors of their children, and tax-payers in relation to the expenditure of public funds; whether, in a republican government, it is necessary to interpose an independent corporation between the people and the schoolmaster; and whether it is wise and just to disfranchise an entire community of all control over public education, rather than suffer a part to be represented in proportion to its numbers and contributions. Since such considerations are now involved, what has hitherto been discussed as a question of benevolence and of universal education, has become one of equal civil rights, religious tolerance, and liberty of conscience. We could bear with us, in our retirement from public service, no recollection more worthy of being cherished through life than that of having met such a question in the generous and confiding spirit of our institutions, and decided it upon the immutable principles on which they are based." *

This noble appeal in behalf of the rights of conscience and equality of the laws fell upon indifferent ears. But the agitation of the school question led to this good result: the abolition of the Public School Society, and the introduction of the present school system by the Legislature of 1842, by which changes sectarianism was at least legally abolished, though no guarantee was provided against its reintroduction practically into the schools. Bishop Hughes advocated this bill as one rendering the public school system not quite so objection-

---

* *Assembly Documents*, 1842, i. 9, 10, 11, 12, 13.

able as before, and as, perhaps, the beginning of a more thorough reform, though false in principle and affording no immunity to Catholics from double taxation for the education of their children. Quite recently the public schools have been confided to the jurisdiction of a Department of Education. The system is virtually the same. During this struggle the Bishop was kept constantly engaged in conducting the discussion by sermons, speeches, letters, and controversies, and his productions on this subject constitute a valuable and important portion of his published works. He now devoted his energies to the establishment of Catholic schools for Catholic children, endeavored to secure the assistance of the Brothers of the Christian Schools for this purpose; facts which prove that no redress had yet been accorded to Catholics for the grievances complained of. In 1852 he assembled together the clergy of New York and Brooklyn, and read to them an address on this all-important subject, urging them to renewed efforts in the erection of parish schools. The Catholics of New York have ever since continued to pay their proportion of taxes to support schools, in which they cannot conscientiously educate their children, and at the same time to provide and support other schools for the education of their offspring. While their contributions have been used in erecting palatial school-houses in the various wards of this city, their own children are sent to school in the humble parish school-houses, and in some cases in the basements of their churches, where they are compelled frequently to study by gas-light, and are deprived of most of the modern appliances and improvements in education. It is hoped the day will yet arrive when American institutions will be relieved of this gross inequality and injustice by the adoption in all the States of a fair and equal system of public schools.

In the fall of 1840 the Seminary was removed from Lafargeville to Fordham, and placed under the patronage of St. Joseph, and the College was opened in June, 1841, and placed under the patronage of St. John the Baptist. Bishop Hughes was untiring in his labors and solicitation of aid for this institution. A large portion of his own salary went to its relief and support. In April, 1846, the College was chartered by the Legislature, and raised to the rank of a University, and in July of the same year the Bishop transferred its management and ownership to the Jesuit Fathers. In 1841, the Ladies of the Sacred Heart, whose services he had engaged during his visit to Europe, arrived in the diocese and founded their first school, the foundation of the present splendid institutions of that excellent Order. Five years afterwards the Bishop introduced the Sisters of Mercy, whose institution, from small beginnings, has expanded into one of the greatest ornaments and blessings to the country.

The devastating spirit of Know-Nothingism, which had perpetrated such outrages and sacrileges in Philadelphia, was disposed to break forth also in New York, and but for the undaunted courage and bold spirit exhibited by Bishop Hughes, scenes still more disgraceful and fatal would probably have been enacted in the latter city. The New York leaders of this church-burning faction invited their brethren from Philadelphia, more experienced in their favorite occupation, to visit the metropolis of New York. These willing patriots readily accepted the invitation, and a delegation, bringing with them the identical national flag which, it was alleged, had been trampled upon by the Irish Catholics during the riot in Kensington, were expected in New York in May, 1844, and a public meeting of their friends and a grand procession were arranged in their honor. Bishop Hughes saw at once that the secret object of this movement was to re-enact the horrid outrages of Philadelphia, and he resolved to defend with his flock the churches to the last extremity. But in the interests of peace he called upon the Irish Catholics of the city to avoid all public assemblies, especially the contemplated meeting of Know-Nothings, and to shun the occasion of outbreak. He called also upon the Mayor, Robert H. Morris, and advised him to prevent the proposed demonstration. "Are you afraid," asked the Mayor, conscious of the real tendency and object of the movement, "that some of your churches may be burned?" —"No, sir," replied the Bishop; "but I am afraid that some of *yours* will be burned. We can protect our own. I come to warn you for your own good."—"Do you think, Bishop, that your people would attack the procession?" —"I do not; but the Native Americans want to provoke a Catholic riot, and if they can do it in no other way, I believe they would not scruple to attack the procession themselves, for the sake of making it appear that the Catholics had assailed them."—"What, then," inquired the Mayor, "would you have me do?"—"I did not come to tell you what to do," said the Bishop. "I am a churchman, not the Mayor of New York; but if I were the Mayor, I would examine the laws of the State, and see if there were not attached to the police force a battery of artillery, and a company or so of infantry, and a squadron of horse, and I think I should find that there were; and if so, I should call them out.

Moreover, I should send to Mr. Harper, the mayor-elect, who has been chosen by the votes of this party. I should remind him that these men are his supporters; I should warn him that if they carry out their design there will be a riot; and I should urge him to use his influence in preventing this public reception of the delegates."

It is sufficient to say that no demonstration was made by the Know-Nothings. New York was saved from a fearful riot, and the credit was justly accorded to Bishop Hughes' prompt and decisive intervention. The apprehended outbreak spent itself in threats of assassination against the Bishop, and in a fierce paper warfare, in which the instigators of Know-Nothing violence against Catholics found in him a champion able to defend his own camp, and capable of carrying the war into the enemy's country.

In February, 1844, the present Most Rev. Archbishop of New York was consecrated coadjutor to Bishop Hughes, and in 1845 the latter visited Europe, in the interests of his diocese, and chiefly to obtain suitable teachers for the Catholic schools of his diocese. He returned in April, 1846, and in May of the same year attended the Sixth Council of Baltimore, whose deliberations resulted, by the subsequent concurrence of the Holy See, in dividing the Diocese of New York, by the erection of the new See of Buffalo, to which the Rev. John Timon was appointed; and of the new See of Albany, to which the Right Rev. Coadjutor of New York was translated. While attending the Council, Bishop Hughes was summoned to Washington by Mr. Buchanan, then Secretary of State under President Polk, to confer with the Administration in reference to the appointment of Catholic chaplains to the army then invading Mexico, a result which was accomplished in the appointment of Fathers McElroy and Rey to those positions. The project of sending Bishop Hughes to Mexico, on a mission of peace in behalf of the Government, was also discussed on this occasion, and in several private interviews between the President and the Bishop; but it is supposed that the latter finally declined the proposed mission.

In 1846 and 1847 the Sisters of Charity in the diocese of New York were organized into a separate institution from the parent house at Emmittsburg. This event had its origin, as was stated at the time, in the withdrawal of the Sisters from the Male Orphan Asylums then under their charge, the unwillingness of the Bishop to see these institutions abandoned, and his opinion that the authority of the parent house at Emmittsburg was too remote. He would not consent, however, that any of the Sisters should remain in New York in violation of their obedience to their own Superiors; for he was unwilling that his separate organization should have its origin in disobedience. Permission having been granted by their Superiors to such as wished to remain, they were formed into an independent Sisterhood under the jurisdiction and authority of the Ordinary of the diocese.

Bishop Hughes' love of his native country was manifested by the profound interest he took in all that concerned the welfare of its people. In 1847, when the famine was raging in Ireland, he sent the collections just taken up for his Theological Seminary, amounting to fourteen thousand dollars, to relieve his starving countrymen. He was a warm admirer of Daniel O'Connell, and friend of emancipation, and was greatly disappointed and mortified by the failure of the movement of 1848. To elevate the moral, social, and intellectual condition of his countrymen in America was one of his most earnest and constant efforts. In this generous effort he accomplished more than any other individual in this country. One of his means of attaining this end was to render their religion understood and respected, and for this purpose he entered frequently the arena of public controversy, and was regarded as foremost among the expounders and defenders of Catholic faith, practices, and morals. He allowed no attack upon the Church, or upon the Catholic body, which came under his notice and appeared to need or deserve refutation, to pass unanswered. His letters on "The Importance of being in Communion with Christ's one, holy, Catholic, and Apostolic Church," published in answer to the attacks of the Rev. Nicholas Murray, over the *nom de plume* of "Kirwan;" his reply to Senator Cass on the Madiai case, and his controversy with Senator Brooks on the Church property question, are well-known instances of his warfare for the principles and welfare of the Catholic Church in this country. In 1847 he preached, by invitation from such distinguished public men as John Quincy Adams, John C. Calhoun, Thomas H. Benton, and others, before Congress, in the Capitol at Washington, selecting for his subject "Christianity, the only Source of Moral, Social, and Political Regeneration." He delivered at various times and in various cities courses of lectures on Catholic doctrine, in vindication of Catholic interests, in refutation of historical calumnies, and in advocacy of the claims of the Catholic Church to the respect, confidence, and spiritual obedience of mankind. His sermons at the dedication or consecration of new churches were marked by eloquence, vigor, depth of argument, and remarkable appropriateness for the places and occasions that called them forth. He also published several essays on important and grave questions of current Catholic interest, such as the "*Catholic Press in this Country,*" "*The Catholic Chapter in American History,*" *Toleration, Immaculate Conception,* and other religious topics. His works have been published since his death, and present a valuable collection of polemical, historical, moral, theological, political, educational, and ecclesiastical writings. His life was one of activity, not of study or composition; his efforts were sermons, speeches, lectures, and essays, addressed to, and designed to influence the conduct of the living; not studied compositions for future perusal, but the soul-stirring appeals and acts of a leading spirit in that actual contact, and often unavoidable conflict of the moral and religious interests and duties of mankind, with the world and the passions of men. The Church was to him the embodiment of moral good, heavenly truth, and human regeneration; it was his highest ambition to be one of her champions, eulogists, and defenders, and it was by general accord that he was looked to by Catholics to meet the many attacks made upon them and their Church. His published works are a noble monument of his zeal, courage, and industry, and are destined to exert an influence long after the voice of the author has been hushed in the grave.

In May, 1849, the Seventh Council of Baltimore was convened, and amongst its proceedings was a recommendation that the Sees of New York, New Orleans, and Cincinnati should be erected into Archbishoprics.

On the 3d of October, 1850, Bishop Hughes received from Rome the papal brief advancing him to the archiepiscopal dignity, with the Bishops of Boston, Hartford, Albany, and Buffalo as his suffragans. He determined to go to Rome to be invested with the *pallium* by the Holy Father himself, and before leaving paid a parting visit to his friends in Philadelphia and Washington. In the latter city he dined with President Fillmore. He announced his intention of going to Rome from the altar of St. Patrick's, in New York, and on the same occasion alluded to the intended erection of a new Cathedral. On the 10th of October, 1850, he delivered a lecture in the Cathedral, on "The Decline of Protestantism, and its Causes," for the benefit of the Sisters of Mercy, which elicited replies from " Kirwan " and other Protestant ministers, and which, after his arrival at Rome, was translated into Italian, and published in the principal journals. While at Rome he took part in the celebration in honor of St. Thomas à Becket, at the English College, and in January, 1857, he delivered a course of controversial sermons, in English, to large congregations of English, Irish, and American residents of Rome, in the Church of St. Andrea delle Frate. He was also chosen to pronounce the panegyric of St. Agatha, on her festival, which was celebrated at Rome with great magnificence. It was customary for the Cardinal-Vicar of Rome to bestow the *pallium*, the emblem of the archiepiscopal dignity, upon newly created Archbishops; but in the case of Archbishop Hughes the Holy Father himself performed the ceremony, which took place April 3, 1851. This was a distinction which the Archbishop alluded to with pleasure and gratitude. He received from the Holy Father every mark of attention and admiration, and his apartments became the resort of cardinals, prelates, priests, and noblemen. He visited Vienna, where, on the morning of his departure, he celebrated Mass in the ancient subterranean chapel of Santa Croce in Gierusalemme. From Germany he crossed over to England, and at Liverpool was entertained at a banquet, given by the Catholics in his honor. He arrived in New York June 22, and on July 1 he preached in the Cathedral, giving an interesting account of his visit to Rome. On July 21, the Catholics gave a grand entertainment at the Astor House in his honor. The visit of Kossuth to this country gave occasion to the Archbishop to come out openly in opposition to revolutions, and to the mission of the Magyar to this country. The Catholics of the United States did not take part in ovations accorded to this then prominent political agitator.

In 1853, Monsignore Bedini,* the Papal Nuncio to the Court of Brazil, arrived in the United States, and was received with every honor by Archbishop Hughes, whose guest he was while in New York City. The Archbishop and Nuncio made an extensive tour through the north-western cities and Canada. The Archbishop was anxious to have established a permanent nunciature in this country, and sounded the Administration on the subject; but, while willing to receive a diplomatic representative from the Papal States, in the same manner as ministers were received from other countries, the Administration did not seem to favor a regular nunciature, lest it might involve some embarrassment in consequence of the ecclesiastical character of such a relation.

---

* See Appendix III.

In 1854 Archbishop Hughes was one of the American Prelates who accepted the invitation of Pope Pius IX. to attend the assembly of Bishops from the whole Catholic world, gathered together to take part in the consultations and ceremonies attendant on the definition of the dogma of the Immaculate Conception of the Blessed Virgin Mary. He was an earnest and devout member of that august assembly, and was greatly attached to the dogma and devotion of the Immaculate Conception. On his return he gave an interesting account of the whole proceeding in a sermon he preached at the Cathedral of New York. He immediately commenced the erection of a church in honor of the Immaculate Conception, which he solemnly consecrated on the 15th of May, 1858. This was the ninety-ninth church erected and dedicated under his personal guidance and responsibility.

Such had been the active and laborious life of Archbishop Hughes, and such the exciting scenes and contests through which he had passed, that his health, naturally very robust, began to fail in 1848, when he was about fifty years old. Many years of his life, during which he made some of his most brilliant efforts and performed great labors, were years of suffering and relaxed physical and mental energy. His natural vigor and activity of character resisted the encroachments of disease. After the year 1855, he made but few efforts like those of his former career. In September, he visited St. John's, Newfoundland, to preach the consecration sermon at the new Cathedral, and traveled considerably through the province, preaching, laying the corner-stone of a new church, and witnessing the general growth of the Church. He was received throughout with extraordinary honor and respect, and his journey was one series of ovations, banquets, and celebrations. In his sermon at St. Patrick's, after his return, he spoke with admiration of the faith, piety, and heroism of the people whom he had just visited. In January, 1856, he delivered at Baltimore, before the Young Catholic's Friend Society, his fine lecture on "The Present Condition and Prospects of the Catholic Church in the United States," and at Pittsburgh, before St. Paul's Institute, that on "The Relation between the Civil and Religious Duties of the Catholic Citizen." In December of the same year he published in *The Metropolitan*, of Baltimore, his striking article entititled, "Reflections and Suggestions in regard to what is called the Catholic Press in the United States." In 1858 he made a detailed and masterly report of his administration to Rome, which was greatly admired there by the ecclesiastical functionaries for its comprehensiveness, admirable order, luminous descriptions, and for the penetrating grasp of mind which it displayed. In the same year rumors were occasionally current of a competition for ecclesiastical honors between the Archiepiscopal Sees of Baltimore and New York; rumors, however, as unfounded themselves as the Prelates presiding over those sees were incapable of commencing such an issue, or tolerating it even on the part of others. Archbishop Hughes lost no time in writing to Rome to recommend that Baltimore rather than New York should be erected into a primatial see; but the Holy See contented itself with conferring upon the Archbishops of Baltimore a "prerogative of place," entitling them tc precedence in the councils or assemblies of the American Hierarchy.

In 1857 and 1858 Archbishop Hughes, weighed down by his labors and cares, and enfeebled in health, not only thought of resigning, but communicated his views on this subject to Rome. The Holy See would not listen to his resigning, but expressed a willingness to allow him a Coadjutor. He next thought of selecting a Coadjutor, but as this plan seemed to necessitate the withdrawal of one of his suffragans from a see, for which it would be difficult to find a suitable successor at that time, it was, after consultation and correspondence, abandoned. It was about this time that the Holy Father purchased at Rome the ancient convent of the Umilta for an American College, and appealed to the American Bishops to furnish it and provide for the current expenses. Archbishop Hughes entered into this noble work with the energy and courage of his former days of health and strength, and advanced five thousand dollars for the college in anticipation of the collections to be taken up for this purpose. He communicated his intention of providing a fund, the investment of which would support in the American College seven ecclesiastics, whether he had that number there or not. All this was done on the eve of the great undertaking, which the Archbishop had contemplated, in the commencement of the new and magnificent Cathedral for his own metropolitan city. The corner-stone of this grand structure was laid August 15, 1858, in the presence of seven Bishops, one hundred and thirty priests, one hundred and twenty cassocked and surpliced youths well trained to chant the psalms alternately with the clergy, and at least one hundred thousand people. Everything passed off in the most perfect order, without an accident, and amidst the praises and admiration of all, including many Protestants, as was cordially testified by the accounts given of the occasion by the secular press. Some idea of the Archbishop's still wonderful energy, and of his influence with his flock, may be formed from the single fact that he paid visits to the most wealthy Catholics to solicit contributions to the new Cathedral, and in one hundred of these visits, which did not take him over twenty hours to make, he found one hundred who gave him a thousand dollars each. Before his death the walls were advanced twelve or fourteen feet high, and the noble structure is now rapidly advancing towards completion, under the vigorous exertions of the present Most Rev. Archbishop of New York. The success of Archbishop Hughes in this and in all the great undertakings of his administration was in great measure owing to the personal force of character of the Archbishop, his indomitable energy, and the magnetic influence he exerted upon the minds and hearts of men. The good and generous rallied to his support, and while many of his best friends and supporters among the laity are still living to enjoy the fruits and blessings of their generous co-operation, many have passed like him to their great reward. Among the latter the names of Daniel Devlin and Terence Donnelly should be particularly mentioned as among the foremost and most generous promoters of the noble and magnanimous works of Archbishop Hughes.

In the same year he was invited to take part in the celebration of the laying of the ocean telegraphic cable, and was requested to write one of the addresses on the occasion. He was designated to ride in the same carriage, at the celebration, with Lord Napier, the British Minister; Edward Everett, and the venerable Rev. Dr. Nott, then eighty-six years of age, and for fifty-four years President of Union College;* and was invited to the grand banquet given in honor of the event. In 1859 he made an exception to his rule then for some time past adopted of not preaching or lecturing out of his own diocese, and accepted the invitation of the Jesuit Fathers at Washington to preach the sermon at the blessing of the new Church of St. Aloysius in that city. He was invited to be the guest of President Buchanan on this occasion, but declined in favor of the pastor of St. Patrick's Church, where it was his habit to stop in his visits to the capital. In 1859 he took an active part in manifesting sympathy for the Holy Father in his trials; issued an inspiring Pastoral on the subject, which was so gratefully received by the Pope, that he ordered it to be printed at the Propaganda in English and Italian, a distinction never conferred upon any other pastoral at Rome. He subsequently proposed calling public meetings of sympathy, but abandoned this plan in favor of a collection in aid of the Holy Father's depleted treasury. The collection amounted to fifty-three thousand dollars. On receiving this present, and the letter of sympathy which accompanied it, the Holy Father was moved to tears, and, as a mark of his grateful appreciation, he sent to the Archbishop "a first-class medal, for his zeal for religion, and singular and devoted attachment to the chair of Peter."

In 1861 Archbishop Hughes, at the request and by appointment of the Administration at Washington, visited Europe on business connected with the then disturbed and distracted condition of the country. The precise nature of his duties in this mission were not made public, but his own words, in a letter addressed to Cardinal

---

* The same individual who advocated the denominational system of public schools.

Barnabo, show that he regarded it as a mission of peace, and as one not inconsistent with the character of a follower of the Prince of Peace:—" My mission was, and is, a mission of peace between France and England on the one side, and the United States on the other. . . . The time was so brief between my visit to Washington and my departure from New York, that I had no opportunity of writing to your Eminence on the subject, or of consulting any of the other bishops in regard to it. I made known to the President that if I should come to Europe it would not be as a partisan of the North more than of the South ; that I should represent the interests of the South as well as of the North ; in short, the interests of all the United States, just the same as if they had never been distracted by the present civil war. The people of the South know that I am not opposed to their interests. They have even published that in their papers, and some say that my coming to Europe is with a view to bring about a reconciliation between the two sections of the country. But, in fact, no one but myself, either North or South, knows the entire object of my visit to Europe." While abroad he preached at the laying of the corner-stone of the Catholic University in Dublin. In Paris he preached several times to crowded congregations in the Church of St. Roch. At Rome he took part in a number of ecclesiastical ceremonies, and officiated at the devotion of the stations of the cross in the Colosseum, followed by about five thousand pilgrims. He was also present at the canonization of the Japanese martyrs at Rome, June 10, 1862. After his return he founded the Theological Seminary at Troy, the last of the ecclesiastical institutions established by him. His last sermon was delivered in June, 1863, at the dedication of St. Theresa's Church, New York. His last attempt at public speaking was his address to the anti-conscription rioters in July, 1863, in which he endeavored to quell the spirit of disorder and calm the passions of the hour. He spoke from the balcony of his residence in Madison Avenue, and remained seated, in consequence of the feeble state of his health.

The disease from which Archbishop Hughes had been suffering for several years, Bright's disease of the kidneys, had now made such rapid inroads upon his once powerful constitution, that he was for some time before his death an invalid. He made great exertions in July, 1863, to attend the funeral of Archbishop Kenrick of Baltimore, and while there, and on the morning of the funeral, he was saying a low mass for the repose of the soul of the deceased Prelate, when his frame began to totter, and he was only prevented from falling by some one who caught him and supported him from the altar. He made several journeys in pursuit of health, but with little success. The autumn of 1863 was passed in a state of almost entire prostration. About the middle of December he took to his bed, and towards the last of the month, when informed that he could not recover, he received the intelligence with perfect calmness and resignation, and spent his remaining days in communion with God, and in preparation for his last end. On Wednesday, December 30, he received the last sacraments from his confessor, the Rev. William Quinn, and from that time none spoke to him on any but spiritual subjects. On Sunday morning, January 3, his old friend the venerable Father McElroy, S.J., who had come on to visit him, offered up the holy sacrifice in his room. On the evening of the same day he breathed his last, while Archbishop McCloskey was reciting the prayers of the Church for a departing soul. Among those present during his last hours were his two sisters, Bishop Loughlin, Fathers Starrs and McNeirny, and other clergymen, and Henry L. Hoguet, Esq., his friend, on the part of the laity. His funeral took place at the Cathedral of St. Patrick's, January 7, and was the most imposing funeral ceremony ever performed in the city of New York. It was attended by eight bishops and nearly two hundred priests, and a countless multitude thronged the church and neighboring streets. Testimonials of respect were offered from every quarter, among which were the adjournment of the courts, and the passage of resolutions of sorrow and condolence by the Legislature of New York and the Common Council. The latter body subsequently had prepared and presented to the diocese a very handsome *Memorial* in his honor, which stands in the Archiepisopal residence. It was universally acknowledged that in the death of Archbishop Hughes the Church lost a devoted and laborious Prelate, an able and dauntless champion, and a brilliant ornament. Let the controversies and struggles of the past be forgotten, for it must be acknowledged that the motive of his actions through life was the promotion of God's glory and the extension of His Church.

RIGHT REV. MATHIAS LORAS, D.D.,

First Bishop of Dubuque, A.D. 1837.*

BISHOP LORAS was one of those exemplary French clergymen who, having been reared in the church of their native country, volunteered for the modest, yet glorious work of the American missions, and whom Providence prepared in the crucible of labor and poverty to become rulers and patriarchs of the Church in the new world. Appointed Bishop of a new and extensive see, which possessed but a single priest and a single church, the work of building up an entire diocese was before him. He entered upon a task, humanly speaking devoid of promise, but one which, to his happy and practical talents, was full of hope and encouragement. Not only is the church of Iowa indebted to him as its founder, but the State is under untold obligations to him, as the promoter of immigration, by attracting to her forests and prairies an honest and industrious population, whom he organized into Christian communities and congregations as they arrived. In this great work he seemed to have a special vocation. No differences of nationality entered into his thoughts; a Frenchman himself, he was a friend of both Irish and German immigration, and there are few, if any, in our history, who did so much to favor the westward tide of population, and, at the same time, confer so many solid benefits and blessings upon the settlers after their arrival. He illustrated forcibly the union between Catholicity and civilization. His life, character,

---

* Compiled from numerous contemporary publications and periodicals.

virtues, and services were worthy of the best ages of the Church.

Mathias Loras was born at Lyons, France, in July, 1792. His parents enjoyed a high social position, and were distinguished for their piety, talents, and wealth. They were too prominent, not only in their loyalty and virtues, but also in their wealth and respectability, to escape the destroying hand of the "Reign of Terror," which entered upon the destruction of everything good and noble in France. His father being an adherent of the royal family, was an early victim of the Revolution. The pious family grew in devotion and zeal as persecution gathered around them. The mother alone remained to guide the household in the path of virtue, amidst the wreck of altars and shrines. The accounts we have received represent young Mathias as one who fully corresponded with the pious efforts of so good a mother, and the virtues of his saintly life were the fruits of the chastening and exalting school of persecution. She watched most tenderly and scrupulously over his education, and from his tenderest years he was distinguished for his piety, generosity, and fidelity. A religious vocation was the result of this careful training, in co-operation with the designs of Providence. He was ordained at Lyons about the year 1817 or 1818, and was soon afterwards, though very young, appointed Superior of the ecclesiastical Seminary of Largentière. He presided with success over this institution for several years, rendering a service to religion inferior to none other in training good and worthy priests for the sanctuary. The more immediate labor of saving souls had, however, always commended itself to his zeal, and seemed to be his vocation. He accordingly resigned his position in the Seminary, for the more active and laborious one of the mission, and became an active and zealous member of an excellent society of priests, who devoted themselves chiefly to the holding of conferences and missions in the different parishes of the diocese of Lyons.

He was thus engaged when Bishop Portier, of Mobile, visited France in 1829, to procure colaborers in the missions of Alabama and Florida. Father Loras saw in this apostolic field one to which the voice of heaven seemed to call him. He therefore joined the little colony of the Bishop of Mobile with whom he sailed from France, November 1, 1829, arrived at New Orleans December 24, and at Mobile January 3, 1830. He celebrated mass immediately on his arrival, united with the Bishop in a *Te Deum*, and assisted in installing Bishop Portier in the newly created see of Mobile. Among the companions of Bishop Portier in the voyage from France were several young ecclesiastics. To train these candidates for the august duties of the priesthood, a task in which he was well experienced, became the charge of Father Loras. He was also appointed Vicar-General of Bishop Portier, and pastor of the Cathedral at Mobile. He was engaged in these duties seven years, during which he ably and zealously promoted the excellent measures of his Bishop, and by his labors and devotion illustrated the true character and life of the holy ministry, and by his charity and goodness of heart endeared himself to the people of Alabama.

The fathers of the Third Provincial Council of Baltimore, in April, 1837, recommended the erection of the new episcopal see of Dubuque, for the Territories of Iowa and Minnesota. The Holy See approved, created the new see, July 28, and, at the recommendation of the Council, appointed Dr. Loras the first Bishop of Dubuque. He was consecrated at Mobile by Bishop Portier, assisted by Bishop Blanc, of New Orleans, December 10, 1837. His diocese was a vast unknown region to him; the unfinished church of St. Raphael, at Dubuque, was the only Catholic church in the Territory, and the Rev. Samuel Mazzuchelli, its pastor, was the only Catholic priest; the Catholic population of Dubuque was about three hundred. But Bishop Loras saw in this great Territory, then in its civil, political, and social infancy, great States in the future. There must be, he thought, Catholics in distant isolated and unfrequented localities, who were wandering from the faith, and the future waves of population would certainly set in towards its fine expanse of meadow, prairie, and forest. The work·at once marked out by his zeal and devotion far exceeded the capacity of himself and his only colaborer; he resolved, therefore, to procceed at once to France, and seek volunteers in this glorious field. He succeeded in obtaining two priests, Rev. Joseph Cretin, afterwards Bishop of St. Paul, and Rev. A. Pelamourgues, and four Seminarians. Leaving France with his companions in October, 1838, he arrived at New York in the following month, and started westward. They were detained in Missouri by the inclemency of the season and the want of traveling facilities, and did not reach Dubuque before April 17, 1839. Bishop Loras was installed as Bishop of Dubuque, April 29, in the new and unfinished Church of St. Raphael, which the zeal and labors of Father Mazzuchelli had erected.

Bishop Loras thus commenced his episcopate with three priests, Fathers Mazzuchelli, Cretin, and Pelamourgues, and four deacons, Messrs. Causse, Petiot,

Ravoux, and Galtier; the first named of the dea..., was ordained by the Bishop during the first year after his arrival. Stationing Father Cretin with himself at the Church of St. Raphael, which became his Cathedral, Father Pelamourgues at Davenport, as the centre of an extensive mission, and Father Mazzuchelli at Bloomington, with another extensive mission around him, the Bishop himself commenced the laborious work of surveying his vast spiritual domain, investigating its condition and necessities, and struggling to provide for its wants. With prudent foresight he purchased at once a lot of three acres adjoining his church at Dubuque, designed to be used as soon as practicable for literary and charitable purposes; also a large lot improved with a house for a school, to be placed under the care of the Sisters of Charity; and he erected in the rear of his Cathedral church a large and substantial building, designed to answer the double purpose of episcopal residence and Ecclesiastical Seminary. Thus he had the consolation of having his young Levites under his own roof, and under the immediate instruction of Father Cretin. He very soon started an academy for boys, and one for girls, Sunday-schools in various places, a country school near Dubuque, and a Catholic society designed to raise funds for the erection of a Cathedral. These institutions accomplished much immediate good, and were the pioneer institutions of the present flourishing diocese of Dubuque.

Scarcely had he commenced these works when this zealous prelate became solicitous for his whole flock, and anxious to carry to its most remote members—descendants of the old French settlers of the Northwest, and of the Catholic Indians—the light of religious instruction, the sacraments of the Church, and the renovation of their faith and zeal. The Territories of Iowa and Minnesota lay before him. Vast and rough was the field, but missionaries of his own faith and nation had, two centuries before, traversed its fields on foot, and its rivers and lakes in canoes; the Church which had sent them forth had now cast upon him its cultivation, and the same undying zeal which she infused into their hearts, she had also communicated to him. It was thus with a cheerful and buoyant soul that he went forth to make the visitation of his diocese. Like Marquette, he took the Mississippi as the great channel of his mission of love and benediction, and its banks again resounded with the Latin office and prayers of the Church. He was accompanied by Father Pelamourgues, a devoted missionary. They reached Fort Snelling, where they found numerous French settlers, and the Indian half-breeds, who were Catholics more in name than in reality. The Bishop and his companion commenced here a glorious mission; instructions, baptisms, confessions, and incessant administration of advice, consolation and stirring appeals, constituted the busy employments of day after day, until fifteen days were spent in the noble work. Abundant fruits rewarded their generous toil. At the end of the fifteen days the Bishop was disappointed by the non-arrival of a boat, and as there was no prospect of the speedy arrival of one, he longed to commence the work in other places, purchased a canoe, and with his companion commenced the descent of the river. After incredible hardships and fatigues they reached Prairie du Chien. Here the mission was again opened; the same daily and untiring routine of zealous labor was gone through with, and the same abundant harvest rewarded the toil of the laborers. Such was a sample of his life, commenced the first year of his episcopate, and continued for many subsequent years.

His four deacons were, in the course of a few years, ordained priests, and greatly augmented the Bishop's means of doing good. A mission for the Sioux Indians was established about two hundred and fifty miles above the Falls of St. Anthony, and Father Ravoux, the missionary in charge, preached in French and Sioux. Also the mission of the Sacs and Foxes was established and placed in charge of Father Pelamourgues, and that of the Winnebagoes under Father Cretin. A valuable property was acquired in Davenport, with the view of applying the revenue from it to the support of the missions.

During the first ten years of his administration, Bishop Loras was chiefly engaged in calling into active organization the Catholic elements already existing in his diocese, for as yet the tide of population had not set in for Iowa, which was then comparatively unknown. Missions, stations, and churches were increased, and a laborious body of clergy provided. It was during these years that St. Mary's Female Academy for boys, at Dubuque, was established, and placed in charge of the Sisters of Charity of the Blessed Virgin. St. Raphael's Academy for boys was also established, and placed under the care of the clergymen of the Cathedral. The Church of St. Raphael, known as the old Cathedral, was finished during the first year of his administration, and consecrated by the Bishop, August 15, 1839. Numerous Temperance Societies were formed in various parts of the diocese, under his special patronage and encouragement. He was an ardent advocate of this excellent virtue, and for the hardy and industrious settlers of the West, he regarded and advocated temperance as an indispensable safeguard. During this same period, St. Philomena's Academy, under the care of the Sisters from Dubuque, was established, and the Bishop purchased a valuable tract of eighty acres of land for a Catholic cemetery. He also purchased St. Joseph's Prairie, a valuable tract one mile square, near Dubuque, which was improved with suitable buildings and dedicated to the uses of a Mother House for the Sisters of Charity of the Blessed Virgin. The Mother House of these Sisters had been at Philadelphia, and from that city the first of the Order went to Iowa. But their House at Philadelphia was destroyed in the conflagrations in 1844, and from that city the means were generously provided for the establishment of a Mother House near Dubuque. A boarding academy was connected with St. Joseph's, and hither came the children of the surrounding country early on every Sunday morning for instruction and Mass, and on these occasions the Very Rev. Superior entertained and provided for them with true Catholic hospitality. The Very Rev. T. C. Donaghoe was the founder and Superior of this excellent order, and our Holy Father, Pius IX., in 1847, conferred unusual favors and indulgences upon it. Bishop Loras also obtained generous aid for his diocese from Europe, and with consummate prudence expended it, while land was cheap, in the purchase of about three square miles of land; a splendid domain for religion and charity, which subsequently became studded with educational, religious, and charitable institutions, and proved of infinite service to the diocese. A writer alluding at the time to these enterprises of Bishop Loras, said: "This has all been accomplished by alms obtained from Europe. Thus his college and future Seminary, etc., will in time form one continuous line of ten miles from the new Cathedral to St. Anne's. May we not, then, entertain the hope that humble hearts, with the blessing of God and the aid of His admirable Mother, will afford the consolations of religion to a thickening Catholic population."*

Bishop Loras, by his travels throughout the Territory of Iowa, had ample opportunities of knowing, and he became convinced, that no section of the country possessed a finer soil or climate, or presented more favorable opportunities for an industrious agricultural population than that embraced within his diocese. To his regret he saw large numbers of the European immigrants tarrying in the Atlantic cities, where want, sickness, and crime beset their path, and he became deeply interested in giving to this worthy population the more healthful and vigorous direction of the West. The lands of Iowa and Minnesota were as yet comparatively unknown, so that one of his first measures was to do all in his power to cause the fertility of the soil, its cheapness and facility of cultivation, and the salubrity of the climate, to become known, not only among the immigrants arriving at our Eastern ports, but also in Europe. Articles were prepared and published setting forth these attractions, and at the same time holding out to Catholics the advantages of religion, which the vigorous conduct of Catholic interests in that section, under Bishop Loras, enabled him to promise. An immense correspondence, both with persons in this country and Europe, resulted from the well-known interest which Bishop Loras took in these subjects, which, in the midst of his pressing duties, he found time to keep up. Letters from great numbers of individual

---

* *Catholic Almanac*, 1859.

immigrants, desiring his advice and assistance in settling their families, and from small colonies of settlers desiring to have lands selected for them in one body, were received and punctually answered by him. At one time we read of his visiting a small German colony, in 1846, numbering seventy-four persons, and in less than two years afterwards we find him spending eight days in the midst of the same community, counting its population by hundreds, all Catholics, and receiving from the Bishop the highest praise for their piety, temperance, and devotion to the faith. Such was the town of New Vienna in 1846 and 1848. Next we hear of his dedicating a fine brick church at Fort Madison, then a frontier town on the Mississippi, surrounded by a large and thriving population of French, Americans, Irish, and Germans, with some Indian half-breeds; and again of his going to the Big Maquoketa, or to the head waters of the Little Maquoketa, to organize the Irish settlers in those fine regions into congregations, and to commence in person the work of building for them churches, instructing them in the faith, and administering to them the sacraments. The boundaries of the Church and of the States have since advanced far beyond these positions; but in the early days of the episcopate of Bishop Loras they were on the remote frontiers of both. Such are but individual instances of his almost constant occupations and exertions, and so vast were the labors entailed upon him, that he was frequently absent from his episcopal city for large portions of the year, organizing congregations among new settlements, commencing new churches, dedicating others, establishing schools and academies, and laboring for the temporal and eternal welfare of his people. It became necessary for him to notify the public interes in Western immigration, and consequently in his own movements, through the Catholic newspapers of the Atlantic cities, of the temporary changes of his residence, which these labors rendered necessary. Neither did the more distant regions of Minnesota escape his zealous exertions. As early as 1848 his missionaries, conspicuous amongst whom was Rev. Father Bellecourt, penetrated the most remote sections of that country, and carried the consolations of religion to the French and Catholic Indians residing there. The foundations of the future diocese of St. Paul were laid, amidst labors and privations worthy of our ancestors in the faith. A tide of Catholic population began to flow into Iowa and Minnesota, which was brought under the beneficent influences of the Church as soon as it arrived, and while good members of the social and political community were virtuously trained, they were also prepared for the citizenship of Heaven.

In 1847, Bishop Loras sent Father Ravoux, the first whom he ordained of the young deacons who accompanied him from France, into the most northern portions of Iowa, on missionary duty. His principal points of delay and labor were Fort Pierre, Pembina, and Council Bluffs; his journey lay through the country of several Indian tribes, whom he went to evangelize, such as the Ioways, Sioux, Mandanes, Black-Feet, Ricarices, Shiennes, *Gros Ventres* (known in our day by their English name of *Big Bellies*), and Pawnees. The following extract from a letter of Father Ravoux to Bishop Loras, dated from Fort Pierre, August 4, 1847, which was then published by the Bishop, will show how sad have been the effects of European and American association with the Indians, how the Catholic Church strove to arrest the evil, and how little the warning has been heeded; and it is but too well known in our own day, that what the *fire-water* of the whites left undone to destroy the above-named Indians, has now been nearly finished by fire and sword :—

"We fell in with some Indians on the 14th with a horse laden with casks of whiskey. They were going to sell it among the *Ioways*, a tribe of the Sioux. The price of a keg, containing three or four gallons, is a horse. Three or four days after, we met some more Indians, who were also carrying whiskey to the *Ioways*. Unless the sale of liquors to the Indians be soon arrested, we must expect to hear of the most terrible crimes. Last winter six persons at least were killed, in the neighborhood of the river St. Pierre, by the fatal consequences of drink. The intoxicated savage is beyond control: friends are slain by friends, and brothers fall by brothers' hands. What monstrous crimes! It is the duty of the government to make every exertion to put a stop to this dreadful abuse. I think that if Congress were well informed of the innumerable evils resulting from the sale of liquor to the Indians, it would find some method to enforce the laws which prohibit such sales. Oh! that the Lord would open the eyes of those who, in defiance of all laws, human and divine, pursue this infamous traffic! What a disgrace for civilized men! What a crime for Christians! who instead of laboring to enlighten these poor unfortunates, plunged in the darkness of idolatry, do not scruple, for the sake of a paltry gain, to debase them to the level of the brute! I hope that you, Rt. Rev. Sir, will take every means in your power to put an end to such a great scandal. It is almost impossible to hope for any good among the Indians, where the sale of intoxi cating liquors is permitted. You might write to some member of the Senate, and beseech him, together with his colleagues, to adopt some remedy for this wide-spread contagion. They can do it; they have the power; they have made laws, and it is their duty to enforce them."*

Allusion has already been made to the early efforts of Bishop Loras to provide the means of Catholic education for his flock, not only in his episcopal city, but in various and distant portions of his diocese. The light of Christian instruction, blended with secular education, dawned in many and even remote parts of Iowa with the advent of its first Bishop. A single instance, in addition to those already cited, may be referred to, out of many. As early as 1847, a very fine school was in successful operation at Westport, ten miles from Fort Madison, in which were then taught arithmetic, geometry, and algebra, and the English, German, French, Latin, and Greek languages. The fine schools at Davenport, under the care of Father Pelamourgues, also merit a special allusion. Bishop Loras had to employ in his schools at Dubuque and other places, male and female teachers from among the laity, until he could secure the services of the necessary religious Orders. After securing the Sisters of Charity, he next procured the services of the Brothers of Christian Instruction, a colony of whom came to Dubuque in 1851. The Bishop generously provided them with a large and fine brick building, capable of accommodating from fifteen to twenty brothers, at Dubuque; and soon afterwards the Brothers established a novitiate of their Order on a farm of two hundred and fifty-one acres, about five miles from Dubuque, and

---

* *Catholic Magazine*, 1848, p. 19.

called it New Paradise. The Bishop expended large sums of money in building schools and in employing teachers, and when the Brothers and Sisters became located in the diocese, he bountifully provided for their comfortable settlement. A large number of poor scholars were educated at his expense in the school of his own parish, and in several instances he both boarded and educated them.

From the beginning of his episcopate he took steps for the foundation of a Theological Seminary. The young candidates who accompanied him from France were accommodated in his own residence. Subsequently he commenced a few small buildings for his ecclesiastical students on St. Joseph's Prairie, and soon we behold these beginnings expand into the Seminary of Mount St. Bernard. This was a favorite institution of the good Bishop, who loved the society of his young theological students. Whenever his duties permitted, he spent much time at the Seminary, and took part in the instruction of the students. During the latter years of his life he seemed never so happy as when sojourning amongst the professors and pupils of Mount St. Bernard.

In 1851 Minnesota became erected into a separate diocese. Not content with having founded its churches and institutions, he now gave to the new diocese of St. Paul his friend and Vicar-General, Dr. Cretin, as its first Bishop.

Bishop Loras also received into his diocese a colony of the Sisters of the Visitation, who were located at Keokuk. In 1849 a small colony of Cistercian Monks of Our Blessed Lady of La Trappe, after failing to secure a location in the State of New York or Canada, proceeded to the West and were kindly received by Bishop

Loras. He generously gave them a valuable tract of prairie and woodlands; they acquired in all about sixteen hundred acres of land near Dubuque, and founded their monastery of New Melleray. At the Bishop's request the good Trappists extended their labors through the neighboring settlement, and soon they had a flourishing congregation, reared by their zeal, instructed by their preaching, and edified by their holy example. In 1856, when Bishop Loras' health became so impaired that it was necessary for him to secure the aid of a Coadjutor, it was the Monastery of New Melleray which gave him its prior, Father Clement Smyth, who shared generously with him the episcopal charge and became his successor.

The increase of Catholics in his episcopal city, even within a few years after his arrival there, admonished the Bishop of the necessity for a new Cathedral. Such were the demands upon his resources for religious and educational assistance in the various and distant portions of his diocese, that he was for many years content with the old church built by Father Mazzuchelli as his Cathedral. He, however, laid the corner-stone of the new Cathedral on Sunday, November 14, 1848, but for want of means he suspended its erection. In the mean time a neat and spacious church was erected in the upper part of Dubuque, under the patronage of St. Patrick, in order to accommodate the Bishop's congregation, while the Cathedral was under construction. It remained, however, for his Coadjutor to assist him in this undertaking; but Bishop Loras had the consolation of seeing it dedicated before his death.

In 1849 and 1850 Bishop Loras visited Europe, and was engaged there more than six months in perfecting arrangements for the still greater promotion of the religious and educational interests of his diocese. He visited Rome and France; spending most of his time in the latter country. The emigration from Ireland to his diocese had been so great, and he had become so much attached to his children of that nationality, that for their sake he would not return home without visiting Ireland. The chief objects of interest visited by him there were the College of Maynooth, which had sent so many good missionaries to America, and the old monastery of Melleray, which had sent forth the good Trappists, then so usefully located and employed in his own diocese. His tender heart was greatly moved by the miseries and sufferings of the people under British misrule, and he published a letter in the London *Tablet*, expressive of his sympathy for that suffering people. A brief extract from it will prove interesting in our own day:—

"I assure you, dear sir, the scene of poverty and misery in some quarters was wonderful, and I am told it is still worse in other counties. I saw many poor cottages covered with straw, half buried in the ground, and occupied by poor Catholic tenants, who cultivate in the sweat of their brow small fields divided by poor green hedges or half-tumbled walls. The manner in which many were clothed was a sure indication of great poverty and unavoidable sufferings. At every station, at least in towns, the stage was surrounded by whole families of beggars, who, by their pressing demands, would elicit charity from the most hardened heart. Many of those cottages were crumbling in ruins and abandoned by their tenants, who had emigrated to some more hospitable shore. As I was traveling along I saw occasionally some of those extensive and princely estates occupied by rich English lords, whose dwellings and parks are surrounded by old lofty walls and shaded by quite annuated trees. The contrast between great opulence and extreme poverty was truly appalling, and one is at a loss to understand how this state of things can be tolerated in this age of light and philanthropy Another contrast I cannot help noticing. As soon as I crossed the Channel from Dublin to Holyhead, in England, I perceived a great change for the better in the face of the country, and in the look of the people; so much so, that one could hardly believe that Ireland and England were both under the same laws, and protected by the same government; and more than that, the poor Irish are either incarcerated or transported, whenever they make any attempt to better their truly miserable condition."

While abroad he addressed to his flock the following affectionate pastoral letter:—

"PARIS, Easter Sunday, 1850.

"DEARLY BELOVED IN CHRIST:—As after a long abscence a tender father earnestly desires to see again his beloved children, so is it our desire to return among you, whom we love so tenderly; for, 'although' as St. Paul says, 'we be absent in body, yet in spirit we are with you' (Coloss. ii. 5). These six months' absence we have found to pass heavily, and if we had not spent them entirely for the sacred interests of our holy mission, we could not have remained away from you so long.

"In answer chiefly to your fervent prayers for us, the Lord has blessed our pious undertakings. A little colony of young and zealous missionaries; the certainty of having next fall in our diocese some of those truly admirable Brothers of Christian Doctrine, with various other arrangements, less or more complete, for the good of our diocese, which we will more fully detail to you upon our arrival in your midst, are so many causes of gratitude to the Divine goodness, and consolations for the labors we have undergone.

"We could now, beloved friends, relate to you many edifying things that we have witnessed in Europe; but 'we hope speedily to be with you, and to speak face to face' (2 Ep. John) about them; for we intend to leave Havre for New York on the eighth of April, and to lose no time in being soon among you, in that fruitful field entrusted to our care by the Divine Husbandman.

"Now we are sure that you will not neglect to pray for us, that we may pass the boisterous ocean in safety, and reach home in peace. To that end we request our reverend and truly dear clergy to say at mass the *Oratio pro perigrinantibus* every day for four weeks after the receipt of this letter. We wish also that every Catholic in our diocese would recite for the same space of time, and the like purpose, the Lord's Prayer and the Hail Mary.

"For the rest, beloved brethren, rejoice, be perfect, take exhortation, be of one mind, have peace, and the God of peace and of love will be with you. . . . . 'The grace of our Lord Jesus Christ, and the charity of God, and communication of the Holy Ghost be with you all. Amen.'" (2 Cor. xiii.)

"✠ MATHIAS, Bishop of Dubuque."

After a passage of thirty-three days, Bishop Loras arrived at New York, May 13, 1850, and was soon afterwards in the midst of his devoted and joyous flock.

Bishop Loras occupied a venerable position in the American Hierarchy. His energy, character, fruitfulness of resources, extensive services to religion, and his sound judgment, gained for him the respect and veneration of his colleagues. He sat with them in the Fourth, Fifth, Sixth, and Seventh Provincial Councils of Baltimore, and in the First Plenary Council, in 1852. His relations with his own clergy and flock were of the most amiable and affectionate character. In an article on *Immigration to the West*, published in 1842,* the following mention is made of him:—" The See of Iowa, located at Dubuque, is fortunate in having such a head as the Right Rev. Mathias Loras, whom none, however much opposed to his religious principles, can fail to admire. He is a man of great strength of mind, of rare scholarship, of gentlemanly and popular manners, and of most exemplary piety. A true follower of his Saviour, his only aim is the prosperity of his Church; his only ambition, the spiritual happiness of his flock. The Bishop is wedded to his flock, and his flock are united in their love for him."

Bishop Loras was one of the most benevolent and charitable of men. He was accessible to all. The poor found him with an open hand; the afflicted with a generous heart and soothing word; the applicants for alms were never turned away, for he was frequently known to deprive himself of necessaries that he might relieve others. He quite commonly appropriated a portion of the Sunday's collection for the relief of the poor, and was scrupulously nice in distributing it to the most needy. His charities, too, were most unobtrusive, and even secret; seldom did any but the recipient know of

---

* *Freeman's Journal*, 1842 and 1843, p. 93.

his bounty. He provided an hospital for their relief and treatment in sickness in 1857. He encouraged the introduction of the Society of St. Vincent de Paul, of which there were a number of Conferences established in his diocese.

Mention has already been made of his efforts in behalf of Catholic immigration to Iowa. In 1855, the Catholic population of Iowa increased one hundred and fifty *per centum* in a single year. It seems almost incredible to relate that the churches and stations provided for their accommodation increased in the same time nearly one hundred *per centum*. The Catholic population reported in 1855 was twenty thousand, and the churches and stations fifty-two; the Catholic population in 1856 was rated at forty-nine thousand, and the churches and stations at ninety-seven, showing an increase of churches and stations of forty-five. He commenced his episcopate in 1837, with one church, one priest, and the only Catholic population reported, that of Dubuque, three hundred. In 1851, Minnesota was taken from his diocese; yet in 1858, the year of his death, the diocese of Iowa alone possessed one hundred and seven priests, one hundred and two churches and stations, and a Catholic population of fifty-five thousand. There were at this time also eleven clerical students, three male and six female religious institutious, and three male and six female literary institutions. What talent for affairs, what resources of enterprise and industry, what energy of character and zeal for the glory of God and the good of man, must not this good Bishop have called into action in accomplishing such results!

Such labors of mind and body would have long before exhausted the health of any ordinary man. Bishop

Loras attained the age of sixty-six. For the last few years of his life his health began to decline; but he continued his labors to an extent far beyond his years and strength. Early in February, 1858, he had an attack of illness, from which he seemed to recover; but on the evening of February 18, he retired to his room about eight o'clock, in his usual health, and shortly afterwards was found lying on the floor in an insensible state. Paralysis had done its work. Lingering in the same condition until the following morning, he expired without a struggle. It is stated that fully nine-tenths of the entire population of Dubuque, on hearing of his death, turned out to show their respect for his memory and express their sorrow at his death.

RIGHT REV. RICHARD PIUS MILES, D.D.,

*First Bishop of Nashville, A.D. 1838.**

RICHARD PIUS MILES was born in Prince George's county, Maryland, May 17, 1791. At that time there was a considerable emigration from Maryland to Kentucky. The celebrated Daniel Boone had advanced the frontier of civilization in that region, and Bishop Miles' parents, themselves connected with the Maryland branch of the Boone family, which was of the same stock with that of the great explorer and pioneer, were among those who followed in the westward current. Young Miles, then at the age of five years, emigrated with his parents to Kentucky, in 1796. With many instances of religious vocations in his family before him, and educated in piety from his infancy by his good parents, as soon as he was capable of choosing a vocation he chose the better part, and resolved to enter the Dominican Convent of St. Rose, Washington county, Kentucky. He received the white habit of St. Dominic, October 10, 1806, being then only fifteen years old. During his entire life he was most affectionately attached to his brethren of the Dominican Order.

Ten years of study and application to the various offices of the Order prepared him for the sacred ministry, to which dignity he was raised in September, 1816. For twenty-two years he devoted himself with great zeal and untiring energy to the missions of Ohio and Ken-

---
* Authorities: *Louisville Guardian;* contemporaneous Catholic magazines and papers, and original private sources.

tucky, having been pastor of the congregations of Somerset and Zanesville, where the memory of his labors and of his kind and genial manners is still cherished. The models after which his missionary life was formed were such men as Bishops Flaget and David, and Fathers Nerinckx and Badin, all missionaries of the severest and most laborious apostolic schools, and men of the most pious, simple, and humble lives. From the earliest days of his priesthood he was a favorite companion of, and valuable assistant to, Bishop Flaget, in some of those great visitations of his diocese, each of which was a fruitful and consoling revival of faith and piety in the country through which they passed. In 1830 he accompanied Bishop Edward Fenwick, of Cincinnati, in a visitation of the State of Ohio, which was fruitful in great results, and rendered invaluable services to that venerable and good Prelate. Like the other missionaries of the West in those early days, Father Miles had to hunt up the scattered Catholics of his mission; long journeys on horseback were the usual task of the priest, and the severity of his labors was greatly increased by the roughness of the roads and the inconveniences of the traveling vehicles. It was under such circumstances that Father Miles performed his missionary labors in the various parts of Kentucky and Ohio.

The Dominican Fathers of St. Rose were anxious to establish houses of their Order for nuns, to satisfy the religious vocations of many pious ladies of the West. The Superior, Father Thomas Wilson, approved this suggestion, and regarded the rules of the Third Order best suited to the country and the circumstances. It was with his approbation that Father Miles established the Convent of St. Magdalen, now known as St. Catharine of Sienna, near Springfield, Kentucky. Miss Mary Sansberry, herself a Marylander, and Miss Mary Carrico, were the first nuns; the former of whom, under the name of Sister Angela, was the first prioress. Father Miles' wisdom and prudence in the establishment and guidance of this institution, of which he was the ecclesiastical Superior, were much commended. An academy and day-school were commenced by the Sisters of St. Catharine's Convent at the same time, and have ever since proved the sources of immense good in the West, through the exertions of the good Sisters of St. Dominic, in dispensing a Catholic education to many thousands of young ladies. The first branch from the Convent of St. Catharine was that of St. Agnes, at Memphis, introduced during the episcopate of Bishop Miles in the diocese of Nashville, of which Memphis is a part, at the solicitation of Father Thomas L. Grace, now Bishop of St. Paul, Minnesota. Since then its branches have multiplied, and its blessings to the community have increased a hundredfold.

The Council which assembled at Baltimore in 1837 proposed to the Holy See the erection of several new episcopal sees, and amongst these the See of Nashville for the State of Tennessee, and nominated Father Miles as its first Bishop. His labors in the West, his zeal for religion, and the high and responsible offices he had held in his Order, of which he had been provincial, marked him out as eminently qualified for this exalted station, and though his loss was severely felt by the Order of St. Dominic, all acknowledged that his capacity for good would be enlarged in the more extensive field of the episcopate. He was consecrated in the Cathedral of Bardstown, September 16, 1838. The venerable Bishop Flaget was engaged to perform the consecration, but his infirmities rendered him unable to do more than assist by his presence. Bishop Rosati became consecrator in his place, assisted by Bishops Bruté, David, and Chabrat. The Very Rev. John Timon, afterwards Bishop of Buffalo, preached the consecration sermon.

Bishop Miles proceeded at once to Nashville and took possession of his see. No new diocese ever erected in this country, probably, was so destitute as that of Tennessee when its first Bishop entered it. He stood alone in that large diocese, without support, sympathy, or means. There was not a priest in the diocese; occasionally it was visited by some zealous missionary from Kentucky in search of the few scattered Catholics, to strengthen them in their faith and console them with the sacraments of the Holy Church. One or two miserable sheds, in a dilapidated and falling condition, were the only places in the State in which the faithful could assemble to attend divine service. The bishop, having no residence, was compelled to take board at Nashville, and commence the work of organizing, or rather of erecting the Church of Tennessee. At this disheartening crisis the Bishop was taken ill with the prevailing fever of the climate, so fatal to the unacclimated. "Stretched upon a bed of sickness," writes one who received these particulars from the Bishop's mouth, "he was looking hourly for his dissolution, with no familiar face to cheer him, no priest to minister to his spiritual wants, or to aid him with his corporal works of mercy. Thus he lingered on for several days, with a high fever raging upon him, till at last, as if by a special mercy and providence of God, a priest, traveling through the Southern country, casually stopped at Nashville, and in accordance with duty as well as with courtesy, his first thoughts were to report himself to the Bishop. His presence at so critical a moment sent a thrill of joy through the house. God did not forget the Bishop who had so often administered the consolations of the Church to the sick and dying. From the moment the good priest appeared at his bedside, the fever began to abate; he saw in the minister of his religion a friend and a comforter; he no longer felt alone in his new habitation. His health soon returned, and with it his proverbial energy; an energy which is manifested in the increase of his flock and in the number of churches built under his auspices." *

Bishop Miles immediately commenced his arduous mission. Not only was he without a priest to share his labors and take part in his counsels, but the labor of reaching the members of his flock, who did not exceed one hundred families, was immeasurably increased by their being scattered all through the entire State. He began by traveling over his extensive diocese on horseback in search of his children, finding here and there an isolated Catholic, " to whom his visit brought hope of a better day for the Church in Tennessee." Religion, from this moment, began to look up in that extensive region. When the people heard their religion preached in fervid and eloquent terms by a consecrated ruler in the Church, in the court-houses and other places, where it was never heard before, and assisted at the divine service before altars, improvised though they were, began to rally around their pastor, and small congregations of pious Catholics soon began to form in various parts of the State. During this, his first visitation of the new diocese, the Bishop paid his first visit to Memphis, where he was

---

* *Catholic Magazines*, 1844 and 1845.

received with great joy by the people; he preached three times for them, and made arrangements for a church and priest. He experienced great difficulties in getting priests, so great was the demand for them throughout the country, and so little means for their support were available in Tennessee. The Rev. Mr. Clancy, from Spring Hill College, near Mobile, was the first priest who generously volunteered to attach himself to this poor and arduous mission. The Bishop visited Somerset, Kentucky, where he was surrounded by the fruits of his own generous labors in that State, and here he ordained two young priests, who nobly resolved to work in the new diocese of Nashville. A beginning being once made, in a short time new churches began to spring up, and Tennessee seemed at once to experience a new creation. He had an arduous task in sustaining these struggles of the infant Church of Tennessee. For several years he was only able to assign one priest to several counties, and in 1844 a single missionary, Father Schacht, had as many as eight large counties to attend. It may also be mentioned, as an instance of Bishop Miles's labors for the benefit of the Catholic population of his diocese, that he provided a large tract of land in Humphry county, as a place of settlement for them, where they soon began "to enjoy the comforts of a peaceful and independent home."*

In March, 1840, Bishop Miles revisited St. Rose, in Kentucky, one of the scenes of his former labors. Here he joined Bishop, now Archbishop, Purcell and Rev. Father McElroy, S.J., who were then also paying a visit to that interesting place. Bishop Miles accepted the

---

* *Catholic Magazines*, 1844 and 1845.

earnest invitation of his brethren of St. Rose to spend a few days with them, and while there he ordained, at the request of Bishop Flaget, several young priests, conferred confirmation, and conducted in person the examination of the young ladies of the Academy of St. Catharine, which, as has been stated, was founded by himself. His visit to his former children, after the severe and exhausting labors of his first few months of episcopal administration, was one of unalloyed pleasure; and fervent indeed were the prayers of all for his health and prosperity, and for a safe return from the visit to Europe which he was then about to make. Proceeding at once to the East, he embarked for Europe, to visit Rome and other places on business for his diocese.

Bishop Miles took part in the ceremonies of consecrating the Cathedral at Cincinnati, on November 2, 1845, and chanted the solemn *Requiem* Mass, which occupied one of the days of this great gathering of Bishops, priests, and people. On his way to embark for Europe he also took part in the ceremony of laying the corner-stone of the Church of St. Vincent de Paul at Baltimore. He was ever fond of the historical glories of his native State, and was on several occasions, after attending the Councils at Baltimore, one of the most delighted guests at the celebrations of the landing of the Pilgrim Fathers of Maryland, so nobly gotten up by the Philodemic Society of Georgetown College.

At a spiritual retreat, which he gave in Nashville shortly after his arrival there in 1839, there were but nine communicants; in a few years the number of communicants was increased to four hundred, and the number of Catholics reached nearly a thousand. In a visitation of the diocese, which he made in 1847, he confirmed nearly four hundred persons, of whom nineteen adults were converts. In the same year he had the consolation of dedicating the Church of St. Peter at Memphis, erected by the exertions of Rev. M. McAleer, and of preaching and giving confirmation on the same day. In the following year he had the happiness of dedicating his own Cathedral, under the name and patronage of the *Blessed Virgin of the Seven Dolors*, at Nashville, assisted by Bishops Portier and Purcell, and a large body of clergy. This fine structure cost thirty thousand dollars, and its erection was due to the indefatigable exertions of the Bishop. He also succeeded in erecting a fine episcopal residence, and in enriching it with a well-selected ecclesiastical library. He established a charity hospital at Nashville, under the care of the Sisters of Charity from Nazareth, and gave them the old church, which he caused to be fitted up for that purpose. The Academy of St. Mary, under the care of the Sisters of Charity, which became in his lifetime one of the most useful and flourishing educational institutions of the West, is a monument of his zeal. He rallied around him thirteen zealous priests, as sharers of his labors and rewards; he built fourteen churches and six chapels, and established thirteen stations for the mission. He also established a Theological Seminary, three female religious institutes, nine parish schools, a colony of the Dominican Order at Memphis, and a fine orphan asylum, under the care of the Sisters of St. Dominic. The Catholic population, which at his appointment was counted by individuals, increased under his energetic administration to twelve thousand. The first ordination ever witnessed in Tennessee was that performed by Bishop Miles, November 29. 1842, when he raised to the priesthood Rev.

John O'Dowd, a student of the Bishop's Theological Seminary at Nashville.

Bishop Miles took part in the Councils which assembled at Baltimore, in 1840, 1843, 1846, and 1849, and at the First National Council, which assembled there in 1852. At the first of these there were twelve Prelates assembled, representing that number of dioceses; at the last there were six Archbishops and twenty-four Bishops in session, facts showing the great progress of the Church during Bishop Miles' time.

During several years, Bishop Miles' health was very feeble, owing to a chronic cough with which he was greatly troubled. Many of the labors of his arduous mission were performed by him while thus in infirm health. The assistance of a Coadjutor became necessary to him, and the Right Rev. James Whelan was appointed to that office, and consecrated May 8, 1859.

Bishop Miles was remarkable through life for his cheerful disposition, which he preserved to the last, although his decline became more and more apparent every day. On February 17, 1860, he was kept awake all night by his cough; on the following morning he was found sitting before the fire in the position he usually occupied while reciting the sacred office; on raising him from his chair, it was found he could not stand; he was carried to his bed, from which he never arose; he departed this life on the 21st. He received the last sacraments from the hands of his Coadjutor, and his death was calm and resigned. His loss was universally lamented in Nashville and throughout Tennessee, and by all religious denominations. A profound respect was manifested by the entire community for his memory and virtues. His remains were interred under the high altar of his Cathedral. It has been well said of him: "Never morose, and seldom low-spirited, Bishop Miles had the happy faculty, in his social relations, to be able to impart to all around him a portion of his own cheerful spirit. He was pious without affectation, charitable to the poor, and kind and affable to all."*

* *Louisville Guardian.*

RIGHT REV. FRANCIS GARCIA DIEGO Y MORENO, D.D., O.S.F.,

Bishop of Both Californias, A.D. 1840.*

FRANCIS GARCIA DIEGO Y MORENO was born towards the close of the last century of a very respectable family in the city of Lagos, State of Jalisco, Mexico. He was piously instructed from his first years, and he made his collegiate course of Latin, rhetoric, and philosophy, at the Seminary of Guadalaxara, with marked success. It was his great privilege to consecrate himself to religion at an early age, and it was thus that he made his studies at Guadalaxara a preparation for higher and holier aims. He went immediately from the Seminary to the Apostolic College of Our Lady of Guadalupe, at Zacatecas, where he assumed the habit and made his solemn profession of the rule of St. Francis, at the age of seventeen. He was ordained priest about the year 1824. He continued throughout his after-life, not only while residing in the convent of his Order, but also amidst the varying and trying events and sufferings of the mission, and while exercising the episcopal office, a rigid observer of that rule. In the Franciscan Convent of Our Lady of Guadalupe, he became successively Master of Novices, Bachelor of Arts, and Vicar of the Convent. At such times as he was not engaged in the duties of these offices, he labored most zealously for the

---

* Authorities: *History of the Catholic Missions*, by J. G. Shea; Capron's *History of California*; and original materials furnished by Archbishop Alemany and by the Rev. Secretary of Bishop Diego y Moreno.

spiritual good of others, and devoted most of his time to giving missions to the faithful in many towns and cities of the Republic of Mexico. His labors were productive of abundant fruits. He never spared himself in these apostolic services, which were animated by a sublime zeal, assisted by a high order of oratorical talents, and, more than all, supported by a pure, devout, and exemplary life. His signal services to religion in Mexico won for him the veneration and gratitude of his countrymen.

In 1832 Father Garcia was appointed Prefect of the Missions for the Conversion of the Indians in California. These missions had flourished for years under the Franciscan Fathers, and presented a spectacle at once pleasing and instructive—a lesson of peace and prosperity, from which our statesmen might learn how to organize and conduct the Indian Bureau. The Indians of both Californias were gathered together in Christian communities, forming a commonwealth of prayer and industry, in which the chapel, the school, and the mission-house were the central points of civilization, and in which a noble race, redeemed from barbarism and peacefully conquered to the Christian faith, commenced the day at each village like one family, assisted in prayer, devoted their hours to the cultivation of the soil, the raising of cattle, and the weaving of cloth and fine cotton; labors mingled with devotions to God, and sanctified by dedication to His honor. Two Franciscan Friars directed each mission: one as the spiritual Father, the other as the conductor of the labors in the field and factory, in which he took a leading part with his own hands. The Fathers were both civil and religious rulers, or rather guides. The life of the missionary and the Indian was regular, simple, frugal; yet abundance blessed their industry, and innocent recreations refreshed both mind and body. Modesty of dress and purity of life were as conspicuous features among the Indians, as the opposites of these had been amongst them before their conversion, and were still so revoltingly seen amongst the heathen Indians. The products of their industry were breadstuffs, wine, oil, hemp, cordage, hides, and tallow, which were sold or shipped to convenient ports. The vineyards of St. Gabriel and other missions yielded an excellent wine, and ships sailed regularly for Lima and San Blas, loaded with products of the missions. The most enlightened enterprise prevailed; an instance of which is found in the fact that Father Zalvidia, of St. Gabriel, opened negotiations with an Americian house to supply the Mission with iron fences. The members of these happy and peaceful communities were not even all of the same tribe, but of divers tribes, who worshipped and labored together under the shadow of the Cross. Truly was the tomahawk buried. The Great Spirit was their only God, the Franciscans were truly their Fathers, whom they most tenderly loved, and they were brothers amongst themselves. Twenty such missions flourished at the time of which we write, whose names, so expressive of Christian faith and piety, were as follows:—San Diego, San Carlos, San Gabriel, San Solidad, San Luis Obispo, San Antonio, San Juan Cepistrano, Santa Clara, San Francisco, Santa Buenaventura, Santa Barbara, La Purissima Conception, San Fernando, San Miguel, San Juan Bautista, Santa Cruz, San José, San Luis Rey, San Raphael, and Santa Ynez. A Catholic population of 30,650 inhabited these consecrated spots, and in each was a Cross elevated high above cabin and tent, an in each an altar, sanctified by the clean oblation of the Christian law. They possessed 424,000 head of cattle, 62,500 horses, 321,500 sheep, and their annual production of wheat was 122,500 bushels. With the returns of the sales of these, clothes, tobacco, agricultural implements, tools, and other articles were purchased for the Indians, and with the surplus were purchased necessaries for the mission, furniture for the churches and Indian dwellings. The missionaries had voluntarily embraced a life of holy poverty, and confirmed it with monastic vow—their food and clothing were all they received from the common fund.

Such was the field over which Father Garcia was now appointed as Prefect of the Missions. He started immediately for California, accompanied by ten missionaries from the College of Our Lady of Guadalupe; but owing to the great distance, and the difficulties of the journey, he did not reach his missions until January 15 of the following year, 1833. He took up his residence at Santa Clara, from which point he endeavored to revive and sustain all the missions of Upper California, already yielding to the pressure of secular and political interference and persecution. He arrived among the missions at a critical period of their existence, and had it been possible to save them from the destroying hand of the secular power, they certainly would have been rescued by the powerful exertions and untiring labors of Father Garcia.

Echandia, the first Governor sent to California by the Mexican Republic, became the scourge of the missions. He plundered the Indians, scattered and broke up their peaceful settlements, and expelled the missionaries. His removal gave the missions only a short respite, under the mild and friendly administration of Don Manuel Victoria, when soon again the work of plunder and outrage was resumed. The missionaries were the only friends of the Indians, and their only protectors against such wrongs; but the missionaries were themselves the chief objects of the hatred and ill-treatment of the tyrants. The undaunted Martinez was driven from his church and flock, and the venerable Sanchez, after the most cruel sufferings and banishment, died of grief in 1831. The celebrated Father Peyri, who for thirty-four years had conducted the Mission of San Luis Rey, which he had founded, was torn from his children, amidst the mingled tears of pastor and flock. Missionaries who had been for forty years amongst the Indians were expelled, and in some instances their lives were in danger. Their number was so reduced that, in 1832, when Father Garcia was sent out to California as Prefect, he was compelled to carry ten missionaries to recruit their ranks. One of his first acts was to make a wise and efficient distribution of his co-laborers amongst the Indians, giving to each of them instructions in relation to the spiritual guidance of the flock committed to his care, and for the administration of the temporal interests of the Missions. His own labors at the Mission of Santa Clara were untiring and without rest. He devoted himself especially to his neophytes, and had the consolation of baptizing with his own hands many Indians in the Missions of Santa Clara and San José. His solicitude, however, extended to all the missions of Upper California, and he exhorted the missionaries stationed at the various missions, by frequent communications he addressed to them, to increase their fervor and enkindle their zeal. In the disordered and persecuted condition in which the missions were, and the maladministration of the secular power, many delicate and embarrassing questions arose, which the missionaries referred to him to solve or decide, and by his wisdom and prudence he warded off or mitigated many of the misfortunes of the Indians.

It was while thus engaged in laboring for the good of the missions that he witnessed the severest blow they had yet received, in the passage, by the Mexican Congress, of the wicked and fatal decree for the secularization of the missions. The work of secularization had, in fact, been long progressing, and much damage had already been done; but the decree was passed in August, 1834, and although not finally and officially sanctioned and promulgated until 1837, the missions were already doomed. The property was now handed over to the political authorities; the missionaries, who had heretofore been called presidents or governors of the mission, were now deprived of all civil and religious power, and received the name of prefects; and while a small part of their property was allotted to the Indian families, the missionaries received only rations from the government agents, and frequently not even these—for Father Sarria died of hunger and misery at his mission of Solidad, which he had refused to abandon, falling on the very steps of the altar, which he was ascending to offer the Holy Sacrifice for his flock. Father Garcia Diego's heart was pierced with grief at the sight of the sufferings and persecutions of his flock and their pastors. He saw the cultivated fields desolated, the property of the missions destroyed and consumed day by day in the most lawless and scandalous manner, the Indians scattered and flying to the woods and mountains; in many instances their minds were poisoned against their own spiritual fathers, and they began to return to their former vices and barbarism. Apostasies became frequent, thefts of horses and cattle repeated, and immorality stalked abroad over the fair regions which had been consecrated to religion and peace, to industry and innocence. Father Garcia Diego, after struggling for some time in vain to arrest the work of pillage, destruction, immorality, and secularization, resolved to go in person to Mexico, and appeal directly to Congress for redress and remedy of these and many other evils which afflicted the country, and were blighting the good which a century of toil, sacrifices, and prayer had accomplished. He made his journey to the capital in the middle of the summer of 1836, and by his earnest and eloquent appeals to the Supreme Government and to Congress he secured the repeal of the decree of secularization, and the issue of an order for the restoration of the missions to the church. While grateful for these results, the good missionary felt that this tardy change of policy came, alas! too late to restore the country to even a shadow of its former peace and prosperity.

Having finished his work in the city of Mexico, he was anxious to be reunited to his flock; but so great had been his labors of mind and body, and so harassing his cares and anxieties, that a severe and protracted illness detained him at the Convent of Our Lady. Upon his recovery he was elected President and Visitor of the College at Zacatecas, and as such he was obliged to hold the Chapter of Guardian at the Convent and College in 1839.

Having concluded these duties, he was again preparing to return to his missions in California, when he received tidings of his appointment as Bishop of both Californias, having been elected and proclaimed in the

Roman Consistory, April 27, 1840. He was consecrated October 4, 1840. The ardor with which he sighed, now more than ever, to be with his children, and to labor for their preservation and protection, was again doomed to suffer, disappointment, by the delay in reaching and taking possession of his new diocese, and he did not reach San Diego before December 11, 1841. Sad was the sight he beheld on his return after several years' absence. The mission and church of San Diego were reduced to ruins; such, too, was the condition of the once splendid mission of San Gabriel. The faithful missionaries at San Fernando, Santa Clara, and Santa Ynez, during his absence, had succeeded in saving what remained of the missionary property; but he beheld nothing but ruin or desertion at San Buenaventura, Santa Cruz, San Juan Bautista, San Miguel, Carmel, La Purissima Conception, and San Raphael. Santa Barbara still possessed its mission and its devoted missionary. San Luis Obispo was in ruins, and its missionary reduced to almost nakedness and starvation, but still clinging to his altar and his flock. La Solidad, from having been an earthly paradise, was now a wilderness of ruin and devastation. At San José, the devoted Prefect of the Northern Missions subsisted upon the scant rations doled out to him by the officials; and at San Francisco Solano everything had been destroyed, and the materials of the mission-house and chapel sacrilegiously used in building the palace of Don Mariano Vallejo. The Indian population was reduced from over 30,000 to 4,450; their herds of cattle and flocks of sheep almost annihilated, their agriculture destroyed, and themselves mostly scattered and demoralized.

Bishop Garcia Diego y Moreno stood in the midst of

desolation, and but for his apostolic zeal and robust courage, would have despaired. He commenced the difficult task of saving what he could of his missions and Christians, and of doing all in his power to repair the ravages of secularization. Complete success was impossible; but it was wonderful how he accomplished so much. While some of the missions were totally destroyed, others were partially restored by him, and many souls at least rescued from crime and barbarism. The new Bishop made long and difficult journeys in accomplishing the episcopal visitation of his extensive and devastated diocese; he exhorted all by word and example. His energy and self-sacrifice enabled him to undertake the erection of a seminary at Santa Ynez, in which he was soon able to count a goodly number of students. His appeals to the Supreme Government of Mexico, inspired by a father's love and grief, and enforced with a becoming eloquence, were incessant in behalf of the Indians, the missionaries, and the Church. That he should have stayed for awhile the arm of devastation, under such appalling evils, is saying much; but his generous heart sank under the pressure of evils to his Church and people, which neither his apostolic zeal nor his appeals to the government could avert. Towards the close of 1845 he began to perceive his health failing, and he retired to Santa Barbara. His life had been an example of zeal and sacrifice; so his last moments were full of patience and conformity to the will of God. He received the last offices of the Church with profound piety and devotion. He peacefully resigned his soul into the hands of his Creator on the night of April 13, 1846, leaving behind him a glorious example, his labors and his sufferings, a precious inheritance to his Church.

RIGHT REV. JOHN MARY JOSEPH CHANCHE, D.D.,

*First Bishop of Natchez, A.D. 1841.**

DURING the insurrection of the negro population of St. Domingo, at the close of the last century, many of the white inhabitants of the island took refuge in this country. Among those were John Paul Chanche and his wife, Frances Elizabeth Harding. They were accompanied by John Chanche and his wife, Catharine Provost, the parents of the Bishop; they settled in Baltimore. The Bishop's mother was the only child of Frances Elizabeth Harding, by her first marriage with Mr. Provost, of St. Domingo. The Bishop's family were possessed of considerable wealth in St. Domingo, his father having been one of its most extensive and successful merchants.

John Mary Joseph Chanche was born at Baltimore, October 4, 1795, and was baptized there by the Rev. William Dubourg, afterwards Bishop of New Orleans, August 13, 1796. At the early age of eleven years he entered St. Mary's Seminary. It is said that at this tender age he had made choice of the sanctuary for his vocation, and piously directed all his studies to this exalted purpose. Happy indeed was his choice in thus consecrating to God the purity and innocence of his youth, as well as his manhood and mature age. His preparatory

---

* Authorities: Chiefly original sources and documents furnished by Bishop Elder; also, *Catholic Almanac*, 1853; *Catholic Magazines*, etc.; De Courcy and Shea's *History of the Catholic Church in the United States*, etc., etc.

studies were accomplished with great success. He received the holy tonsure from the hands of Archbishop Carroll, at the age of fifteen ; a few years later he received minor orders from Archbishop Neale, and was promoted to the holy priesthood June 5, 1819, by Archbishop Maréchal. Three successive Archbishops of Baltimore thus contributed to his ordination. During his ecclesiastical studies he had been a professor in the Seminary. He was now a member of the Sulpitian Order, and continued his duties as professor in St Mary's College. He was subsequently made Vice-President of the College. He became President in September, 1834, as successor to Dr. Eccleston, who was then appointed to the archiepiscopal office.

"As principal of an establishment of learning," writes one who was personally acquainted with him, " Mr. Chanche exhibited much wisdom. While he enforced the observance of discipline with a firm hand, his bland and gentle manner conciliated the esteem of all under his charge, and rendered him highly popular in the community at large. At no period did the institution over which he presided enjoy a better name or more prosperity than under his administration. The same qualities continued to win for him a general esteem, when he was called to a higher sphere of duty." *

When the question of selecting a Coadjutor to Archbishop Whitfield was mooted, Bishop Fenwick, of Boston, warmly urged the name of Dr. Chanche for that position. The latter having heard this from the Archbishop himself, with whom he had considerable influence, used his best efforts for the appointment of Dr.

---

* *Catholic Almanac*, 1853.

Eccleston. There always subsisted a warm friendship and mutual esteem between Bishop Fenwick and Dr. Chanche. When the former came to Baltimore to confer the *pallium* on Archbishop Eccleston, in 1834, Dr. Chanche preached on the occasion; after Mass, Bishop Fenwick, approaching Dr. Chanche in his own affectionate manner, and taking both his hands in his own, earnestly begged him to accept the office of Coadjutor of Boston. Dr. Chanche kindly but firmly persisted in declining this, as he had shrunk from former offers of promotion. This was while the young and gifted Fitzpatrick was at St. Sulpice, in Paris, before his ordination, and of course before he could be proposed or thought of for the episcopal office. Bishop Fenwick subsequently urged the name of Dr. Chanche as Coadjutor to Bishop Dubois of New York; but here again he used his arguments and persuasions with Archbishop Eccleston to secure his escape from the mitre.

Dr. Chanche was an eloquent preacher, a profound theologian, and a man of fine administrative abilities. He was tall, commanding, and handsome in his appearance, and in the performance of the sublime ceremonies of the altar he was peculiarly imposing and distinguished. He acted as master of ceremonies at the Second Provincial Council of Baltimore, in 1833; was one of the promoters at three subsequent councils; and at the First National Council was chief promoter, and celebrated the solemn Requiem Mass for the deceased Prelates. He was urbane and cultivated in his manners, always accessible, courteous, and kind, and there were few clergymen in his day who had more numerous or more ardent friends and admirers among the Bishops, clergy, and laity. His services were frequently called into requisition as a preacher on important occasions. Among his most eloquent and powerful sermons were two which he preached in the Cathedral at New Orleans, at celebrations of the anniversary of the battle of New Orleans; one on infallibility, preached at the blessing of St. Paul's Church, at Vicksburg; and one preached on his return from Europe, in his own Cathedral. The last of these created, at the time, a profound sensation in the South, and he was bitterly denounced by the sectarian press.

When the necessity for creating new episcopal sees arose, it was not possible for so worthy and prominent an ecclesiastic, one who had several times been already proposed for older sees, to escape nomination. The Council which assembled at Baltimore in 1837 proposed, among others, the erection of a bishopric at Natchez, comprising the State of Mississippi. No portion of the country was in greater need of churches and priests; the vineyard had gone untilled for want of laborers, and a Bishop was wanted, not so much to preside over an existing church, as to call one into existence. The Congregation of the Propaganda, by letter of September 2, 1837, transmitted the pontifical briefs, bearing date July 28, founding the three new dioceses of Natchez, Dubuque, and Nashville, for the first of which the Reverend Thomas Heyden, of Pennsylvania, was appointed. His declining the episcopal office caused some delay, and it was not until December, 1840, that Dr. Chanche was called to occupy the see of Natchez. In February, 1841, he received the Papal Bulls appointing him, dated at Rome, December 15, 1840, in the tenth year of the Pontificate of Gregory XVI., and signed by Cardinal Lambruschini. He was consecrated on March 14, in the

Cathedral at Baltimore, by the Most Rev. Archbishop Eccleston, assisted by Bishops Fenwick, of Boston, and Hughes, of New York. Bishop Hughes preached the consecration sermon. On April 27, he started for his see, accompanied by his brother as far as Cincinnati; thence he proceeded to New Orleans, from whose Bishop he desired to obtain detailed information concerning the state of religion in Mississippi, its resources and necessities. In this he was disappointed, as that Prelate was not at home, and Bishop Portier, of Mobile, who kindly went to New Orleans to meet him, could not accompany him to Natchez. He was thus obliged to go to his diocese alone. He made the passage from New Orleans to Natchez in thirty hours, on the Mississippi, was treated with the kindness and respect due to his official rank and personal character on board the steamer, the clerk of which, a Mr. Fitzgerald, who was a Catholic, refused pay for his passage. He arrived at night; a colored porter, who carried his trunk on his shoulders to the hotel, was the only one to meet him, and the Bishop entered his see without reception or ovation, after the manner of the apostles of old. His heart was sustained by faith and the love of souls.

Desolate as appeared the Church of Mississippi when entered by its first Bishop, it was not without its sacred traditions. Its foundations had been laid in the blood of martyrs. As early as 1727 the fierce tribe of the Natchez heard with amazement, from their wigwams and canoes along the banks of the Mother of Waters, the mingled hymns of Jesuit and Capuchin: the men of God landed on the mysterious shore; the Jesuit pushed his way to the scattered Indian hamlets, the Capuchin, by an arranged division of labor, ministered to the French settlers at Natchez. In 1729 this infant church, thus bravely begun, had its glorious martyr; its first beginnings were cemented in the blood of the illustrious Jesuit, Father Du Poisson, in the famous massacre of the Natchez. The Jesuit missions probably continued till the society itself succumbed under the violence of infidelity in France, in 1763. Subsequently, under the treaties by which Louisiana was ceded to England, numerous colonies of emigrants from all the English colonies in America poured into Mississippi. We have an account of one of these emigrant companies, which left New England to settle in Natchez, early in 1776, under the leadership of General Lyman, of Massachusetts, and Captain Phelps, of Connecticut. Amongst them was the Rev. Mr. Smith, their chaplain, and his family. They suffered great hardships on the way. The boat containing the Lymans and Smiths finally arrived at Natchez in August, 1776; but most of the immigrants were exhausted, and many deaths are chronicled. We do not know to which of the prevailing sects of New England Mr. Smith belonged, nor did he have an opportunity of becoming a missionary either at Natchez or among the Indians, for we are told that "a few days after (his landing) the worthy minister closed his earthly career." * After the recognition of our independence by Great Britain in 1782, American emigration from all the Atlantic States commenced flowing westward and south-westward, and must have carried with the tide some of the Catholic element then in the country. The treaties between England, France, and Spain left the boundaries somewhat uncertain, for though claimed by our government as included

---

* Pickett's *History of Alabama*, vol. ii. p. 20.

in the cessions, the region about Natchez remained in the possession of the Spaniards till about the year 1797. The king of Spain, true to his religious education, felt a deep interest in providing priests for his Catholic subjects in that country; and in 1787 it was decreed "that parochial stations of Irish priests should be established in Natchez and such other places in said province (then all called Louisiana) as might be deemed suitable, for the purpose of attracting the English and American settlers, their children and families to our region." * The Bishop of Salamanca was requested "to select four clergymen of the Irish nation, of recognized zeal, virtue, and cultivation," as the proposed missionaries. The choice fell upon the Rev. Constantine McKenna, Rev. William Savage, Rev. Michael Lamport, and Rev. Gregory White, of whom the first-named was appointed Superior of the Mission. Articles were signed by these Rev. gentlemen and the agent of the Spanish Government, by which the former bound themselves to proceed to their missionary posts, and serve therein without any limit as to time; and the Spanish king, on his part, engaged to give to each of them three thousand reals for an outfit to defray the cost of the voyage, from the royal treasury, and to allow to each the sum of forty dollars a month during his stay, as a support. Three at least of these missionaries, Rev. Constantine McKenna, Rev. William Savage, and Rev. Gregory White, embarked from Cadiz, safely arrived at Natchez, and were duly installed in their respective stations. The Spanish Government, then worthy of the name of Catholic, performed faithfully the articles, for we have evidence of the payment of the salary to these three priests as late

---

* *Spanish Documents* collected by Bishop Chanche.

as 1791, which was no doubt continued to the end. Measures were also taken by order of the king for the purchase of land and buildings to accommodate them. A tract of land of three hundred arpens, in the immediate vicinity of the fort, was purchased for this purpose from one William Carpenter, for the sum of two thousand dollars, and the missionaries were placed in possession. Upon the land was a house, fifty feet in length by forty feet deep, including the galleries, supplied with furniture and all necessary conveniences, and orders were issued for the erection of a suitable church. These clergymen conducted their missions and remained in possession of the Church property until 1797 or 1798, when the American Government took possession of the country and the property of the Church. It is difficult to comprehend the ground upon which our Government took possession of these Church lands, unless it be upon the narrow ground that the legal title was vested in the Spanish Government, and that the United States, on acquiring sovereignty over the country, succeeded to all the rights and property of their predecessor. It is certain that Carpenter deeded the land to the Spanish Government, and there is no evidence extant that any deed was given by the Spanish Government to the Church, and it is quite probable that at the time of the change of nationality, the legal title to the land was in the Spanish Government. It is without doubt, however, that the title was thus held by that Government merely in trust or for the benefit of the Church, and that the purchase and dedication of the land to Church purposes were intended to be, and were virtually a grant of them to the Catholic Church. By the Treaty of Florida, as it is called, provision was made for asserting title to lands in that territory, before a commission, within a given time. But at the time of the change of government, and the occupation of the missionary lands by the Government of the United States, the missionaries themselves had departed, and there was no proper head or representative to prosecute the claim in behalf of the Church until 1819, when it was too late. In the mean time the lands were sold by the Government to private individuals, and they are now subdivided and owned by numerous persons. These lands now embrace a considerable portion of the city of Natchez. In January, 1844, Bishop Chanche embarked at New Orleans for Havana, with the intention of seeking among the Spanish archives of the island of Cuba the evidences of the grant. He was received and treated with great kindness by the Most Rev. Ramon Francisco Casaus, Archbishop of Guatemala and Administrator of the Diocese of Havana, by Captain-General O'Donnell, by General Campbell, the American Consul, by the French Consul, by Counts Villanova and Fernandino, by Don José Maria Morales, a former schoolmate of the Bishop at St. Mary's College, in Baltimore, and by the Right Rev. Dr. Mendo, Bishop-elect of Sicovia, in Spain, then Superior of the Seminary at Havana, with the last of whom, by invitation, he made his home while in Havana. From the Government archives he obtained authentic copies of all the documents relating to the diocese of Natchez, and more especially to the land-grant to the Church. On March 1 he returned to New Orleans, and on the 11th to Natchez. He subsequently petitioned Congress, either to return to the Church of Natchez the original sum of two thousand dollars which the King of Spain had invested for that Church, or to grant other lands of equal extent or value with those originally granted. He was warmly supported in his efforts by Señor Calderon de la Barca, Spanish Minister at Washington, and by others; but his petition was never granted.

The first priest that visited Natchez after the withdrawal of the Irish missionaries sent by the Spanish Government, of whom tradition speaks, was the Rev. Father Boudin, who went to Natchez in 1802, and remained till 1803. In the latter year he went to conduct some nuns from New Orleans to Cuba; he returned for his effects, and then went to Point Coupée. He lost his life while visiting the sick, by the upsetting of his canoe near Lafourche, in the Bayou. In 1807 Natchez was visited by a German priest from Pennsylvania; but there was neither chalice nor the other indispensable articles for divine service, so that he only remained a few days and then proceeded to New Orleans, after having baptized some Catholic children of the place. Again, in 1810, Natchez was visited by a priest, whose name, however, has not been transmitted to us. In 1817 a pious Spaniard left fifteen hundred dollars for the church at Natchez, provided a priest were obtained within two years, and the church repaired, otherwise the bequest was to go to the hospital of the town. These conditions were complied with; a venerable Catholic citizen named McGraw advanced the money to repair the church, and in 1819 a priest came from the diocese of Bardstown, Kentucky. He went to New Orleans and procured a chalice and other necessary church service, and in June of that year the Catholics of Natchez had the consolation of assisting at holy Mass. The name and nationality of this clergyman are not given in our documents; but it is presumed he was a Frenchman, for it is related that the people complained of his bad English, whereupon he told them he could speak good French, and immediately gave them a severe sermon in that language, which the oldest inhabitants remember to this day. In the Lent of 1820 the Rev. Father Blanc, afterwards Archbishop of New Orleans, visited Natchez, and remained four months. During his stay the Rev. Mr. Maenhaut, then recently ordained at St. Louis, came to Natchez, and remained as pastor till 1824. During his mission in 1821, Bishop Dubourg administered confirmation, assisted by the pastor and the Rev. Mr. Vidal—the latter was brother to the Governor, and resided on the opposite side of the river, where he led a life of voluntary retirement and poverty. He visited Natchez occasionally, and offered Mass for the congregation. In 1825 the Rev. Mr. Gallagher, of New Orleans, a very aged man, was there; after his death, which occurred the same year, his fine library and even his church vestments were sold; the vestments were ripped to pieces by the purchaser, for the silk and other materials of which they were made—an evidence of the poverty of the Church of Natchez at that early period. From 1828 to 1829 the Rev. Mr. Ganillo officiated; Rev. Mr. Doyle in 1831; and in 1832 Rev. Mr. Kinderling; the last of whom possessed ample means, and cheerfully devoted them to charitable and religious objects. He offered to give four hundred dollars towards rebuilding the church, and to serve as pastor without salary. His offer, for some reason not related, was not accepted, and he repaired to New Orleans; but occasionally returned to Natchez to perform marriages and administer other sacraments. He continued his liberal charities at New Orleans.

The only church at Natchez, which was located in Commerce Street, was destroyed by fire, December 28, 1832, and with it was consumed an organ, said to have belonged to Louis XVI., and to have been presented by Louis XVIII. to Bishop Dubourg. After the consecration of Archbishop Blanc, of New Orleans, he sent a priest from time to time to Natchez; and in 1838 the Rev. Mr. Vandevelde, afterwards Bishop of Chicago, and still later Bishop of Natchez, went to prepare the way for the Rev. Mr. Hayden, the Bishop-elect of Natchez. In 1839 Rev. Mr. Timon, afterwards Bishop of Buffalo, gave one of his most successful missions at Natchez at the request of Archbishop Blanc. In the same year the Rev. Mr. Brogard became the pastor there, and remained until, and some time after, the advent of Bishop Chanche.

The church of Natchez had been, from the earliest period, dedicated to the Holy Family. That Catholicity made some progress there, during these long years of poverty and of interrupted and transient missions, is shown by the fact that Father Brogard found his chapel too small for the number of the faithful, and had rented the Mechanics' Hall for the divine service. The Father himself resided in a single room attached to the chapel.

Such had been the history of the Church of Natchez, and such was its condition when Bishop Chanche arrived there in 1841. The title of the only church property was vested in trustees; there was no house provided for the Bishop, so that he gladly accepted the offer of a pious lady, Mrs. Gireaudeau, to give him one-half of her house as his episcopal residence; she had seen her husband die without priest or sacraments, and she was now overjoyed at seeing a Bishop at Natchez, and in welcoming the hope of a happier day for religion in Mississippi. The Bishop lost no time; the day after his arrival, Ascension-day, he officiated at Mechanics' Hall, the usual place of worship, and took advantage of this early occasion to announce to his assembled flock his intentions in their regard. He informed them that his movements would be guided by the encouragement he received at their hands; that he was not tied down to the city of Natchez, but was only bound to the State of Mississippi, and that if his efforts met with little support he would not remain, but would seek a more promising field elsewhere in the State. The Catholics of Natchez and vicinity were assembled together on the following Saturday, and, cordially responding to the Bishop's appeal, they promptly directed the trustees to convey to him the large and fine lot at the corner of Main and Union Streets for the erection of a church. Bishop Chanche may be said to have commenced the organization of his diocese without church, priest, or school, and without the means of providing them; for the chapel had been abandoned in consequence of its small size. Father Brogard was only temporarily in Natchez, and when he proposed to the trustees the building of a church he found them without means, and was forced to delay the commencement of the building. His people, in common with their fellow-citizens, were suffering from the ravages of a recent tornado, which destroyed considerable portions of their city, the news of which calamity, by a singular coincidence, reached the Council at Baltimore on the very day that Dr. Chanche was nominated as Bishop. Fortunately Bishop Blanc came to the relief of Bishop Chanche, and placed about eight thousand five hundred dollars at his disposal, which enabled him to go to the North in the summer of 1841, and purchase the necessary church articles for his diocese.

While at Baltimore, on this trip, he consecrated eighty-seven altar-stones for the various missions he contemplated establishing in his diocese, and for priests going to distant stations to say Mass. He also consecrated, on November 7, 1841, the fine church of St. Vincent de Paul in the same city. His thoughts had been engaged, from the moment of his entry on his episcopate, on the important subject of providing Catholic education for the young of his diocese; and with this view he carried back with him from Frederick, Maryland, several pious and accomplished ladies, two of whom were his nieces; and Natchez soon beheld with satisfaction the opening of an academy for young ladies, under the auspices of its Bishop. The erection of a Cathedral church also engaged his early thoughts, for he had been long accustomed to see the noble services of the Church performed with due solemnity and grandeur, and he had a special love for the honor of God as expressed by the Christian temple and its solemn rites. In his own case he had a special motive for desiring to render this service to the Almighty, inasmuch as what he proposed to erect as a Cathedral was greatly needed as a parish church. By February 24, 1842, he had gathered sufficient resources to justify the commencement of his Cathedral, and on that day he had the consolation of laying its corner-stone, and of placing the new temple under the special invocation of "The Transfixed Heart of the Blessed and Immaculate Mary ever Virgin." The ceremony was performed by the Bishop, assisted by the Rev. Mr. Desgualtiere, accompanied by the mayor and select-men of the town, several gentlemen of distinction, and in the presence of an immense concourse of citizens.

The sermon preached by Bishop Chanche on this occasion is the only one of his sermons of which even an outline has been preserved. He alluded in an impressive manner to the time which had elapsed since the burning of the Catholic church at Natchez, to that day, when the congregation were cheered with the prospect of soon seeing another erected. He compared his little flock to the people of Israel returning from captivity, and zealously undertaking to rebuild the Temple of God in the city of Jerusalem. He spoke of the ceremonies he was about to perform, which were new to all present, and to many might appear strange. But he reminded them that they were the same ceremonies which were performed by an Augustine in England, and by a Patrick in Ireland; the same ceremonies with which were laid the corner-stones of the lofty Cathedrals of York and Westminster; the same ceremonies with which the cross was planted by our forefathers on the proud bluff of our own Natchez. He said this not in a spirit of controversy, but flattered by the reception he had met from persons of all denominations since his arrival in Natchez; and anxious to retain their esteem as well as their good feeling, he would thus speak of ceremonies which otherwise, perhaps, would not be appreciated. Indeed, when he saw the brilliant assembly by which he was surrounded, composed of persons of every denomination, who came to encourage the undertaking by their presence, his heart prompted him to exclaim, Oh! it is good for children of one family to dwell together in unity! And why should it not be so? he said. Are we not Christians? men redeemed, therefore, by the same precious blood which was spilt on Calvary for all? Are we not children of the same Father, who is in Heaven? The heirs, therefore, of God, and the co-heirs of Jesus

Christ? Are not our breasts animated by the same joyous hope of meeting in the kingdom of our heavenly Father? Must our sojourn in this vale of tears be embittered by strife and bad feeling? He then eulogized the virtue of fraternal love, which Christ called his own commandment, and engaged all to the diligent practice of it, and to banish from their society the demon of discord. After speaking of the purposes of the Church, in which their immortal souls were to commune with their Almighty Creator, in which they were to come to ask his blessing and avert his indignation, in which they were to pray for the favors of Heaven for themselves, for their families, for their city, and for the whole country, he concluded by a prayer for the speedy completion of the edifice, and that all who were present, after living in this world consoling one another in fraternal love, might meet and live forever in the bosom of the God of charity.

This fine church, which Bishop Chanche's energy and zeal rapidly pushed forward, was dedicated December 25, though not quite finished, and was for many years regarded as the most beautiful church in the West. Some years afterwards he received as a present, from Prince Alexander Torlania, a fine bell for the Cathedral, which he notices in his journal as follows:—

"On the 26th March, 1849, Trinity Sunday, I blessed the beautiful bell presented to me by Prince Alexander Torlania, of Rome. This bell had reached Natchez the Monday before in the boat *Natchez*. It came to me free of all expense. Such had been the direction of the Prince to the different merchants through whose hands it was to pass. I blessed it according to the ceremonial of the Roman Pontifical, and called it *Maria Alexan-*

drina, in honor of the donor and his lady. The bell is the work of Giovanni Lucenti. It is beautifully decorated, and weighs over three thousand pounds. It is related that the night it was cast, about 12 o'clock, the Prince left the company whom he entertained, went with his wife and a few friends to the foundry, and knelt with them, reciting the Litany of the Blessed Virgin and other prayers during the fusion. It was suspended in our Cathedral on Monday, March 27. The sound is soft and sweet, but not so loud as might have been expected from the size of the bell. Some attribute this to the smallness of the clapper. I was attended on the occasion by Father Mathew, Mr. Moricet, Mr. Grignon, and Mr. Fierabras."

On the Feast of Pentecost, 1842, Bishop Chanche celebrated the first Pontifical High Mass at Natchez, administered confirmation to about thirty persons, and concluded the ceremony by imparting the Papal benediction, of which he gave an interesting explanation to the congregation. It was during this year, also, that he caused a mission to be held for the especial benefit of the colored people, thus proving his paternal zeal for the humblest no less than for the more exalted members of his flock. At first only two or three persons attended the instructions; but this did not discourage Father François, who conducted the mission, and soon his audience increased to sixty, and among the fruits of this truly charitable work may be mentioned the conversion and baptism of fifteen adults. At this time there were but two priests to share the ministry with Bishop Chanche in the whole diocese, and the Easter communions of this year amounted to one hundred. Small as these figures appear, they show a great increase of good since his arrival in the diocese, and give us the means of approximating the great good he accomplished during the entire time of his episcopate.

He made long and laborious visitations of his diocese, and discharged every work, however humble and fatiguing, which pertains to the Christian ministry. His visitations were more like the usual visits of a missionary amongst a scattered Catholic population, which needed at his hands every function of the priesthood. He organized new parishes and congregations, made preparations for the erection of churches, and did all that charity, energy, zeal, and earnest eloquence could accomplish in so large and unprovided a field of labor. He soon began to reap the fruits of his labors in the increase of priests and organized congregations.

Bishop Chanche had a remarkable devotion to the Blessed Virgin Mary, and succeeded, after a very short time, in establishing in nearly every parish in his diocese the "Confraternity of the Most Holy and Immaculate Heart of Mary," in union with that of the parochial church of Notre Dame des Victoires in Paris.

Bishop Chanche started in company with Bishops Blanc and Odin, April 24, 1843, to attend the Council at Baltimore, and we are informed that he took an active part in the venerable assemblies of the American church. He twice accepted the invitation of Bishop Blanc to preach the annual sermon at the celebration of the battle of New Orleans, on the 8th of January, the last of which occasions was in 1844. On January 26, of the same year, he sailed from New Orleans to Havana on the business connected with the Spanish land grant already mentioned. By March 11 he was again in Natchez, and on the 15th opened the memorable retreat given there under the guidance of Dr. Timon. It is not necessary to detail all the missions, visitations, church dedications, and other labors of Bishop Chanche, for these, together with the other varied duties of the episcopate and of missionary life, were his constant occupations. The flourishing condition in which he left his diocese is the best evidence of the success of his episcopate. An account taken from a cotemporary publication,* of a single visitation of his, will serve to show the condition of the Church in Mississippi, the labors of its first Bishop, and the state of social and religious feeling there in 1844 :—

"On the morning of Wednesday, the 24th of April, the Bishop of Natchez arrived at the interesting town of Yazoo. The city of Yazoo, as it is now called, formerly Manchester, is situated on the Yazoo River, about one hundred miles from its junction with the Mississippi. It is a promising town, filled with an active and industrious population, amounting to about one thousand souls. The stores are numerous and well stocked, and furnish supplies to a very considerable extent of country. The exports of cotton from this town last year were from fifty to sixty thousand bales. This export must necessarily increase every year in proportion as the fertile banks of the Yazoo and the country around are brought into cultivation. The Catholics in this town are not very numerous, but earnest and zealous. As soon as it was known that the Bishop had arrived, the Honorable E. C. Wilkinson invited him to his residence, where he received the visits of the gentlemen, Protestant as well as Catholic, of the city. He was invited to preach in the evening, and the Methodist meeting-house was obtained for the purpose. The Bishop complimented them for

---

* *Catholic Magazine*, 1844.

their zeal, dilated on the importance of religion, and announced that the next day he would discuss the grounds upon which Christianity was founded. The next evening the Methodists refused the use of their meeting house, so did the Presbyterians, so that the gentlemen were obliged to have recourse to a large hall at the Phœnix House. On Friday the Bishop preached on Transubstantiation. It was an able argument and produced a great effect upon the people. On Saturday he preached on the Sacrament of Penance with equal effect. On all these days the rooms were very much crowded. The Catholics, assisted by several liberal Protestant gentlemen, are determined to build a church at once. The choice of four or five lots has been offered to the Bishop, and a subscription raised of more than four thousand dollars. How much good could not an active and zealous priest do here! The people are just prepared to receive instruction and are willing to do so. How great would be the fruit of his labors! The Bishop celebrated Mass on Sunday morning at the residence of Judge Wilkinson, in the presence of from forty to fifty Catholics; he administered the holy Eucharist to several persons, and baptized several children. After Mass the Bishop started, accompanied by Judge Wilkinson, for the town of Benton, where he was expected to preach. He preached in the Methodist meeting-house, and though the weather was bad, his audience was large. This is the first time that a Catholic Bishop has been seen in these quarters, and his reception everywhere is most flattering and promising."

Bishop Chanche, from having so often in his younger days, at Baltimore, served as master of ceremonies at great ecclesiastical feasts and celebrations, acquired a thorough knowledge of, and devout appreciation for, the splendid ritual of the Church. His fine appearance, dignified carriage, and devout manner added much to the effect of the ceremonies he participated in. At his Cathedral in Natchez, he took care to present to the people the solemn services of the Church with all the imposing ceremony and grandeur in his power, and he united with the Church at large on all occasions of those celebrations, which are so beautifully expressive either of her joys or sorrows. He mentions several of these in his journal, and amongst them were the Requiem Mass and funeral service for the soul of Bishop Fenwick of Boston; the same on the occasion of the death of Pope Gregory XVI., in July, 1846; and the celebration of the jubilee proclaimed by Pope Pius IX., in 1847. On the very day that he heard the news of the election of the Holy Father, Pius IX., he received as a present to himself, from that illustrious Pontiff, a handsome chalice, which had been brought from Rome by Bishop Odin. In the Sixth Council of Baltimore, in 1846, he performed the duties of one of the promotors of the Council, and celebrated the Requiem Mass for the deceased Prelates of the American Church. In 1848 he visited Europe on business for his diocese, and traveled through several of the principal countries of the continent. He returned in time to take part in the Council which assembled at Baltimore in 1849.

Among the invaluable services rendered by Bishop Chanche to the diocese of Natchez, was the introduction of the Sisters of Charity, from Emmittsburg, Maryland. Three sisters came at first, and arrived at Natchez towards the end of January, 1848, and immediately opened their school. The Bishop purchased for them the fine residence of Mr. Farriday, and Sister Martha, the sister-servant, gave her notes for the deferred payments. They found a generous friend in Col. Rice C. Ballard, who endorsed the notes and took the payment of them upon himself. The following year this institution was incorporated by the Legislature of Mississippi, and before the Bishop's death, in 1852, had expanded into St. Mary's Orphan Asylum and School, with its six sisters, thirty orphans, and seventy day scholars, and was then about to send forth from its own community the colony that was to establish a similar asylum and school at Vicksburg.

When he went to Europe, in 1848, the question of securing a union of the Sisters of Charity in America with those instituted in France by St. Vincent de Paul, was seriously considered. This object had been greatly desired by Mother Seton herself, and was now earnestly approved by Archbishop Eccleston and Father Deluol, and by the good sisters made a special object of prayer. On the eve of his departure for Europe, Bishop Chanche, who was a warm friend of this noble sisterhood, accepted from the proper authorities the commission of making application for the desired affiliation. Father Etienne, the Superior-General, to whom Bishop Chanche made the application, gave at first rather a positive refusal; but this did not discourage the Bishop. After a short pause, the Bishop replied: "Father, suppose it were the will of God that such a union should take place, would you still refuse?"—"Of course not," was the answer; "but I do not see that it is God's will." —"What proofs would you require to be convinced that God desires such a union?" inquired the Bishop. "First," replied the Superior, "that the sisters should desire to be affiliated, and make to that effect a formal application, through their Superiors. Secondly, that the Archbishop of Baltimore, and the majority of the Bishops in whose dioceses the sisters are established, should consent to the measure. And, thirdly, that the sisters should be willing to adopt the rules and customs of our sisters in Europe." Whereupon Bishop Chanche presented to the Superior the formal application, signed by Archbishop Eccleston, Father Deluol, and by Mother Etienne, the Superior of the American sisterhood, in the name of all the sisters; and added that he was pretty sure of the consent of the Bishops generally, having himself spoken on the subject to several of them. As for the third condition, the Bishop said it had been already acknowledged as a necessary result of the proposed union. The point was already virtually carried, and after due correspondence and consultation between France and America, this noble union was accomplished.*

Bishop Chanche had now, though with very limited resources, brought his diocese to a prosperous state of development and strength. He had built eleven churches and established thirty-two stations. He had increased the number of his priests to eleven. We may judge how the Bishop and his priests labored, by adverting to the fact that these eleven churches and thirty-two stations were attended by one Bishop and eleven priests. At this time, also, there had been established at Natchez a fine orphan asylum, with a Sunday-school attached. Another asylum was then also projected for Vicksburg.

While undertaking and forwarding the foregoing and

---

* *Life of Father De Andreis.*

other similar works for the promotion of religion and education, he left Natchez to attend the First National Council at Baltimore, which was held in May, 1852. He was appointed chief promotor of the Council, and otherwise took an active part in its deliberations. It was well said of Bishop Chanche, in connection with this first Plenary Council in the United States: "There was no one present in that venerable assembly, whether Bishop or priest, who could witness with more heartfelt interest the wonderful progress of Catholicity in the United States, which the National Council exhibited. He had beheld the Church in this country in its feeble commencement, when but one Prelate was charged with the spiritual care of all the Catholics in the United States, few indeed in number, but extending from the Atlantic border to the far West, and from Maine to the Gulf of Mexico. He had watched its steady and rapid advancement, and he now contemplated an increase of its force, which was calculated to excite equal astonishment and admiration."*

After the close of the Council, Bishop Chanche visited Emmittsburg, and returning stopped in Frederick, Maryland, to make a brief stay with some of his friends in that city. He was here suddenly attacked with a violent form of cholera morbus, which baffled all medical efforts, and, after a severe illness of two weeks, this· distinguished ornament of the Catholic Hierarchy breathed his last. He, whose life had been so zealous, so laborious, and so exemplary, was equally an example of Christian virtue and resignation at the hour of his death. Stricken down with sudden disease in the midst

---

* *Catholic Almanac* of 1853, p 53

of robust health, when human nature is less reconciled to bear and suffer, he bore and suffered, and met his fate, with heroic patience and cheerful acquiescence in the divine will. His last days were truly worthy of a Christian Prelate. The trial of being separated from his diocese and flock, at that moment so dread and appalling to him and to them, he bore with meek acceptance. During his painful illness he never allowed a murmur or complaint to escape his lips. He met death with that same courage and hope in God, which had carried him so successfully and usefully through his arduous life. He died July 22, 1852, in the fifty-seventh year of his age and the twelfth of his episcopate. His remains were interred, at his own request, in the Cathedral cemetery at Baltimore, where his many friends immediately made arrangements to erect a suitable monument in his honor. The funeral service was performed in the chapel of St. Mary's College, with solemn Requiem Mass, at which the Most Rev. Archbishop Kenrick took part and pronounced the absolution. While the Hierarchy and the whole American Church mourned his loss, Baltimore, his native place, and Natchez, his episcopal city, especially felt his death; and in both of these places his memory is treasured in tender affection to this day.

RIGHT REV. PETER PAUL LEFEVRE, D.D.,

Bishop of Zela in part., and Administrator of Detroit, A.D. 1841.*

TRANSFERRED from one of the most remote of our Western missions to the episcopal office and city of Detroit, Bishop Lefevre, in his successful administration and inestimable services to religion in his new field, presents a striking example of the resources of the Catholic Church, of the wonderful devotion of her children, and of the guiding presence of the Holy Ghost in her councils.

Peter Paul Lefevre was born April 30, 1804, at Roulers, a town in the province of West Flanders, near Ghent. He was very young when he resolved to embrace the life of the sanctuary, and from that time directed all his efforts and studies to that high end. He pursued his studies in the best schools of Paris, where he graduated in 1828. In the same year he came to the United States, and attached himself to the diocese of Missouri, then governed by that distinguished Prelate, Dr. Rosati. Continuing his theological studies for three years longer at St. Louis, he was ordained deacon by Bishop Rosati in 1831, and priest in the same year. He commenced his missionary labors at New Madrid, Missouri, in that year, and after a few months was transferred to Salt River, Ralls County, Missouri, which he made the central station of one of the largest, most difficult, and laborious missions ever attended by a single

---

* Compiled from the *Catholic Almanacs* and other periodical publications, and from original sources.

priest. It embraced the northern part of Missouri, the western part of Illinois, and Southern Iowa. His church at Salt River was dedicated to St. Paul. Besides this, his head-quarters, he attended nine other stations at great distances apart: these were, Cincinnati, Ralls County, where the church was dedicated to St. Mark; Louisville, Lincoln County, where the church was dedicated to St. Simeon; Penno Creek, Pike County; Indian Creek, Monroe County, where the church was dedicated to St. Stephen; Wyaconda River, Lewis and Clark County; Cedar Creek; North Santa Fé, Clarke's County; Marion City, and Half Indian Tract. His mission over this large region was full of hardships, long and dangerous journeys, severe humiliations, uncomplaining and cheerful sufferings. The few Catholics within his mission were scattered at great distances, requiring long and exhausting journeys to reach them. In one of these expeditions over the rough roads of the West he sprained his ankle, from which he never entirely recovered. He had to deal with the most difficult of all flocks—for he had to bring to the Church and to the sacraments families and individuals originally Catholics, but then strangers to their faith and the sacraments, indifferent to religion, and frequently addicted to improper and disedifying courses of life: unbaptized adults; Catholics married out of their Church, and large families of children growing up in ignorance of the faith of their forefathers. This young priest devoted himself with apostolic zeal and courage to this difficult field; for ten years he labored without sparing himself, and his success was both abundant and permanent. The mission thus attended by him was prepared for future harvest of a hundredfold increase, and is now the home of a large and flourishing Catholic population, the seat of many churches, and religious and educational institutions. It was not surprising that such vast labors and privations began to undermine a constitution not inured from early manhood to them, but which had encountered them with undaunted courage, and endured them with unwavering fortitude.

With health impaired by his exposures, labors, and sacrifices, Father Lefevre visited his native country in 1841, in order to recruit his strength for renewed exertions in the same field. It was while abroad that the Holy See appointed him Bishop of Zela *in partibus*, and Administrator of the Diocese of Detroit, the incumbency of which had been resigned by Bishop Resé. He returned to the United States, and was consecrated in St. John's Church, Philadelphia, on Sunday, November 21, 1841. The ceremony was solemn and impressive in the highest degree. The Right Rev. Francis Patrick Kenrick, then Bishop of Philadelphia, was consecrator, assisted by the illustrious Bishops England and Hughes. The latter Prelate preached the consecration sermon, which was regarded as one of his most eloquent and effective efforts.

Immediately after his consecration he addressed to his diocese, from the city of Philadelphia, a pastoral letter, inspired by the loftiest zeal and purest charity. A brief extract from this apostolic address will give some idea of the entire document. "We feel ourself pressed forward by the charity of Christ," he writes, "and we are ready to make every sacrifice, and to endure all hardships, to supply in our own person what may be wanting for the application of His sufferings and death to the souls of men. The piety and zeal of our venerable brethren the clergy, who have labored with such fidelity and perseverance, encourage us; and we trust, with their co-operation, to cultivate successfully the portion of the vineyard committed to our care. We shall endeavor with them to be the models of the faithful in word, in conversation, in charity, in faith, in chastity. Having been inured to the labors of a missionary life for many years in a remote part of the diocese of St. Louis, we feel ready to share with you, venerable brethren, all the labors of the ministry; and we are ambitious of no distinction, except that imposed on us by our station, of greater solicitude for the souls intrusted to us, and of greater zeal for our own perfection."

Bishop Lefevre repaired at once to his diocese, and entered upon his long and active episcopal career with energy and good-will. The entry of a Bishop, called from a distance of many hundred miles, into a diocese where he could not behold a single familiar face or feel the personal sympathy and support of a single old friend, must have been a most trying event. The natural inclination of men under such circumstances is to tolerate existing and long-recognized evils, and await the opportunities of time and circumstances to correct them. But with one reared in the school of conscience and discipline, as Bishop Lefevre had been, it was but a duty to considerately but fearlessly advance to the work before him. The tenure of church-property in Detroit, from the early days of the French settlers, was not according to the laws of the Church. The valuable and venerable church property of old St. Anne's was the principal ecclesiastical possession. The Bishop required a settlement of this property in accordance with those laws. He encountered opposition and even estrangement from some of the laity, but, supported by the sense of his own right and duty, he bore down all resistance and vindicated the laws of the Church. Whatever may have been the feeling entertained at the time by a few, all must now at least concede the tribute of approval and applause to his wisdom and firmness. The church of St. Anne and that of Holy Trinity were the only Catholic temples in the city of Detroit, while in the whole diocese, the State of Michigan, and the Territory, now State of Wisconsin, there were twenty-five churches and chapels, and the same number of stations, at which Mass was occasionally said. During his administration the number was increased in the city of Detroit to eleven, and in that part of the State of Michigan alone which is called the Lower Peninsula the number of churches with organized congregations was increased to one hundred and sixty. The Upper Peninsula and Michigan, in the mean time, became separated from his see and formed into new dioceses. Among this number are many large and handsome temples. The Cathedral of Saints Peter and Paul was built under his direction and with his resources, though the plan, with which he was never pleased, was the choice of others. It is a large and substantial building, calculated to accommodate the growing congregation attending it for generations to come. Leaving the exterior comparatively unfinished, Bishop Lefevre took great pride, and went to great expense, in preparing and decorating the interior as a fit dwelling-place for the Most High. A number of new churches were begun before his death, and others were projected, and the land already provided. Besides the great increase of churches in his episcopal city, with a provident and prudent forethought, he had purchased sites for future churches in localities where the inevitable growth of the city rendered their future necessity quite sure. The valuable ecclesiastical property in the heart of the city of Detroit, with its handsome income, was most jealously guarded and preserved by Bishop Lefevre, through all the eventful vicissitudes in business and in fortunes which he witnessed, and handed down intact and unencumbered to his successors and to posterity. Too much praise cannot be accorded to him for his energy and good management in thus laying broad and deep the foundations of his Church, and in providing an unfailing source of support and strength for the innumerable charities and educational institutions, which the genius and mission of the Catholic Church are ever calling into active life and fruitfulness.

The privilege he claimed in his first pastoral to his flock, to share with his priests, and even to lead them forward, in the labors and privations of missionary life, was no outburst of exuberance or vain display. A missionary by dedication and long years of service, he saw in his elevation to the episcopal office no release from, but rather a stronger attraction to, the hard work of the missions. Neither the vastness of his diocese, nor lake, morass, mountain, nor prairie, though all of immense extent, deterred him from the glorious work which Marquette and Richard had commenced and rendered famous within his own diocese. Amongst the clergy of his diocese was the apostolic Baraga* in the Upper Peninsula, whose fame and merit as a missionary, like those of Lefevre, placed a mitre on his head, and whose splendid labors compare with those of the most distinguished

---

* See his Life, *Post.*

early French missionaries. The Indian missions of Father Baraga were objects of special interest and encouragement with Bishop Lefevre. His references to them always showed that he regarded them as the brightest glories of his diocese. His episcopal visitations were indeed missions among his flock, in which not the least happy and zealous portions were with his Indians. These, together with a considerable portion of the descendants of the old French population scattered through the country and lost to the Church, were prominent in his solicitude and in the glorious fruits of his labors. He established stations at a multitude of small, far distant, and obscure points, so that all might have the consolations of Mass and the sacraments at stated days. A witness of his visitations has thus described them:—" In his day he has traversed the State from one extent to the other; now in the open boat from Mackinack around the coasts and islands, where dwelt the poor relics of the red man's race, to farther up amidst the rocks and hills of Lake Superior, to seek out the poor miner and see to his spiritual wants; again in the miserable stage-coach, over roads intolerable for man or beast, to serve his flock, to baptize the little ones, and to bring the sacraments to the poor isolated settler in the backwoods. All this he underwent in God's service."

The private life of Bishop Lefevre was that of a true missionary. Simplicity, voluntary poverty, frugality, temperance, and personal austerity were the virtues of a lifetime with him, no less in the episcopal city of Detroit than in the backwoods of Missouri. He was an early riser in winter and summer; he was ever punctual at the altar of the Cathedral or chapel at half-past five in summer, and six in winter, every morning of the week, commencing a day of labor and devotion with the august sacrifice of the immaculate Lamb. He was as regular in his attendance at the confessional as any priest, spending hours in this painful and confining service. The poor flocked to his confessional, as they did to his altar; for none were repulsed from either, but rather welcomed as the representatives of Christ, and as the proofs of His presence with his Church. The cathedral congregation, under his immediate eye, was as numerous as it was edifying, and it was a pleasing sight to behold, on Sunday morning, the crowded throngs which successively filled the Cathedral at the various Masses.

To provide his flock with good pastors was a leading study and endeavor in Bishop Lefevre's life. It has already been stated that he labored with great energy and success in erecting churches throughout his diocese. The providing of priests to officiate in them, and supply to the most distant and needy congregations the regular and punctual offices of the Church, and administration of the sacraments, was a work to which he devoted his best energies. Thus we learn of the arrivals of priests and seminarians from abroad, and chiefly from France, from the commencement of his episcopate. By a punctual and judicious distribution of these co-laborers, he supplied not only many towns with permanent pastors, but a great many stations with regular periodical missions and celebrations of the divine service. The ground rendered sacred by the toils, sacrifices, and sufferings of the first French missionaries was traversed by the Bishop and his priests; missions that had ceased for nearly two centuries were revived, and the woods and lakes that resounded once with the litanies and offices of Druilletes and Marquette, again awakened their echoes to the same sacred notes, nature's union with man in adoration of their common Creator.

The Redemptorist Convent at Detroit is one of the ecclesiastical institutions established during Bishop Lefevre's administration, with the intention of supplying in part the Diocese of Detroit with educated and zealous priests. The American College of Louvain, Belgium, was also another of his means, adopted in common with others, for the especial purpose in part of supplying his diocese with clergymen. The President, Very Rev. John De Neve, and the Vice-President, Very Rev. Edmund Dumond, of this fine institution, are from the Diocese of Detroit, and were Vicars-General of Bishop Lefevre. The success of Bishop Lefevre, in supplying this great necessity in his diocese, may be judged from the fact that, in 1841, when he assumed the administration of the Diocese of Detroit, then embracing all Michigan and Wisconsin, the whole number of priests within these extensive limits was eighteen; and at the time of his death, in 1869, the clergymen within the Lower Peninsula alone numbered eighty-eight.

The subject of education, so dear to the Catholic Church, and to her Prelates and ministers, was one of paramount importance with Bishop Lefevre. He sympathized ardently with the noble efforts of Archbishop Hughes, to obtain for Catholic free schools a fair share of that common school fund, raised by the contributions of Catholics as well as Protestants, for the purposes of free education. He was not behind-hand in claiming the same just rights from the State of Michigan, and from his fellow-citizens, and in presenting his claim with all the ardor, force, and ability he possessed. But the day had not come in his time, nor has it yet arrived, when the public authorities and people of the United States can be induced, by arguments even drawn from the fundamental principles of our free system of government, to see this question in its just light. In their zealous pursuit of what appears to them the greatest necessity and blessing of a free State, they lose sight of the appalling fact that the means adopted for the purpose are destructive of the very freedom of the State itself. But Bishop Lefevre, as a devoted lover of education and of freedom, and as a shepherd charged with the guardianship of that portion of the freedom of his flock which more immediately affects the conscience, has left on record his earnest and unflinching protest against the wrong done to his people, by which they are compelled in fact, not only to provide for the education of the children of others, but for conscience sake to provide an independent system of education for their own children. It is not surprising, then, that he took such energetic measures to provide Catholic education for his Catholic flock. The statistics of his diocese present an honorable list of parish and free schools, attached to various congregations. It was to meet this great work that he introduced into his diocese the Sisters of Notre Dame, Sisters of Charity, and Sister-Servants of the Immaculate Heart of Mary, for the female schools; and the Brothers of the Christian Schools, for the male schools of his diocese. Besides these, the Ladies of the Sacred Heart have their place in the diocese, and address themselves to the higher branches of academic education. The Sisters of the Immaculate Heart of Mary have also a flourishing academy at their Mother-House in Monroe. They also teach St. Augustine's School for colored children at

Detroit. Not only have convents, academies, and schools arisen under his benevolent sway, but charitable institutions have also sprung into existence and usefulness under his active administration. Four orphan asylums—conducted either by the Sisters of Charity or Sister-Servants of the Immaculate Heart of Mary--St Mary's Hospital and Insane Asylum, the Michigan State Retreat, are among the charities originating in his zeal.

Bishop Lefevre enjoyed the great confidence and veneration of his colleagues in the episcopate. He sat with them in the Fifth, Sixth, and Seventh Provincial Councils of Baltimore, and in the National Council in 1852; also in the Provincial Councils of Cincinnati. Archbishop Purcell, in pronouncing the funeral oration over his remains said: "The Bishops who have sat with him so long, and have recognized his wise counsel in the administration of the affairs of the Holy Church, will mourn over his departure; fathers and mothers, whom he united in the holy bonds of matrimony; children whom he baptized, and friends of the deceased, whom he prepared for the last of earth, leading them up to the very gates of immortality—how can all these assist in this sad scene without the deepest emotion." He enjoyed in an especial manner the friendship of Archbishop Kenrick, of Baltimore, and Archbishop Purcell, of Cincinnati. In the august assemblies of Prelates, at the altar, as well as amid the solemn ceremonies of religion, and in the walks of private life, Bishop Lefevre was distinguished by his dignity, fine ecclesiastical bearing, benevolence of expression, and dignity of manner. With a heart abounding in charity, he was unsparing of himself, uncompromising with wrong, falsehood, and bad example. He pursued the path of duty without human respect, and while ever ready to modify his plans and measures according to the experiences of the past, he was firm in his good purposes, and undeviating in his pursuit of them. He was a father to his flock, a provident guardian of the rights and possessions of the Church, and an earnest originator and promoter of works of charity.

In his sixty-fifth year, he was attacked by erysipelas in his ankle, the same that was sprained nearly thirty years before in the rough missionary journeys of the West. His disease was a long and painful one. When he saw his case was hopeless, and his last end approaching, he calmly and cheerfully resigned himself to the will of Him who had sent him. He laid aside all the emblems of his dignity, and went to the hospital established by himself for the poor and afflicted, and there in a little room, divested of furniture, except the bed which he occupied, he prepared himself for death. The good Sisters of Charity gratefully and reverently rendered their gentle services to one who had so long been serving others. He received with great devotion those offices of religion which, at that hour, are for Pontiff, priest, and layman alike the sources of celestial grace; and after bestowing his blessing upon the friends, clergy, and Sisters present, expired March 4, 1869. He was buried under the Cathedral sanctuary at Detroit. Archbishop Purcell, Bishops Rappe and Luers, a large body of clergy, and an immense concourse of laity assisted at his funeral, and Archbishop Purcell pronounced an eloquent and glowing eulogy on the life, character, virtues, and services of the deceased Prelate.

MOST REV. JOHN MARY ODIN, D.D.,

First Bishop of Galveston and Second Archbishop of New Orleans, A.D. 1842.*

THE name of Odin is destined to fill an honored place in the Catholic history of the United States; a name worthy of being inscribed in our annals with those of Marquette and Jogues; a name ever to be associated with the recital of heroic deeds of missionary life and labor, and with examples of exalted virtues, exhibited by the Church in her saints. Instances are rare of such humility, united with such exalted services; of such sanctity, with such constant contact with the active world; of such charity, with the exercise of authority; of such faith, in a skeptical age; of such zeal and benevolence, in the midst of personal sufferings and sacrifices. The Sons of St. Vincent may well be proud of such a name; the Church of the South may well hold it in veneration, as it is held in honor by the Church of America and of France. It is a name that is indissolubly associated with the brightest chapter in the history of the American Church, that which relates to her glorious missions, and with loyal devotion to the chair of Peter, the centre of Christian faith and unity.

John Mary Odin was born at Ambierle, in the Department of the Loire, France, February 25, 1801. His parents, while highly respected in the social world,

---

* Authorities: *Propagateur Catholique; N. Y. Freeman's Journal; N. O. Morning Star and Catholic Messenger;* Deuther's *Life of Bishop Timon; Life of Rev. Felix De Andreis; Catholic Almanacs; Catholic Magazines* and *Metropolitans;* De Courcy and Shea's *Catholic Church in the United States,* etc., etc.

were still more esteemed for their Catholic virtues. Their good example and religious training moulded the character and habits of their son after the purest and best Catholic models. Devotion to the Blessed Virgin was a prominent virtue in this pious family; their son bore, together with the name of the beloved apostle, that of his Holy Mother, and in her little chapel at Ambierle, he learned to love and invoke her name and intercession in his childhood, at the same time that he acquired his first lessons in Christian doctrine. Throughout his whole life, this venerable servant of God was remarkable for his devotion to the Mother of God. From his childhood he evinced a gravity of character, an earnestness and seriousness of purpose and pursuit, a studiousness of habit and piety of life, which withdrew him in a great measure from the frivolous world, and attracted him to the temple of religion and to the companionship of the good and learned. His love for a recollected and devotional life was united with great zeal and charity for the religious advancement of others. It was thus that when, at an early age, he resolved to give himself to religion, he found his vocation in the congregation of Priests of the Mission, commonly called Lazarists, and entered this Order when quite young. This excellent religious body was founded by St. Vincent De Paul, and had for its chief objects the sanctification of its own members, the promotion of the salvation of the rural population by giving missions amongst them, and the advancement of the spiritual interests of ecclesiastics. They had been approved by the Most Rev. John Francis De Gondi, Archbishop of Paris, in 1626; by Pope Urban VIII., in 1632; and chartered by Louis XIII., of France, in 1642. In 1632 they received possession of the old Priory of the Knights Hospitalers of St. Lazarus of Jerusalem, in Paris, from which circumstance they received the popular name of Lazarists, a name which has clung to them, notwithstanding their expulsion from the house of St. Lazarus by the French Revolutionists in 1792. In 1642 a house of the Order was established at Rome, and a province founded, with its seat in that city. The general government of the congregation is located at Paris.

It was among the good Lazarists at Paris, that young Odin spent the first years of his religious life. In 1822, in his twenty-second year, while yet a deacon, he dedicated himself to the foreign missions, came to America, and entered the Lazarist community at the Barrens, near St. Louis, Missouri, a house which had been founded by Fathers de Andreis and Rosati, from the Roman province of the Congregation. Here he taught logic to the younger students, while pursuing his own studies in theology, and subsequently assisted Dr. Rosati in teaching theology. During the frequent journeys of the latter through his diocese, his classes of logic and theology were entirely confided to Mr. Odin. The latter was raised to the dignity of the priesthood about the year 1823, or the beginning of 1824.

While pursuing the double duties of pupil and professor at the Barrens, Father Odin was associated with men of learning and piety: with the zealous and accomplished Dr. Rosati, with the saintly and talented Dr. De Neckere, with the indefatigable and laborious Father Timon, who afterwards was Bishop of Buffalo. The last, though older in years than Father Odin, entered the Congregation after him, and was a student under him in logic and theology at the Barrens. They afterwards became companions and co-laborers in arduous missions, and through life a holy friendship subsisted between these excellent and distinguished Prelates.

Scarcely was he raised to the priesthood, than he began the fulfilment of the vocation, which he had chosen for himself while a novice at the house of the Lazarists, in Paris. At first his missionary labors were exercised at the Barrens, and within a circuit around it of about twenty miles. Abundant fruits rewarded the zeal and labors of the young priest, and he was encouraged to enter upon more extensive and arduous fields. In 1824, Father Odin, and Mr. Timon, then a subdeacon, started from the Barrens upon a missionary tour to Texas. They traveled on horseback, and the journey as far as New Madrid, in Missouri, was performed without more than the ordinary fatigue and hardships of such traveling at that time in that country. At New Madrid, Father Odin, assisted by Mr. Timon, gave a most effective mission ; one which was long remembered by the people. Beyond this place their journey lay over swamps and sparsely settled regions, and every kind of hardship and privation, were encountered. A night spent upon the wet ground of the swamp, rivers which could only be crossed by swimming, hunger and thirst, presented no insurmountable impediments to these holy men. The desertion of their guide only aroused their energy and perseverance the more. A scanty refreshment at a log hut, and a few moments rest to their feet, were the only physical comforts they accepted, and as they passed through the rugged country, they sought out the Catholics and administered to their long-neglected spiritual wants. At a fine mansion, to which they humbly applied for a drink of water, they answered the objections of the family against the Catholic faith, especially the charge of idolatry, with such fervor and eloquence that when one of the missionaries produced from his bosom his crucifix, and pointed out the sufferings of Christ upon the cross for man's redemption, all were overcome with devotion; and the mother, who had never seen a crucifix, called to her children to "come and see how much their Saviour had done for them." Their painful journey was full of the most comforting results, both among Catholics and Protestants. Marriages were validly renewed, numbers of children and adults were baptized, confessions heard, and many who had not been to the sacraments for forty years now approached. The Indians were not overlooked. The missionaries visited the Quapaws, near Arkansas Post, on the Arkansas River; the word was announced through an interpreter, a rustic altar was erected before the wigwam of the chief, and the holy Mass offered by Father Odin for them. The return of Father Odin to the Barrens was not for the purpose of taking rest, but to plan and execute more missions among the people. Mr. Timon was now raised to the priesthood, and the two young Lazarists went upon frequent excursions of apostolic zeal and love. They visited New Madrid several times, penetrated repeatedly into Texas and Illinois, and several times canvassed a region of two hundred and fifty miles north and south. After the consecration and departure of Bishop Rosati from the Barrens, the priests of the Mission were sent forth on permanent duty at various stations, and Father Odin was for long periods of time the only priest at the Barrens. On such occasions everything devolved upon him. He was provisional Superior of the Seminary, parish priest, confessor also to the brothers, seminarians, collegians, and Lorentine Nuns; and besides all these duties, that of directing the general course of studies in the College devolved upon him. It was no unfrequent occurrence for him to be engaged on most arduous duties, involving distant sick calls and other important duties, all day, returning to the Seminary frequently after ten o'clock at night, and if it should be Saturday night, he would find at this late hour all the members of the community waiting to go to confession to him, and he would be occupied with this and other duty the remainder of the night. The cheerfulness with which he discharged all these arduous duties was the admiration of all. The happiness of doing good sustained the zeal and physical health of this servant of God, and prevented even his robust constitution from succumbing under so heavy a burden. His health was severely tried; and his labors and over-exertion of mind and body caused him to suffer excruciating headaches for several days without intermission. Some relaxation and relief to his endangered health were now fortunately presented to him. He was called upon by Bishop Rosati to accompany him to the Second Provincial Council of Baltimore, which assembled October 20, 1833, as his theologian. After discharging this duty, he sailed for Europe, for the purposes of recruiting his health and visiting his relatives, to solicit aid for the Lazarist Mission in America, and to attend to important interests of the Congregation of the Mission. He was at this time President of the College at the Barrens. The love and veneration in which he was held by the community, which had for nearly ten years witnessed his heroic labors and sacrifices, and to which he had rendered such signal services, are the best human tribute that could be paid to his eminent virtues.

Whilst abroad Father Odin attended a general assembly of the Lazarists at Paris, and represented the community of the Barrens. At this assembly the American mission was erected into a province, and Father Timon was appointed Visitor. The same assembly decreed the suppression of the College at the Barrens. This measure was earnestly opposed by Father Odin, and after his return to Missouri, by his earnest and energetic correspondence with Paris, he greatly assisted the new Visitor in rescuing the College from annihilation.

While abroad "his simplicity, amiability, and gentle deportment gained him many friends, and he succeeded in collecting a considerable sum of money, besides ornaments for the altar. He also obtained a number of ecclesiastics, some belonging to the Congregation, others secular priests; many of them accompanied him on his return, and the rest followed at a subsequent period."*

He remained on duty as before, at the Barrens, until 1836, when a permanent mission was established at Cape Girardeau, for which he was selected as the pastor. On March 24, of that year, the mission was opened by the celebration of Mass by Father Timon, the Visitor, who after Mass introduced Father Odin to the congregation as their pastor, and in doing so paid an exalted tribute to the services he had already rendered to religion, and augured the most favorable results from his mission at the Cape. He labored at this post with his unfaltering energy and perseverance for a year or more, and to the great benefit of the people there and in the surrounding country, when he was again recalled to the Barrens.

---

* *Life of Father De Andreis.*

For several years he filled various offices and professors' chairs, either at the College, Seminary, or Novitiate. During these years he was the companion and helper of the untiring Visitor, Father Timon, in his great labors. At the retreats given by the Lazarists, Father Odin's services were always most effective; his sermons were most successful, and his example most inspiring. Missionary labors, such as we have already described, were performed by him in addition to his duties at the Barrens, and the good he accomplished during these years of toil and self-sacrifice were but imperfectly known or remembered by men, and can find a faithful record only in the Book of Eternal Life. It was during this period of his life that Father Odin, in his missionary travels, had the happiness of meeting the celebrated missionary of the West, Father Nerinckx, for whom he entertained the greatest veneration, and from whose great experience and wisdom he derived important advantage. A letter addressed by Father Odin to the Society for the Propagation of the Faith, makes allusion to Father Nerinckx' last visit to Missouri, in terms which give an admirable insight into the ardent zeal and simplicity of Father Odin, and show how the devotion to Mary, imbibed in his youth, remained unchanged in his maturer years. "Oh! how I loved to be with him!" he exclaimed. "He prescribed for me all sorts of little practices for the advancement of souls, communicated to me all that his own experience had discovered to be most advantageous for the conversion of heretics, and above all, he spoke to me frequently of the Blessed Virgin."

In 1840, Father Timon was appointed Prefect Apostolic of Texas, and immediately appointed Father Odin Vice-Prefect, and confided to him the Church and Missions of Texas. Father Odin lost no time in repairing to his new field of duty, a field, however, with which he was not unacquainted. He was accompanied by a single assistant. While descending the Mississippi they were overtaken by a violent tornado opposite Natchez, which destroyed a great part of the town, and immediate destruction seemed to threaten the steamer and all on board. Father Odin and his companion, falling upon their knees, supplicated the protection of Heaven; all on board joined in their prayers; a sudden and miraculous interposition rescued them all from their peril, amidst a general thanksgiving. After their own rescue they were able to save a number of poor passengers on other steamers from the waves. Arriving safely at his destination, the Vice-Prefect Apostolic hastened to repair to San Antonio, where a grave scandal required his immediate action. The two Mexican priests of that place were leading open lives of profligacy and violation of their vows, and were performing no service but saying Mass. The Prefect Apostolic had, before his departure from the Barrens, delivered to Father Odin a letter suspending them from all ecclesiastical functions, and requiring their submission on pain of excommunication. Father Odin acted with vigor, yet with great prudence, in so delicate a case. "But," pleaded these unhappy men, "at least, Mons. Odin, permit us to say Mass, the *honorarium* of which is the only support we have for our families."—"I cannot," said Father Odin; "here are my orders. But I will do for you whatever is in my power. Receive the Masses which your friends offer you, keep the *honorarium*, and I will say, or have said, the Masses for you." This judicious course had the desired effect. The scandal was arrested, the sanctuary purged, and the unworthy priests, after about three months, retired from Texas into Mexico.

Towards the close of the year Father Odin was joined by Father Timon, and a missionary destined for the Texan mission. A place of worship was soon secured in Houston, and Father Timon offered the first, and Father Odin the second Mass ever said in that city. Religion now began to revive and extend in Texas, under the energetic administration of Fathers Timon and Odin. The latter continued, as Vice-Prefect, to give his untiring labor to the work before him. The Legislature, on the petition of Father Odin, granted to the Church the ecclesiastical property of Texas, and also ordered a survey of several leagues of land in different sections to be appropriated for the uses and purposes of Catholic schools. Measures were taken for the promotion of Catholic immigration to Texas, and even at this early date it was announced to the immigrants, that they could find in almost any part of the country the consolations of their religion. The public men of Texas were greatly encouraged in their hopes for the future of their newborn Republic, by the prompt and energetic measures of Fathers Timon and Odin to cement the interests of the State and of society with the sanctions and blessings of religion, and to restore the ancient Church of Texas. They extended every attention to those venerable priests, entertained them at complimentary dinners, and, as we have stated, bestowed substantial benefits upon religion. Father Odin, however, was intent only on his missions. He visited various sections of the republic, aroused the long-neglected religious sentiments of the people, and carried the sacraments to the homes of many distant families and settlements.

In May, 1841, Father Odin, in obedience to his Superior, started from Texas for the Barrens, in order to concert more effectual plans for the promotion of religion in Texas, and for the regulation of the missions of that country. On reaching New Orleans, the holy missionary was actually in rags, such was his generosity in giving to others more needy than himself, and such his love of poverty. But such are the apostles of the faith, and from such the rulers of the Church are selected. Bishop Blanc received the servant of God with veneration and tenderness; and, while chiding him for his neglect of himself, presented to him the Bulls from Rome appointing him Coadjutor Bishop of Detroit. So great was Bishop Blanc's attachment to Father Odin, that he insisted upon his remaining with him, in order that he might himself consecrate the new Bishop of Detroit. The humble Lazarist, however, replied that he could take no step without first consulting his Superior. On arriving at the Barrens, Father Odin placed the bulls and the urgent letters from Rome in the hands of Father Timon, and submitted the whole matter to his decision. The two priests offered their Masses the following morning in supplication to God for light and guidance. After Mass, Father Timon said: "Mons. Odin, good men can easily be found for the Bishopric of Detroit, where things are already in a prosperous way; but it would be difficult to find a competent person now to take so poor and difficult a post as yours in Texas; hence I think it more for the glory of God and the good of souls that you send back the bulls and return to your post." Recognizing in that of his Superior the voice of God, the humble Apostle of Texas returned to the labors and hardships of his arduous mission. While thus engaged, he was again surprised by the arrival of other bulls from Rome. Father Timon, after the occurrences above related, recommended the erection of Texas into a Vicariate Apostolic, and the appointment of Father Odin as Vicar-Apostolic. Accordingly, Pope Gregory XVI. appointed the latter Vicar-Apostolic of Texas, under the title of Bishop of Claudiopolis *in partibus*. He was consecrated at New Orleans by Bishop Blanc, on *Lætare* Sunday, March 6, 1842. The present Archbishop of New Orleans, in announcing the death of his venerable and beloved predecessor, makes the following allusion to this event in the life of the latter:—" It was on this occasion, dearly beloved brethren, that it fell to our happy lot to take a closer view, and form a more adequate estimate, of this beautiful and saintly character. When he came to New Orleans to receive the Episcopal consecration, at the hands of the Right Rev. Anthony Blanc, the Bishop of this Diocese, on the 6th of March, 1842, he selected the modest retreat we occupied, as Chaplain, adjoining the Ursuline Convent, to prepare for his consecration; and it was there were formed those relations so honorable and advantageous for us, which grew more and more intimate from year to year, rising as they did out of extreme benevolence on his part, and profound veneration on ours."

The origin of Texas, as a civilized country, is wholly Catholic. La Salle, the Catholic explorer of the Mississippi, was shipwrecked on its banks, while attempting to found a Catholic colony. This event attracted the attention of the Spaniards of Mexico, who extended their posts from Mexico and Florida towards each other, until they included Louisiana and Texas; they established Franciscan missionaries on its coast La Salle himself had been accompanied by zealous Recollects from France, who were ardent for the conversion of the Indians. In the year after La Salle's misfortune, there were fourteen Franciscans laboring to convert and civilize the Indians of Texas. Many good results were obtained; but the Missions finally succumbed to disease and famine among the tribes. In 1717 the Texan Missions were again restored, under Father Augustine Padron de Guzman, among the Adayes, and under another Father among the Texas tribe. San Antonio was a thriving Spanish town, and here the Fathers were forced to take shelter, when wars among the Indians suspended the missions. The revival of the missions, between 1721 and 1746, was more lasting; and thriving missions were established by the Franciscans from Querétaro and Zacatécas at San Francisco, in Central Texas, San José among the Nazones, Nuestra Señora de Guadaloupe among the Nacogdoches, and Nuestra Señora del Pilar among the Adayes, and other missions among the Asinais, the Aes, Cocos, Osages, and Missouris. The missions of Texas extended as far as those of New Mexico, and flourished as late as 1812, when they were suppressed by the Spanish Government, and the Indians dispersed. Notwithstanding this disastrous policy, many of the Indians retained their faith and piety. In 1832, Father Diaz was sent to Nacogdoches by the Bishop of Monterey, but he soon fell a martyr to his zeal, beneath a hostile tomahawk. The colonization of Texas from our States, the declaration of Texan independence, and the war that followed, checked every effort at restoring the missions.* The Church of Texas had numbered

---

* *History of the Catholic Missions*, by J. G. Shea.

her children by many thousands, from various tribes; the monuments of their piety and civilization remain to this day in ruins, but silent witnesses of what the Church was gloriously accomplishing for them. The Church of Texas, too, had her martyrs, whose blood, we trust, is destined to fructify for future good.

The oldest town of Spanish Texas is San Antonio de Bexar, founded in 1698. At the time of Father Odin's advent to Texas, this town contained a population of two thousand, sixteen hundred of whom were Catholics. The state of disorder reigning there, and the wise measures of the Vice-Prefect Apostolic, have already been stated. In this town was a beautiful church of Spanish origin, the cost of erecting which was estimated, in 1840, at $120,000. Austin was founded in 1821 by an American of that name, while Mexico was under Spanish rule; and still later Houston, named in honor of the military hero, Gen. Sam Houston, who afterwards represented Texas in the United States Senate. Soon after the founding of Austin, Mexico declared her independence of Spain, and in 1836 Texas announced her separation from Mexico, and maintained it by arms. At the time of Father Odin's Vice-Prefecture, Houston had a population of five thousand, of whom several hundred were Catholics. In the County of Nacogdoches there were six hundred Catholics, and others were thinly scattered over the country in various directions. The entire population of Texas, at the time of its erection into a Vicariate-Apostolic, and the consecration of Bishop Odin, was something over 200,000. His diocese contained 500,000 square miles. There were four priests laboring in the Texan mission besides the Bishop. San Antonio was in the beginning the principal centre of religious activity. The work had already been commenced by Fathers Timon and Odin, and signal success achieved—but how vast was the field of labor, how few the laborers, and how scattered the flock! Texas needed an apostle to restore and create all things. Such she found in her saintly and devoted Bishop.

Bishop Odin commenced the vast work before him with holy zeal, and with a resolute purpose. The ancient church at San Antonio was repaired; new churches were erected at Galveston, Houston, on the river Labaca, at Fort Bend, St. Augustine, and Nacogdoches. Several ancient churches, restored to the Church by the Texan Congress, were taken into possession, repaired, and returned to their original uses; schools were opened in various places, and were encouraged by grants of land from the government, and the religious wants of the people supplied, as far as Bishop Odin, by his own unsparing labors and those of the few priests he had, could supply them. The labor of visiting the churches and stations of this vast region, at that early period, was attended with incredible hardships, privations, sufferings, and dangers. So much was the good Bishop among his flock, scattered as it was, that he was on every side impressed with the great necessity of procuring more priests. He had exhausted all his resources at home, and was now compelled to look abroad for relief. He accordingly went to Europe in 1845, sailing from Boston in April of that year, in company of Bishop Kenrick of Philadelphia. The two Prelates visited Ireland, and traveled together through France to Rome. Bishop Odin succeeded in procuring both priests and resources for his diocese, and returned to renew, with redoubled effort and hope, the great work before him.

Ten priests now assisted him in his difficult missions and he labored with them and took part in every work and privation of the ministry, while at the same time his energies and resources were severely taxed in governing and providing for his flock. In the beginning of 1847 he procured three more priests, who accompanied him from New Orleans to Texas in January. At the same time, having made arrangements before leaving his diocese for their reception, five professed Sisters and three Novices of the Ursuline Community, near New Orleans, started for Galveston to establish a foundation of their Order in that city, and to open boarding and day schools for young ladies. This was the first community of religious established in Texas.

In 1847 the Holy See erected Texas into a Bishopric, with its Episcopal See at Galveston, and Bishop Odin was installed as Bishop of Galveston. Henceforth his official residence was at that city; but such was the extent of his diocese, such his zeal for the religious advancement of every part of it, and so numerous were the undertakings he embarked in for this end, that he was more in his saddle or buggy than in his own residence. No part of his spiritual domain failed to receive his special attention. His personal efforts for the good of his people were everywhere felt. But the task of providing priests and churches, for the many new and growing communities that were constantly springing up, was a heavy and difficult one. Until priests could be provided adequately, the Bishop undertook by his travels and labors to supply their places. Besides these efforts, he was engaged in the great work of providing institutions for the education of youth, also pious and charitable associations. In addition to the Ursuline Convent at

Galveston, another Convent of the same Order was commenced at San Antonio. Also a Convent of the Ladies of the Incarnate Word was founded at Brownsville, and the Brothers of Mary were established at San Antonio, where they opened a school for boys, as they did also at Brownsville, Laredo, and Brazoria. In November, 1854, Bishop Odin commenced the College of the Immaculate Conception, and placed it under the charge of the Order of Oblates of Mary, which, in 1857, was erected into an university. In the early part of 1852 he visited Europe for the second time, in order to procure more priests for his needy diocese, and returned in May of that year, having secured six priests and sixteen young men preparing for the priesthood. They embarked at Havre in the latter part of March for New Orleans. The Bishop himself arrived at New York May 3, 1852, and proceeded to Baltimore, to attend the Council which was assembed there at that time.

It was by his missionary labors, performed during the episcopal visitations of his diocese, that Bishop Odin accomplished so much good, and acquired a fame equal to the most distinguished missionaries of our country. An account of some of these extensive, dangerous, and laborious tours of mercy and benediction should not be omitted, as they constitute a distinguished feature in his noble career. In the fall of 1851 he was engaged over five months in visiting the most remote and the wildest regions of Texas. During the first three months of this visitation, the Bishop's health became prostrated under the severe travel, privations, exposures, and labors he underwent, and he was in consequence detained for some time with illness at San Antonio. Scarcely was he convalescent, when he resumed his perilous and toilsome journey to seek out and console, by his presence and by the sacraments, the scattered members of his flock. His course lay through the wild country of the fierce Camanches and other hostile Indian tribes. For two months no tidings could be received of him, and the most saddening apprehensions were felt for his safety. But God preserved his own, and the good Bishop made his way in safety to Nacogdoches on November 19, 1850, to the great joy of his people. At Nacogdoches he remained five or six days, preached repeatedly in French, Spanish, and English, and confirmed at this place alone one hundred and thirty persons. He next returned to Galveston amidst the enthusiastic rejoicings of his faithful flock. He had traveled over two thousand miles, through wild and hostile tracts, over bad roads, and without the comforts or even necessaries so essential to preserve health under such fatigues and labors.

In the summer of 1854 he started upon a visitation which occupied four months, during which he traversed the Valley of the Rio Grande, all the border of the Gulf of Mexico as far as Laredo, and returned by way of San Antonio. The principal towns he visited were Point Isabel, Brownsville, Rio Grande City, Roma, and Laredo, and here he found proportionately the greatest number of Catholics, twelve thousand Catholics having emigrated from Mexico to those towns within a few years. He also visited more than thirty *ranchos*, or little hamlets, inhabited by from ten to thirty of these emigrant families. He was delighted with these people, and bore testimony on his return to the purity and simplicity of life and sincere faith of the Mexican Catholic population of Texas. So eagerly did they respond to the Bishop's word, that he was accustomed, after spending all day, to devote large portions of the night to hearing their confessions. The Oblate Fathers at Laredo and Brownsville he found laboring under many difficulties, but consoled by the abundant fruits of their generous labors. At Laredo he gave a retreat, which was very successful, and drew great numbers to the sacraments. In the Valley of the Rio Grande he confirmed eleven hundred and twenty-three persons. He next proceeded to San Antonio, over a road one hundred and eighty miles long, and attended with great fatigue and danger. But he was fortunately invited to travel in company and under the escort of Captains Lyons and Jones, U.S.A., and fifteen soldiers, who treated him with every possible attention and kindness. He also visited Bramfels, thence proceeded to Austin, and from Austin to Houston. In these latter places he confirmed two hundred and eighty-seven persons, making in all fourteen hundred and ten confirmed during the visitation. He visited, and was greatly pleased with the prosperity and success of the Ursulines at San Antonio, who had one hundred and forty pupils; the Brothers of St. Mary, whose school numbered one hundred and fifty, and the Sisters of the Incarnate Word at Brownsville, who had a flourishing convent, with thirty boarders and a large attendance of externs. From Austin to Houston the whole country was inundated, and travel was attended with great hardships and danger. It took him ten days to accomplish this part of his journey, which was usually accomplished then in five days. When the Bishop returned to his episcopal city, the ruinous state of his buggy, bound up and held together by leathern thongs and flexible twigs, attested the hardship of the roads and the difficulties of his journey. The vehicle had been broken several times. He had been compelled to sleep in the open air, to fast for many days, and endure hunger and many privations in a vast land of wilderness, which, to add to its terrors, was infested by hostile Indians. While engaged in this visitation, Bishop Odin formed an agreeable acquaintance with Bishop de Verea, of Monterey, who was also engaged in visiting his flock on the opposite side of the Rio Grande; the two Prelates met at Las Tortais, on the Mexican side, and were mutually consoled and encouraged by each other's labors and successes.

This truly apostolic Bishop continued these arduous visitations throughout his episcopate in Texas, and though they were not all as long as those above described, he made them annually. A brief allusion to some of his subsequent journeys, and to some of the incidents connected with them, will suffice to illustrate the life of Bishop Odin.

In the visitation which he made in the summer of 1857 he was providentially saved from drowning. Having reached San Antonio from Powder Horn, he took passage on a small boat for Sheldon Mansion. When in sight of Indianola, he was knocked overboard by the shifting of the boom; the boat passed rapidly on, and was not able to return to his rescue for twenty minutes. Though unable to swim, he was supported on the waves until the boat returned to his relief. The first effort to draw him up failed; at the second he was drawn under the boat; and when, after some moments of painful suspense for his safety, he reappeared on the surface, it was with delay and difficulty that he was finally rescued. He was almost suffocated with the salt water he had swallowed, and greatly exhausted and bruised. He was compelled to remain at Fort Lavaca for medical aid, but was soon afterwards again traversing the wilds of Texas in quest of souls.

In the visitation of 1858 he went to eighteen *ranchos*, twenty-eight villages, and to the more important towns of Houston, Fillsburgh, San Bernard, Hallettsville, Victoria, Goliah, Refugio, Lamar, l'Amita, l'Arkansas, San Patricio, and Corpus Christi. Then descending the Rio Grande, he visited Point Isabel, Santa Rosalia, Arenal, San Raphael, Suez, and Brownsville; and at the request of the priest of Matamoras, Vicar-General of Tamaulipas, he crossed the Rio Grande four times, and administered confirmation at Reynosa, Camargo, Mier, and Guerrero. He traveled eighteen hundred miles, and confirmed *three thousand four hundred and fifteen* persons, many of whom were adults. At Brownsville he met the exiled confessor, Bishop of San Luis Potosi, and the twenty faithful priests, companions of his exile. Bishop Odin was deeply moved at the persecutions of these holy men, and with a heart full of sympathy and heroic admiration, he lavished every attention and kindness upon them. He invited the venerable Bishop to accept a home in his own house at Galveston. The Bishop of Monterey, whom Bishop Odin had met in 1854, was now also an exile from his own country, and a refugee in Texas. In crossing the Rio Grande, to give confirmation to some of the flock of the exiled Prelates, Bishop Odin was received by the people with joy and gratitude, and crowds flocked to accept his generous ministry.

To attempt descriptions of the many remarkable visitations which Bishop Odin made through his vast diocese, and to recount the abundant and precious fruits which he reaped from them, would swell this tribute to his wonderful career to too great a length. We will merely add an account, written by himself, of a portion of his visitation in 1860, in order to show how he labored to recover and restore the ancient and sacred shrines of Texas, and rebuild the venerable temples erected during her Spanish period :—

"I returned to Galveston the beginning of this month (November). During my stay at San Antonio, I confirmed over two hundred persons, and exerted myself to bring about the repair of the Church of the Conception, built by the Spanish settlers in 1754. I have hopes that the work on this edifice will be so far advanced by the 8th of December, the Feast of the Immaculate Conception, as to be ready on that day for the celebration of the holy sacrifice of the Mass. This church, distant about two miles from San Antonio, is destined to become a place of pilgrimage. There is an excellent farm of one hundred acres of land attached to the church, of which I obtained possession in 1841, and which I have given to the Brothers of Mary. As soon as they can get the means, the Brothers propose to build an orphan asylum on the site of the ancient convent built by the Franciscans, who formerly had charge of this mission. The Benedictines have undertaken to revive the ancient Mission of San José. Father Priem, with some Brothers, has established his residence there. I hope after a while that we shall have there an abbey and a college. Little by little I expect to purchase a large part of the lands which formerly belonged to this mission, which is about five miles from San Antonio. The Churches of the Conception and San José are the only remaining relics of ancient times which we have. They are two magnificent edifices, solidly built, and which, under no circumstances, should be suffered to go to destruction."

The general growth of the Church of Texas, during the episcopate of Bishop Odin, was truly wonderful, especially when we recall the inadequate means at his disposal. He increased the number of his priests to twenty-nine seculars, thirteen religious, in all forty-two priests on the mission. He left to Texas fifty churches, a fine college, four academies for young ladies, and five fine schools for boys. In his beautiful Pastoral on the death of Archbishop Odin, the Most Rev. Archbishop Perché makes the following mention of his services in Texas: " Unnecessary for us is it here to give the minute details of Mgr. Odin's labors as Vicar-Apostolic of Texas. The vicariate was in a few years erected into a bishopric, of which he was the first incumbent, with the full title of Bishop of Galveston. We need merely to state a fact, as well known to the Catholics of Louisiana as of Texas, that he was constantly and unremittingly one of the most intrepid pioneers of Christian civilization, one of the most ardent apostles of the Gospel of Jesus Christ. Unwearied by fatigue, undeterred by danger, he kept himself ever traversing his vast diocese, founding Christian communities in places hardly reclaimed from the wilderness, building churches, and stationing priests at the outermost posts, as the vanguard of civilization, and always leading the advance himself, exposing his own life in the encounter with danger and the endurance of privations from which an ordinary man would have recoiled. In a word, and without detracting in the least from the well-earned reputation of his active and energetic successor, it can be affirmed that the Catholic Texas of to-day is the Catholic Texas which bishop Odin established. A glorious achievement is this, and one which must occupy a distinguished place in the ecclesiastical annals of the nineteenth century."

The Archiepiscopal See of New Orleans was made vacant in 1861 by the death of Archbishop Blanc. It was with one accord, that all eyes were turned to the venerable patriarch of religion in Texas, as the most worthy successor to that lamented Prelate. His humility had failed to conceal the splendor of his services to religion—splendid in the midst of his humility—and his own modest silence had not hushed the voice of fame. At Rome he was as much appreciated as in America, and the decision of Rome confirmed the verdict of America. By Papal Bull, bearing date February 15, 1861, Dr. Odin was appointed Archbishop of New Orleans. His appointment was to him as unexpected and startling as it was merited and applauded. He yielded only to the urgent demands of others, and with tears in his eyes; because, as he himself said, he "supposed God had some mysterious purpose to accomplish by it." On his arrival in New Orleans, he was received with extraordinary veneration and joy by both priests and people. In the beautiful Pastoral which he addressed to his new flock, were mingled touching sentiments of sorrow at his separation from Texas, which was so dear to him, with a lively and generous acceptance of his new and trying position, and a paternal adoption of his new flock. A few extracts from this admirable document will serve to illustrate the amiable and noble character of the venerable Archbishop:—

"During a residence of more than twenty years in Texas, we have received from its inhabitants nothing but evidences of kindness and affection. Our spiritual children, scattered throughout that immense region, ever greeted us with a heartfelt welcome! How painful has it been to us, to separate ourselves from a people to whom we had consecrated all of our affections! What a heart-rending sacrifice to us to leave that land of Texas, to which we had devoted our life, and in which we hoped our ashes would find a resting-place! Neither could we part without bitter feelings of regret from those venerable priests, both secular and regular, who were associated with us in our labors with the noblest devotedness, who made the most generous sacrifices, submitted to every privation, fatigue, and hardship to aid us in planting the Cross of Jesus Christ in a country where God was so little known. Loving them with all the tenderness of our heart, we ever fondly hoped that death alone could separate us.

"And how could we have left without deep regret those worthy Brothers of Mary, or of the Christian schools, or those devoted daughters of St. Ursula and of the Incarnate Word, who came to Texas with such alacrity at our earnest solicitations, for the instruction of youth? Their noble zeal for the interests of religion and society, was for us an object of admiration and gratitude. Their various establishments, though yet in their infancy, are producing such rich fruits and give such bright hopes for the future, that we have never ceased blessing the Lord for having procured us, in those chosen souls, such powerful auxiliaries. Yes, dearly beloved brethren, everything contributed to render the ties that bound us to Texas both dear and sacred; and to see them torn asunder without a pang would prove us devoid of that heart of a father and pastor, which every Bishop, who is the vicar of the tenderness of God for man, must necessarily possess towards the people intrusted to him. You will, I trust, pardon this tribute of affection to the past, which is replete with so many sweet memories, nor will you reprove the tears we shed over a wound that is still bleeding."

The sentiments with which he regarded the new flock committed to his care, are so beautifully portrayed in the same elegantly written and truly paternal Pastoral, that we cannot refrain from quoting them:—

"We are fully aware of the importance of a province which enjoys one of the first ranks in the territorial divisions of the New World. We know that Louisiana combines within herself all the elements of greatness, on account of her numerous population, the fertility of her soil, and the genius of her inhabitants. And we who, up to the present moment, have been accustomed to live as it were in the desert, beneath the humble cabins of our hardy pioneers, behold, we are suddenly transported to the centre of a great and opulent city! Is not such a change calculated to frighten us?

"Our only resource is to be so deeply impressed with a lively sense of our unworthiness, that Almighty God will be moved to compassion in our weakness. Faith teaches us that the Lord is pleased to make use of the weakest and vilest instruments in the accomplishment of His designs, showing us thereby His power, which out of nothing brings forth something, that no flesh should glorify itself in His sight. Far from casting an ambitious thought on, or seeking the mission which has been intrusted to us, He knows that we have accepted it with fear and dread; and we therefore hope that, knowing our weakness, He will give us strength.

"We also place our confidence in the knowledge we

have of your devotion to the Catholic cause, of your love for the Church of Jesus Christ, and of your filial attachment for its august Chief, the Roman Pontiff. We have not forgotten the touching proofs you have given of this attachment, in the noble demonstration which followed our last Provincial Council.

"We likewise feel encouraged by reflecting on the pious fidelity, with which you have preserved the sacred deposit of doctrines and traditions, which you received from your fathers. In the beautiful soil of Louisiana, from the time she was first discovered, the Christian faith took deep roots. The grain of mustard-seed has become a powerful tree, which has produced abundant fruits of Catholic fervor. Charity, the inseparable companion of faith, has multiplied here, under every form, with an exhaustless fecundity, all institutions suited to the removal of ignorance, to the curing of vices, and to assuaging the miseries of poor suffering humanity.

"The fertility of her soil, and the conquests of her industry, have not cooled in her people their zeal for the precepts and maxims of the Gospel. There is found amongst you, in the midst of the perfectness and prosperity of the material life, that simplicity of manners, those hospitable customs, those religious habits, and that respect for divine things, which have always won the admiration of strangers who visited your charming valley.

"'How beautiful are the fruits of civilization,' saith an illustrious writer, 'when they grow beneath the influence of religious beliefs and manners, and are nourished and take their hue from the sun of faith. Religion, which warms them into life also, alone preserves them. Oh, whilst you pursue those labors and discoveries which may add to your well-being on earth, cease not to have your eyes fixed on heaven, which is your true country!'

"If the knowledge which we have of your character, your principles, and your sentiments, encourages us in the tremendous ministry which is imposed on us, we can also promise you, on our part, devotion the most unbounded; we may say to you, in the language of our Lord, 'All that is ours is yours.' We place at your service all that we have, all that we are, our thoughts, our affections, our time, and our strength; we would wish even, after the example of the Sovereign Pastor, to sacrifice our life for the salvation of your souls.

"Our first duty is to know our flock; and we will have no sweeter enjoyment than in its fulfilment, by visiting each and every one of all the parishes of this extensive diocese. To go through your towns and villages, announcing the word of salvation; to extend our hands over your children, to communicate to them the gifts of the Holy Ghost; to gather from their innocent lips the proofs of their proficiency in the law of God; to bless your persons, your houses, and your fields; to pray with you over the tombs of your fathers; to watch over the beauty of the house of the Lord, and to attend to the dignity of divine worship—all this shall be to us, not a painful labor, but a most pleasing occupation."

A tender love for his priests was one of the noble traits of Bishop Odin's character. While Bishop of Galveston he treated them all as his children, shared their severest labors and sacrifices, was a true friend and father in their troubles, and shed the tears of paternal love over their graves. We have seen a letter, written to announce the death of one of his priests in 1861, which pours forth the love and sorrow of a parent's heart. While Archbishop of New Orleans he was no less distinguished for this gentle and amiable trait. In his first Pastoral, already quoted, he says of his clergy: —"We entertain for them a sincere and profound esteem. It is not by display of power, but rather of love, that we will show the authority with which, notwithstanding our unworthiness, our character invests us. In New Orleans, as well as in Texas, it will be our happiness to love the priests, the ministers of Jesus Christ, our glory to honor them, and our triumph to merit their confidence."

There was something providential in the appointment of so saintly a Prelate for New Orleans at the trying period of the history of that city, at the time of his arrival there. His child-like simplicity, straightforwardness of purpose and conduct, his openness, sincerity, and benevolence, challenged the respect of the world and its followers, and elevated him above the breath of censure or suspicion, amid the shifting fortunes of war. "We witnessed," writes his successor, "the unrepining patience with which he bore the excruciating pains to which he fell a victim, shortly after his arrival in this city. This patience, this meekness, this calm unruffled resignation, accompanied him to the last."

Archbishop Odin practised the virtue of poverty in an eminent degree. His life in Texas was one incessant example of this. He not only bestowed everything upon his church, but even his own clothing he shared with his impoverished priests. He appeared once at the Council of Baltimore, that of 1849, in such poverty of raiment, as to elicit remarks from his friends. This led to the discovery of the fact that the good Bishop possessed but a single shirt. This discovery forced from him the reluctant explanation, that such was the poverty of some of his clergy, that he had given all, except the one he wore, to them. At New Orleans he had ample opportunities of acquiring worldly means and comforts; but no, he preferred to give rather than to receive, and he died in the same exalted poverty in which he had lived. His charity was the companion-virtue of his poverty; a charity tender and solicitous even more for the soul than for the body of his neighbor; a charity united with the utmost humility, and with a saintly rigor towards himself. "What shall we say now," writes Archbishop Perché, "of the private virtues of Archbishop Odin? In spite of all his ingenious attempts to conceal from men that which would have elicited their homage, we had an opportunity to see the lengths to which he carried the spirit of Christian mortification, and how severe and harsh he was to himself, when the slightest want or the lightest pain experienced by his neighbor awakened his most anxious solicitude and enlisted his tenderest compassion, and not rarely furnished a vent for his tears." *

The services he rendered the cause of religion in Louisiana were extraordinary. Assuming as he did the government of the archdiocese of New Orleans at an advanced age, and with health impaired by the long labors and exposures of his episcopate in Texas, he labored for his new flock with the zeal and energy of his younger days. Every portion of his diocese received his paternal and untiring attention. The institutions erected under his predecessors were fostered and strengthened, and new ones were added to their num-

---

* Pastoral of Archbishop Perché, of July 3, 1870.

ber. Churches were multiplied, educational institutions increased, and charitable establishments erected in various parts. He made repeated visits to Europe in the interest of his diocese, but especially for procuring more priests for his diocese, the number of whom were nearly doubled during his Archiepiscopate. In France and at Rome, in both of which places he was greatly respected, he always secured important succors and advantages for his church; and those long and painful voyages and journeys, which he performed with so much labor and inconvenience to himself, were productive of most substantial and effective relief and benefit to his flock. Amidst the demoralizing influences of war and military occupation, he exerted all his energies in promoting piety and religion among his people. Great numbers of reformations were effected, through his efforts and those of his clergy, during those trying times, embracing the adoption of a reformed and good life by many indifferent or irreligious Catholics, and a large number of conversions from the sects. The good Archbishop himself could not refrain from noticing, and expressing his happiness at witnessing, the improvement in morals and devotion, not only in his episcopal city, but in other parts of the diocese. A single example, that of a New Orleans regiment in the Southern army, may be mentioned. In this regiment, the *Guards d'Orleans*, "every person connected with it, without one exception, from the colonel to the youngest drummer-boy, went to confession and communion, just before leaving New Orleans. This regiment particularly distinguished itself in the battle of Shiloh, by deeds of the most desperate valor. Within the forty-eight hours before that battle, they all once more went to confession. It was not only during the march from Corinth to Shiloh, but wherever there was a halt, the good priest that accompanied them was surrounded by a little crowd, till they had all in turn made their confession."* It was at sights like these, the harvest of the Lord's vineyard, even more than at the external grandeur of the Church and her temples, that Archbishop Odin rejoiced. Not only did he thus labor for the good of his own people, but afterwards, during the military administrations of Generals Butler and Banks, he extended his solicitude for souls to all; and amidst the din of arms and the promulgation of military proclamations, his gentle voice was raised to plead for the cause of God and of religion. A noble example of this is found in the admirable Pastoral he issued in 1864, announcing and inculcating the penances of Lent, the proper observance of the Lord's day, and abstinence from all vice and immorality.

He took a lively interest in the Church Universal, and his truly Catholic heart acted always in sympathy with whatever concerned or affected her interests. His visits to Rome, though rendered necessary by the wants and interests of his flock, were performed by him in the spirit of devotion and loyalty, and as pilgrimages to the shrines of the apostles and saints. He was distinguished in his attachment to the Apostolic See, and to the saintly Pontiff who now so gloriously fills the chair of Peter. In 1867 he repaired to Rome at the invitation of Pius IX., though in very feeble health, to take part in the canonization of the Japanese martyrs; and there were few of the venerable fathers, assembled in St. Peter's on that solemn and glorious occasion, who re-

---

* *New York Freeman's Journal*, July 5, 1862.

joiced more in the conquests of the Church throughout the world, or in honoring her illustrious and martyred sons. On his return to his home in the South, he was welcomed by his clergy and his flock with outbursts of joy and love; and although the ovation then gotten up in his honor was unexpected by him, and foreign to his simple and humble tastes, he was overpowered by this evidence of his people's affection, regarded it as a tribute to the Sovereign Pontiff whom he represented, and as an act of religion and homage to the Church. Those who participated in this enthusiastic and dutiful demonstration, can never cease to cherish a remembrance of the scene when the venerable Prelate, bowed down with infirmities and labors, yet supported by a vigorous and generous spirit, with a countenance beaming with joy and goodness, with an uplifted hand that was never raised but to bless, bestowed upon that devout assembly the Papal benediction.

It is impossible, in this brief biography, to detail the many services rendered by Archbishop Odin to the archdiocese of New Orleans, or to do justice to the good he accomplished for the Church in the United States, and especially of the South-west. It will be sufficient to give a general summary, and for this purpose we prefer quoting the language of his distinguished successor, who was a witness of what he relates:—" You, beloved brethren, know as well as we, how steadily religion advanced in this diocese during the nine years of Archbishop Odin's administration. In the most troublous times, the commotions which heaved this country up from its very foundations never checked or diverted the uniform industry of his zeal. The number of priests and churches almost doubled, the religious and charitable in stitutions multiplied and developed, the wise reforms introduced, the salutary ordinances put in force, are so many monuments, as glorious as they are enduring, erected in the living temple of the Church in America, to the spirit in which he was animated, to his singleness of purpose, the purity of his intentions, the soundness of his judgment, and his administrative ability."

For many years before his death, and in fact during his entire administration of the archdiocese of New Orleans, Archbishop Odin's health was not only feeble, but during those nine years he suffered from a painful and distressing disease, contracted under the exposures and privations of his missionary life in Texas. There was scarcely a day that he did not suffer intensely from neuralgia. The ravages of this malady were manifest in his face and shoulders, but never in the least impaired his cheerfulness or interfered with his labors. He labored up to the last moment, and finally fell a victim to duty. Summoned by the Vicar of Christ to the Œcumenical Council of the Vatican in 1869, he hastened to obey that supreme voice. His health had become much worse before his departure from home; the voyage to Europe completely undermined it. Notwithstanding his feebleness and his sufferings, he was constant in his attendance at the sessions of the Council, amongst whose records he solemnly and reverently deposited his *credo*. It was becoming impossible, under his increasing malady, for him to continue his attendance, and the Holy Father, on being made acquainted with his condition, readily consented to and advised his departure from Rome and a sojourn in his native France. While at Rome he obtained the appointment of Dr. Perché as his coadjutor Bishop and successor. He was in a dying condition when he left Rome, and on reaching Ambierle, his native place, he was extremely ill. He cherished to the last, hopes of being able to return to his beloved flock. His last moments were replete with excruciating sufferings; but his uniform calmness and serenity were never disturbed by his pains. He received the holy Viaticum on the day of his death, and as his soul departed, he fixed his eyes steadily on Heaven, and an angelic smile rested on his lips after the spirit had gone. He died in the midst of relatives and friends, and amongst a population who revered him as an apostle, and who, on the announcement of his death, came in procession, with pious veneration, to claim the privilege of touching his hands, his rosary, and his medals. It was said by an eye-witness that the public voice canonized him as a saint. They insisted on watching and praying by his corpse for days, and on having his remains borne through the streets of the town instead of carried directly to the church. Father Chalon, the pastor of the Cathedral of New Orleans, who accompanied him to Europe, requested his remains, or at least his heart, that he might have it preserved as a precious relic amongst his flock; but the people of Ambierle would not consent to give up what they too so tenderly and reverently esteemed. His death occurred on the eve of the festival of the Ascension, May 25, 1870. He was buried in a tomb prepared for him in the chapel of the Blessed Virgin at Ambierle, the same shrine in which he had worshipped and learned his catechism when a boy. "We have learned from trustworthy sources," writes Dr. Perché, "that the people living round about the town in which he lay sick and went through so terrible an agony, dazzled by the splendor of his virtues, already venerated him as a saint, and that his funeral was a triumphal march, in which the faith and piety of the people bore witness to his eminent sanctity."

The following tribute to the virtues and services of Archbishop Odin is from the pen of one of his flock, and is beautifully expressive of the sentiments in which he was held by those whom he had loved and served so well:—

"In the death of Archbishop John M. Odin, religion, though it has gained a martyr, has lost a confessor, humanity has lost a benefactor, and our poor afflicted country a true and real friend. With the longing eagerness of the exile, our good Archbishop pined for his flock in our beloved Southern land, and until the last moment almost he indulged the hope, growing stronger every hour in proportion to the impossibility of its being realized, that in that dear land his bones would moulder into doubly kindred dust: the dust of the land he had adopted as his own, and the dust which in its living forms he had made kin to God, in supernaturalizing it by his sacred ministry. That hope was baffled; John Mary Odin died where he was born; like that other John, whose life could hardly have been more austere, he died among his own people—the members of his own family; a confessor by right, a martyr by merit, but without the *éclat* of martyrdom. His was a strange and eventful life. It was a drama, perfect in its minutest details, though the casual observer may see little in its development to surprise or startle him. The explorer of Missouri's sombre forests, the Boones of western civilization —those who first penetrated the frowning wilderness of the Far West—have their Coopers, their Longfellows, and a host of inferior writers to wed their daring to immortality. Father Odin did as much as they did, and

Bishop Odin did much more than they ever thought or dreamt of doing; and where is his panegyrist? Through the vast prairies of Texas—across the American steppes, the dreary solitudes of which were unbroken save by the savage war-whoop of the Comanche or Arapajo—that humble servant of a crucified God rode tranquilly on his mule, undismayed either by the awful loneliness or still more awful society around him, with no weapon but a crucifix, no commission but his trust in God. Yet with these slender resources he performed wonders, which formidable armies have in later times covered themselves with ridicule for attempting; by this meek influence he proved to the savage red man that the white man, need not be essentially a brute, and gave the white man himself, who came to announce in those regions the evangel of lust and the bowie-knife, a lesson of genuine Christian civilization. Somebody ought to write the life of Bishop Odin in Texas. Texas was his home, because his legitimate mission; and some veteran Texan ought to give us the minutest particulars which a mission so fruitful of good to human nature can furnish: . . . there we saw in him only the self-sacrificing, fearless missionary, who might vie with St. Paul himself in his tribulations; while in both dioceses we can claim for him that combination, so rare in modern times, of the indefatigable zeal of the apostle with the serene austerity of the anchoret and the angelic meekness of the recluse." *

---

* *Morning Star and Catholic Messenger*, June 26, 1870.

RIGHT REV. WILLIAM QUARTER, D.D.,

First Bishop of Chicago, A.D. 1844.*

IT may be said not only of countries, but also of families, in which the full influences of the Catholic faith have prevailed, that a vocation to the holy ministry is esteemed as among the highest and best of honors and blessings on earth. Thus in Catholic Ireland, no less than in Catholic France, and our own Catholic Maryland in its early days, parents esteemed it the glory and benediction of their families to contribute one or more of their sons to the sanctuary of the Most High, and of their daughters to be the spouses of the Immaculate Lamb. There is no family probably of the same period, that presented in this spirit of the faith more of its members to the Church, than the maternal branch of the family of Bishop Quarter. The beautiful example and pious training by which his excellent mother instilled the spirit of devotion and the traditional love of the faith into the heart of her son, and the generous manner in which he corresponded to these gentle teachings, present at once to parents and children a noble example of true Christian life. We are told that there were, at the time of the Bishop's ecclesiastical life, nearly twenty members of his maternal family of Bennet in the ministry, and that they presented an unsullied name, "while there have never been any men in the ministry more firm in upholding the rights of the priest-

---

* *Life of Bishop Quarter*, by Dr. McGirr; *Catholic Magazines* of 1844, 1845, 1846, 1847, and 1848; *Metropolitan*, 1858; Shea's *Catholic Missions*; De Courcy and Shea's *Catholic Church in the United States*, &c., &c.

hood." Of this truly sacerdotal family, the subject of this memoir became the most distinguished.

William Quarter was the third son of Michael Quarter and Ann Bennet, a very respectable family of King's County, Ireland. He was born in Killurine, January 24, 1806. Of four sons three embraced the holy ministry: Walter Joseph, who was the Bishop's Vicar-General, and administrator of the diocese on the Bishop's death; the Bishop himself, and James, who died before ordination. Their pious mother devoted herself untiringly to their moral training and religious education. Their first efforts at articulation were directed to the pronunciation of the blessed names of Jesus, Mary, and Joseph. The habit of morning and evening prayer became ingrafted upon their lives both by precept and example, as all the members of the family circle assembled regularly for this purpose, and never retired at night without reciting the Rosary of the Blessed Virgin Mary. The mother's great devotion to Mary made a deep impression on the heart of William. Her piety must have been extraordinary, for the Bishop in after-life used to say, "I never saw but one, and that one was Bishop Bruté, who exhibited so tender a piety as my mother." At the tender age of seven, he was taught to wait upon the priest at the offering of the Holy Sacrifice, and his mother would say to him after he had been thus engaged, " My son, it does my heart good to see you serving at the altar. I consider your place there more honorable than if you occupied the first station in a kingdom; now you are truly in the service of your God." Having herself received a thoroughly Catholic and good secular education, in an academy attached to one of the convents of her native country, she knew the value of such an education, and was competent to bestow its advantages upon her. She accordingly, in the midst of her other engrossing and laborious domestic cares, took upon herself the early education of her children, in order that a good foundation for the life of the future Christian and citizen might be laid, solid and deep in their hearts. William corresponded fully and generously with the efforts of his parent, by eagerly and earnestly embracing her lessons of virtue, and by applying himself industriously to his studies. Home was thus made a nursery for the college and the sanctuary. Young William at this early age showed the promise of his future eminence. His studies were earnest beyond his years; and even his pastimes were expressive of his after-choice in life; for we are told that while his companions were at play with their toys, he was in the habit of retiring to his room, where he erected his miniature church and altar, "offering up to God upon it the sacrifice of his young and spotless heart." *

In the mean time, his mother was offering her son to God in her daily prayers; and as the time was approaching for him to leave home for school, she determined to fortify his heart in virtue and grace, that he might encounter the temptations of the little world he was about to enter, by preparing him to receive the Holy Eucharist. He received his first communion with such piety and devotion, that all who witnessed the scene were impressed with an admiration which never passed from their memories. It was at this early period of his life that he resolved to dedicate his whole existence to the service of his Creator, and declared his resolution of embracing the holy ministry.

---

* Dr. McGirr's *Life of Bishop Quarter*.

Leaving home for Tullamore, he entered the school of Mr. Derar, one of the best classical scholars of the country, and spent two years there in the study of the classics and mathematics. He next entered the academy of John and Thomas Fitzgerald, in the same town, where he remained till his sixteenth year. During these years of study the young scholar was an example to all his companions. His application to his books and his exemplary conduct were as exact and untiring as they had been while the parental eye rested upon him. His example and manly virtues gave him great influence with his companions, which he always exerted to encourage virtue and repress vice. It was a singular proof of his fitness for the benevolent and disinterested pursuits of his after-life, that at that early age he experienced the greatest happiness in doing charity among his companions, and in giving alms to the poor: for we are told that his allowance of pocket-money at school was expended by him in relieving the sufferings of the indigent and afflicted. Such was the marked career of this youth among his companions, such too was the clear and prophetic appreciation of school-boys for what is good and noble in human life and character, that he was generally known at these two academies of Tullamore by the title of the "*little bishop.*" He closed his academic course by a very creditable public examination, and returned home preparatory to entering upon his studies for the priesthood at Maynooth.

The finger of Providence at this juncture pointed out a new career to the future priest and Bishop; and the earnestness and steadfastness of purpose with which he entered upon it, and followed it, present us an example worthy of contemplation and imitation. While at home, preparatory to his entrance into Maynooth, the Rev. Mr. McAuley, a brother of Count McAuley, of Frankfort, King's County, Ireland, returned to his native country from the United States, where he had been on the mission. This reverend gentleman, who spent much of his time at the house of Mr. and Mrs. Quarter, spoke frequently of the vast and needy missionary field of America; of the scattered condition of the Catholics, the scarcity of priests, the deplorable condition of Catholics in remote regions, without church, priests, or sacraments; the many who were in danger of losing the faith, and of the many allurements, in a new and non-Catholic country, to tempt the best inclined to lose sight of God and of their souls in the pursuit of wealth, and in the hurried and eager current of a new and adventurous existence. His accounts of the necessitous spiritual condition of the country, and of the rich harvest of souls that it presented to the zealous laborers in the vineyard of the Lord, made a deep impression on the mind and heart of young William Quarter, whose thoughts were now intent upon his sacred vocation. He regarded these words of Father McAuley as the words of God addressed to his heart, inviting him to go and enter this vast and suffering portion of the fold and labor for its salvation. He resolved to obey the call of conscience and of duty. The remonstrances of his devoted parents, who had willingly offered him to the Church of his native country, and who felt keenly the dreaded pang of separation from so young a son; the regrets of his good Bishop, the Right Rev. Dr. Doyle, who beheld, in his intended departure for America, a serious loss to the church of Ireland, and of his own diocese especially; the persuasions of friends and relatives—all had no effect in weakening his generous purpose. The Bishop gave him the requested *exeat*, and accompanied it with his blessing. His parents were too good and conscientious to stand between their beloved son and his God. The example of the Roman mothers, who sent their sons forth to battle for their country, glorious as it was, cannot be compared with the sublimer heroism of this Christian mother, who sent forth her son on a voyage of peril and a mission of labor, hardships, and sufferings, with these noble words: "My son, I have given you to God; go whithersoever He calls you, and may His and your mother's benediction ever attend you!"

Our young candidate for the American mission sailed from his native country April 10, 1822, when he was in his sixteenth year, and landed at Quebec. Presenting himself to the Bishop of that city, he applied for admission into the ecclesiastical seminary, but his request was not granted, because of his youth. His earnestness and perseverance next carried him to Montreal, and here again his youth brought upon him a repetition of the disappointment. He next journeyed through the United States until he came to Mt. St. Mary's College, at Emmittsburg, Maryland, that mother of priests and Bishops, and presented himself, undaunted by refusal and disappointment, to the Rev. Mr. Dubois, its founder and president. Mr. Dubois, admiring his youthful zeal, and knowing how acceptable to God is the offering of young and innocent hearts, received him as a son. The holy friendship thus formed in the union of sincere hearts in God, their common centre, continued through life.

On examining his pupil, Mr. Dubois found him so thoroughly prepared in classical and mathematical learning, as to warrant his immediate reception into the ecclesiastical Seminary, and he selected for his entrance therein the 8th day of September, the Feast of the Nativity of his patroness, the Blessed Virgin Mary. He was found competent at once to take charge of the classes of Latin, Greek, and Algebra in the College, and in the following year was appointed Professor of the Latin and Greek languages. As a reward for his piety, he was, after one year's residence in the institution, appointed sacristan, a position for which he made an especial preparation by approaching confession and Holy Communion. When he entered upon his office it was with awe and fear, remembering how much more sacred was the Chalice of the Body and Blood of the Lord, which he was to handle, than the Ark of the Covenant, for which, even with good motives, a servant of the Lord had been severely punished under the old law. Before he would enter the Holy of Holies, even as its servant, he humbled himself at the door of the church, and would not approach the Tabernacle for the first time except upon his knees, upon which he went from the door to the sanctuary. This virtue of veneration for sacred things he preserved through life, never allowing familiarity to diminish it; and, as a Bishop ordaining priests, he ever reminded them of this important lesson, and warned them against the least thoughtlessness or familiarity in presence of the Blessed Sacrament. From the learned and saintly Bruté he learned not only the lessons of theology, but was confirmed in his virtues and stimulated in the practices of piety he acquired under the parental roof. It was a commendation well worthy of preservation, that Dr. Bruté said of him, that "Among all the professors and students he was highly esteemed for his clear mind, sound judgment, gentle disposition, firm friendship, and perfect devotion. Associating the external beauties and earthly friendships of the mountain college with his own dedication to the service of God, he cherished for them ever after the fondest attachment." His biographer * portrays this lively sentiment in the heart of the Bishop by the following spirited passage: " Often have I been seated with him for hours, forgetting all else, while he spoke of the men and things there; of the little church away up upon the mountainside; of the beautiful valley that stretched out in front of it from the base of the Blue Ridge, and extended away as far as the eye could reach; of the graveyard and the friends of his that lay mouldering there; of the cottage, and the garden, and the grotto, and the ravine, bridged over by 'Plunket's Folly;' of the crystal fountain bubbling up at the mountain's base, pure, sparkling, and bright, and distributing its liquid treasures; of the old wooden college that has been long since removed and replaced by the tall stone one, with its majestic steeple, with its cross above the clouds, its terraces, and its trees fringing their borders; of the hunting-grounds, and the rabbit-dens and their trappers; of the little gardens of each student's industry, nestled like birds'nests amid the tall trees upon the mountain-side; of these and a thousand other topics, that may be readily imagined by any one who has spent his college years at Mt. St. Mary's. In this regard for the memories of those years, we behold how unchangeable were his affections."

On the appointment of Mr. Dubois to the See of New York, he carried with him the *exeat* and other papers

---

* Dr. McGirr.

which Mr. Quarter had placed in his keeping, intending to enlist him, when ordained, in the service of that diocese. The exertions of the Archbishop of Baltimore to retain him in his diocese, the brilliant offers made to him by the faculty of the college, in order to secure his valuable services to that institution, could not prevail upon him to abandon his first and best friend; that one, above all others, who accepted and received him in the service of God, when others refused. He finished his theological studies at the age of twenty-three years, and on September 4, 1829, he departed from the cherished scenes and friends of Mt. St. Mary's, amid the regrets and benedictions of all, and arrived in New York on the 16th. Bishop Dubois removed by dispensation the impediment of want of years, and having conferred on him the clerical tonsure, minor orders, and sub-deaconship on the 17th, deaconship on the 18th, raised him on the 19th to the dignity of the priesthood, the young levite thus attaining the highest aspiration of his soul. The Bishop soon after departed for Europe, leaving the Very Rev. Dr. Power to administer the diocese in his absence. The Rev. James Smith was appointed to the pastoral charge of St. Peter's Church, and the Rev. William Quarter was appointed his assistant. After laboring zealously in this field for two years, Father Quarter went to pay a visit of affection to his Alma Mater at Emmittsburg, in 1831. But his visit was also one in the interests of religion, and we are indebted to his exertions on this occasion for the first introduction of the Sisters of Charity into New York. Three of these good Sisters went to take charge of the female free school attached to St. Peter's Church, which, after enduring many early years of discomfort and shifting accommodations, was permanently established in its present comfortable schoolhouse, and has continued for nearly forty years to dispense the blessings of a religious education to thousands of poor children. This was the germ from which sprang the present numerous and splendid institutions of the Sisters of Charity in the States of New York and New Jersey.

Father Quarter had soon presented to him the severest test of the true servant of God. That fell destroyer, the Asiatic cholera, desolated the city of New York in 1832 and 1833. The sufferings, the horrors, the mortality, and the afflictions of that dread season will be recalled by many. The charitable heart of Father Quarter was stricken with grief for his people. With an unbounded generosity and an heroic self-sacrifice, he devoted himself to their temporal and spiritual relief. He was unceasing in his attendance on the sick and dying. The hovels of the poor and the mansions of the rich shared equally his paternal care and kindness; but as his flock was composed chiefly of the poor, the scenes he witnessed were those of the deepest and most unmitigated suffering and woe. Day and night he was engaged in his visits of mercy and religion, and considered himself quite fortunate if he could secure for himself three hours from the twenty-four for repose from his exhausting labors. He resided during this period in the house of Mr. Snowden, publisher of the *Courier and Enquirer*, and such was the effect of the self-sacrificing and Christian example of this devoted priest upon the family, that Mrs. Snowden and her three daughters and two sons embraced the faith of the Church "that taught such heroism for God's sake." This good lady, in order that the indefatigable priest might obtain the rest necessary to the discharge of his arduous and exhausting labors, used to watch for the sick-calls, and communicate them to him after he had secured a little repose and refreshment. Thus no calls went unanswered, no patients or penitents unattended. Not content with his ministrations to the sick and dying, Father Quarter gathered together the orphan children of such members of his flock as fell victims to the pestilence, placed them in charge of the Sisters of Charity, and bestowed all the means he possessed upon their maintenance. He procured for this purpose a house from Mr. Cornelius Heany, a true benefactor of the orphan, who, after the making of a permanent provision by Father Quarter for the little ones, whom he thus sheltered until they could safely be provided with situations, donated the house to the Sisters of Charity, as a refuge for the fatherless. It was thus that Father Quarter went, like a messenger of comfort and heavenly benediction, among the pestilence-stricken people, saving the lives of such as could be saved, bestowing the last consolations of religion upon the dying, and providing a home for the orphans of those who fell victims to the visitation.

> "Think not the good,
> The gentle deeds of mercy thou hast done,
> Shall die forgotten all ; the poor, the pris'ner,
> The fatherless, the friendless, and the widow,
> Who daily own the bounty of thy hand,
> Shall cry to heav'n, and pull a blessing on thee."

Father Quarter became pastor of St. Mary's Church, in New York, in 1833. The old Church of St. Mary's, in Sheriff Street, had been destroyed by fire, November 9, 1831, and, in the opinion of all, the hand of an incendiary applied the torch to this shrine of the living God, and scattered the flock that worshipped there. This congregation was still further afflicted in the following month by the death of their beloved pastor, the Rev. Luke Berry. But before his death he had selected and purchased the lots at the corner of Grand and Ridge Streets, as the site of the new church. The congregation left no exertion untried to rebuild their church and re-erect their altar. In the midst of their generous exertions the cholera came and prostrated all enterprise and paralyzed their work. By dint of renewed exertions, after the cholera disappeared, they succeeded at length in completing their church, which was dedicated by Bishop Dubois, June 9, 1833, and at the conclusion of the service the Bishop announced the appointment of Father Quarter as pastor of St. Mary's. It was no easy task to reorganize the flock that had been dispersed, to collect the children together again in schools, and to set on foot the numerous instrumentalities of devotion and zeal so necessary in every congregation. But the new pastor set about his difficult task with his accustomed courage. The heavy debt resting upon the church rendered it impossible for the Trustees to embark in new enterprises; these the pastor had to undertake at his own expense, so that Father Quarter, seeing the necessity of securing the services of the Sisters of Charity for the female school of the parish, applied, with the consent of the Bishop, for, and obtained three Sisters of Charity from Emmittsburg, and by the 1st of September, 1833, had St. Mary's free school in operation. He also permitted the Sisters to open a select pay-school at their residence, as a means of aiding in their support and the maintenance of the free school. The free school commenced with a hundred, and soon had five hundred scholars, and the pay-school soon had a hundred. It was not long before the trustees had sufficiently recovered from debt, to be able to unite with their pastor in purchasing the house they occupied in Grand Street as their permanent residence. Father Quarter addressed himself earnestly to the formation of pious confraternities and sodalities amongst his flock, and had the consolation of seeing rosary and scapular societies springing up around him, to edify by good example, and to send up the incense of pure devotion to Heaven. The fruits of Father Quarter's zeal are still manifest in this fine parish. Under the pastoral care of Rev. E. J. O'Reilly, the church has been greatly enlarged and beautified, the works of Father Quarter developed far beyond their original plans, and many new and noble works of religion and charity undertaken.

One of the most gratifying occurrences connected with Father Quarter's pastoral charge of St. Mary's, was the conversion of the Rev. Mr. Œrtel, a Lutheran minister of New York. Earnest in his pursuit of truth, and ardent in the desire for his own and his neighbors' salvation, this gentleman had labored both in Prussia and the United States to these ends. But on a closer comparison of the tenets of his communion with the writings of the Fathers he discovered the widest differences, and even in regard to the Lutheran tenets he found the greatest want of accord among Lutherans, and a total want of union in the Church. His visit to the Lutheran Bishop, Dr. Stevens, of Missouri, only resulted in drawing from that official the admission "that the Lutheran Church is extinct, not only in Germany, but throughout all Europe." Nor did America present a different spectacle, and the minister became conscious to himself that he was not a member of the "one fold," established by Christ and perpetuated by the Apostles and Fathers. About this time he became acquainted with Father Quarter, who received him with kindness and Christian charity; explained to him the doctrines of the Catholic Church, divested of the misrepresentations heaped upon them by opponents, and supplied him with Catholic books. The grace of conversion took effect in his heart; he embraced the truth, and "wept for very joy that he had at last found the secure haven, wherein he could anchor the frail bark of his mortality."

Father Quarter continued the devoted pastor of St. Mary's, whose congregation is said to have become, under his zealous and paternal care, a model of piety and good example, until 1844, when he was called to a more extended and laborious field, as the chief pastor of the Church of Illinois.

The tradition is still preserved, that the first European foot that traversed the soil of Illinois was that of a Catholic priest. Many of the Illinois warriors and traders had met the zealous Father Allouez at Chegoimegon, where he had established his Ottawa mission in 1667. They were thus prepared to welcome the illustrious Marquette, who devoted himself to the Illinois mission, of which he was the founder, and in the service of which he spent his last breath. Father Allouez afterwards planted his gigantic cross in their midst, which long stood as a monument of his zeal and of their faith. Three missionaries accompanied La Salle in 1680, in his exploration of the Mississippi, and preached the Gospel to the Illinois on its banks; and one of them, the vener able Father Gabriel de la Ribourde, watered their soil with his blood as a martyr of Christ. In 1691 the Jesuit missions were resumed, and Fathers Douay, Gravier, and the celebrated Father Rale, became the teachers of these noble tribes. Under the latter a Christian community grew up, in which all attended the daily Mass, and morning and evening prayers. Father Gravier, again becoming their missionary, reaped great fruits, in spite of the opposition and persecutions of the medicine-men. Among the Peorias he trained up fervent Christians; and it was a precious fruit of his labors that they trained up such a Christian as Mary, the daughter of the chief of the Kaskaskias, who dedicated herself, in that rude state of society, as a virgin to the Most High, and who afterwards, by a still higher exercise of virtue, sacrificed this her chosen dedication for one of mercy for her Church and people, by consenting to marry a Christian, in order to save the infant church of the Illinois from persecution, and to pave the way to the conversion of her people to Christianity. A succession of missionaries followed— glorious apostles of the Faith—so that in the first quarter of the eighteenth century nearly all the Illinois were Christians, and were devoted to their European friends, through whom they received the light of the Gospel. Under the influence of religion they became less wandering in their habits, and more industrious, cultivating the soil, and raising poultry and live stock, which they sold to the French. The women became ingenious weavers, working the buffalo hair into a fine thread, which they afterwards wove into a fine glossy cloth for dresses for themselves. Some of these Christian Indians, descending the Mississippi, visited New Orleans, and Father Le Petit bears the following testimony to their deportment:—"They charmed us by their piety and edifying life. Every evening they recited the beads in alternate choirs, and every morning heard my Mass, chanting at it, especially on Sundays and holidays, prayers and hymns suited to the day. They are well acquainted with the history of the Old and New Testament. Their manner of hearing Mass and approaching the sacraments was excellent. The missionaries do not suffer them to grow up in ignorance of any of the mysteries of religion or of their duties, but ground them in what is fundamental and essential, which they inculcate in a manner equally sound and instructive." Why, we may well ask again, should this happy state of things not have been fostered by the government, and why should not the Indian tribes have been preserved to honor and serve God on earth as Christians, instead of being doomed to annihilation? But alas, the Illinois mission was destined to decline; the mismanagement of Louisiana impaired the prospects of the whole Mississippi Valley; the pernicious and corrupting examples of the dissolute soldiers garrisoned among them, unsuccessful wars, and neglect of the government, demoralized and thinned them. The final dispersion of the Jesuits by Choiseul, and the transfer of the French possessions to the English, completed the work of decay. But Father Potier, "the last Jesuit in the West," continued to visit the Illinois from Detroit to the time of his death, in 1781. In later years, the remnants of this Christian nation were occasionally visited by Catholic clergymen, when opportunity offered. Bishop Rosati baptized the brother of their great chief, and afterwards Bishop Blanc ministered among them. While many of them relapsed into barbarism from neglect, others retained their religion and their civilization, and some even, like John B. Richardville, or Piskewah, son of the heroine who led the Miamis at Harmar's defeat, demonstrated the practicability of civilization for the Indian, by adopting the costume and habits of the white man, and acquiring ease and competence. The subsequent transfer of the remnants of the Illinois clans to the countries west of the Mississippi has again brought them within the present western missions of the Jesuits, who are still zealously laboring for their salvation.

But the attention of the missionaries was not confined to the Indians; the French settlers in Illinois were also the object of their care. In 1750 there were five French villages in Illinois and upper Louisiana (Missouri), containing one hundred and forty families. The Bishop of Quebec had charge over this remote and scattered flock of French and Indian Catholics, and the succession of priests who attended these missions seems never to have been interrupted for any considerable time. Prairie de Rocher was generally the residence of the clergy, but they resided occasionally at Kaskaskia. Rev. M. Gibault was Vicar-General of the Bishop of Quebec for Illinois from 1770 to 1789; Rev. M. de la Valinière occupied that position in 1789, and Rev. M. Levadoux in 1793. After the appointment of the first American Bishop at Baltimore, the Rev. Gabriel Richard and Rev. John Janin were the missionaries of this region, and in 1799 the Very Rev. Donatian Oliver, as Vicar-General of Bishop Carroll, took charge, and continued to do so till 1827. In 1833 the episcopal see of Detroit was established, and embraced within its vast jurisdiction the whole of Illinois. Shortly afterwards the See of Vincennes, Indiana. was created, and this diocese embraced the northeastern part of Illinois, and continued to do so until the erection of the See of Chicago.

The Fifth Council of Baltimore, which assembled May 14, 1843, proposed to the Holy See the erection of several new episcopal sees in the United States, including that of Chicago, and transmitted nominations to fill the new bishoprics. The Holy See approving of these proposals, the Congregation of the Propaganda, by letters of September 30, 1843, transmitted the Pontifical briefs appointing the nominees of the Council, and among these was the appointment of the Rev. William Quarter as first Bishop of Chicago. He was consecrated together with Bishop Byrne of Little Rock, and Bishop McCloskey, now Archbishop of New York, in the Cathedral at New York, by Archbishop Hughes, assisted by Bishop Fenwick, of Boston, and Bishop Whelan, then of Richmond, March 10, 1844. This ceremony, at which there were present six Bishops and about fifty priests, was one of the most brilliant and imposing sights ever witnessed in this country.

It was with a pang of sorrow that Bishop Quarter tore himself away from his beloved flock at St. Mary's; but his solicitude for his new flock in the West hurried him on to his See. He arrived at Chicago on Sunday morning, May 5, and on the same day offered up the Holy Sacrifice in the old church, and preached in the new, the latter being then unfinished. The Bishop found the church which was to become his Cathedral scarcely half completed, and burdened with about five thousand dollars of debt. Knowing the inability of the congregation, composed mostly of the poor, to discharge this debt, the Bishop and his brother, the Very Rev. Walter J. Quarter, united their private means and paid it. Stimulated by this generous example, the congregation commenced a systematic plan of collections, and it was not long before the first spire erected in Chicago bore aloft the glittering cross, to receive and reflect the first rays of the sun arising above the bosom of the lake, and before long the pious flock worshipped at the foot of the new altar at which their Bishop officiated. But the Bishop was sorely tried by the scarcity of priests to attend to the various congregations of the State. The whole northeastern part of his diocese, having until now been under the care of the See of Vincennes, was supplied from that diocese with priests, and these were recalled to their own diocese on the separation of Illinois from the See of Vincennes. The Bishop had thus to create around him the means necessary for supplying the wants of his needy and extensive diocese, and began at once by bestowing minor orders upon several candidates, and before many weeks had ordained four priests. Among the priests ordained by him were the Rev. Messrs. Kinsella, Breen, and Clowry, now of the archdiocese of New York.

Conscious of the importance of education, especially of that system of education which goes hand in hand with religion, Bishop Quarter commenced opening Catholic schools for the proper education of the Catholic children of his congregation. His schools were the special objects of his solicitude and pride. He founded also the College, which afterwards became the University of St. Mary's of the Lake, and received a charter from the Legislature of Illinois. He also obtained from the Legislature an act incorporating the Bishops of Chicago as a corporation sole, with power of holding property in trust for religious purposes. The visitations of his extended diocese were a prominent feature in the labors of Bishop Quarter, on which occasions he aroused the piety of the people, confirmed many hundreds, including numbers of converts, and initiated movements for the erection of new churches. In his episcopal city of Chicago he opened a retreat towards the close of Lent, 1845, conducting the exercises himself, and preaching twice a day. So fruitful of good were these efforts of the zealous Bishop, that it was impossible to hear the confessions of the crowds that flocked to the holy tribunal. Being desirous of uniting to his University an ecclesiastical Seminary, and finding the resources of his diocese inadequate to this end, he went upon a tour of collection to New York, in April, 1845, and, after an absence of four months, returned with a handsome amount, with which to commence his Seminary. Laying the foundations of his new College and Seminary, October 17, the work was so rapidly pushed forward as to be under roof by November 22. The new Cathedral was finished and solemnly consecrated by the Bishop, on Sunday, October 5, 1845, and from every quarter of his diocese the most encouraging accounts were received of the progress of religion. In September, 1846, desiring to enrich his diocese with the presence and services of the good Sisters of Mercy, he applied to Bishop O'Connor, of Pittsburgh, for a colony of this community, and obtained his request. It has well been said that "the new convent of Chicago prospered to such a degree that it has since covered the face of Illinois with its filiations." In the latter part of the same year he appealed in the most earnest manner to his clergy and laity for aid in raising funds for the new College and Seminary, to which they generously responded. Some extracts from this letter are here introduced as samples of his style, and as evidences of his paternal solicitude for his flock:—

"Although our holy religion advances daily and steadily under the protecting care of Divine Providence, and although the number of the clergy has been considerably increased within the last two years, still are there several congregations in the diocese deprived the whole year round of the consolations of their religion. There are many who have not the happiness to assist even once in the twelve months at the Adorable Sacrifice of the Mass, and numbers die annually without receiving the last rites of the Church, especially in those months when sickness is most prevalent in these Western States; and all this because the clergymen are not sufficiently numerous in this diocese to have one stationed in each congregation. Another melancholy evil, arising also from the scarcity of clergymen, is that the children of Catholic parents in various sections of the State are suffered to grow up without any religious instruction. If the present, in their regard, be painful to reflect upon, the future presents a dismal and a dreary aspect."

. . . . . .

"Are these evils to remain, or shall an effort be made to remove them? Will no effort be made to send to our brethren that are far away from their Father's house, and toiling in bondage, an adviser,—a consoler,—yea, a deliverer? Will no effort be made to secure a pious, a disinterested, a zealous clergy, who may go to the exile in his lone hut, in his solitary and desert home, with words of peace on their lips and blessings in their train, to offer the Adorable Mysteries, to administer the Sacraments, and to instruct in the ways of Salvation? To enable the

Bishop to send missionaries where they are most needed, will not the faithful generously co-operate and assist with their means? Can any alms be better bestowed than those which are given to have the poor relieved, the sick visited, the afflicted and sorrowing soothed and consoled, the ignorant instructed, and the seeds of virtue planted in the youthful breast? Can any alms be more meritorious than those which tend to preserve the soul from eternal ruin? Without the charitable co-operation of the faithful throughout the diocese, little, comparatively can be done by the Bishop; with it much can be effected. Were every adult Catholic in the diocese, or even every head of a family, to contribute but one dollar annually towards the support of the Diocesan Ecclesiastical Seminary, that has been in existence about two years, soon could missionaries be sent to every congregation in the diocese. As yet, however, the Catholics of the diocese have contributed but little towards the support of this Ecclesiastical Seminary. They are now requested to be more considerate hereafter. They are emphatically requested to turn their attention, and to direct their charitable donations to an institution, where the future priests of the diocese are being, and are to be, educated, and from whence many have already gone forth to labor in the vineyard of the Lord. The Ecclesiastical Seminary of the diocese has to depend for support on the voluntary contributions of the faithful. To it, in their turn, are the faithful to look, both now and hereafter, for a supply of zealous missionaries. Will they refuse, then, their fostering care? Will they deny to it support, and still expect to have clergymen sent to them when they are in need?"

The Bishop then closes his letter by a strong appeal

to the clergy for their co-operation and support in a work which he had so much at heart.

He had the consolation of seeing his new Seminary completed and put in operation; and the new University was opened, with appropriate ceremonies, for the reception of pupils, July 4 of this year. The Sisters of Mercy, to whom the Bishop had given up his own residence on their first arrival in Chicago, were now removed to a new convent built for them by him. He had commenced the erection of a number of new churches, which were progressing successfully; and the Church of Illinois was advancing with rapid strides under his active and zealous administration. As an evidence of the growth of the Church within the short period during which he had presided over it, it may be stated that when he summoned his clergymen around him in diocesan· synod, there were thirty-two priests who attended, and nine who were prevented from attending by ill-health or bad roads, making forty-one priests in the new Diocese of Chicago. The Bishop's labors were rewarded, even in his lifetime, by the grateful acknowledgments of his flock; and we are told that when, in 1847, he went on his visitation of the Diocese, he was received with every demonstration of honor and veneration; troops of gentlemen on horseback and in military uniform welcomed him on the roads, as far as sixteen miles from their town, and escorted him into it, amidst the ringing of bells and the hymns of the Catholic school-children. He was thus escorted from town to town, and received everywhere as a father and benefactor of the people.

Bishop Quarter introduced amongst his clergy theological conferences, said to have been the first of the kind in this country, which were held twice a year at

Chicago, Alton, and Galena. At these conferences questions concerning the holy calling and ministerial duties of the clergy, the Rubrics, the Roman Missal, and the Statutes of the Diocese were discussed, and the greatest advantages were derived from this excellent practice. He also encouraged the formation of devotional and pious societies and confraternities for all ages and both sexes, amongst which were Sodalities of the Blessed Virgin, Confraternities of the Immaculate Heart of Mary, and St. Joseph Societies. He labored earnestly for the improvement and advancement of his countrymen, the poor emigrants, who made their way in great numbers to the West, and established benevolent societies for their benefit.

During the Lenten season of 1848, he delivered a course of Lectures on the Marks of the True Church, in his Cathedral; and on Passion Sunday he lectured, as usual, at the last Mass, with ardent and burning eloquence and fervor. After descending from the pulpit he felt indisposed; at Vespers of the same day it was observed that his voice was feeble when he bestowed his benediction upon the people. It was his last blessing; his health failed rapidly from this moment, and yet his death was sudden. He expired on the 10th of April, 1848, after receiving the last rites of the Church, with these words on his lips: "Lord, have mercy on my poor soul!" His death was so calm and peaceful that it was at first mistaken for slumber. He was meditating important enterprises and improvements for the benefit of his diocese, when God called him to his reward in the midst of his labors. Catholics and Protestants united in doing honor to his memory, for they all knew and appreciated his virtues, his labors, and his sacrifices.

RIGHT REV. ANDREW BYRNE, D.D.,

First Bishop of Little Rock, A.D. 1844.*

BISHOP BYRNE was born at Navan, in Ireland, December 5, 1802. His parents were pious and exemplary Catholics, and of a respectable social position. They secured for their son a good primary course of instruction, preparatory to his studies for the ecclesiastical state, which he had at an early age determined to embrace. He next entered the Diocesan Seminary at Navan, founded by the Very Rev. Eugene O'Reilly, Archdeacon of Meath. He was here engaged in his ecclesiastical studies, when Bishop England, who had lately been consecrated for the new See of Charleston, South Carolina, was seeking recruits for that poor and unprovided mission. Young Byrne was one of those who volunteered for this field, and in 1820 he accompanied the Bishop to America. His studies henceforth were prosecuted under the masterly direction of Bishop England. He received from that Prelate the order of deaconship in April, 1827, and on Sunday, November 11, of the same year, the holy order of priesthood. He entered at once upon active missionary duties, and at different times was stationed at various arduous posts in South Carolina and North Carolina. The few Catholics of these States were scattered over an extensive country, and Father Byrne, in administering to their wants,

---

* Authorities: *Catholic Almanac*, 1864; several Nos. of the *Catholic Magazine, Metropolitan, Freeman's Journal, Catholic Diary*, etc., etc.

was compelled to go on frequent, long, and fatiguing journeys, and to endure the fatigues, hungers, and privations of a truly missionary life. His labors and travels sometimes exposed him to exhaustion and disease; and he was on one occasion overtaken by a severe illness, at the residence of Judge Gaston, under whose hospitable roof he received, for several weeks, the most tender and untiring attention. In 1830 he was pastor of St. Mary's Church at Charleston, and was for several years the Vicar-General of Bishop England. In 1833 he went with Bishop England, as his theologian, to the Second Provincial Council of Baltimore.

In 1836 he removed to the city of New York, and was for some time one of the assistant pastors at the Cathedral. He was subsequently appointed pastor of St. James's Church, the duties of which position he zealously and successfully discharged. While pastor of St. James's he was sent by Bishop Hughes, in 1841, to Ireland, on an important mission. While Bishop Hughes was in Ireland, in 1840, he saw, for the first time, some of the schools conducted by the Christian Brothers, and was so much pleased with them that he resolved to make every effort to obtain a community of the Brothers for New York, where such schools were much needed. For this purpose he sent Father Byrne to Ireland; but so few were the teachers and so great the demand for them, that his mission, for the time, proved unsuccessful. His visit to Ireland, his native country, to which he was very warmly attached, was a source of great pleasure to him. and only served to strengthen his conviction of the great political wrongs under which she then suffered, and from which the noble O'Connell was then struggling to emancipate her. Soon after his return, he publicly testified his sympathy and co-operation in the cause of repeal. and became a member of the association organized in this country for that purpose.

The next mission of Father Byrne was at the Church of the Nativity, in New York city, of which he continued the pastor till he opened, March 19, 1841, the new St. Andrew's Church, which was the fruit of his own zeal and energy. This building had long been known and venerated in New York as a temple dedicated to the cause of liberty and justice; it was now to become the holier and more peaceful shrine of the Almighty. It was owing to the untiring exertions and labors of Father Byrne that this commodious building was, in an incredibly short time, altered and transformed into a Christian church. It was dedicated by Bishop Hughes, with solemn ceremonies; Pontifical Mass was celebrated by Bishop Fenwick, of Boston. The former preached on this occasion a sermon, which was long remembered as one of his most brilliant and ablest efforts. A large body of the clergy assisted, and it is remarkable that three of those present, Messrs. Byrne, Quarter, and Bacon, afterwards became Bishops of the American Church. It was in St. Andrew's Church, on Sunday, May 1, 1842, that Father Byrne pronounced an eulogy on the life, character, and services of Bishop England, which was at the time pronounced to be an effort of great power and eloquence. He had himself labored for thirteen years as a missionary priest under the leadership of Bishop England, and was well qualified to recount his splendid labors, to portray his exalted character, and to eulogize his great genius. During the various missionary positions filled by Father Byrne in the city of New York, he was commended alike by Bishop, priest, and layman, for his earnest labors, his priestly and edifying life, and for his sound judgment.

The new diocese of Little Rock, comprising the State of Arkansas, and the Cherokee and Choctaw nations in the Indian Territory, was created in 1844, and Father Byrne, who had gained so much commendation as a priest, was now promoted to the episcopal dignity, and appointed for this new and unprovided see. He was consecrated at St. Patrick's Cathedral, together with the Right Rev. John McCloskey, then Coadjutor to Bishop Hughes, now Archbishop of New York, and the Right Rev. William Quarter, Bishop of Chicago, March 10, 1844, by Bishop Hughes, assisted by Bishop Fenwick, of Boston, and Bishop Whelan, then of Richmond, and a numerous body of the clergy.

The Very Rev. Dr. Power delivered one of his most eloquent and thrilling discourses. The ceremony, which lasted five hours, is thus described in part by an eye-witness: "We cannot attempt to do justice to the scene presented during the performance of this rite. The immense multitude that filled the vast pile, hanging hushed and awe-struck—the high altar, a perfect blaze of radiance—the floor of the sanctuary covered with the kneeling Bishops and clergy, their vestments splendid with gold and colors—the prostrate Bishops elect—the sunshine and air of a most serene heaven streaming in, warm and clear, through the southern windows—the intense stillness within and without, broken only by the thrilling and almost unearthly chant of the choir, amid which it seemed as if the voice of the consecrator ascending on high brought down a present blessing from Him, of whom he seemed at the time a most fitting minister, as in the midst of a flood of light he stood at the great altar, looking more than mortal, so august and glorious was he to behold—his pontificals, chasuble, mitre, and crosier flashing back from their gold and jewels a dazzling effulgence—and with outstretched arm he made the saving sign over the suppliant forms before him ; all that could inspire the painter's hand and the poet's pen, and elevate the Christian heart, combined to form a spectacle to be witnessed with awe, recalled with emotion, but not to be adequately described. . . . . . The ceremony and other services of the day proceeded as described in the *Form*. The *Te Deum* was given with great effect by the choir in the sanctuary. Making the circuit of the church and blessing the people was a rite of very touching character. From the manner in which the nave was thronged, it seemed a hopeless task to attempt to obtain a passage through it; but by the almost incredible efforts of the officers in attendance, admirably seconded by the people, at great personal inconvenience to themselves, a way was made for the five Bishops (the consecrated and the assistants), the entire congregation kneeling, wherever it was possible, to receive the blessing. It was striking to see how, at the approach of the Prelates, the multitudes that had been a moment or two before heaving to and fro in their anxiety to catch a glimpse of the ceremonial, and apparently impenetrable as the stone walls of the Cathedral, slowly receded right and left, and subsiding at once into perfect quietness, knelt, old and young, to receive the episcopal benediction. It was one of those sights, tender, touching, and holy, with which only the Church of Christ, loving mother as she is, can console her children."

In the midst of such a scene, how thrilling to Catholic

hearts and ears must have resounded those glorious words of the *Te Deum* :—

> " Thee, the glorious choir of the apostles,—
> Thee, the righteous band of the prophets,—
> Thee, the white-robed army of the martyrs,—
> Thee, the Holy Church throughout the earth,—
> Oh! Father of infinite majesty, doth praise!"

Immediately after his consecration he repaired to his diocese, and commenced as Bishop the performance of missionary labors, more arduous even than those which he undertook as a young priest in the Carolinas. Some idea may be formed of his occupations and duties from the following account given by himself: " He said the extent, as to space, of his diocese, was at least half of that of all Europe put together; that it would at some remote period be the seat, not of one, but of six dioceses; that in some cases he had to travel, on his visitation from one mission to another, from 700 to 1,000 miles." One of his first undertakings was a trip to Ireland to obtain priests, nuns, and catechists for his diocese, and it was not long before the new Bishop performed the first ordination which had ever taken place in that extensive region of country. This occurred on the Feast of all Saints, November 1, 1845, in the Church of St. Ambrose, at the post of Arkansas, when the Rev. Thomas McKeone was raised to the holy priesthood. In May, 1846, Bishop Byrne repaired to Baltimore and took part in the Sixth Provincial Council, one of the most important in the history of the American Church. He also visited Ireland a second time, to procure additional colaborers and assistants in the cause of religion and education. He procured a colony of Sisters of

Mercy from the Convent of Mercy, in Baggot Street. Dublin. They established St. Mary's Academy at Little Rock, one of the finest educational houses in the West. This became a parent institution in the diocese of Little Rock, and its numbers soon increased so as to enable them to found other institutions of their Order in other places. One of these was at Fort Smith, then on the confines of a frontier civilization, and when Bishop Byrne received the solemn profession of, and conferred the black veil on, three Sisters at this house, in 1853, " he congratulated the community on the successful progress of their Order, then to be found as far as the utmost borders of civilization, close by the encampments of the wild sons of the forest." The Bishop's labors were constant and wide-spread. At one time we hear of his being in New York raising funds for a projected College of St. Andrew, at Little Rock, and next we hear of his being at some remote part of Arkansas dedicating a new church. An account of one of these new churches, erected as recently as 1858, relates to the church at Napoleon, Arkansas, on the banks of the Mississippi, and informs us that there was then no other church or priest for two hundred miles on either bank of the river, and that the congregation were obliged, for three months in the year, to reach the church " in skiffs and dug-outs." Yet in such a remote and scattered congregation the erection of their church, and the providing of the money to pay for it, was only the work of three months. In 1856 Bishop Byrne attended the first Provincial Council of New Orleans. In the midst of his active and useful labors he was, in the wise and inscrutable ways of Providence, called to receive his reward in a better world. His death occurred in 1862. The growth of the Church in the Southwest was wonderful during his episcopate. In the very year of his death he himself stated, "that whilst, in 1842-43, the number of churches or chapels was in the whole but four, in 1862 there were seventeen, with fifty stations; that whilst the priests then were only four, they are now twenty-four, with six ecclesiastical students; that whilst there was then no religious institute, there are now four, with twelve schools and seminaries for both sexes; and that whilst the Catholic population was but five thousand, it now numbers upwards of fifty thousand."

Bishop Byrne's zeal projected many noble works, which his untimely death arrested. Among these was the intended College of St. Andrew, at Fort Smith, for which he procured a fine tract of land a mile square, with funds contributed entirely by collections made by him outside his diocese. To the College was to be attached a diocesan house, in which the faithful missionary, exhausted by labor or disease, could always find a home for rest and restoration to health. He also proposed to establish immediately, in connection with the College, a colony of Christian Brothers. He had also obtained the promise of a fine female religious foundation for Van Buren. His efforts to promote Catholic immigration to his diocese were unceasing, and his intelligent and well-exerted measures to this end proved in his day, as well as afterwards, a great benefit to the Southwest.

RIGHT REV. WILLIAM TYLER, D.D.,

First Bishop of Hartford, A.D. 1844.*

THE antiquity of the Church, over which Bishop Tyler presided, extends back to the days of Vikings and Northmen, and to the twelfth century.† The ages of pagan darkness which followed left the continent of America virtually undiscovered; and although it was Catholic faith, zeal, and enterprise that afterwards gave the New World to mankind, this portion of it passed under the harsh but earnest sway of Puritanism. Although the labors of Bishop Eric, the Latin hymns of the early Church, and the Holy Mass, had consecrated the land to God while England was Roman Catholic, and before the disastrous days of the religious revolt of the sixteenth century, the permanent settlement of the country was left for a class of English Protestants, who appropriately called their colonies *New England*, for the heresy of the mother-country had grown old, as all heresies do, in a short time, for want of true vitality; and her sons soon discovered that heresy, in order to maintain itself, must be ever in a state of revolt, novelty, and variation. Discarded by its mother-heresy in England, and persecuted by its unnatural parent, Puritanism sought a new home; but it brought with it the lessons of its infancy, a hatred of Catholicity, an abomination for the Church of Rome. The Puritans and their descendants for cen-

---

* Compiled chiefly from Bishop Tyler's Journal, and other original sources; *The Catholic Almanac*, 1850, etc., etc.

† See Life of Bishop Eric, *ante*.

turies were educated to regard the Church of Bishop Eric as the Anti-Christ, the mother of error and sin; and it was regarded as a service to God to persecute His own Divine Spouse. The American Revolution prepared them for toleration, although toleration was not universally enacted by the law; while socially intolerance prevailed. There was much ignorance in New England as to what the Catholic Church really was. But events were maturing which tended greatly to remove this ignorance and banish intolerance. In the course of time Catholic bishoprics sprang up in and around New England; the saintly examples of such men as Cheverus and Matignon at Boston, and the zealous labors, sermons, and writings of such men as Kohlman and Fenwick, Varela and Power, at New York, produced a profound impression upon the more thoughtful and earnest minds of New England, resulting in numerous conversions, especially among the New England ministers. Among these there was no instance so remarkable as the conversion of the Barber family, to which Bishop Tyler belonged. It was thus that New England supplied from her own sons future priests and Bishops to labor for the conversion of their countrymen, and the Church, in her wisdom, selected such to struggle with and labor to overcome that mass of prejudice and ignorance, which seemed to present insuperable barriers to the progress of the Faith. Bishop Tyler was one of those who literally had to evoke from nothing that Church which he was appointed to govern; and who, embarrassed by his own and the poverty of the Church, with few priests, churches, or schools, without resources, and with the united sentiment of the community arrayed against him, had to struggle with untold obstacles.

in the service of religion. With a constitution already impaired by an insidious disease, the cares, labors, trials, and solicitudes of the episcopacy exhausted his remaining strength, and it was with humble and uncomplaining submission that he devoted his sinking energies and expiring labors to his people, his Church, and his God.

William Tyler was born June 5, 1806, in the town of Derby, Vermont, and removed with his parents to Claremont, New Hampshire, in his early youth. His father was a respectable, well-to-do farmer, who was, like the farmers of New England generally, accustomed to perform the labor of his farm with his own hands, assisted by his sons. William was a devoted son, and took great pleasure in relieving and assisting the toils of his father, whose health was feeble. His mother was a daughter of the Rev. Daniel Barber, and sister of the Rev. Virgil Barber, who had been Congregational ministers of repute in New England, and afterwards became ministers of the Episcopal Church. Their change from Congregationalism to Episcopalianism was but a step in their progress to Rome, the centre of Christian truth and unity. Their minds once set upon the inquiry, and their hearts earnestly longing for peace and union with God, they eagerly read the controversies which occurred between some of the eminent Catholic divines of that day and prominent Protestants, and which created quite an "awakening" to the truth among many of the Protestant ministry. Thus, about the same time, 1816, the Rev. Mr. Kewley, formerly of Middletown, but then rector of the Protestant Episcopal Church of St. George, in the city of New York, the Rev. Mr. White, of Waterbury, the Rev. Daniel Barber, of Claremont, and his son, the Rev. Virgil Barber, with their families and several of their friends, received the light of divine grace, and earnestly and gratefully followed, till led by it to the bosom of the Catholic Church.

The conversion of Miss Allen, daughter of the distinguished American general, Ethan Allen, a former follower and parishioner of the Rev. Daniel Barber, seems to have made a deep impression on his mind. In 1807, Mr. Barber, a Congregational minister at that time, baptized Miss Allen, then twenty-one years of age, in that sect; this young lady soon afterwards went to Montreal and entered the Academy of the Sisters of the Congregation of Notre Dame; there she became a Catholic, and devoting herself to God, joined the Community of Hospital Nuns at the Hotel-Dieu. Such was the impressive character of her piety and devotion, that in 1819, when on her death-bed, her example and saintly resignation led to the conversion of the Protestant physician who attended her. Her singular example and exalted virtues deeply affected her former pastor, Mr. Barber, who generously sacrificed all for the truth of which he became convinced. The sacrifice of all worldly considerations, which he and his associates made, was complete. Among their friends and former parishioners was sorrow and deep lament, that minds so pure, pious, and fervent, should have been demented. In the farewell address which the Rev. Daniel Barber made to his congregation, who heard with tears the announcement of his intended departure from amongst them, he said: "I now, my friends, retire to the shades of poverty. May the faults which I have committed while among you be written on the sands of the sea-shore, that the next returning wave may wash them into oblivion."

Mr. Daniel Barber had two sons and one daughter. His oldest son, the Rev. Virgil Barber, had one son and four daughters; all of these were received into the Church by the illustrious Bishop Cheverus, of Boston. Mr. and Mrs. Virgil Barber with one accord resolved to abandon all, to separate from each other, in order to become united with God, and to enter into His exclusive service. For this purpose the husband went to Rome in 1817, to obtain the necessary permission, which was granted by the Sovereign Pontiff. He there embraced a religious life, was ordained priest, and after two years returned to America with the proper permission for Mrs. Barber to enter and become a member of a religious house. She became a novice of the Visitation Nuns at Georgetown, in the District of Columbia; their four daughters were received as scholars in the Visitation Academy at Georgetown, not knowing that their mother was a novice in the adjoining convent; and their only son, Samuel, was received as a scholar at Georgetown College. When the mother's time of probation had expired, "the five children were brought to the chapel to witness her profession, and at the same time, on the steps of the altar, their father devoting himself to God as a member of the Society of Jesus! At this touching and unexpected sight the poor children burst into sobs, believing themselves deserted on earth. But their Father who is in Heaven watched over them; He inspired the four daughters with the desire of embracing the religious state; and three of them joined the Ursulines, one at Boston, one at Quebec, and one at Three Rivers. The fourth made her profession among the Visitandines of Georgetown; their brother Samuel was received into the Society of Jesus," pursued his studies at Georgetown.

Frederick, and Rome, and he and his venerable father became useful and distinguished members of the Society, in which they died with every sentiment of tender piety and exalted devotion.

A year or so after the reception into the Church of her father, the Rev. Daniel Barber, and of her brother, the Rev. Virgil Barber, Mrs. Tyler followed their example, accompanied by her three sons and four daughters. All these were received into the Church at Claremont. Of her sons, William afterwards became a priest, and was created first Bishop of Hartford, and the four daughters became Sisters of Charity. It was thus that God rewarded the faith and sacrifices of this excellent family in an extraordinary manner, by bestowing upon them vocations to become His own.

William Tyler was about fifteen years old when he became a Catholic. His uncle, the Rev. Virgil Barber, in aid of what was most needed at the time, and wherein he considered he could do the greatest amount of good, opened near the former parochial residence of his aged father a Catholic classical seminary. Here William Tyler became the first student, not only in point of time, but more especially in point of excellence. His merits soon raised him to the responsible office of prefect of the school and conductor of the studies. At this early age he developed not only his characteristic industry and earnestness, but also his devotion to the interests of others. His recreations and holidays were devoted to manual labor on his father's farm, and in assisting his parents to support the family. The pride with which he recorded at the time the fact, that when about the age of eighteen years, he obtained his father's permission to depend exclusively upon his own labors and exertions for his support, is a proof of his native independence and energy of character. While thus engaged in mental and bodily labor, he found time to join in the innocent sports, the social amusements, and out-door exercises and enterprises of the neighborhood. He also cultivated instrumental music, less as an amusement than as a means of adding to the effect and beauty of the divine service, at which he was accustomed to accompany the organ with his flute or French horn. His amusements were mingled generally with religious sentiment, for he informs us that he used to employ some of his leisure hours in stringing rosaries for the pious neighbors; and on one occasion he lost the ticket or reward in his French studies, by the intentness and zeal with which he was engaged in making little crosses for his companions and friends. Shortly after he became a Catholic he began to keep a youthful journal, in which he recorded the thoughts and incidents of each day, a habit which he resumed to some extent when he became a Bishop. In this little journal religious subjects constitute a prominent feature, and it opens with an account of the remarkable conversion of a man, who, while traveling from Boston to Claremont, was beset by robbers, and other imminent dangers, and who, though a Protestant, knew of no other means of extricating himself than by the sign of the cross; impressing this sacred sign upon his forehead and breast, he passed safely from amidst the dangers which beset him, and from that moment was a Catholic. He notes from time to time the occasions when he had the happiness of approaching the sacraments, of listening to impressive sermons, or of assisting in decorating the church for divine service at Christmas and other holy seasons. With true devotion to his father, whom he tenderly loved, he offered up for his spiritual benefit, now a penitential fast, and again a Holy Communion. He generously attributes the first suggestion of these pious offerings to his good mother. The earnestness and strong religious tendency of his mind at this early period of his life, are well exemplified in a letter which he wrote to his brother, then living in Georgia, from which we take the following extract:—

"Now, my dear brother, let me warn you not to place too much affection and dependence on the things of this life. Although you now are prosperous, still you may meet with a reverse of fortune; and even if you could be sure of prosperity and all the blessings this world could afford, what comparison could they bear to the happiness or misery of eternity? . . . . Our time here at the longest is but short, and we are daily liable to the strokes of Death. At the longest our life here is but short; a striking proof of this lately occurred in Cornish: a young man, who had lived in a Catholic family, and had obtained a knowledge of the Catholic religion, but for reasons known to himself deferred his conversion. But the tyrant Death did not wait for him, and he was ushered into the other world, unprepared as he was. I hope that you find some leisure from your business for serious meditation; and there is one time which, of all others, is perhaps the most productive of meditation—I mean the silent hours of night, after we retire to rest. Of this you cannot be deprived, and I hope you employ it for the benefit of your soul. How do you pass the season of Lent? As a Catholic, or as a Protestant? I know that it is difficult for one in the situation you are in to live a regular life, but I hope that God will give you grace to walk in the path of duty."

Under the instruction of his accomplished uncle, William Tyler became a fine classical scholar. Latin was the prescribed language of the school, all others being prohibited in the conversations of the students. French and Greek were also studied, and young Tyler's journal shows that he received many tickets of merit in all these. His proficiency in Latin and French, and his fondness for his studies, were exhibited in the Latin and French letters which he addressed to his brother in Georgia, in preference to writing in English.

But it was chiefly with religious subjects that his mind was at this time occupied. The exciting scenes through which his grandfather and uncle had passed, the religious controversies of the day, the conversion of so many of his family and relatives, the sacrifices made by them for the Faith, the social ostracism to which on many occasions they had to submit, and the zealous efforts they engaged in to establish a congregation, build a church, and attain the enjoyment of the sacraments, all tended to impress the mind of young Tyler deeply with religious sentiments, and to identify him with the Catholic Church in New England. He who at the age of sixteen had to defend the Catholic doctrines and practices which he had embraced, among his companions and school-mates, felt at the maturer age of twenty an inward vocation to the Sanctuary, and to the service and propagation of the Church of his adoption. Without means or resources, and necessitated to work for his support, he encountered many obstacles in attaining this cherished object. The following letter to his brother reveals the anxious sentiments and noble perseverance with which he encountered the obstacles standing in the way of his great purpose:—

"How often do we meet with disappointments, when our hopes and expectations are at their highest point! You have seen how various and changeable the course of life is, how vague and fluctuating fortune, and how great inconstancy among friends. You have been made acquainted with my intention of becoming a priest, and that the means by which I expected to attain this was by the assistance of the Rev. Superior, Mr. Barber, in retaining and promoting me as his assistant in the school. I have already informed you of the loss of expectation. Now, what course shall I pursue? For myself, I know not where another year will find me. Pa thinks that I had better agree with uncle Daniel to procure me a situation in a store at Boston, where he is soon going. This is far from my wishes, since I have so seriously engaged my mind in the pursuit which appeared to me to be the one pointed out for me by Divine Providence. I do not like to give out; but if it is the Divine will that I should become a priest, there will be some way for my attaining it."

That Divine Providence, in whom he so confidently trusted, did provide for him a way that led to the Sanctuary. A friend, and one of the best and truest of friends, was raised up for him in the person of the Right Rev. Benedict Joseph Fenwick, Bishop of Boston, who had already been favorably impressed, by observation and report, of his assiduity in study and of the goodness of his life. About this time the Rev. Virgil Barber went upon the mission among the Indians of Maine. Invited by the Bishop to Boston, young Tyler proceeded to that city in August, 1826, and commenced the new life before him by a fervent approach to the Holy Sacraments. He continued his preparatory studies at Boston, residing with the Bishop, and it is said partly in Canada, until the attainment of his twenty-first year. June 5, 1827, and two days thereafter his journal states that he commenced the study of dogmatic theology. He prosecuted his theological studies under the immediate eye and instruction of Bishop Fenwick, by whom he was raised to the dignity of the priesthood in Pentecost week, 1828.

He was stationed, after his ordination, at the Cathedral Church of Boston, and discharged the pastoral duties in that congregation for several years with devotion, zeal, and edification. He also spent one year on missionary duty, at the Catholic settlement of Aroostook, Maine. The remaining years, before his consecration as Bishop, he spent at the Cathedral of Boston, where he is still affectionately and gratefully remembered by the elder members of the congregation. The zeal with which he performed his sacred duties, and his unostentatious charity to the poor, rendered him very much esteemed and popular amongst his people. He exercised a great and most beneficial influence over the youth of the congregation. His sermons were pleasing and effective, not long, and were delivered from carefully prepared notes before him. He was appointed by Bishop Fenwick his Vicar-General, an office which he filled up to the time of his consecration. "From the moment of his ordination," as is well said in his obituary,* "it may be said with truth that '*he had been delivered, through the grace of God, unto the work which he accomplished.*' All who knew him felt at once, and may testify, that, unmindful of himself, and of all human applause, and of all worldly

---

* *Catholic Almanac*, 1850.

advantages, he had constantly but one object in view— the salvation of souls and the greater glory of his Divine Master; and the Catholics of Boston will well remember how, during many years, in sickness and in health, by day and by night, he was ever ready to serve their souls in a never-changing spirit of meekness and of zeal; and '*how he kept back nothing that was profitable to them, but preached to them and taught them publicly, from house to house, testifying to all penance towards God and faith in our Lord Jesus Christ.*'"

The Fifth Council of Baltimore, which assembled May 14, 1843, in order to meet the increasing demands of the Church, requested of the Holy See the erection of several new episcopal sees, and amongst these was the erection of a new see at Hartford, embracing within its jurisdiction the States of Connecticut and Rhode Island, for which they nominated the Rev. William Tyler as its first Bishop. The Holy See approving, the Congregation of the Propaganda sent their letters of September 30, 1843, containing the Pontifical briefs making the appointments requested, and amongst them was the appointment of Bishop Tyler to the See of Hartford. The new Bishop received the bulls of his appointment February 14, 1844, and was consecrated March 17, at the Cathedral in Baltimore, by the Right Rev. Benedict Joseph Fenwick, assisted by the Right Rev. Richard V. Whelan, then Bishop of Richmond, and the Right Rev. Andrew Byrne, Bishop of Little Rock. The Most Rev. Archbishop Eccleston was present only at the commencement of the ceremony, in consequence of the death of his mother on the day previous.

Bishop Tyler arrived at his see, Hartford, April 12, 1844. His Cathedral, the only church in Hartford, was that of the Holy Trinity, a wooden structure seventy feet long and forty feet wide, and yielding from its pew rents about eleven hundred dollars per annum, of which three hundred and fifty dollars were paid to a schoolteacher. The pastoral residence adjoining belonged to the priest in charge, from whom the Bishop arranged to purchase it. Leaving Hartford under the pastoral care of Rev. Mr. Brady, the Bishop proceeded in a few days to Providence, Rhode Island, which, as the principal city of the diocese, he selected as his episcopal residence. The whole diocese contained but six priests. Providence contained four times as many Catholics as Hartford, and the Church of Sts. Peter and Paul became the Cathedral. The Bishop commenced at once the arduous work before him, a prominent part of which consisted in providing churches and priests, schools and teachers, where there were none. He lost no time in laying the needy condition of his diocese before the noble Leopoldine Society at Vienna, and on August 7, 1844, received a remittance of valuable aid from the Most Rev. Vincent Edward, Prince and Archbishop of Vienna. He not only performed all the duties of priest at Providence, hearing confessions, visiting the sick, and instructing the ignorant, but he began visiting all the portions of his diocese, and acted as the pastor of congregations which had no pastor of their own, visiting them as often as he could. He administered confirmation at various points, and made it a practice to record the name of every person confirmed by him. In May, 1846, Bishop Tyler took part in the Sixth Council of Baltimore, one of the most important councils held in this country. Notwithstanding the poverty of his diocese and the many demands upon his meagre resources, he succeeded in greatly enlarging and improving his Cathedral of Sts. Peter and Paul, at Providence, and in rendering it one of the finest churches in the country. He dedicated it on Sunday, April 11, 1847, on which occasion the Right Rev. Bishop Fitzpatrick celebrated a Pontifical Mass, and the Rev. Dr. Ryder, President of the College of the Holy Cross, preached the dedication sermon, in the presence of an immense crowd that flocked to this spacious temple. Bishop Tyler labored with untiring zeal to lay the foundations of the Church in New England, and to present her dogmas, services, and ceremonials, in the most becoming and imposing manner possible to him, before a people unaccustomed to them and greatly prejudiced against them. By his efforts the clergy of the diocese were doubled in number, and many congregations received the services of pastors; several churches were erected and new missions opened. One who knew him well writes to us, alluding to his episcopal career, that, "In this dignified position he was beloved on account of his meekness, humility, and charity. He was respected by all on account of his dignified and religious manners; in his conversation, and even in his dress, it was evident to all that he was a holy and devoted Bishop of the Catholic Church." Bishop Tyler was venerated by all who knew him well "as a truly saintly man." He was a man of great simplicity and purity of character, kind, gentle, and charitable; yet one who knew how to be stern when necessary. No Prelate could have given greater evidences than he did, under the trying circumstances in which he was placed, of self-denial and devotedness to his people. He was also remarkable for his humility, which in one of his fine appearance, blended with a retired manner and saintly expression of countenance, deeply impressed all who saw him. The opportunity for achieving results brilliant in the sight of men had not arrived in Connecticut and Rhode Island during the time that Bishop Tyler occupied the episcopal chair in that diocese. To have attempted these would have elicited an opposition that might have checked the progress of the Church in New England for several years. The solid foundations for the future superstructure were to be quietly and modestly laid, and the minds of the people gradually made familiar with the existence and benign influence of the Church in their midst. The way was to be opened for more showy and productive results thereafter. Bishop Tyler, having himself sprung from the people among whom he was appointed to perform this difficult mission, knew well how to proceed in its accomplishment. While zealous in the discharge of his episcopal duties, he never appeared as an obtruder or propagandist, preferring to reach the minds and hearts of men by example and by charity. While regardful of the dignity of his office, he humbly and devoutly discharged all the duties and labors of a missionary priest, and went every month to perform missionary duties in some unprovided portion of his diocese. The want of means greatly diminished the results of his zealous efforts, but he accomplished great results with the means at his disposal. His feeble health greatly embarrassed his labors, but did not diminish them, for he labored with unabated industry and devotion through many years of ill-health, and to the last. That he led a somewhat retired life resulted from the necessity of his position and the feebleness of his health. Towards the last he seldom went out, except on duty or business. These never went neglected, even when his strength was scarcely equal to the occasion He was scrupulously exact in the performance of every religious duty. The same fidelity with which he discharged his office as Master of Studies in the Seminary at Claremont, he evinced during his priesthood and episcopacy. His crucifix and books were his companions ; mental prayer his delight. In the confessional, ever zealous, he was a father and true spiritual guide; at the bedside of the sick ever attentive ; and to the poor, though always in secret, he was most generous. His devotion to the Blessed and Immaculate Virgin was remarkable during life, and conspicuous in his last moments.

About the time of his appointment to the episcopacy he caught a severe cold, which settled on his lungs, and from that time was gradually, but painfully, undermining his constitution, so that during the five years and three months of his episcopate he labored and suffered in the cause of religion. His anxiety for his flock, the difficulties growing out of the poverty of his diocese, and the double labors of priest and Bishop which he underwent, hastened the ravages of consumption. He attended the Seventh Council of Baltimore, which assembled May 6, 1849, with certificates of his physicians that he could not survive much longer, and he requested permission to resign. The Prelates there assembled sanctioned, instead of his resignation, the appointment of a coadjutor, and recommended for that position the choice of Bishop Tyler himself, the Right Rev. Dr. O'Reilly.

Returning from the Council, he was taken ill with a rheumatic fever, which terminated his existence. On the morning after his return to Providence, which was Pentecost Sunday, he attempted once more to offer up the august sacrifice of the Mass. When he arrived at the sanctuary his strength of body was unequal to the devout desires and holy longings of his soul. Sitting near the altar, he assisted at the sacred mysteries which he was unable to celebrate. Immediately afterwards he laid himself upon the altar of his own death-bed, from which he was to offer the sacrifice of his being. During his last illness his only thoughts were God, his people, and his own salvation. The disease proceeded to the brain two days before his death, and deprived him of reason. In his moments of delirium, his only care and his only sorrow were that he could not work for the souls intrusted to his care, and he frequently implored for permission to return to the labors of his office, from which he imagined himself withdrawn.

A remarkable circumstance occurred just before his death. For two days he was unconscious, and did not recognize any of the devoted and sorrowing members of his clergy that attended at his bedside. The Right Rev. Bishop Fitzpatrick now arrived and was also unrecognized. Kneeling in prayer at the side of his departing friend and colleague, Bishop Fitzpatrick, to his delight and surprise, saw the dying Prelate open his eyes, and with his accustomed smile recognize his friend. He enjoyed four hours of as perfect consciousness as he had ever had during health, and availed himself of it to communicate to Bishop Fitzpatrick all the necessary information as to how he had arranged the affairs of the diocese, where all was to be seen recorded, and other matters of a spiritual character which he desired his col league to know. "At the end of which," says one who witnessed the impressive scene,* "he closed his eyes

---

* Letter of Rev. James Fitton to Right Rev. Bishop McFarland.

and never spoke audibly more, save at times those pious aspirations and holy ejaculations of a departing saint." He died June 18, 1849, in the forty-fifth year of his age. The funeral services of the deceased Prelate were solemn and affecting. The Right Rev. Bishop Fitzpatrick celebrated the Requiem Mass, assisted by the venerable Father McElroy, S.J., and the Rev. John J. Williams, now Bishop of Boston, and other clergymen. The sermon, by the Rev. Mr. Wiley, of Providence, was frequently interrupted by the tears and sobs of the eloquent speaker, and by those of the crowded congregation, who showed that they felt the loss of a devoted father and friend.

"In the episcopacy," writes a cotemporary of the Bishop,* "he was distinguished by the same unassuming worth, the same deep wisdom, the same untiring zeal, which had marked his career in the priesthood. Under his prudent care and assiduous labor, religion grew up with silent but rapid growth in every part of his extensive diocese, and his piety, his union with God, drew down from heaven those graces which gave increase to that which he had planted and watered with apostolic toils. . . . . He was thus proceeding in the discharge of his episcopal duties with unremitting assiduity, and with a success proportioned to his zeal, when it pleased the Lord of the Vineyard to call him from his labors and invite him to sweet repose. Although enfeebled and almost exhausted in strength, he attended, with great edification to his colleagues, the late Council at Baltimore.

"After the absolution, the body was borne on the

---

* *Catholic Observer*, June, 1849.

shoulders of six priests to its final resting-place, a tomb under the high altar of the church. There will the mortal remains of the sainted Bishop Tyler repose till the last trump shall sound. His spirit, we trust, is in the bosom of God, reaping the reward of many years of devotedness, charity, zeal, faith, and unfeigned piety—of all those virtues which distinguished him even among the most pious; and often will his devoted flock come to offer on his tomb a prayer for his repose, and a resolution to imitate his virtues. May our souls also die the death of the just, and may our last moments be like unto his."

RIGHT REV. IGNATIUS ALOYSIUS REYNOLDS, D.D.,

Second Bishop of Charleston, A.D. 1844.

THE parents of Bishop Reynolds emigrated from Maryland, and settled in Kentucky, towards the close of the last century. Attracted by the religious and educational advantages which the Abbé Flaget's exertions had called into existence at Bardstown, they selected a farm in Nelson County, near that city, as their home, and here the future Bishop was born, August 22, 1798. The cabin in which his birth took place, situated about three miles from Bardstown, was, until within a few years past, pointed out as an object of interest to Catholics visiting that neighborhood. The parents of Bishop Reynolds were remarkable for their piety, and the humble home in which he was reared was a nursery of virtue and devotion. To these excellent parents, and especially to the tender and pious teachings of his good mother at home, while the father was engaged in the honest toil of husbandry on his farm, he attributed through life, under God, all that he possessed of devotion, religious training, and nobility of character. The affectionate and grateful tributes which he so delighted to pay to the memory of his parents in his after-life,

---

* Authorities: *Reminiscences of a Lay Catholic in Kentucky*, by B. J. Webb; *Catholic Almanac* of 1856; *Substance of a Discourse on Bishop Reynolds*, by Rev. C. I. White, D.D., published in *The Metropolitan*, Vol. III., 1855; *Life of Bishop Flaget*, and *Sketches of Kentucky*, by Archbishop Spalding; *Catholic Magazines, Metropolitans, Freeman's Journals*, etc., etc.

were at once an honor to parents and son. It was under their Christian training that young Reynolds' earliest thoughts and aspirations were turned heavenward, and that the holy vocation to the sanctuary was first infused into his soul. They also bestowed the greatest attention in their power, not only on his religious education, but also on his instruction in human learning. Gifted with a ready power of acquisition and a high order of intellect, he availed himself successfully of all the means of education within his reach. One of the first fruits of the exemplary influences by which he was surrounded was a religious vocation, embraced with alacrity and zeal by himself, and hailed no less by his worthy parents with joy and gratitude to God for so signal a favor and honor bestowed upon their name and household. At an early age he entered the Theological Seminary at Bardstown, and was probably one of the first students of that institution. Here, under the saintly Father David, its founder, he received the best of instruction in sacred lore, and the purest teachings in Christian virtue. In December, 1821, he repaired to St. Mary's Seminary at Baltimore, then in charge of the good and able Father Tessier. Here he not only made a complete course of theology, under the zealous and learned Sulpitians, which he accomplished with great success, but also enjoyed the advantages of a thorough and profound training in the physical sciences, under such professors as Wheeler and Chevigné. It was thus that to the learning of the theologian he added the accomplishments of the chemist and mathematician. Having made his course with distinction, and acquired every qualification for the sacred ministry, he was ordained by Archbishop Maréchal, at Baltimore, October 24, 1823.

Immediately after his ordination Father Reynolds returned to Kentucky, and was soon afterwards appointed Professor in St. Joseph's College, Bardstown, and was subsequently president of this institution for several years. By his energy and able management he cleared the College of its pecuniary difficulties, and by his wise administration and firm and judicious discipline he elevated the character of the institution, and secured its permanence and future usefulness. On the appointment of Dr. Francis Patrick Kenrick as Bishop Coadjutor of Philadelphia, he was appointed by Bishop Flaget Professor in the Theological Seminary, as successor to Dr. Kenrick. He was thus compelled to resign his presidency of St. Joseph's College, in which institution, however, he never ceased to take the liveliest interest. In addition to his duties as professor of theology, he labored also on the mission. Bardstown and vicinity became, for several years, the scene of his labors; and by his zeal, energy, self-sacrifice, and noble example, as well as by his fine eloquence and brilliant talents, he accomplished great good among the people. He did not confine himself to mere parochial duties; there was no service for the good of his neighbor, and the relief of temporal or spiritual distress, that he did not render with a generous hand and heart.

When the cholera broke out at Bardstown and in the neighboring counties, in 1833, Father Reynolds was among the foremost to devote himself to the care of the sick and dying, and to their spiritual and temporal relief. He not only devoted himself to this charitable cause, but went to bring Sisters of Charity to recruit the ranks of those angels of mercy, already thinned by the pestilence. In the midst of disease and death he stood firmly at his post, like a good pastor, and even forcibly interposed himself between danger and the saintly Bishop Flaget, who, at the first outbreak of the pestilence, rushed to the relief and consolation of his flock. The Sisters of Charity, who ever distinguished themselves in the diocese of Bardstown, as they did everywhere in times of public calamity, were always sure to find in Father Reynolds not only a warm and active friend, but also an indefatigable co-laborer in their works of relief and mercy. It was thus a welcome charge, added to his already heavy missionary duties, and an appointment most agreeable to the Sisterhood of the diocese, when he was designated as their ecclesiastical Superior, on the resignation of Bishop David.

He was also for many years Vicar-General to Bishop Flaget, between whom and himself a warm and mutual friendship subsisted. He labored to lighten the burden and cares of his aged and holy Bishop, while, at the same time, the pious example of the latter and of Bishop David, and the lessons of experience and wisdom that fell from their lips, were treasured in his heart, and served to prepare and sustain him in the arduous episcopate, which was so soon to be placed upon his own shoulders. When, in 1841, the Episcopal See of Kentucky was transferred from Bardstown to Louisville, Father Reynolds, who was then Vicar-General, paid a visit to Europe in the beginning of 1841, to recruit his health, which severe missionary labors had impaired, and on his return preceded the Bishop to Louisville, and was most zealous in preparing everything for his reception. From this time till 1844 Louisville was his mission, to which were also united the duties of Vicar-General. In the congregations of Louisville, as in those of Bardstown, his zeal and eloquence accomplished good results for religion; and few among the host of eminent missionary priests produced by Kentucky succeeded better in leading sinners to penance, and in winning souls to God.

It was while thus engaged that he received from Rome the bulls of his appointment as Bishop of Charleston, and successor to the illustrious Bishop England, having been named for this high honor by the Fathers of the Fifth Provincial Council of Baltimore, in May, 1843. The reluctance with which he accepted the mitre, and the sacrifice such acceptance necessitated, are thus expressed in the first Pastoral he addressed to the Diocese of Charleston:—

"The mysterious Providence of God has sent us among you as your Bishop, to watch over and govern you, 'as being to render account of your souls.' (Heb. xiii. 17.) It were difficult to express the feelings and thoughts that fill and even overwhelm our heart and mind on this occasion. We had many sacrifices to make in accepting the awful duties of the episcopacy; nor was it one of the least to give up our own judgment, and suffer ourselves to be guided and directed by others in an affair so important to us and to you. And surely we had never obtained our consent to assume the mitre, if faith did not teach us that the Saviour of men is pleased to choose 'the foolish things of this world, that he may confound the wise; and the weak things, that he may confound the strong; and the things that are not, that he may bring to naught the things that are; that no flesh may glory in his sight. For Christ Jesus is made unto us *wisdom*, and justice, and sanctification, and redemption.' (1 Cor. i. 27.) And yet it is only with fear and trembling that we appear among you, clothed in the full vesture of the priesthood, and holding the staff of pastoral authority. Our hope is in Him who enlightens the blind, strengthens the weak, heals the infirm, and raises even the dead to life. And oh! how consoling it is, in the sorrows and doubts of our pilgrimage here, 'to cast our care upon the Lord,'—to feel and cherish the sense of our nothingness,—of our entire dependence upon God; and in the human loneliness of our sorrows and anxieties, to throw ourselves upon the bosom of divine love—to seek comfort, strength, and light in the eternal and infinitely perfect Being from Whom we received existence, and in Whom alone we can find repose. Divine faith! how inestimable thy gifts! how cheering thy heavenly influence! Thy light is upon every path, and thy comfort to every state and condition of life; the rich and the poor, the learned and the unlearned, the great and the small, the master and the slave, the priest and the layman, are alike taught, guided, and cheered by thee."

Bishop Reynolds was consecrated in the Cathedral of Cincinnati, on the Feast of St. Joseph, March 19, 1844, by Archbishop Purcell, assisted by Bishop Miles, of Nashville, and Dr. O'Connor, then Bishop of Pittsburgh. The following allusion to this event, and description of Bishop Reynolds, is from the pen of one of his intimate friends: "*—

"In person, Dr. Reynolds was a noble specimen of dignified manhood. . . . . . . He was a natural orator. Together with an excellent mind, enlightened by study and research, a good voice, and a distinct articulation, he possessed, as well in his manner in the

---

* *Lecture* by B. J. Webb, of Louisville, 1867.

pulpit as in his method of arranging the matter of his sermons, that peculiar power of fixing and retaining the attention of his hearers which gives force to oratory. I was present at his consecration, which took place in conjunction with that of Dr. Henni, the present pious Bishop of Milwaukee, in the Cathedral Church of Cincinnati. It was his wish to receive this rite at the hands of his own Bishop, Dr. Flaget. The great age and the weak physical condition of this saintly Prelate prevented the accomplishment of his desire. He was present, however, at his consecration, and I shall never forget a circumstance that took place immediately after the benediction given by the newly-consecrated Prelates. I observed, from where I sat, the tottering figure of our late saintly Prelate, supported on either side by the consecrating Bishop and one of his assistants, being led up the steps of the high altar. A moment after, in accents so feeble that they could scarcely be heard where I sat, he intoned the initiatory words of the solemn episcopal benediction—*Sit nomen domini*. When he turned to give the blessing, every knee in the vast Cathedral was bent to receive it, whether of Bishops, priests, or people. I could but remember at the time what was said by one of the Popes to a young Englishman, who appeared to hesitate when others accompanying were kneeling to receive his blessing: ' Kneel down, my son; an old man's blessing will not hurt you.' "

After his consecration he proceeded by way of Baltimore to Charleston. His first act was a feeling and eloquent Pastoral Letter, addressed to his new flock, breathing all those sentiments of humility, faith, love of souls, and inspiring hope, which were well calculated to edify and console the clergy, religious, and laity of a diocese still plunged in grief at the loss of their great Prelate. His own personal sentiments on assuming the care of the Diocese of Charleston, as expressed in this fine document, have already been quoted. His appeal to the clergy and to the laity, in which he also made a most touching and effective allusion to his noble predecessor and his precepts to his flock, is full of the most earnest eloquence, solicitude for the good of his people, and holy zeal. That portion which was addressed to the Sisters of St. Ursula and the Daughters of Charity, the two female religious Orders of his diocese, is too beautiful to be omitted :—

" And what shall I say to you, chaste virgins of Christ —daughters of the pure and saintly Ursula—and to you, handmaids of charity, angels of heaven to the afflicted of earth ? Happy thrice your lot ! Secluded from the dangers, vanities, and defilements of the world, sanctified and consecrated to God, you commence even here, in the sweet and retired shade of your own altars, the holy canticle of praise and love, which you will chant eternally in the heavens, ' following the Lamb whithersoever he goeth ; ' a canticle, which none others may sing, save those ' in whose mouth no lie is found,' and ' who are without spot before the throne ' of God. (Rev. xiv. 4, 5.) To you we forbear exhortation ; for surely *you* will not suffer ' the serpent, which seduced Eve by his subtilty,' to glide into the Eden of your innocence and your happiness, invade the privileges of your holy state, sully with slightest stain the white robes of your consecration, or *even tempt* you to fall from the simplicity which is in Christ ! (2 Cor. xi. 3.) Yours is the pleasing task to cultivate the mind and heart of female youth, and rear the young daughters of the South to science

and refinement—to virtues bright as our vernal skies—
and manners as bland as our evening breeze. Or yours
is the still happier lot to cherish the orphan with a
mother's love, smooth the pillow of affliction with more
than woman's kindness, and bathe the fevered brow with
the gentle hand of the 'Sister of Charity;' prayer for us
and for a sinful world being your repose, and sanctify-
ing the hours that intervene."

The visitations of his diocese, which Bishop Reynolds
prosecuted from year to year with unremitting zeal,
honorably illustrate the history of his episcopate. The
Diocese of Charleston at this time embraced the three
States of South Carolina, North Carolina, and Georgia.
It must also be borne in mind that the populations of
these States, when Bishops England and Reynolds commenced their arduous labors in them, were very different
from those of the other States, then and now. The Church
had scarcely a foothold within them; no Catholic traditions could be appealed to; no Catholic population, either
native or immigrant, beyond a very few isolated families
or individuals, was there; and a small, and in a worldly
sense obscure congregation, in a few of the cities, constituted the Church of Georgia and the Carolinas. The
Episcopalians of South Carolina, the Baptists of North
Carolina, and the Methodists of Georgia, were the predominating sects. The slaves of those States usually
followed the creeds of the families to whom they belonged. Hence, when Bishop England or Bishop Reynolds went upon an episcopal visitation, it was not to
crowded audiences of expectant and eager Catholics, who
longed for the presence of a Bishop or priest; but it
was mostly like the mission of Peter and Paul at Rome,
who addressed strange audiences of cultivated and acute

unbelievers, or who in the quiet walks of private life addressed the words of truth to some earnest and inquiring soul. Bishop England was the man in the Church, of all others, to present in glowing terms of eloquence, and with invincible power of thought and argument, the truths of the Catholic Church to such an intelligent and fair-minded population, whose opportunities had afforded them no means of information concerning them. Bishop Reynolds continued, with admirable tact and prudence, the work Bishop England had commenced. His successes were real gains to the Church, and in the cotemporaneous accounts of his visitations, it is no uncommon occurrence for him to have received into the Church and baptized two, four, or six adults, all of whom were converts. These converts, together with a few native or immigrant Catholics, formed the little congregations, which are now expanding into the most encouraging proportions. In the cities particularly, the Church made rapid progress under the zealous labors of Bishop Reynolds. The Church at Newbern, North Carolina, had been planted before the Revolution, by the Gaston family, and there a flourishing congregation had nobly preserved the Faith. Bishop Reynolds understood the people amongst whom he was sent, as did Bishop England, and his generous and charitable efforts were rewarded with signal success,—a success which may be somewhat measured by the fact, that he prepared the way for the erection of three dioceses where in his day there was but one.

Bishop Reynolds, like his predecessor, had to struggle for his Church against many obstacles, and, as may naturally be concluded from the foregoing account of the fewness and sparsity of the Catholic population, the greatest of these obstacles was poverty. The following account of the condition of his diocese, addressed to his clergy in 1846, by Bishop Reynolds, is an interesting and important page in the history of the Diocese of Charleston :—

"The difficulties witn which my lamented predecessor had to contend are known and appreciated by few, perhaps adequately by none, not even his most devoted friends and warmest admirers. Of his administration no one can form a correct judgment, for the motives, and perhaps uncontrollable causes of much that he did—his anticipations and ultimate intentions—were known only to himself. God, in His mysterious Providence, called him to rest from his labors and receive the reward of his zeal, without requiring the sorrows, toils, disappointments, and embarrassments which his successor so deeply feels, and which he too, notwithstanding his splendid talents and great energy of mind, would have experienced, had heaven left him still in the field of labor and of trial. He died at the hour, truly, 'least expected' by others and even by himself; and at the very time when the resources of his powerful mind, and his extended fame and influence, seemed most necessary to devise and apply the means of paying the heavy debts he had contracted, and for accomplishing the designs and undertakings of his zeal. He left a debt of thirty-four thousand dollars : annual pensions—most justly due—to the amount of six hundred and fifty dollars ; two hundred and fifty dollars in the bank, and the same sum in the hands of his grief-stricken Vicar-General and administrator of the diocese. To meet the above liabilities, the proceeds of all the property he had owned, and all the donations received from Europe, were by far insufficient.

His successor, upon arriving in this diocese, found about fourteen thousand dollars of debts unpaid, besides the annuities above mentioned—without property, without income from any source, without means of support for himself and for the few clerical students, other than the voluntary contributions of the Catholics of the diocese— few in number, poor in worldly goods, and scattered over a territory of one hundred and sixty-three thousand square miles.

"The three States composing this diocese contain a population of (including persons of color and slaves) upwards of two millions; and of this population not more than twelve thousand are Catholics, counting children, slaves, and all colored persons. Of the Catholics very few are wealthy, and of these few, some, alas! are only nominal members of our Church. The priests on the missions have immense labors, in a sickly climate, and several of them do not receive enough for the necessaries of life. Hence, I am forced to use the greater part of the small (proportionably very small) appropriations from Europe, to support the Seminary and the priests of the mission. And yet I have the pleasure of informing you that through the exceeding liberality of the people of this diocese, and with the aid I have received from abroad, the Bishop's debt is now reduced to the sum of five thousand dollars.

"In Charleston and Charleston Neck there are not Catholics enough to form one numerous congregation; and yet circumstances, beyond the control most probably of my predecessor, induced the erection of three churches —two in the city and one on Charleston Neck—thus dividing and thereby diminishing the means of maintaining three churches and their respective pastors.

"The present Cathedral, sinking into decay beyond the possibility of repair, has only sixty pews, and of these, six or seven are generally not rented. The house occupied as a Seminary is actually falling into ruins, and is not only uncomfortable, but unhealthy and unsafe.

"The present Cathedral, Seminary, house of the Bishop, and lot on which these buildings stand, were, a few days since, valued by gentlemen entirely disinterested, and of much experience and long residence here, at nine thousand dollars. This valuation I requested to be made to obviate, if possible, the erroneous statements regarding this property, and from sources we should have little expected, making it one hundred and fifty thousand dollars!

"*These are facts;* and yet there are some who say that we are well off, and have more abundant means than many of the other dioceses of this ecclesiastical province. I acknowledge, and with feelings of gratitude and admiration, that in this city and several other parts of the diocese, the generosity of the Catholic people, and on some occasions of our separated brethren, is almost unbounded. In no part of America or Europe are the Catholics and people in general so liberal as in Charleston and the greater portion of my diocese. They are a generous and noble-minded people, and would that I might acknowledge their dispositions in some way more adequate to their merits and just to my own feelings, than the poor tribute offered by this expression of my grateful regard."

In May, 1845, Bishop Reynolds visited Baltimore, and at the request of Archbishop Eccleston, administered confirmation at the Visitation Convent to a number of the young ladies of the Academy, and on the same day, at the Cathedral, to about two hundred persons. He was then on his way to Europe, whither he sailed, accompanied by the Rev. Mr. Sullivan, of Charleston, on business of interest to his diocese. After an absence of several months, he returned in November of the same year. Having made an extensive visitation of his diocese, especially in North Carolina, he called his clergy together in spiritual retreat from December 10th to 18th, the Bishop himself presiding at the exercises, which were followed by the clergy with great earnestness and piety. He held several meetings of the clergy before their departure to their respective missions, promulgated to them the decrees of the several Councils of Baltimore as henceforth to be in force in his diocese; measures were also taken in aid of the diocesan paper, the *Catholic Miscellany*, and in furtherance of the important undertaking he was about to commence for the erection of a new Cathedral.

The old Cathedral of St. Finbar, erected by Bishop England, was a temporary frame structure, which it was always the intention of that Prelate to replace by a larger and more permanent one, as soon as his resources enabled him to do so. With this view he had provided an ample lot of ground in the most eligible part of the city. But Bishop England had a great work before him, which the circumstances of his diocese required him to meet first. This was two-fold: first, to provide immediate, though temporary church accommodations, for a flock composed of small and scattered congregations; secondly, to exert the vast resources of his intellect and the matchless powers of his eloquence in defending and explaining the dogmas and practices of the Catholic Church, before a public who were strangers to it. It has seldom fallen to the lot of any Bishop to succeed in removing prejudice and in allaying hostility to the Church to the same extent. For twenty years he toiled; but it was not given to him to realize his long-cherished hope of building and dedicating the new St. Finbar's. This was reserved for Bishop Reynolds, whose mind was forcibly impressed with the necessity by the dilapidated condition of the old church. He announced this great work to his clergy in the retreat of 1845, and in 1847 he made a similar appeal to the clergy and people of Savannah, and not without a cordial and substantial response. A treasurer of the Cathedral fund was appointed, and for four years he appealed to the Catholics of Charleston and of his whole diocese to contribute. In the early part of 1850 the treasurer announced that he had twenty-one thousand dollars towards the work, and in May, 1850, the Cathedral was commenced. During the four years of its construction Bishop Reynolds continued his appeals and exertions with increased energy, making collecting excursions occasionally into other dioceses. In 1853 he returned from one of these excursions to Louisville and St. Louis, with the handsome sum of two thousand three hundred dollars towards the completion of the Cathedral. On April 6, 1854, Bishop Reynolds had the consolation of seeing his new Cathedral consecrated; the consecrator was Bishop Gartland, of Savannah, and the sermon was preached by Archbishop Hughes, of New York; Bishop Portier of Mobile, Bishop McGill of Richmond, and Bishop Reynolds assisted at the imposing ceremony, together with a large body of clergymen and a great concourse of people. St. Finbar's is a noble structure, built of Connecticut brown stone, in a style of Gothic which is called the "ornamental English style;" is one hundred and fifty feet long, seventy-two feet wide, and has a tower and spire two hundred feet high. It stands a worthy temple of Christian worship, and a fine monument of the zeal, piety, and labors of Bishop Reynolds.

Another important undertaking of Bishop Reynolds, and one which does great credit to his ardor for truth, zeal for the Church, and devotion to the memory of his predecessor, was the compilation and publication of the voluminous and invaluable works of Bishop England. He was aided in the compilation by Dr. Lynch, the present Bishop of Charleston; but the arduous and unrequiting task of publication he accomplished at the cost of great care, labor, and personal sacrifice; for the aid he expected having almost entirely failed him, he was compelled to draw upon his own scanty means to enable him to prosecute the work. These valuable writings, in five volumes, are now before the public, and constitute one of the most important and useful contributions ever made to the Catholic literature of the country.

Bishop Reynolds took part in the Sixth Council of Baltimore in 1846, at which he was selected to preach the concluding sermon. He took for his subject "The Unity of the Church," and handled it in a style of eloquence, argument, and erudition that won universal admiration. He also took part in the Seventh Council of Baltimore in 1849, and in the First National or Plenary Council in 1852, in all of which his wisdom, zeal, and eloquence gained him the respect and confidence of his colleagues. As a pulpit orator Bishop Reynolds achieved a high reputation in the American Church, as is shown by the notices of his sermons in cotemporary publications, and testified by now living witnesses. His sermon for the orphans of Louisville, in 1844, was particularly mentioned as a splendid effort, and brought the largest collection ever taken up there on any similar occasion. His pastoral letters are fine specimens of ecclesiastical writings, and two of them particularly are worthy of perusal and admiration: that which he addressed to his diocese in 1844, on occasion of his taking possession of his see, from which some extracts have been given above, and that which he issued in January, 1854, in which he treated of the important subjects of matrimony, mixed marriages, banns, baptism, Christian burial, episcopal administration, ecclesiastical districts, and the catechism: in this able letter he emphatically discountenanced mixed marriages, and promulgated the acts of the Councils respecting the publication of banns and solemnization of marriage between Catholics; and finally that, probably his last official act, which in his solicitude for his flock he issued from his bed of sickness, and in which he announced the jubilee of 1854 and 1855. In this last he made the following allusion to his own health:

"It is a source of deep affliction to us that we are unable, at this time, to address you at greater length and with more earnestness; and still more do we regret our inability to speak to you in person and from the fulness of our heart, as we were wont to do, the words of instruction and exhortation. God has been pleased to afflict us by a long and severe illness, and we must and do endeavor to resign ourselves entirely and perfectly to His holy will, knowing that His thoughts are not like the thoughts of man, and that His providence is above our comprehension, but, nevertheless, always full of mercy and wisdom. We are consoled by the pleasing confidence that our zealous co-operators in the holy ministry will, by their increased zeal and fervor, more than supply our deficiency."

The disease which had so long afflicted Bishop Reynolds, and the sufferings which he bore with such admirable patience and resignation, carried him off finally to a better and a happier world. His death occurred March 9, 1855. The following notice of his life and death is from a cotemporary publication :—

"During the eleven years of his episcopate he labored with untiring zeal to promote the cause of religion. He watched with solicitude over the Catholic institutions, and strove earnestly and anxiously to encourage their growth and to extend the sphere of their usefulness. His parental kindness, courtesy, and generosity, endeared him to his clergy; his urbanity and gentle, yet dignified demeanor towards all, won for him respect, not only of Catholics, but even of those who belonged not to his spiritual jurisdiction. In him the poor, the afflicted, and the distressed found a father, a consoler, and a friend. The virtues which had distinguished him during thirty years of a laborious ministry shone more conspicuously as his life drew to a close. The patience and resignation with which he bore his suffering, especially during the last and painful stages of his disease — the congestion of the lungs—elicited the admiration of all who approached him. Even in his last hour, during the moments immediately preceding his dissolution, when his eyes unconsciously wandered around as if in quest of solace and aid, they ceased their wanderings the moment they rested upon the image of his crucified Lord. He has passed from the scene of his labors; he sleeps by the side of his illustrious predecessor; yet his virtues survive, his memory is cherished in the hearts of the Catholics of Charleston."*

It was well said of him by one well acquainted with his life and virtues : " Dr. Reynolds, though not demonstrative in manner, was one of the most charitable of men. He loved to perform acts of kindness in secret, and no one deserving of his aid ever appealed to him in vain, whether for temporal assistance or for counsel." The Fathers assembled in the Eighth Council of Baltimore, in May, 1855, in a feeling letter to the *Councils of the Propagation of the Faith* in Europe, announced the death of Dr. Reynolds, regretting the loss of his talents in the future Councils of the American Church, and stating that he had "worn himself out in the service of his church "—a tribute to his memory more truly grand than the most costly and magnificent monuments of bronze or marble.

---

* *The Metropolitan*, 1855, p. 199; *Catholic Almanac*, 1856.

RIGHT REV. JOHN BERNARD FITZPATRICK, D.D.,

Third Bishop of Boston, A.D. 1844.

JOHN BERNARD FITZPATRICK was born at Boston, November 1, 1812. His parents emigrated from Ireland and settled in Boston in 1805. Possessed of energy of character, good judgment, and sterling virtues, they soon won the confidence and esteem of all who knew them. Their personal appearance is described as venerable and prepossessing. They inspired respect in all who saw them. But their comeliness of person was only a reflection of the more exalted beauty of their souls. Their family circle was adorned by the halo of faith, purity, and religion, and the many good qualities of these exemplary Christians caused them to be looked up to and consulted by their fellow-Catholics and countrymen in trials and difficulties. They also enjoyed the friendship of the illustrious Bishop Cheverus and the saintly Father Matignon, both of whom, on the occasion of the baptism of the future Bishop of Boston, honored by their presence the circle of friends assembled to celebrate the Christening.

The education of John Bernard was commenced at home, under the instruction of his parents. That home was not only a school for the mind, but it was also a temple for the soul, where good parental example and

---

* Authorities: "*In Memoriam of Right Rev. John B. Fitzpatrick;*" *Catholic Magazines*, etc., etc., and original sources.

early religious inculcation made a lasting impression upon the young members of that happy household. The first lessons he received were of prayer, love of God, abhorrence of sin, the practice of good deeds, devotion to the Church, and the love of his neighbor. His intellectual training was mingled and kept pace with these, and he profited well from his instruction. As a boy and as a man, he could say that he never in his life uttered a curse or an oath, nor would he ever associate with those who swore or used profane language.

The first lessons in secular learning that he received outside of his own family were imparted in the primary and grammar schools of Boston, in which he greatly distinguished himself, and gave promise of his future eminence. These were then the only schools of which he could avail himself. At the Adams and Boylston schools he was pre-eminent among the pupils, and all who beheld him foresaw that he was marked out for some great future. While he excelled in every study, he was especially apt in mathematics, rhetoric, and declamation. At the public exhibitions of each of these establishments he received the Franklin medals, rewards of his assiduity and good conduct. In 1826 he became a pupil in the Boston Latin School, where he studied Latin, Greek, and the higher branches of mathematics, for three years. He was here, as he had been in the primary and grammar schools, at once a model student, a favorite companion, and an exemplar of Christian youth. In this school Mr. Leverett was then master, and Mr. Samuel Parker sub-master, and between these gentlemen and young Fitzpatrick a life-long friendship was maintained. The latter ever spoke of them, and of all his teachers and companions, with gratitude and affection. On the other hand, all who were connected with the schools of Boston, or felt an interest in them, pointed long afterwards to Bishop Fitzpatrick as an *alumnus* of whom they might well be proud.

Frank and sincere as were the admiration and friendship of these persons for young Fitzpatrick, they failed to see his character in its most admirable light—that of a conscientious Catholic. In the midst of elements most hostile to his faith and Church, he clung to these with unwavering fidelity and love. From the school-house he usually repaired to the church and catechism class, and his proficiency in secular studies was only surpassed by his attainments in Christian doctrine, and by the practice of Christian piety and devotion. Sunday was his favorite day, because it was the Lord's day. On that day he did not, like so many others, yield to self-indulgence; but arose at an earlier hour than usual, and repaired to the temple, where he enjoyed the presence of his Redeemer; and he was never more happy than when engaged in serving the priest at the altar. He became a teacher in the Catechism school, and took delight in imparting to others those lessons he had experienced so much pleasure in learning.

The quick and solicitous eye of Bishop Fenwick soon perceived the treasure which the Church possessed in young Fitzpatrick, whose noble bearing and solid virtues attracted his attention, gained his confidence, and won his affection. The good Bishop was not long in discovering that God called to Himself this pious youth, who, on his part, had already dedicated himself to his Maker. It was well said of him, that "no work appeared to him so worthy of man as the service of God his Creator; no examples so worthy of emulation as those of apostles, martyrs, and confessors; no place so attractive and so beautiful as the courts of the house of our God." Under the advice and patronage of the Bishop, he took leave of his family and friends—some of whom, his venerable father and loved brother and sister, he was destined never to see again—and, at the age of seventeen, entered the Montreal College in September, 1829. Here he made a thorough course of classical studies with honor and distinction. His deportment was edifying and his life pure; his piety and love of virtue became the admiration of all. In 1833 he held a public disputation in four languages, Latin, Greek, French, and English, at the public exhibition of the College, in the presence of four Bishops and the Governor of the Province, and signally won the applause of all present. His proficiency was so great, that he was withdrawn from the ranks of the pupils, and promoted to a professorship of rhetoric and *belles-lettres*. This promotion, unasked and undesired, greatly increased his duties and cares, and for four years he discharged these new labors with untiring industry and scrupulous exactness. In a letter to one of the members of his family he gave the following account of his occupations at this time:— "Four hours' class every day. One hour conference of Theology. Two and a half hours' recreation, at which I am *obliged* to be present. Three-quarters of an hour meditation. Half an hour spiritual reading. Mass, meals, time required for preparing my class lessons and explanations, revision and correction of exercises, learning my own lesson in Divinity, various calls and interruptions from my scholars. To say nothing of the additional occupations that the incidents of every day may give rise to. Add all together, and subtract from twenty-four, and then scold me, if you can in conscience, for not writing oftener."

In 1837 he completed his course of eight years' study at the College of Montreal. As an evidence of his thoroughness of study in the languages, it may be mentioned that he acquired such a mastery of the French, that in his conversations and correspondence he was usually taken for a native Frenchman. It was now determined by his ecclesiastical superiors that he should go to the Grand Seminary of St. Sulpice, at Paris. Before departing for France he revisited Boston. He was now of the canonical age for ordination, and was fully qualified by his attainments for the holy ministry; but he esteemed himself unworthy of such an honor, and not sufficiently instructed in sacred learning. He therefore humbly declined, for the time, the proffered elevation to the priesthood, and prepared for further study in the divine sciences.

His reputation as a scholar, and as one who had done honor to his native city abroad, preceded his return to Boston, and he was received by many of his old friends and former schoolmates with distinguished attention. The following account of his reception at the Annual School Dinner of 1837, is given by the Rev. George F. Haskins, then a Protestant, and an Overseer of the Poor for the city of Boston, and now a zealous member of the Catholic clergy:—" It was on the 24th day of August of that year that I first saw the Bishop. It was under the following circumstances: I was at that time Overseer of the Poor for the city of Boston, and as such had received an invitation to be present at the Annual School Dinner in Faneuil Hall. The Hon. Edward Everett, then Governor of the Commonwealth, Hon. Samuel A. Elliot,

Mayor of the city, President Quincy, of Harvard College, Adjutant-General Dearborn, and other distinguished persons were present, and made eloquent addresses. There sat upon a raised platform, under the painting of Washington, and in the midst of them, a tall young man, who attracted the notice of the guests upon the floor and in the galleries by his dignified bearing, his splendid head, and intellectual, beaming countenance. All around me were asking who he was and whence he came. But no one was able to answer. At length, however, a rap was heard from the Mayor's table, and Major Benjamin Russell rose and said, in substance: 'Mr. Mayor, I wish to introduce to you and to these assembled guests my respected fellow-citizen, a young man, a native of Boston, of Irish parentage, and a Roman Catholic. He has been educated in our public schools, and is a medal scholar in more than one of them. This young man has just graduated with the highest honors at the celebrated College of Montreal, in Canada. He is now about to visit France, with a view to perfect his education. Boston and her schools may well be proud of such a man and such a scholar. Mr. Mayor and gentlemen, I have the honor of presenting to you Mr. John Bernard Fitzpatrick.' The response of young Fitzpatrick was characteristic. It was modest, manly, dignified, and graceful. It was listened to with marked attention, and elicited frequent and enthusiastic applause."

The Seminary of St. Sulpice at Paris had long been the nursery of profound learning and exalted virtues. Many of the most illustrious members of the French church had been its pupils, and this venerable shrine of learning and sanctity had sent forth from their own sunny France many saintly men, gifted with eloquence and zeal, to illumine remote regions of the world. Our own country particularly had been blessed by the presence and labors of many of these great and good men, who at the close of the last century came to us in our need as apostles of the Faith. To enter this illustrious school, young Fitzpatrick sailed for France in September, 1837 At this time over two hundred students, the flower of France and of Europe, were studying within its hallowed walls. It is related that in this choice assembly our American levite soon became conspicuous, and in less than a year was regarded as the ornament of the Seminary. His quickness of perception, acuteness of intellect, power of analysis; his ready wit, varied learning, classic attainments, and withal his close application to study, gained for him here as elsewhere the respect and admiration of professors and students. His society and friendship were sought by all, and his humility, unassuming manners and modesty, caused all to rejoice in his success and preferment. He was the only representative at St. Sulpice from the United States at that time, and as all eyes were turned upon him with inquiring and friendly interest, the gaze soon became riveted in admiration. He was selected to teach Catechism at the Church of St. Sulpice, to the sons of the aristocratic families of the Faubourg St. Germain. He expounded the doctrines of religion to these noble youths, in their own language, with such ease and elegance, that all were astonished and delighted. He was also selected one of the four or five "Masters" to preside at theological conferences. In this honorable office he equally astonished and delighted all by the readiness with which he solved the most difficult theological propositions, by the logical precision of his arguments, and by the solid learning and clear perception and force with which he vindicated the truths of religion. The Right Rev. Dr. De Goesbriand, Bishop of Burlington, Vermont, who was one of his companions at St. Sulpice, has stated that the venerable Superior of the Sulpitians then predicted that young Fitzpatrick would one day rise to a high position in the Church of God, and become an ornament to its Hierarchy. During his sojourn in Paris he was accustomed to improve his time of vacation by visiting the monuments and works of art in that cultivated and brilliant metropolis. He studied pulpit oratory by attending the sermons of the most celebrated preachers, and cultivated a fondness and appreciation for the grand and beautiful, by listening to the inspiring music and witnessing the gorgeous ceremonies of the churches. The advantages of these pure and ennobling pursuits were evidenced in his after-life by the refined and cultivated taste for which he was remarkable.

His studies were now completed, and he was ripe for the holy calling which had been the great object of his studies, prayers, and disciplines. He was accordingly promoted to the order of sub-deacon in May, 1839, and to that of deaconship in the following December; and on June 13, 1840, the eve of Trinity Sunday, at the age of twenty-seven years, he was ordained in the priesthood. His first desire was to enter the Society of St. Sulpice, a secure harbor, where he could work out his salvation with greater safety to himself. But he consulted rather the will of God than his own, and as soon as that will was known in his regard, he cheerfully and ardently embraced it. Bishop De Goesbriand, who knew him well at this time, has said: "I can testify, from my intimate acquaintance with him, that he had but one object at heart—the glory of his Creator and the conversion of his countrymen. And when I had myself determined to come to America, I well recollect how he used to express his joy at my determination, lament over the spiritual destitution of Catholics in this country, deplore the deeply-rooted prejudices of Protestants, and desire that God would send worthy missionaries to open their eyes." He expressed his own sentiments at this time, in a letter to a friend, thus: "I am now wholly and irrevocably consecrated to God. The Lord is my portion and my inheritance, and His house will be my dwelling forever. You must pray that every day, by increase of fervor, I may supply what may have been wanting in the sincerity and universality of my offering; that my sacrifice may be without reserve, and, above all, without return to anything that this world can offer; that all my toils and labors, all my talents and capacities, all my days of life, may be to the last breath devoted generously and exclusively to the service of God and the salvation of souls."

In November, 1840, he returned to Boston, the chosen field of his labors. To an ardent and well-regulated zeal he united thorough preparation for the ministry. Shunning the flatteries and pleasures of the world, which through life seemed to surround his path as so many tests of his strength, he immediately commenced his work. No time was spent in personal ovations and social gratulations. His first mission was at the Cathedral. Here he devoted himself to hearing confessions, instructing children, the poor, and the ignorant in their religious duties, and in visiting 'the sick. He was also during this period assistant pastor of St. Mary's Church. A year spent in these labors was a good preparation for more arduous and responsible duties. He was appointed pastor of East Cambridge. Here the people were in want of a place of worship, and his zealous efforts soon supplied them with a substantial stone church, in which his fervid eloquence and truly priestly life and labors accomplished much good. Such were his prudence and good judgment, and his ever-ready desire to be of service, that he was now employed and intrusted by Bishop Fenwick with a difficult and responsible commission, in which he succeeded in composing dissensions of long standing, and in substituting peace and good-will in their stead.

In 1844 the declining health of Bishop Fenwick, and the increasing labors of his arduous office, rendered it impossible for him to postpone longer the appointment of a coadjutor to assist him in his administration. From the time of the return of Dr. Fitzpatrick to Boston, the Bishop's hopes in this regard had been fixed in him. The zealous and competent manner in which he had discharged every office imposed on him had more than realized the promise of his early life. The Bishop's wishes were concurred in, and the priest of his choice was given to him as his coadjutor and successor. The humility of the young Bishop elect was greatly tried by this event. It was evident to all that he would rather retire from the dread ordeal to which his elevation to the episcopal dignity would subject him. His real sentiments may be gathered from a letter written to his sister in 1839, long before he had the least intimation of what was in store for him. He wrote: "Pray for me that I may be ever free from that ambition which covets the esteem and applause of men, for these are the most dangerous enemies that can beset a priest, and for thousands have been the rock on which they split and perished." To accept such an office was to embrace in truth the cross; but the cross had become his choice forever. His acquiescence was an act of obedience to God, to the Sovereign Pontiff, and to his own immediate superior. He was consecrated at Georgetown, on Sunday, March 4. 1844, by Bishop Fenwick, assisted by the Right Rev. Bishop Whelan, then of Richmond, and the Right Rev. Bishop Tyler, of Hartford. Once consecrated, his gifted soul and generous nature came fully up to his new position. It was well said of him, that " his misgivings vanished, his doubts were dissipated. Serenity and joy now rested on his noble brow, and he was every inch a Bishop." The glittering cross which he wore upon his breast was a true emblem of that cross of the spirit which weighed upon his heart. Though he felt this more than others knew, it was always remarked that his cheerfulness and gayety never deserted him. " At first it was not so much to carry his own as to lighten the burden of him whom it was his office to assist, and it was his consolation to know how great was the relief which he afforded, and how many a thorn he removed from his pathway to the grave."*

On entering upon his new career, he commenced by prescribing rigid rules for his own conduct and management of affairs, which he carefully observed, and which guided him with remarkable safety and success through the many spiritual and temporal cares of his journey. Amongst these rules was the law of labor, the most wholesome of all discipline. He immediately took up his residence at the episcopal mansion in Franklin

---

* *Funeral Sermon*, by Archbishop McCloskey.

Street, and the old Cathedral became the field of his zealous toil. "In the dark basement of that church you might find him punctually attending the confessions," as it has been remarked, "being the first to enter it and the last to leave it." The number of the clergy, especially at that time in Boston, was wholly inadequate to the labors of the missions they conducted. This led to the introduction of that admirable system of appointing days for the instruction of children, for hearing their confessions, etc., in all which Bishop Fitzpatrick was conspicuous for the labors he performed. He relieved Bishop Fenwick of the heavier and more laborious portions of his episcopal charge, such as visitations of the diocese, management of temporalities, creation of new parishes, building new churches, etc.

His sermons were very impressive, eloquent, and convincing, and were attended by great numbers of Protestants, many of whom became converted to the faith. In August, 1844, he confirmed on one occasion sixty persons, nearly thirty of whom were native converts. In 1846 he took his seat in the Sixth Provincial Council of Baltimore, which Bishop Fenwick was prevented by illness from attending. He also took part in the subsequent Provincial Councils, and in the First National Council of the American Church. In 1846 the venerable Bishop Fenwick died, and henceforth the whole responsibility of this immense and populous diocese, embracing all New England, devolved upon Bishop Fitzpatrick. His tender ministrations towards his dying colleague and friend were those of a son to a father; nothing could be more touching, more noble, more untiring, or more delicate.

Now the cross which he had embraced bore heavily upon his shoulders, with no one to share it but Him who bore it for us all. He performed his work in person; it was not till 1855 that he appointed a secretary to assist him; he had no Vicar-General till 1857. During these years of single-handed labor his heart was on many occasions greatly afflicted. It was his lot to witness on the *Fourth of July*, 1854, a day that might have been spared such a scene, the blowing up of the Catholic Church, then in course of erection at Dorchester, by some unknown ruffians. On the fourth and fifth of the same month, a fanatic named Orr, but who irreverently assumed the title of "Angel Gabriel," went through the streets of Bath, denouncing Catholics, their church and clergy; under his frantic appeals an anti-Catholic mob of several hundreds turned out and proceeded to the Catholic Church, broke in the doors and windows, demolished the pews, rang the bell, tore down the cross, and then fired the temple of God, which was wholly destroyed. The mob then paraded the streets in triumph; no arrests were made. On the morning of the third and fourth of the same month a "Know-nothing" riot broke out at Manchester, New Hampshire; about five hundred armed men attacked the quarter of the town inhabited by Irish Catholics, expelled the peaceable inhabitants from their homes, which they gutted, and destroyed the furniture; they then attacked the Catholic Church, breaking the stained glass windows, and were proceeding to its destruction, when, to the credit of the town, the mayor and police arrested their progress. In October, 1854, the "Ellsworth outrage," as it is known, occurred, in which a mob of citizens assaulted a holy priest, and inflicted upon him most cruel and inhuman outrages and injuries, for exercising that inestimable right of Americans, that of discussing a question of public policy and justice, which is to this day a subject of discussion, and in which men of various politics and religions are arrayed on different sides. It fell to his lot to behold the appointment, by the Legislature of Massachusetts, of a special committee to intrude upon the sacred privacy of the Sisters of Nôtre Dame, in Roxbury, and grossly insult them in their own asylum; those pure and holy daughters of religion, whose prayers and charities arose like incense to appease the anger of God against sinful man, and for whose existence and maintenance the Bishop had so earnestly struggled; that asylum of sanctity and devotion, erected on property purchased by him and given to them, to promote the greater honor and glory of God, and the welfare of man. These and other afflictions and injuries he had to bear. Heavy were his cares and anxieties, many the trials and contradictions he had to endure. By his wisdom, forbearance, and charity, angry passions were allayed, dissensions healed, animosity reconciled, and harmony restored. Such were the wrongs which the Church endured in her ministers and temples, that public feeling reacted in favor of the Bishop, and on some occasions he received marks of sympathy even from Protestants. His own feelings, under the persecutions his Church endured, may be gathered from the sublime words he used at the dedication of St. Martin's Church, at Templeton, Massachusetts, while alluding in his sermon to the prevailing outcry against Catholics: "They may deprive us of the privilege of being citizens of the Commonwealth, but they cannot deprive us of the privilege of being citizens of Heaven." In 1854 he visited Rome on business for his diocese. We may well imagine with what heartfelt relief he poured forth his soul, and laid his trials at the feet of the gentle and sympathizing Pius IX., the good and illustrious Fathei of all the faithful. Rome was to him then moie than ever, and more than it is now permitted to be to us in these unhappy days, a shrine of pilgrimage and a city of benediction :—

> "Oh Rome! my country! city of the soul!
> The orphans of the heart must turn to thee."

There are many who remember now the joy with which he returned to his diocese and people in October, 1854, bringing with him and bestowing upon them the apostolic benediction of the Holy Father, and delivering the characteristic message of Pius IX. to the Catholic people of New England, "*Persevere under afflictions.*"

The celebrated school controversy in Boston also deserves mention. It is well chronicled by an eye-witness in these graphic terms : "And could I find adequate words in which to express my admiration of his consummate prudence, foresight, and sagacity, I might advert to an event that occurred in March, 1859, the like of which never occurred before or since in this country, nor probably in any other, and which at the time imperilled our churches and the free exercise of our religious worship. I refer to the Eliot School rebellion, when five or six hundred boys in one section of the city rose in open and defiant resistance, and thousands more in other quarters were on the point of doing the same, because a Catholic boy had been whipped for refusing to recite the Lord's Prayer and the Ten Commandments in the Protestant form. Excitement was becoming intense; the worst of feelings were beginning to be developed; the

City Hall, where the School Committee held their sessions, was getting to be an arena of acrimonious controversy, when at this critical moment Bishop Fitzpatrick, who ever before had shrunk from public notice, felt it now his duty to interfere, and accordingly addressed a communication, dated March 21, 1859, to the School Board, at the time when the indignation of the community was at its height, and the rallying cry was raised, 'To the rescue of the Bible.'"

The reproduction of the leading passages in this admirable letter alone can do justice to the subject:—

"The undersigned would, therefore, first state, in general, that the objections raised by the Catholic pupils, and by their parents, are not affected scruples—are not, as some would seem to think, fetches or pretences devised simply for the purpose of creating a difficulty. They are serious and solid objections, founded in individual conscience and individual faith.

"To show this, it may be well to divide the matter, and set apart for consideration three particular points, out of which and against which, mainly, those objections arise.

"These points are—1st, The enforced use of the Protestant version of the Bible; 2d, the enforced learning and reciting of the Ten Commandments in their Protestant form; 3d, the enforced union in chanting the Lord's Prayer and other religious chants.

"On these three points the undersigned respectfully begs leave to remark, as follows:—

I. Catholics cannot, under any circumstances, acknowledge, receive, and use, as a complete collection and faithful version of the inspired books which compose the written Word of God, the English Protestant translation of the Bible. Still less can they so acknowledge, accept, or use it, when its enforcement as such is coupled expressly with the rejection of that version which their own Church approves and adopts as being correct and authentic; and yet this is required of them by law. The law, as administered, holds forth the Protestant version to the Catholic child, and says, '*Receive this as the Bible.*' The Catholic child answers, '*I cannot so receive it.*' The law, as administered, says, '*You must, or else you must be scourged, and finally banished from the school.*'

"II. The acceptance and recital of the Decalogue, under the form and words in which Protestants clothe it, is offensive to the conscience and belief of Catholics, inasmuch as that form and those words are viewed by them, and have not unfrequently been used by their adversaries, as a means of attack upon certain tenets and practices which, under the teachings of the Church, they hold as true and sacred.

"III. The chanting of the Lord's Prayer, of psalms, of hymns addressed to God, performed by many persons in unison, being neither a scholastic exercise nor a recreation, can only be regarded as an act of public worship—indeed, it is professedly intended as such in the regulations which govern our public schools. It would seem that the principles which guide Protestants and Catholics, in relation to communion in public worship, are widely different. Protestants, however diverse may be their religious opinions—Trinitarians, who assert that Jesus Christ is true God, and Unitarians, who deny that He is true God—find no difficulty to offer in brotherhood a blended and apparently harmonious worship, and in so doing they give and receive mutual satisfaction, mutual edification. The Catholic cannot act in this manner. He cannot present himself before the Divine presence in what would be for him a merely simulated union of prayer and adoration. His Church expressly forbids him to do so. She considers indifference in matters of religion, indifference as to the distinction of positive doctrines in faith, as a great evil, which promiscuous worship would tend to spread more widely and increase. Hence the prohibition of such worship; and the Catholic cannot join in it without doing violence to his sense of religious duty.

"These three points the undersigned simply sets forth as facts appertaining to the faith of Catholics, and to their conscience in matters of religion. Any discussion or show of arguments to prove the reasonableness of such belief and of such conscience would seem to him out of place, inasmuch as the question to be solved is not why people believe, but what they believe, save always the laws of common morality and the respect due to all such things as may be essential or integral to the Constitution under which the Commonwealth is governed.

"The undersigned will not bring his communication to a close.without disavowing the slightest thought of imputing to the gentlemen who framed the school regulations any design to disregard the rights or the feelings of Catholics. His personal knowledge of several amongst them excludes such an idea from his mind, and the bare inspection of the rules is, he thinks, enough to prove that good and just and honest intentions presided in their councils.

"The undersigned begs leave to add one word more in conclusion. It has been supposed that, because he was silent, he was satisfied with the state of our public schools. This is not so. He has always entertained the sentiments which he now expresses. But whenever and wherever an effort has been made by Catholics to effect such changes as they desired, the question has been distorted from its true sense, and a false issue has been set before the non-Catholic community. It has been represented that the design was to eliminate and practically annihilate the Bible. This has never been true; and yet this has always been believed, and a rallying cry, ' *To the rescue of the Bible!*' has resounded on every side. Angry passions have been roused, violent acts been committed, and almost invariably the last condition of things has been worse than the first.

"In the light of this experience, any attempt to bring about a change seemed calculated to cause much strife and very little good, and therefore not advisable.

"To-day, however, circumstances known to all seem to make it a duty for the undersigned to act and speak. He does so without reluctance, since it is a duty, and he hopes that what he has said will be received as it is spoken, with a spirit of conciliation and with a true disposition to promote good-will and charity among all classes of citizens."

This letter stunned the School Board. Many of them believed that Bishop Fitzpatrick did not sustain the Catholic view of the common schools. They now found him an impregnable barrier to their plans; they all felt that his letter was unanswerable; the Board wisely postponed the whole subject indefinitely; the tempest passed away, the boys returned to school, the obnoxious rules were repealed, and only a month afterwards, for the first time in the history of Boston, a Catholic priest and several Catholic laymen were elected members of the School Committee.

Under the wise and energetic administration of Bishop Fitzpatrick, churches, parishes and institutions sprang up in all parts of New England; the Catholic population had incredibly increased; the influence of the Church had been wonderfully strengthened. The vast diocese, with its numerous labors and increased population, was more than one Bishop could attend to, and Bishop Fitzpatrick saw the necessity of subdividing it. In the National Council assembled at Baltimore in 1853, he applied for and obtained this subdivision, and two new dioceses were carved out of that of Boston, having their episcopal sees located at Burlington and Portland. Though Bishop Fitzpatrick thus ceased to be Bishop of the States of Maine, New Hampshire, and Vermont, he ever afterwards took a deep interest in their churches and clergy, rendering them every assistance in his power. The most practical test of his labors and their results may be found in these simple facts: from one diocese there were now three; from forty priests and as many churches in 1844, there were at the time of his death three hundred priests and three hundred churches, more than one hundred of each being in the diocese of Boston alone. In addition to these proofs of his wisdom and efforts, may also be mentioned the five-fold increase of religious communities and orders; one of the finest orphan asylums in the United States, costing eighty thousand dollars and containing six hundred orphans; a large and flourishing reformatory; a spacious hospital in charge of the Sisters of Charity; a new college under the learned and pious Jesuit Fathers, and many other excellent foundations of charity and religion. Though comparatively young when first attacked by the disease which finally caused his death, and frequently warned of the constant danger he was in, he continued his personal labors and exertions with unabated energy. He was frequently advised by his friends and colleagues to relax his application to work, but as long as he was capable of laboring he never allowed himself rest. He discovered his error, alas! too late.

Among the great works undertaken by Bishop Fitzpatrick was the erection of a new Cathedral, which should be worthy of the capital of New England. Though deeply interested in this new and necessary work, his warm and generous heart would not allow him to dispose of or part with the old Cathedral without sorrow and regret. His conception of the new Cathedral was vast and grand, like his own mind and soul. It became an object dear to his heart. He purchased a spacious and eligible lot for this purpose, plans for the building had been obtained, and a distinguished architect whom he had consulted declared that he never spoke to a man who had about church-building such grand views as Bishop Fitzpatrick. The generosity and disinterestedness with which he postponed this favorite project for the sake of others, are worthy of our admiration. He saw around him many of his churches still in debt and their zealous pastors struggling under its weight; he nobly went to their relief, and caused the funds destined for the new Cathedral to be applied in liquidation of the debts of the other churches. Acts like these were the constant fruit of his exhaustless charity and heroic self-denial.

His health grew daily more and more precarious. For many years before his death he was an invalid and a great sufferer. These causes were increased by his disinclination to remit his accustomed duties. In 1844 the growing symptoms of disease compelled him to try a trip to Europe for his health, yet not without plans for benefiting his diocese at the same time. In his solicitude for his flock, and in his desire to provide a father for them in case of his death, he gave his attention as long as twelve years before his death to the important matter of selecting his successor. During that time he had fixed his choice upon the present distinguished Prelate who occupies the see of Boston. When finally, during his illness, the news came from Rome that the Holy Father had accorded to him his own choice for this important trust, joy immediately brightened up his noble countenance in the midst of suffering, and he exclaimed: "Now, Lord, let thy servant depart in peace." During his eight years of pain and anguish, his people, who had so much admired and loved him in health, now honored and venerated more than ever the patient sufferer. No murmur ever escaped his lips; he was ever cheerful and always considerate of others, and never even expressed a wish or hope for his recovery unless such should be the will of God. As an evidence of his generous thoughtfulness for others, as well as of his love for the land of his fathers, it is related that while he was an exile from his diocese at Brussels, where he had gone in search of health a few years before his death, the famine broke out in Ireland; his tender heart was melted at the sufferings of that woe-stricken people. "The wail of suffering reached his ear, and immediately from a sick-bed he wrote to Boston a letter of affectionate entreaty, imploring his people to hasten to the relief of the famishing sons of St. Patrick. That letter elicited a glorious response, which sent bowling over the Atlantic wave thousands of dollars in gold to be distributed among the neediest and most deserving." It is also related of him, during one of his severest attacks of illness, that " on the 14th of December, 1864, a short time after his return to Boston, the Bishop was seized in the evening with violent pains; one faithful, but only one, attendant was in the room, who asked to go for one of the priests. ' No,' replied the Bishop, 'this is his week to visit the sick; he has to say Mass early to-morrow; he would stay too long with me and fatigue himself; give him a chance to rest.' Towards midnight his condition became more critical, and his attendant told him again, ' I must go for a priest,' when he told her positively, ' You must not go; those gentlemen need more rest than I do.' He was obeyed; no priest was sent for till the morning, but when he came in he found the Bishop senseless on the floor and bathed in his own blood. It was in this position that extreme unction was administered to him."

It is the silent virtues of men that are as truly sublime in the eyes of God. as many of their heroic acts and words. History should perpetuate the memory of the former as well as of the latter; hence the following extracts from the eulogium of one who knew Bishop Fitzpatrick well will serve our purpose:—

"A beautiful trait of the Bishop's character was a love of truth. This was recognized and felt by all who knew him, and by none more than by those who knew him best. In any assembly, if a dispute or difference of opinion existed, the simple word, '·the Bishop told me,' or, ' the Bishop said so,' immediately produced silence. That silence was devout and sincere acquiescence. Argument was at an end. The Bishop never spoke rashly, never falsely. His very countenance, his general bearing, his conversation, all testified to the truth within him. The hypocrite and dissembler trembled in his presence, and dared not look him in the face. For the contrite wrongdoer he was full of compassion and forgiveness, but the deceiver he would never brook. His displeasure extended even to those who, to entertain a company, invented stories, or exaggerated facts, and he usually manifested it by refusing to join in the laugh, or by adroitly changing the current of conversation. The reproof was felt, and keenly. When he spoke, truth came forth from his lips. When he wrote, from his pen. There was no obscurity in his language or writings, because there was no duplicity in his heart. No one had ever to ask his meaning. It was plain enough to the simplest comprehension. With the wisdom of the serpent he combined the simplicity of the dove." *

The pen that wrote the above has recorded also his testimony to Bishop Fitzpatrick's strong faith; a faith which was not only strong, but was also simple and reliant, a faith that had its whole embodiment in the significant word *Credo*, I believe, and proceeds: " Hence his solicitude in supplying the spiritual wants of his vast flock by sending them learned and good priests. Hence his earnest instructions to erect large and commodious rather than ornamental and costly churches. Hence his deep concern for the training of little children; his zeal in visiting personally every church and congregation, as long and as often as his health permitted; his kind and considerate bearing towards Protestants of whatever sect; his uniform affability, that made all men, even the

---

* *Panegyric* by Rev. George F. Haskins.

humblest, regard him as a friend; and his love of children, which every child instinctively perceived, and which made them run to him with confidence, and play with him as with each other." *

" Decision of character was one of the Bishop's prominent traits. His was a decision proceeding not from self-will or pride, but from confidence in God. In every affair of importance that regarded the good of his diocese, or the happiness of any individual priest or layman, he first invoked the guidance of God, and then, after weighing carefully every consideration, he calmly laid out his course of action, and was seldom known to deviate from his first decision; and if he did, in deference to the opinions of others, he ever after regretted it. In all matters of doubt he felt that there was a right and a wrong; that man might err, but God could not. Hence his decision, formed and made, it was unalterable and irrevocable. I shall conclude by a brief allusion to his patience and long-suffering. It has been my privilege to have been much in his company and to have known him intimately. Yet I never witnessed one solitary instance of anger or impatience. His reproof to the wrong-doer was indeed terrible, but it was administered with the severe dignity of a just judge. In all his sorrows and pains his wonted gayety never left him, nor his smile of welcome or approval." †

His long illness and protracted sufferings only served to bring out with greater lustre his many exalted traits. His death was worthy of his life, calm, resigned, devout and noble to the last. His mental powers remained unimpaired. On one occasion, when the litanies and

---

* *Panegyric* by Father Haskins. † Ibid.

prayers were recited at his bedside, he united in responding to them in his own clear and prompt manner. When the attendants " were reciting that beautiful hymn, 'Jesu dulcis memoria,' there was a momentary pause— the memory was at fault—they forgot the words of one of the concluding verses. The Bishop took up the sought-for verse, repeating it with the freshness and devotion of youth." *

Another remarkable scene is described:—"On the Saturday evening before he died, he had been slumbering quietly, though in a state of very great weakness. He wore on his finger the episcopal ring, the emblem of his fidelity to his Church, and in his hand he held a small crucifix. All at once he was seen to wake up calmly, partly remove the clothes which covered him, and then, turning up his eyes to Heaven, and raising high the hand that held the crucifix, he said in a loud distinct voice:—

"'The dark veil will soon be drawn from my eyes, as the gloomy winter passes before the spring. I shall soon be where there are millions of blessed souls, sanctified souls, beautiful souls, around the throne glorifying God. This land is consecrated to the Blessed Virgin Mary, and I renew the consecration.' And then, stretching his hand as far as he could, he formed the sign of the cross, and actually sang out the episcopal blessing. Before he let fall the hand which held the cross, he added: 'I will follow the cross to the end.'"

Bishop Fitzpatrick expired on Tuesday morning, February 13, 1866, in the fifty-fourth year of his age. His death produced a profound sensation at Boston and

---

* *Funeral Sermon* by Archbishop McCloskey.

throughout New England, and was earnestly felt in every part of the country. Every honor was paid to his memory. As his remains were carried to the church, the bells of the city of Boston were tolled by order of the Mayor, and again during the funeral. People of all religions turned out by tens of thousands to show their sorrowful respect. His funeral was attended by ten Bishops and one hundred and forty priests ; by the Governor, Mayor, and other officials, and by an immense concourse of people, including some of the most distinguished political and literary men of the country. From the day of his death till the Month's Mind, Masses of Requiem for his repose were celebrated not only in the diocese of Boston, but also in other dioceses. Those sacred words were well applied to him: "Beloved of God and men, whose memory is in benediction."

RIGHT REV. JOHN TIMON, D.D.,

First Bishop of Buffalo, A.D. 1847.*

THE Catholic Church in America has always been in advance of civilization. It was the desire of carrying the gospel to men that led the way to most of the great discoveries and explorations on this continent. The cross was planted along the Mississippi, from Canada to the Gulf of Mexico, long before a church was built in any of the Atlantic cities. The historical events which transferred those vast interior regions from France to England, and finally to the United States, occasioned a sad interruption to those glorious missions which preceded the settlements and traffic of the white man in America. But we may hope that those events will lead to a greater aggregate of religious good in those sections.

Scarcely had the century commenced when the Church was again at work on those frontiers, and as early as 1817 one of her Prelates was organizing churches and missions in St. Louis, then a town of merely four thousand souls. At the same time, a colony of Lazarist priests from Rome commenced the evangelization of those extended regions of scattered settlers and roving tribes. One of the first of our own people who joined this small but brave army of apostles was John Timon. Never was missionary better suited to his vocation than he; his heart was fired with an all-conquering zeal. So

---

* Authorities: *Life, etc., of Bishop Timon*, by C. G. Deuther; *Life of Father De Andreis*; Cotemporaneous Catholic periodicals, *Catholic Almanacs, Obituary Notices*, etc., etc.

thoroughly was he imbued with the spirit and inured to the habits of the missionary, that in after life he allowed no obstacle to stand in his way whenever the severest labors of the ministry were within his sphere of good. While his career as a Bishop was most useful and eminent, the history of his life in the main belongs to the missionary annals and traditions of our country. It was the fame of his great labors chiefly that caused him to be so honored and esteemed at Rome, the ever-grateful mother and rewarder of apostolic virtues.

John Timon was born at Conewago, Pennsylvania, February 12, 1797, and baptized on the 17th of the same month. His parents, James Timon and Margaret Leddy, had quite recently arrived in this country from Ireland, and were from Belthurbet, Cavan County. A family of ten children, of whom John was the second son, blessed the Catholic household of these pious parents, and gave ample employment to their zeal and energy in providing for their spiritual and temporal necessities. They did not fail in either of these respects, for the three sons and seven daughters were all trained up to be exemplary Catholics, and a worldly independence rewarded the industry of this good family. The first five years of John's life were spent with his parents at Conewago, and he subsequently, at Baltimore, Louisville, and St. Louis, was the faithful and useful assistant of his father in his mercantile pursuits. In his father's dry-goods store in Howard Street, Baltimore, from 1802 to 1818; at Louisville, in 1818 and 1819; and at St. Louis, from 1819 to 1823, he displayed such aptitude for business that he seemed destined for a merchant, both by education and vocation. But Providence had other paths for him to walk, and the uniform piety of his life as a merchant nurtured in him virtues that were destined for a higher and a holier field. The loss of fortune, and the death of friends dearer to him than fortune, turned his affections from man to God, and diverted his labors from the busy marts of commerce to the cultivation of the heavenly vineyard on earth.

In April, 1823, John Timon joined the congregation of the mission conducted by the Lazarist Fathers at the Barrens, near St. Louis. He entered first the preparatory Seminary of St. Mary's, where he applied himself to his new studies with his native industry, now fired by new and more exalted motives. His course consisted chiefly of the languages, philosophy, and theology. Under such preceptors and superiors as Fathers De Andreis and Rosati, he made rapid progress in learning and piety. Under the inspiring magic of their saintly example he made still greater progress in self-conquest and in the virtues necessary to the ecclesiastical state. With such surroundings the classic Latin did not lose its beauty amidst the hammerings of the community shoemaker on his last; nor did theology, the queen of sciences, savor less of Heaven when mingled with the clippings of the tailors in the adjoining room. His progress in asceticism was not retarded by the intervening occupations of felling trees and splitting wood, of digging potatoes and carrying them in sacks upon his back, and of driving the ox-cart loaded with the corn he had gathered. On the contrary, he is said to have distinguished himself by the cheerfulness with which he performed these services. Seasoned as they were with the high and holy motive he had in view, he regarded them as a part of his spiritual training, and so grateful were they to him under such circumstances, that he sought the opportunities of performing them. Thus it is related, that on a missionary trip which he made with one of the fathers, after he was made deacon, and during which he preached the first English sermon heard by the inhabitants, he was often seen, in the intervals between religious exercises, carrying wood for a poor old widow who occupied a log cabin on the plantation. An eye-witness to this fact, who was then a Protestant, says: "This, in my state of mind then, might have been called affected charity; but, thank God, I imputed nothing of the kind to him, for he was so humble and so kind that the impression made on me then will go with me to the grave." To this testimony let that of Archbishop Hughes be added, as an evidence that his life never changed; that the humility which adorned the young deacon was only increased in the honored Bishop, who had been the guest of Pontiff and Emperor, and who stood in veneration among the rulers of the Church. Archbishop Hughes publicly declared, in the presence of assembled ecclesiastics and laymen, and in the temple of God, that he had never known so humble a man as Bishop Timon.

While pursuing his studies at the Barrens, Father Odin, afterwards Archbishop of New Orleans, was the professor of Mr. Timon, and between these two holy men and laborious missionaries a warm friendship was maintained through life. The latter was ordained subdeacon in 1824, and from that time he preached frequently and with great success. He now accompanied Father Odin on a most extended and exhausting missionary tour in the State of Texas, and in the spring of 1825 he accompanied him on a similar journey through the State of Arkansas, rendering great service by his admirable sermons, his instructions to children, and still more by his saintly example. His studies were so rapidly and so thoroughly prosecuted, his judgment so ripe, his zeal so ardent, and his services so necessary, that Bishop Rosati raised him to the priesthood in 1825. From this time his life was one of constant labor. To the duties of professor in the Seminary of the Barrens were added the more arduous duties of the mission. A circuit of twenty miles was his ordinary field of duty, Cape Girardeau and Jackson being the principal points, at the latter of which places he frequently preached in the courthouse. The country was full of prejudice and hatred of Catholicity, and this zealous priest frequently encountered opposition and ill-treatment, which on one occasion was aimed at his life. These, however, soon yielded to a great extent to his winning eloquence and his exalted virtues. To render his life still more holy he now joined the Lazarists, and formally became one of the sons of St. Vincent de Paul. His expeditions to Texas were repeated during several years, with great success in restoring the faith in Catholic families of Spanish descent, in replanting the cross among the Indians, and in organizing the weak but willing Christian elements of a rude society. He, like the early missionaries on our continent, had a special zeal for saving dying infants among the Indians by the life-giving waters of baptism. His labors now began to extend into Illinois, and Catholic congregations were organized in remote and heretofore desolate spots in the West.

It was at the Barrens, however, and the neighboring counties, that his labors were constantly and regularly performed. The appearance of the Lazarists in that locality had aroused the anger of the sectarian ministers, and on several occasions they came in numbers to the very doors of the little Seminary, and with excited and violent gestures challenged the fathers to meet them in debate. A single occasion, in which Father Timon met six of them in public debate on the stump, and completely silenced them, was enough for the ministers; they gave no more challenges to the Lazarists. The fame of this zealous priest extended in every direction. He became a champion of the faith. He was sent for by Catholics on their death-beds, and even by dying Protestants, to go to remote places to visit and minister to them in their extreme peril, and no one could excel him in the ministration of mercy and hope to the dying sinner. We behold him on one occasion riding a long journey through the rain to bestow the last consolations of religion upon an expiring Catholic woman; and as he journeys on, accompanied by the husband, who had also neglected his religion for many years, his eloquence touches the poor penitent's heart, his confession is heard on the road, and the absolution pronounced amidst the peals of thunder and the torrents of rain. On another occasion we see him in the cell of a criminal condemned to die on the scaffold the following morning; his ministry is interrupted by a number of sectarian ministers, who claim to take charge of the unfortunate man. He boldly maintains his ground, confronts them in controversy, and silences them all; he then turns to the condemned man, who prefers his services to those of the vanquished parsons, and with indescribable tenderness subdues his heart with penance, rewards him with the ever ready pardon of his offended Maker, and sends him to meet death with courage and hope. At another time we hear of his going, at the prompting of his own zeal, to a prison where a murderer was about to be executed, unrepentant and hardened in vice; he enters the cell, expels the liquor with which the poor man was supplied in order to sustain him till his fatal hour, instructs him, and fervently prays with him, and sensibly touches his heart. On leaving for the night, he stations faithful guards to prevent the introduction of the fatal cup again; he returns in the morning, completes the conversion of the sinner, and before the dread penalty of the law is exacted his soul is regenerated in baptism.

His zeal was not confined to these noble acts, but extended to the great work of building up and extending the Congregation of the Mission at the Barrens, that it might become, as it certainly did, the fruitful mother of holy priests and untiring missionaries. His talents and experience were of great service to the community in their trying and disheartening poverty. Some misunderstanding arose between them and Bishop Rosati, in relation to the tenure of property by the community; Father Timon became the mouthpiece and representative of his brethren, and his wisdom, conciliation, and prudence adjusted those delicate questions satisfactorily to all parties; and from that time the Congregation of the Mission was established on a firm basis, became the owner of valuable property necessary to the conduct and furtherance of their glorious work, and greatly expanded in numbers, usefulness, and prosperity. Bishop Rosati did all in his power to promote these results, and that distinguished Prelate entertained the highest esteem for Father Timon's character, respect for his talents, and admiration for his virtues. His missionary labors in the extensive countries above mentioned continued with unabated zeal for the ten years following his ordination.

during which he was simply a member of the Congregation of the Mission. They resulted in numbers of Protestants being brought into the fold of the Church, in reclaiming great numbers also of stray sheep, in the organization of numerous little congregations, and the erection of quite a number of churches and chapels.

In 1835 a general assembly of the Congregation of the Mission was held at Paris, in which it was decided to erect the American Mission into a province of the Order, and Father Timon was appointed its first Visitor. On November 16, of that year, on the return of Father Tornatori, then Superior, and Father Timon, to the Barrens, from a tour of inspection into the state of the Mission, the letters announcing these decisions of the general assembly were received by them. Father Timon's humility would not allow him to accept the office; he requested the contents of the letters to be kept secret till other arrangements could be made, and it was only after repeated efforts to escape the office, and on the unanimous will of his brethren being made known, that he finally accepted it. Having once accepted, he applied himself to his new and responsible duties without regret and without sparing himself. The great pecuniary embarrassments of the Lazarists were relieved by his efforts and energy. Mortgages on old property were paid off, and new property of great value acquired at St. Louis. Disaffection amongst some of the members of the Order was dispelled, and several of their number who had left the community at the Barrens were induced to return, and the school attached to the Seminary was relieved from the decree for its suppression, which had been passed by the general assembly at Paris. One of his early acts as Visitor was to erect a perma nent establishment at Cape Girardeau, and for this purpose he journeyed thither on horseback accompanied by Father Odin and others. On reaching the river its passage was found difficult, on account of recent heavy rains; but Father Timon was afraid of nothing; he plunged in and swam the river on horseback, then searched for a more fordable place, recrossed, and brought the others through in safety. Quite a number of new congregations, organized by Bishop Rosati in various parts of his diocese, were offered to the Lazarists and accepted by the Visitor. He undertook, with great success, the enlargement and completion of the improvements at the Barrens. The old log church at this place, which was still so open and unfinished that, on Holy Saturday, 1837, while Father Timon was officiating, the assistant clergymen were obliged to shelter him and his book from a drenching rain by holding the sleeves of their surplices over him, was the same year, by his great exertions, replaced by a fine stone church, and the latter was consecrated by Bishop Rosati, assisted by Bishop Bruté and a numerous body of clergy, in October.

With the advice of his brethren, Father Timon departed for France, on business for the Mission, in 1837. His journey to Baltimore, Philadelphia, and New York was filled up with zealous labors by the way, for he was never idle, and seemed ever on the lookout for an opportunity of doing good. The spiritual care of the Sisters of Charity at Emmittsburg was offered to his Order by Archbishop Eccleston; but on submitting this proposition to the authorities at Paris it was declined. He remained at the mother house in Paris only a month, but accomplished much for the Mission in that time, and on returning brought ten thousand francs towards paying off the debt on his Seminary, and several zealous priests and brothers as recruits for the American province. Among these priests was Dr. Domenec, the present Bishop of Pittsburgh. Scarcely had he arrived at New Orleans, on his return, and placed his recruits in the houses of various clergymen, than we find him hard at work as usual: a retreat for the Sisters of Charity; the acceptance from the Bishop of New Orleans of his Seminary for the Lazarists, subject to the approval of the mother house; the taking charge of the missions at Donaldsonville, were some of his works here, while awaiting the reopening of navigation on the Mississippi. Thus, although the numbers of the Lazarists were rapidly increasing, the increase was not equal to the increasing works and labors assumed for them by their indefatigable Visitor.

In 1838, at the request of Bishop Blanc, of New Orleans, seconded by Bishop Rosati, Father Timon accepted the missions of Texas, then recently declared independent of Mexico. So deep was his interest in the vast field, in which the state of religion was represented as in a deplorable condition, that he decided in December to go in person on that important mission. So extended and numerous had been his labors in the South-west, that in Texas he met many persons with whom he had become acquainted in his journeys, and amongst them many public men. On the Feast of the Holy Innocents he offered the first Mass ever celebrated in Galveston; he preached in the Hall of Congress, at Houston, and rented a convenient room in the town, and erected the first altar in the place. The streets of Houston soon witnessed the performance of heroic acts of charity by this man of God, and many who had long neg¹ cted their religion received confession and communion at his hands. Having obtained full details of the country and its religious condition and wants, and received from the people proposals and promises of means for building a church at Galveston, he returned to New Orleans. Here he again gave retreats, visited and regulated the affairs of the Seminary and Mission at the Assumption and Donaldsonville, and proceeding to Natchez, at the request of Bishop Blanc, founded a mission there. His time was constantly occupied from this time in giving retreats, establishing new missions, building churches, in working extraordinary conversions both among Protestants and straying Catholics, in organizing religion throughout the country, and in governing the complicated affairs and developing the resources of the growing and already important Congregation of the Lazarists. In 1839 his humility was greatly shocked at news received from the Lazarist house in Paris of his nomination at Rome for the episcopal dignity; and in September Bishop Rosati visited the Barrens, and handed him the Papal Bull constituting him Bishop of Venesi *in partibus*, and Coadjutor of St. Louis, with the right of succession. He could not be prevailed upon to accept this appointment, nor even the administration of the diocese of St. Louis during the Bishop's intended absence at Rome. He returned the documents the following morning to Rome, earnestly recommending Bishop Rosati to select the present Archbishop of St. Louis as his Coadjutor and successor.

In April, 1840, Father Timon returned to the Barrens from one of his fruitful missionary journeys into Louisiana, accompanied by a number of boys, the sons of the most respectable families of that State, as students for the College. On his arrival he found letters from Rome, announcing the separation of Texas from the See of Monterey, and its erection into a Prefecture Apostolic, and his own appointment as Prefect Apostolic of Texas, with power to confer confirmation, and to appoint a delegate. Now again his humility was put to a severe test, but in this case his wishes were overruled by the advice of his brethren of the Mission; he accepted the appointment, and delegated Father Odin to proceed to Texas as Vice-Prefect Apostolic. In this year Father Timon visited Kentucky, at the invitation of Bishop Flaget, and spent some time there in revising the conventual rules of the Lorentine Nuns. On returning to the Barrens he had the happiness of receiving a visit from Mons. de Forbin Janson, Bishop of Nancy, whom he accompanied to 'Kaskaskia, where, after much trouble, he had the consolation of mending a breach between the congregation and their pastor. After various other labors he departed for Texas, accompanied by a missionary to assist Father Odin. At Galveston he was called upon by the Mayor to perform the funeral service over the remains of a Mr. Treat, who had once been Minister from Texas to Mexico, and whose remains were landed on the dock as Father Timon was about to embark. He declined to perform the ceremony, on the ground that the Catholic Church did not allow her ministers to perform the Catholic service for deceased Protestants, and that the deceased, if he could be reanimated, would certainly reject the office. Not only was the Mayor satisfied, but on the trip to Galveston, General Henderson, who had just returned as Minister from Texas to France, approached him on the steamer, introduced himself, and stated that though himself a Protestant, he fully approved of the conduct and motives of Father Timon in refusing his ministry on such an occasion. At Houston he again preached in the capitol as before, and for two hours held his audience entranced by his eloquence and fervor. At Austin he handed to the acting President of the Republic letters from Cardinal Fransoni, of the Propaganda at Rome, which the Texans hailed with joy as a virtual recognition of their independence. He was invited to dinner at the French Minister's, where the acting President, Judge Burnet, and several prominent members of Congress were invited to meet him, all of whom had listened to his sermon in the capitol, and united in pronouncing it a triumphant refutation of the calumnies which they had often heard repeated against the Catholic Church. He delivered another sermon of great power in the Senate chamber, received the compliment of a public dinner from the acting President, Judge Burnet, and prominent members of the Senate and House of Representatives, at which he eloquently and unanswerably vindicated the teachings and practices of the Church. His object in taking part in these festivities was to promote the cause of religion, to promote the desired end of securing a restoration of the extensive and valuable Church lands, and to give a public impetus to the organization of the Church in the new Republic. In the mean time he was busily engaged in securing sites for churches and the means for building them, and in company with Father Odin visited the Colorado, where there was a priest stationed, and then continued the journey through the country to Houston and Galveston, again to Houston, thence to Nacogdoches and St. Augustine. This journey is described as one of the most extraordinary missions on record in this country;* numerous conversions rewarded their labors, permanent missions projected for the future, earnest revivals of religion in many towns, and indeed the whole country on the route seemed to respond to the appeals of these apostolic men, and resound with the praises of God, awakened now for the first time after years of silence. In returning through New Orleans, Father Timon paid off a debt of six thousand francs incurred for the Texas mission, regulated the affairs of the Order of Lazarists there; and at the Barrens, by his advice, saved Texas from the loss of its Vice-Prefect Apostolic, who had been nominated as Bishop of Detroit. On receiving directions to visit the mother house at Paris, he started for France in June, 1841. His fame had preceded him, so that he was received with great honor both by the members of his Order and by the public. In November he sailed from Marseilles for New Orleans, accompanied by more recruits for the American Mission. On the vessel the missionaries prepared a portion of the cabin for a chapel, and in calm weather the holy sacrifice was offered; all on board, even the Protestants, were edified by the Catholic devotions they witnessed, and were greatly moved by the sermons of Father Timon. His little community preserved during the voyage the routine of prayers, meditations, and exercises which are usually observed in Lazarist houses on land. Father Timon was not idle among the passengers and crew; he labored for their souls, and in one instance was the instrument of converting to God an Italian sailor, who had long neglected his religion, and of preparing him for his edifying death, which soon occurred during the voyage;

---

* Deuther's *Life of Bishop Timon.*

and he performed over his remains the sacred office of the Church, in consigning him to his grave in the sea. On returning to the Barrens he resumed his great work, which he prosecuted with his characteristic zeal from year to year, with an energy and vigor which seemed only to increase with his advancing years. Seminaries in various dioceses were placed under his care and that of his brethren; congregations and churches sprang into existence on every side; his laborious journeys, such as have already been mentioned, were repeated in the States of Missouri, Kentucky, Arkansas, Indiana, Louisiana, Mississippi, and Texas. The discipline and efficiency of the Congregation of the Mission, or Lazarists, were greatly promoted by his wise and able administration as Visitor, and still more by his own example to his brethren. Twice, while filling the office of Visitor, he represented the Lazarists in the Councils of Baltimore. During the years that followed now before his appointment as Bishop his labors continued as before. Did space permit, many instances of personal sacrifice, heroic courage, and heavenly charity could be related: the rescue of the Sisters of the Visitation from a terrific flood in Kaskaskia, at the peril of his own life; the midnight journey through ice and snow to some distant penitent *in extremis;* the public oral discussion in defence of the Faith; attending in the prison or standing on the scaffold with the repentant convict; heralding the faith along the banks of the mighty rivers, or over the vast prairies of the South and West, braving the dangers of the Indian war-path; carrying the sacraments over many miles to a solitary family in localities where now thousands receive it at the table of the Lord:—these and many other noble deeds fill up the intervening years of this good man's life.

On September 5th, 1847, Father Timon was informed that he had been appointed Bishop of the new Episcopal See of Buffalo. His astonishment may be imagined from the fact that he had not even heard of the erection of that diocese. He humbly refused to receive the bulls from the Archbishop of St. Louis. His scruples were finally overruled by the counsels of his brethren, and the advice of several eminent clergymen. A spiritual retreat, and a settlement of the titles of the property of the mission completed his arrangements. But such was his poverty, that he had neither money to pay his traveling expenses nor clothing sufficient to keep him warm, much less suitable for a Bishop. A purse with two thousand francs and a well-filled trunk were generously provided for him within a few hours by some friends, who accidentally heard of his embarrassing destitution. The estimate of Bishop Timon, formed by those who had witnessed his remarkable career, is well expressed in a cotemporary print, as follows: —

"*Very Rev. J. Timon.*—The worthy and Very Rev. gentleman whose name appears above has been appointed by the Holy See Bishop of the Diocese of Buffalo, N. Y. There have been few clergymen of the Catholic Church better known or more beloved, throughout the valley of the Mississippi, than the Rev. Father Timon. The purity of his life, the zeal of his ministry, the fervent piety and ardent charity of his principles and practice, have long endeared him to the Catholics of this diocese (St. Louis); and it will not be without strong feelings of regret to them, that the assumption to the important station to which he has been called will necessarily deprive them of the presence of one to whom they have been so long tenderly attached. But whilst they acknowledge the selfishness of this regret, they will not fail to rejoice that the virtues that adorn the character of Bishop Timon will, in the elevated position he is about to assume, exert a wider and more extended influence in the holy cause to which he has so generously and zealously devoted his life.

"We congratulate the Catholics of the new Diocese of Buffalo. They will receive in Bishop Timon a Prelate uniting in his character all that can adorn the man, the Christian, and the clergyman; and in the unostentatious and unobtrusive discharge of his sacred duties combining qualities that cannot fail to win the hearts and command the esteem of persons of all classes and denominations."*

Bishop Timon was consecrated in the Cathedral at New York, by Bishop Hughes, October 17, 1847, assisted by Bishop Walsh, of Halifax, and Bishop McCloskey, of Albany. Archbishop Kenrick, of Baltimore, preached the consecration sermon. He was accompanied to his See by Bishops Hughes, Walsh, and McCloskey, and by the Very Rev. Bernard O'Reilly. Bishop Timon had sent word that he would arrive in Buffalo on the evening of October 22d. The weather was bad, the journey was long and fatiguing. His companions were exhausted, and proposed to remain all night at Rochester; but Bishop Timon, while earnestly requesting them to do so, informed them that he felt bound to keep his first appointment with his people. His companions generously resolved to accompany him. They arrived at Buffalo at night—were received by ten thousand persons in procession with torches. The Bishop, it is said, instead of occupying the coach intended for him,

---

* *News Letter; Catholic Magazine,* 1847.

was discovered during the procession walking behind it, through the mud and rain, carrying his valise in his hand. The Bishop delivered a stirring discourse, and dismissed the joyous multitude at eleven, P.M., with his blessing. He commenced his work by a careful examination into the religious condition of the diocese, and by giving a series of retreats and missions among the various congregations. The fruits of his efforts to improve his people may be judged from a single instance: one congregation, which had usually had three hundred communicants, numbered, after a retreat the Bishop gave them, fifteen hundred communicants. Similar results were accomplished, to proportionate extents, in almost every congregation in the diocese. The Bishop, when engaged in these missions or retreats, preached three, four, and frequently even five times a day. In every temporal point of view his position was gloomy and discouraging. He had neither cathedral nor residence, neither income nor resources. His only consolation consisted in mingling with his congregations and people, and laboring for their good. There might seem to some a want of system in his first efforts; but his system consisted in doing all the good that was possible, whenever and wherever he could. He knew there was more eloquence in the earnest and zealous labors and sacrifices of God's ministers than in the most systematic plans of business. He sought to gain the love and confidence of his people by teaching them the way to heaven. Every portion of the diocese felt the inspiring effects of the Bishop's example and efforts. No severity of the weather retarded his merciful progress. On one occasion he started to make the journey from Oswego to Elmira in a sleigh; the unevenness and difficulty of the roads caused the sleigh to upset, and the Bishop was thrown upon the hard ground, greatly stunned and cut. After a few moments he strove to pursue the journey in the sleigh, which, however, soon broke down; they hired a wagon, but the horse soon gave out. Factoryville was reached, and, to the astonishment of all, he went to the confessional, where he remained late that night, and was on his way again next morning for Elmira.

The trouble with the trustees of St. Louis Church, Buffalo, was the great trial of Bishop Timon's episcopate; it had its commencement under Bishop Hughes' administration, and continued for several years under Bishop Timon's. An illegal claim to control the temporalities of the church on the part of the trustees on the one hand, and the determination to enforce the laws of the Church in respect to temporalities, and to vindicate his own rights and duties thereunder on the part of the Bishop, formed, in brief, the gist of the controversy. Appeals to the public, to the Common Council, and the Legislature, seemed only to result in complicating the trouble. An agreement on the part of the trustees to refer the matter to Mgr. Bedini, the Papal Nuncio to Brazil, then in this country, resulted in their repudiating his decision when it was rendered against them. The decision of the Sovereign Pontiff himself was disregarded by them. Finally, the Bishop excommunicated the trustees and placed his interdict upon the church. At last, through the mediation of the distinguished Jesuit Father Weninger, these troubles were adjusted; the trustees ultimately, in 1855, submitted to the lawful authority of the Church, but not until after they had accomplished a wrong from which it is to be feared the Catholic Church in this State will long suffer. In their malice they in stigated the passage of what is known as the Church Property Bill by the Legislature of New York, by which Bishops and their successors are forbidden to hold property to them and their successors. In doing so they availed themselves of the Know-Nothing or Anti-Catholic persecution, which became dominant about the year 1853. Although Catholics are not particularly mentioned in the law—but, on the contrary, its terms apply equally to all denominations—yet the Catholic Church was the only religious body which suffered from or was intended to be affected by it, and it was designed to force the conveyance of all church property to trustees. In the debate on the bill in the Legislature, many gross slanders and misrepresentations were uttered by members against Catholics and their Church. Bishop Timon, as on other occasions, came forward as a champion of religion, and ably and bravely replied to a speech of a Senator named Babcock, in which he triumphantly defended the Church, thus wantonly assailed; his reply was replete with theological and historical research, which his adversary could not answer, and not free from a withering satire so justly provoked.

Bishop Timon, at the commencement of his episcopate, appointed Rev. Bernard O'Reilly, afterwards Bishop of Hartford, his Vicar-General. This gentleman was a warm sympathizer and supporter of Bishop Timon during his stay at Buffalo. Bishop Timon took great pains in introducing into his diocese various religious orders, and in building up charitable and educational institutions for the benefit of his flock. In March, 1848, he went to Baltimore to secure the services of the Sisters of Charity, and in June of that year he had the satisfaction of welcoming in Buffalo six Sisters, three of whom were for an orphan asylum and three for an hospital. The Bishop's resources were very, slight—indeed, he was extremely poor; yet by his indomitable will and energy he found properties for these two institutions, and soon put them in operation. They are now among the permanent successful charities of the diocese, the asylum numbering its two hundred orphans, and the hospital its seventeen hundred patients in a single year, the average number being three hundred. In 1851 the Bishop undertook a boys' orphan asylum, and obtained from the Legislature of New York the passage of a charter for it, under the name of St. Joseph's, he having himself prepared the charter and other papers during the night, and succeeding in securing its enactment the next day, amidst the hurrying and crowding out of bills towards the close of the session. It is located on a farm near the city boundaries, purchased for the purpose by the Bishop. As early as 1853 he commenced the great charity of a Foundling Asylum; it was ready for entrances in June, 1854, and is now in a prosperous career of mercy. The want of a cemetery was now felt; the Bishop had not a dollar, but that did not stand in his way. He borrowed the amount, twelve thousand dollars, purchased a farm, and consecrated forty acres for the cemetery. The Deaf and Dumb Asylum, St. Mary's German Orphan Asylum, the Magdalen Asylum, and the Providence Lunatic Asylum, were also among the noble works introduced into the Diocese of Buffalo during his administration. These splendid charities were expressive of the personal and private generosity and benevolence of the good Bishop. His private charities were performed without stint and without regard to his own necessities. The poor never applied to him in vain. Not only was his purse drained for their relief, but his wardrobe was also depleted by his alms-giving. He was at one time reduced to a single shirt, the one on his back, and only discovered the fact on sending his housekeeper to his drawer for a shirt for a beggar whom he met at his door. Like another Vincent de Paul, he brought destitute or abandoned infants in his arms to the Foundling Asylum. He possessed a simplicity of character which is the accompaniment of true greatness. He stopped at no act, however simple or insignificant in appearance, which could do good, and he was not content to leave to others the performance of corporal acts of mercy; he always performed his part with his own hands.

He also enriched his diocese with institutions of learning and education, and bequeathed to his successor a glad inheritance in such treasures. In 1848 he established in his diocese an ecclesiastical Seminary at Suspension Bridge, Niagara County; it commenced with two students, was placed in charge of the Lazarist Fathers, and is now a vigorous establishment. The College and Convent of the Franciscan Fathers, at Alleghany, Cattaraugus County, built upon a large farm given by Mr. Devereux, with a considerable donation in funds, was fortunate in having such an advocate in Europe as Bishop Timon when the colony of Fathers was applied for; it was his efforts that secured the desired number, and prevented any delay in forwarding them to America. The College of St. Joseph, under the care of the Christian Brothers, the Redemptorist Convent of St. Mary, the Community of Missionary Oblate Fathers, the Sisters of Mercy, the Passionist Retreat of St. Mary, the Sisters of St. Joseph, the Sisters of St. Francis, the Gray Sisters, Sisters of St. Mary, are among the religious Orders and institutions which, under his energetic labors and fostering care, became ornaments of his diocese. His resources were severely taxed in his efforts to accomplish so much for his flock, but he was one who seemed to grow young in the service of God and His Church.

In 1853 Bishop Timon visited Mexico, in order to solicit aid from the wealthy Catholics of that country for his projected Cathedral, and other costly undertakings for the improvement of his diocese. Though a good linguist, Spanish was not one of his languages; with an energy unusual at his age, he stopped at New Orleans, and, under the instruction of a Spanish priest, acquired that language so well that his mission to Mexico, and afterwards to Spain, proved great successes. His visit to Mexico also enabled him to vindicate the clergy and Catholics of that country from the gross charges with which it had become too common for Protestants, and even some indifferent Catholics, to assail them. His lecture on Mexico, delivered at St. Patrick's Church, Buffalo, is a production of the highest order, and a fine specimen of Bishop Timon's eloquence, industry, and learning.

He also paid several visits to Europe in the interests of his diocese and of religion. The first of these was in 1850, when his eloquence resounded with marked effect in many of the cities of France, and in the Eternal City itself. On this occasion it was his privilege and happiness to be with the Holy Father on his triumphant return to Rome, the witness and sharer of his joy, and to have delivered, in one of the churches of Rome, an address on the occasion before the soldiers of the victorious expedition, which restored to the Church of God and His Vicar the patrimony of a thousand years' transmission. May it soon be a joy realized for the Bishops of the Universal Church, reassembled in the Council of the Vatican at no distant day, to behold that saintly Pontiff, now again deprived of his dominions and a prisoner in his own city, in the providence of God restored to his rights again, and Rome again made the free and undesecrated capital of the Christian world. The Holy Father, on the very day of his return, graciously received a petition from Bishop Timon, asking "for the salvation of souls and to honor the happy return of his Holiness," a special plenary indulgence to the contributors to the work of the Propagation of the Faith, which he answered on the spot, and with his own hand granted the Bishop's prayer. Bishop Timon was also one of the American Bishops invited by the Holy Father to repair to Rome and take part in the definition of the dogma of the Immaculate Conception of the Blessed Virgin Mary, in 1854. The pious zeal and ardor with which he assisted at this grand event, and with which he supported the dogma itself, are beautifully and eloquently manifested in the noble pastoral letter he addressed to his diocese on his return. On this occasion also the ever-zealous Bishop obtained from the Holy Father a special blessing and indulgence; but now the boon sought and obtained was in favor of the benefactors of the orphan asylums of the Diocese of Buffalo. He availed himself of his presence in Europe to solicit in its various countries contributions towards the erection of his Cathedral at Buffalo. His appeals were addressed to all, from the crowned head to the people; and from all he received the greatest sympathy and substantial assistance. The King of Bavaria especially was delighted with the piety, zeal, and eloquence of Bishop Timon, and testified his appreciation by remitting afterwards a handsome contribution towards his undertakings. Again, in 1857, Bishop Timon visited Europe on urgent business for his diocese; was present at the celebration of the great feast of Sts. Peter and Paul, and received from the Holy Father an Apostolic benediction for himself, his clergy, and people. His journey was extended through several of the continental countries, and to England and Ireland. He was the bearer of a special message from the Pope to the Emperor of France. The Emperor Napoleon received him with marked consideration, and admitted him to a protracted audience. The Bishop dined with the Emperor and Empress, and received from the latter a munificent donation for his struggling and needy diocese. His last visit to Rome was made in the spring and summer of 1862, on the occasion of the canonization of the twenty-six martyrs of Japan. He was received by the Holy Father with a paternal embrace; and on his return to his own diocese he was welcomed with the most enthusiastic and joyous demonstrations by his flock. In all his visits to Europe, Bishop Timon took especial interest in visiting the religious and charitable institutions, churches, and cathedrals; his observant and intelligent eye appreciated all he saw in the structure, management, improvements, and architecture of those grand monuments of Catholic faith and charity. In his own young and unprovided diocese everything was yet to be done, and he studied from the older and more venerable models of Europe the best way of doing it. His mind, from repeated travels and an earnest and interested observation, became stored with a fund of useful, practical, and artistic information, which he turned to good account in rearing up the institutions and churches of his own diocese. Frequent personal intercourse had made his virtues known and himself personally endeared to his Holiness, Pope Pius IX., whose guest he was several times at the Vatican, and by whom he was made one of the Prelates of the Papal throne. The Holy Father regarded him as one of the foremost Bishops of America, whose senior he was; and it may be said that he was held in the same estimate by the Bishops of the Catholic Church, both at home and abroad.

Bishop Timon not only took part in those august assemblies at Rome to which allusion has been made, but also had an active share in those Councils, whether Diocesan, Provincial, or National, which assembled from time to time in our own country. In carrying out the decrees and recommendations of the Councils of Baltimore, he was ever earnest and active, as his pastorals well demonstrate, and as his efforts in behalf of the American College at Rome and other general interests of the Church in this country amply prove. He took particular pains in holding retreats for the clergy of his diocese, greatly edifying them by his saintly example. He endeavored both by precept and example to make his clergy models of the virtues which it was their vocation to inculcate in others, and models especially of the virtues peculiar to the ecclesiastical state. He made great efforts to reform the abuses which, contrary to the spirit of the Church, he saw gaining ground in the funerals of some Catholics; the lavish display on such occasions, the extravagant number of the carriages in attendance, and the frivolity and even hilarity which were sometimes indulged in, met with his earnest condemnation and open opposition. The protection and vindication of Catholic marriage was another point on which Bishop Timon was justly sensitive and earnestly active. His pastoral letter, after the retreat of the clergy of his diocese in 1856, is replete with salutary counsels; a brief extract will suffice to show how he handled this important subject:—

"Here, as in every part of our country, we have had to deplore the profanation of the Holy Sacrament of Marriage, the heart-breaking woe and misery, and the awful scandal that ensued. To protect God's people from the occurrence of such evils, we have decreed that whoever, neglecting priestly ministry, or priestly admonition, will be married by a non-Catholic minister, or a magistrate, shall, by the very act, become excommunicated. And also that those wicked persons who attempt a second marriage whilst their first consort is living, deceiving the priest either by culpable silence or sacrilegious falsehood, and all guilty witnesses or abettors to such marriages, which they must know to be unholy and invalid, are, by the very fact, excommunicated; and that absolution from this major excommunication is reserved to the Bishop. Pray to God, dearly beloved, that these regulations may prevent the recurrence of crimes which call down a curse of God upon the guilty parties, their advisers, and abettors."

Bishop Timon adorned his diocese with many noble churches, and undertook frequent and laborious journeys through our own and other countries in aid of them. The splendid Cathedral of St. Joseph, at Buffalo, was with him an object of uncommon zeal and extraordinary labors and trials. Even after he had secured the ground, efforts were made by bigoted persons to get it from him; and even after its erection the same spirit of bigotry compassed its destruction, and there was one at least ready to contribute eight thousand dollars towards its demolition. Commenced in 1852, and persevered with under unparalleled opposition and great pecuniary difficulties, it was a great happiness to the zealous Prelate, in 1855, to dedicate that fine temple to the Almighty, assisted as he was in the grateful ceremony by fourteen Bishops and a hundred priests. May its walls and spires long stand, and its altar send heavenward its incense and oblation in honor of the one true God, and in grateful remembrance of its founder and first Bishop! And may its melodious carillon of forty-three bells long continue to peal forth the solemn hour of the Holy Mass, and call a devout people to that chaste and elegant temple of prayer and sacrifice!

Bishop Timon's episcopal visitations were, like his old missionary tours in Missouri and Texas, full of labor; a labor which bore its glorious fruit as the laborer passed along, and long afterwards. On arriving at a place, he usually went, if possible, immediately to the Church to adore the Blessed Sacrament. He always rose early, was in the confessional at an early hour in the morning and at a late hour at night; he preached several times a day, and found time amidst these and such other duties, as administering confirmation, dedicating churches, laying corner-stones, receiving the vows of religious, instructing children, etc., to perform his own private devotions, and frequently to answer his correspondents. He was never idle. He was only happy in doing good, and no good act, however simple, was too humble for the Bishop to perform. His life was devoted to building up the Church of God on earth. The rich legacy of religious, charitable, and educational institutions which he left to his diocese, attests his devotion to that cause.

From the highest, most sacred, and important functions of the episcopate to the slightest act of charity, from the presence of the Pontiff to that of the beggar, Bishop Timon did all things and treated all men with Christian charity. His advocacy of Catholic rights on the school question was courageous and unflinching. On this and all other subjects his heart was in sympathy with Catholic interests. His devotion to the Apostolic See was very great, and in the swelling tide of sympathy and substantial aid which flowed from the Catholic dioceses of this country to Rome, the diocese of Bishop Timon was among the foremost. He was a great preacher, always ready and willing to preach; he never needed extended preparation, and preaching seemed not to fatigue him. His manner was characteristic; he appeared to be ever pleading for a great end, for some great good; to language highly scriptural and argumentative he added a certain poetic manner and coloring, and this, together with his earnest and noble gestures, made him appear like a being of another world. He seemed to see the things of Heaven, and to be gifted with the faculty of describing them in the language of earth. He lectured and preached to the last. His last lecture was at Dansville, in 1866, and though compelled to sit, from declining health, the effort was one of the finest productions of his intellect. His last sermon was delivered in his own Cathedral not many days before his death, and as he sat and spoke from a chair to the people, he seemed like one descending into the grave, but with the impress of immediate resurrection imprinted on his countenance. On this occasion he predicted his approaching end; and while all others were moved to tears, he alone was happy in the thought of meeting the

Creator whom he had served so faithfully. Instead of requesting the clergymen present with him at morning prayers, on Monday of Holy Week, to pray for some of the many pious objects of the living which he had in view, as was his custom, he requested them on this occasion to pray for his own happy death. He had labored as usual up to this time, and was just previously contemplating another trip to Rome in the interests of his diocese.

Before recording his death, let us briefly recount some more of the virtues that adorned his admirable character, and mention some few additional illustrations of his saintly life. The humility and simplicity of mind and soul which were observed in the young missionary of the Barrens, became more perfectly practised in the venerable Bishop of Buffalo. These virtues were intimately associated with other kindred virtues, such as his unbounded charity for man, and his seraphic love of God. Thus, while he stripped himself of all things, he gave all to the poor and to the service of God; his own clothing he distributed to his poor neighbor, even to the last garment, remarking that even rags were " good enough for the old Bishop;" and his intimate friends found it difficult to keep his wardrobe supplied after these incessant spoliations. In bestowing his best raiment upon the poor, he felt that he was clothing Jesus Christ in their persons. But when he turned to the sanctuary and the altar, where God Himself was corporally present, he was lavish of everything that earth could offer to the King of Heaven and Earth. It was even in the magnificence of the temple that his simplicity of character was developed, for like a child he delighted in giving away all he had, but faith sanctified the offering by directing it to God. That same simplicity caused him to delight in the society of the young ; at the Seminaries and Colleges he visited, he took pleasure in conversing, without reserve, with the students; and at the Orphan Asylums of his own diocese the children felt at home with him, romped with him, and would mount the Bishop's back for a ride. He always traveled in the humblest and simplest manner, departing and arriving unannounced, carrying his valise in his hand, and walking to and from the stations. On visiting a church in any city, he joined the throng of penitents, and took his turn; afterwards he sat in the confessional as long as there was any one to hear. If his zeal caused him to wound the feelings of others, he was prompt to beg pardon, and was known on more than one occasion to ask pardon of his own priests in the presence of others, and on one occasion in the presence of another Bishop. He could bear the grossest insult in public without even noticing it, without a change of expression. His modesty was pained by the acts of veneration rendered to the episcopal office in his person. When retreats for the clergy were given at Buffalo, he was the first to arise and attend the devotions and conferences, after having gone through the episcopal residence, candle in hand, and summoned each one to respond to the invitation of the bell, which had just rung. In the retreats and missions for the laity, he was busy in hunting up those who were the most negligent of their duty, and to sinners returning to the Church his charity and mildness were unbounded; in handing such over to the Fathers conducting the exercises he would say, " Father, I leave this case in your hands. I give you all power, *only save his soul.*" Often, when even priests would kneel to ask his blessing, he fell upon his knees to ask theirs. He sought to make his clergy as perfect as himself, especially in humility, for he had but little hope for a proud priest. He followed the practice of religious orders in changing the missions of his clergy, in order to detach them from human affections. He was a model of prayer; no important decision was rendered by him until he had spent long hours in prayer; and frequently, during the ceremonies of festivals, he spent the hours devoted to them in the shadow of the altar, in the perfect retirement of meditation and devotion. While traveling he was frequently seen kneeling in his place in the cars. His household always commenced and ended the day with family prayers and meditations. He spent little time in sleep, rose early, and spent long hours of the night in prayer, meditations, writing, or other exercises. It was no uncommon thing for the members of a religious community, on assembling at their morning devotions, to find Bishop Timon on his knees in the chapel, the first to arrive, though he had already traveled some distance that morning. His episcopate gave him opportunities of practising in an eminent degree the highest virtues; yet there were not wanting some to accuse him of faults of whose opposite virtues he was a model.*

It is supposed that Bishop Timon contracted the disease of erysipelas, of which he died, from an expiring Sister of Charity, whose last confession he received. He suffered from this trouble two or three years before his death. From the time that he felt his last end at hand, he spent his time in preparing for it. His affairs were always kept in good order, so that no confusion would arise after his death. His approaching end was

---

* *The Catholic World*, April, 1871.

known for some days by the community, and citizens of all religions united with Catholics in testifying their respect and regard for him, both before and after the sad event. His own mind was wholly engaged in prayer, ejaculating to the last, "Lord, into Thy hands I commend my spirit!" or calling on the name of "Jesus, Mary, and Joseph." Bishop Lynch, of Toronto, and Bishop Farrell, of Hamilton, Canada, administered to him the last rites of the Church. His saintly life was closed by a holy death on April 16, 1867. The honors paid to his memory by assembled Prelates and priests, and by the ninety thousand persons who went to view in silent reverence his remains, seem to us but like the things of men and earth, in the contemplation of his exalted virtues, his pure and noble character, and his immortal deeds. These were all of Heaven. His life was a struggle to open the gates of Heaven for all men to enter. Few men have done more in their day to point on earth the road that leads to immortality.

RIGHT REV. JOHN S. BAZIN, D.D.,

*Third Bishop of Vincennes, A.D. 1847.**

BISHOP BAZIN was born in the Archdiocese of Lyons, France, in the year 1796. He received his ecclesiastical education and ordination in the priesthood in France, and came to Mobile, Alabama, about the year 1830. For seventeen years he faithfully and zealously discharged the duties of the holy ministry in that city, and was particularly devoted to the religious instruction of youth, and to the organization and conduct of the Sunday-schools. The cotemporaneous publications mention him as "a most indefatigable clergyman," and as one who "had exercised the holy ministry with great zeal, devotedness, and success." They inform us that "wherever he was known he was universally beloved." They also mention him as a most faithful co-laborer of Bishop Portier, with whom he co-operated "with his wonted impetuous energy." He also filled the important office of Vicar-General of Mobile. He established at Mobile a Catholic benevolent female society, under the direction of a pious lady, which grew under his patronage into a Catholic orphan asylum society. In 1846 he went to France, at the request of Bishop Portier, to obtain from the Superiors of the Society of Jesus a colony of that Order to take charge of the College at Spring Hill, and to secure the services of the Brothers of the Christian

---

* Authorities: *Life of Bishop Flaget*, by Archbishop Spalding; *Life of Bishop Bruté*, by Bishop Bayley; *Catholic Almanac*, etc., etc.

Schools to take charge of the male orphan asylum, and he succeeded in both these efforts.

On the resignation of the Right Rev. Celestine de la Hailandière, Bishop of Vincennes, in 1847, the Sixth Provincial Council of Baltimore nominated Father Bazin for that see, and he was accordingly appointed at Rome. The Catholics of Mobile, on hearing of his election to the episcopate, and of his approaching loss to Mobile, held a meeting and expressed in the warmest terms their sentiments of love and veneration for him, and of sincere regret at his departure from them. He was consecrated at Vincennes, October 24, 1847. The first efforts of his episcopal career gave great promise of usefulness to the Church; but scarcely had he entered upon that career, when he was summoned, after a few days' illness, to his final account. During his last illness he appointed the present Right Rev. Bishop of Vincennes, then one of his Vicars-General, administrator of the diocese during the vacancy of the see. His death occurred April 23, 1848. His remains repose, together with those of his saintly predecessor, Bishop Bruté, under the Cathedral of Vincennes.

RIGHT REV. JAMES OLIVER VAN DE VELDE, D.D.,

Second Bishop of Chicago, and Second Bishop of Natchez, A.D. 1848.*

JAMES OLIVER VAN DE VELDE was born April 3, 1795, in the environs of Termonde, Belgium, of a family high in official influence and social position, the advantages of which he cheerfully renounced in order to embrace the labors and privations of the holy ministry. During his youthful days his native country was greatly disturbed by the convulsions of the French Revolution, so that his character was moulded and strengthened after the examples of the confessors of the Faith. When very young he was confided to the care and instruction of a pious aunt in the village of St. Amand, in Flanders. Here the tender instructions of home were mingled with a personal observation and admiration for the exiles of religion, and the sufferers for justice' sake, who took refuge in Belgium. One of these holy men, an excellent clergyman, a refugee from the revolution in France, happened to be an inmate in the same family with young Van de Velde, and that family altar was at once a retreat for piety and learning, youth and innocence. This good and faithful priest took charge of the education of James, and especially of his moral training. He devoted himself to this grateful task with uncommon care and exactness, and the pupil on his part cheerfully corresponded with the efforts of his preceptor. So much was this the

---

* Authorities: *Western Missions and Missionaries*, by Father De Smet; *Catholic Almanac*, 1856; and various cotemporaneous publications.

case that he attracted the attention of the clergy of the village, with whom he became a favorite. His inclination towards the religious life was manifested at an early age, and even then he found great attraction in the society of good and learned priests. In 1810, at the age of fifteen, he was sent to a boarding-school near Ghent, where he soon became distinguished among his fellows by his proficiency and talents. When eighteen years old he taught French and Flemish at Puers, and continued this employment for several years. But in the mean time great changes took place in the political and religious condition of Belgium, under the treaties negotiated by an European Congress, and designed to settle the state of Europe after the French Revolution—a modern contrivance for adjusting the balance of power, by which the weaker nations are disposed of without their concurrence, and against their interests and traditions, to suit the conveniences or satisfy the jealousies or cupidity of the greater powers; which contrasts strangely with the purer and more Catholic notions of international law and justice which prevailed in the Middle Ages, when a small and weak nation was respected and secured in its individual nationality and independence, and when there was a recognized umpire at Rome, then the actual and glorious capital of Christendom, to whom the weak could appeal for protection against the strong. Thus Catholic Belgium was united by the Congress of Vienna to Protestant 'Holland, and her Catholic people made subjects of the bigoted William I., a Calvinist and violent enemy of the Catholic religion. Young Van de Velde's independent spirit was greatly wounded by this wrong, and he conceived the intention of going to England or Italy. He applied himself to the study of the languages of those countries, and as he had a talent for languages, he readily succeeded. This seemed like a Providential turn in his life, for while the English prepared him for the wide field of usefulness which he afterwards so zealously entered in America, the Italian added to his attainments as a professor at Georgetown College and St. Louis University, and facilitated his intercourse with Italy as a Prelate of the Church. His design of quitting his native country was delayed by the persuasions of his former friend and confessor, the Very Rev. M. Verlooy, director of the Seminary of Mechlin, who induced him to remain and accept a professorship of Latin, French, and Flemish in the new institution that gentleman was then commencing. This same good friend, at the same time, led him to place his name on the list of students of the great Archiepiscopal Seminary at Mechlin. In this double capacity of professor and pupil he learned at one and the same time the great lesson of wisdom involved in governing and being governed; for he knows best how to command and to lead who has himself been trained in the school of obedience. It was also while enjoying these advantages that he perfected himself in the Latin classics. Here too he studied with success the elements of logic, and made good progress in the study of speculative theology.

These interesting and engrossing occupations did not, however, wean his thoughts from the contemplated pursuit of another country and home. His good friend, Father Verlooy, guided these thoughts into a holy channel, and directed his attention to the foreign missions. Providence threw in his way, about this time, one of the most celebrated missionaries of the new world; this was Father Charles Nerinckx, of Kentucky, who had been to Rome in the interests of our western missions, and especially those of Kentucky, and who on his return visited Mechlin. Young Van de Velde was not slow in seeking this saintly man and pioneer missionary, who imparted to him full information on the American missions, their necessities, want of laborers, and of the abundant fruits they produced; and the young follower of the Cross disclosed in turn his fixed purpose of devoting himself to so glorious a work. His self-offering was accepted, and it was arranged that he should accompany Father Nerinckx to America, complete his theological studies at Bishop Flaget's Seminary, at Bardstown, Kentucky, and then devote his life to the labors of the mission.

Father Nerinckx embarked for America May 16, 1817, bringing with him a number of young Belgians, destined for the novitiate of the Society of Jesus at Georgetown. Among them was Mr. Van de Velde. He, however, met with a serious accident on the voyage, which not only greatly impaired his health, but also, in the designs of Providence, greatly changed his destination and the events of his future life. During a violent storm he was thrown down on the ship with such force that he broke a blood-vessel and suffered a great loss of blood. On arriving at Baltimore he was so weak that he had to be carried to St. Mary's Seminary in that city, and was unable to continue his journey to Kentucky. The good and learned Father Bruté, discerning his fine abilities and future usefulness, endeavored to detain him in Baltimore; but Father Nerinckx earnestly advised him to follow his companions, those with whom God had thrown him for some wise purpose, to Georgetown College, and avail himself of that system of training which had given a Xavier to India and a Father Jogues to America—that same field, the mission, which he had selected for himself. Young Van de Velde's soul was ever alive to the inspirations of faith, that faith which brings us in constant contact with God; hence he recognized Father Nerinckx as his providential guide and counselor, and preferred to follow his advice. The Rev. Anthony Kohlman, then Superior of the Jesuits, received him with great kindness, and introduced him into the novitiate of the Society of Jesus. A novitiate of two years prepared him for the reception of Minor Orders, and he then went through the regular collegiate course of poetry, rhetoric, and philosophy. There too, as at Mechlin, he was at once student and professor, and in the latter capacity conducted the class of *belles-lettres*. After ten years spent in these pursuits, and in making the course of theology, he was prepared for ordination, and was raised to the priesthood at Baltimore, by Archbishop Maréchal, September 25, 1827. After his ordination he continued the study of moral and dogmatic theology for two years, and during the same time performed the duties of chaplain to the Convent and Academy of the Visitation, at Georgetown.

Father Van de Velde's first missionary labors commenced in 1829, when, by the appointment of his superior, he served the mission of Rockville and Rock Creek, in Montgomery County, Maryland, contiguous to Georgetown College, where he continued to reside. Thus he traversed the roads which the early Jesuits of Maryland had followed, and attended the missions in which Father Carroll, afterwards Archbishop, himself had labored, one of which, Rock Creek, was the residence of the Archbishop's family, and of himself before his elevation to the See of Baltimore.

The time was now approaching when Father Van de Velde was to enter that great West which had been the subject of his youthful aspirations at Mechlin. The Jesuits, chosen instructors of youth, had established at St. Louis a College, under the patronage of Bishop Rosati, which was in active operation in 1831, when his superiors sent Father Van de Velde to increase the corps of teachers. One who had proved so useful a member of the parent house, at Georgetown, was cordially and joyfully welcomed at the rising College of St. Louis, where almost immediately he filled the professorship of rhetoric and mathematics. In 1833, when the College was raised by the Legislature of Missouri to the rank and name of University of St. Louis, he was appointed Vice-President, and at the same time filled the office of procurator to the institution. He continued these employments until 1837, when, upon making the solemn vows, he became a professed member of the Society. While filling the office of Vice-President of the University, he was also appointed procurator of the vice-province of the Society in Missouri. He was made President of the University of St. Louis in 1840. His attachment to his adopted country, and his admiration for free institutions under constitutional safeguards, are well set forth in a published address which he made at the University, July 4, 1841. In the same year he was selected as the representative of the vice-province of Missouri, in the congregation of procurators of the Society which assembled at Rome. While attending the sessions of this body, he was honored with several audiences by the Sovereign Pontiff, Pope Gregory XVI. Returning to St. Louis, he resumed his office as President of the University, and continued to discharge its duties until 1843, when he was appointed Vice-Provincial of Missouri. While occupying this important office, the interests of religion were greatly promoted by his zeal and energy. Several churches were erected under his auspices, and confided to the care of the Society. The Indian missions received a large share of his efforts, and a great portion of the disposable funds of the vice-province of Missouri was devoted to the relief of the Indians. He also labored personally among the Indian tribes of Missouri Territory. Under his administration a more spacious house of novitiate was erected at the University, and the colleges and missions flourished in a remarkable degree. In 1848 he again held the office of Procurator of the vice-province of Missouri, and was also socius to the Vice-Provincial. In the Sixth Council of Baltimore, 1846, he represented the vice-province of Missouri.

The prominent position occupied by Father Van de Velde in his own Order, the important services rendered by him to the cause of religion in the United States, and the acquaintance which was thus formed between him and many of the Prelates of the Church, who entertained a high appreciation of his talents, piety, and zeal, led to his being selected as the successor of Bishop Quarter in the Diocese of Chicago. Archbishop Eccleston received from Rome the bulls appointing him to that see, December 1, 1848, and immediately transmitted them to him. It was only on the decision of the Archbishop of St. Louis and of three theologians, that the documents from Rome contained a formal command from the Sovereign Pontiff that he should accept the appointment, that he consented to do so. He was consecrated by the Archbishop of St. Louis, assisted by Bishops Loras and Miles, on Sunday, February 11, 1849, in the Church of St. Francis Xavier, attached to the University of St. Louis. Bishop Spalding, of Louisville, preached the consecration sermon.

Bishop Van de Velde did not proceed immediately to Chicago, to take possession of his see, but, as an extensive country lay between St. Louis and Chicago, he visited that part of his diocese lying nearest to St. Louis, and thus commenced at once the work of his Episcopate. He reached Chicago on Palm Sunday. After spending a few months in arranging the concerns of the diocese in Chicago and vicinity, he began his first visitation of the diocese, July 25, 1849. These visitations were journeys of severe labor and unremitting zeal for the spiritual improvement of his flock. Besides administration of confirmation at all practicable times and places, the distances were so great and the means of traveling so inconvenient and uncertain, that he had to pass through the country as a missionary, laboring for the salvation of souls, and performing every kind of clerical and spiritual service. Besides visiting St. Louis twice, where he officiated pontifically and conferred minor orders on several members of the Society of Jesus, and the holy order of priesthood on several of the same Society, one of whom was the afterwards distinguished and eloquent Father Smarius, he visited and officiated in twenty-two other places during this the first visitation of his diocese, and several of them he visited more than once. Many of these places were points of historical interest, and associated with the early Jesuit missions along the banks of the Missouri and Mississippi. Among these were Prairie-du-Rocher, Kaskaskia, Ottawa, La Salle, and Joliet Imbued as he was with the spirit of his Order, Bishop Van de Velde felt and expressed great joy in treading the paths of his brethren of preceding centuries. At Prairie-du-Rocher the Bishop had the consolation of accomplishing a long-cherished object of his, and of rendering a merited honor to an illustrious and departed member of the Society of Jesus, and the last of the resident Jesuit missionaries of the last century in the West. Father Louis Sebastian Meurin, of the Society of Jesus, had spent over thirty years in the mission of the Illinois. He was at Vincennes from 1749 to 1753. His labors for twenty-four years after this were continued at various points in the Illinois country, where he devoted his life to the spiritual care of the Indian tribes and French settlers. He was the only Jesuit missionary left with his flock after the suppression of the Society in France and its dependencies in 1763, and with the exception of occasional visits made by Father Peter Potier from Detroit, as late as 1781, he was the last Jesuit in the West after the suppression. He died and was buried in the midst of his flock, February 23, 1777. Several years before his appointment to the See of Chicago, Father Van de Velde had obtained permission from his predecessor, Bishop Quarter, to search for and transport the remains of this venerable Father. It was not until now, when as Bishop of the diocese himself, and while reviving the labors of the deceased missionary, that he was able to accomplish his pious purpose. From a careful examination of the Catholic records of Kaskaskia, Prairie-du-Rocher, and other stations, he had succeeded in tracing out the exact spot where Father Meurin was buried, which was under the window on the gospel side of the altar of the church of St. Joseph, at Prairie-du-Rocher, then the oldest church remaining in the West. With the aid of the French inhabitants of the village, the floor of the sanctuary was opened by the Bishop, and after they had dug to the depth of a foot they discovered the grave, and within it the remains of the departed missionary. The Bishop gathered them together in a box, on which he placed a suitable inscription, and carried them with him to St. Louis; thence they were "transported," wrote Bishop Van de Velde, "to St. Stanislaus, where exists the first cemetery of the restored Society in the West, a beautiful spot, and where his precious remains, reposing near those of F. F. Van Quickenborne, Zimmermans, Detheny and others, will form the connecting link between the suppressed and revived Society." *

It was during this visitation that he paid a visit to Nauvoo, the first Mecca of the Mormons, where he administered confirmation in the church, which was the same building that was formerly used as the dwelling of one of the twelve apostles of the "Church of Christ of Latter Day Saints." A part of the same house was also the residence of Father Kennedy, the Catholic pastor, which was shared with him by a German family. The scene around was desolate; the country for miles was strewed with the ruins of the once Mormon city; the walls of the grand temple were merely standing, as sad mementoes of human folly and delusion, and in their decay gave evidence of the magnificence of that once proud structure. The city, which had swarmed with its twenty thousand inhabitants, then scarcely contained as

---

* Letter of Bishop Van de Velde, in *Freeman's Journal* of September 15, 1849.

many hundreds. But a stranger feature still in this strange scene was the oft-told lesson of human folly, uninstructed by the experience of others, repeating itself in another form, and in the very presence of the monuments of the silent but teaching past. A colony of Socialists, or Communists, calling themselves very properly Icarians, under the leadership of an elderly Frenchman named Cabet, had purchased the site and ruins of the Mormon temple, and, to the number of about two hundred, were endeavoring to live together in phalanstery, thus repeating a folly more ancient than Mormonism. Distrust and discontent had already begun to undermine their social fabric. Most of them were mechanics who had confided to Mons. Cabet their money, and had expended for him their labor, for which they saw no return. They soon discovered that their trusted leader had been a swindler in France, and was a fugitive from justice. The discovery of these facts at Nauvoo soon stripped the plumes from this soaring follower of Icarus, and the phalanstery went in the way of all its predecessors. But even at the time of Bishop Van de Velde's visit to Nauvoo a more benign influence was rising there, and a more propitious tide of immigration was pouring in. Mingled with the new settlers were not a few Catholics, and the Bishop had the happiness of administering confirmation to forty-six persons.

The Bishop's visit to the ancient town of Kaskaskia, renowned in the history of the early missions, was not devoid of interest. The Catholics came in great numbers, mounted on horseback, and met the Bishop about seven miles from the town; the old gun, whose silence was never broken except on the Fourth of July, was brought forth to welcome his coming, and the whole country for miles around was aroused by his advent. A large but pewless church could scarcely contain the crowds that flocked in to receive the Prelate's ministry, and when he departed, after a brief but fruitful stay, he was escorted by a troop of cavalry, who, on leaving him, dismounted and threw themselves on their knees to receive their Bishop's blessing.

This, his first visitation, lasted five weeks, during which he took no rest; and this is but a sample of his labors. He sometimes only returned from one laborious journey to start on the same day upon another. He was indefatigable in his care for his flock. Before his departure on the visitation above mentioned, his paternal heart was greatly moved by the sad condition of the many destitute orphans who had lost their parents during the cholera. He had gathered them together and boarded them out at his own expense. On his return from his visitation he placed the female orphans, to the number of forty-four, in hired houses, under the care of the Sisters of Mercy, and a house on the lot on which the Bishop lived was given by him for the boys' asylum, which started with thirty orphan boys. His means were too limited to maintain the house as a pastoral residence, yet he found means to fit it up and maintain therein a much larger family of orphans. With means which he collected from both Catholics and Protestants, he procured furniture for his two asylums, and food and clothing for the children. These small beginnings have since expanded into flourishing institutions, and as long as he remained in Chicago he contributed to the full extent of his means to their maintenance. He remained at home only two weeks to attend to these generous works and bring up his correspondence, and then started on a visitation of the southern portion of the State, a missionary journey equal to that just finished, and most productive of consoling fruits.

Bishop Van de Velde's health had not been very good for several years, and he suffered severely from rheumatism, which was greatly aggravated by the cold, damp, and penetrating air of Chicago. It is wonderful how he could have accomplished such labors while enduring such sufferings. His health was still further impaired by the anxieties of his office, and by the hostility and opposition of a small number of his clergy, who seduced to their support a portion of the laity. To one who had devoted himself both to the service of his clergy and laity, it was a severe and unmerited return to find his measures thwarted, and even charges preferred against him at Rome. Very few, however, took part in these unjust and ungrateful measures, and there were few Bishops who enjoyed more than he did the love and veneration of his clergy and people. A few disaffected persons, however, can accomplish much evil, and Bishop Van de Velde frequently found himself without adequate sympathy or support in his charitable efforts.

In consequence of his suffering health, and the unfavorable influence of the north-western climate, he had long desired to petition Rome to release him from the burden of office. The Roman revolution prevented him from having access to the Holy See for this purpose for some time. On the restoration of the Holy Father to the Eternal City he sent his petition, requesting permission to resign his bishopric and return to his brethren of the Society of Jesus. On receiving a reply from Cardinal Fransoni, encouraging him to bear the burdens of the episcopate, he continued as before to labor and to endure with patience and resignation. After some time, a renewal of the troubles and difficulties which had arisen in his diocese had so unfavorable an effect upon his health that he was constrained to renew his petition to Rome. Rome referred the matter to the first National Council, which assembled at Baltimore, May 9, 1852. The Council, while creating a new see at Quincy for the southern portion of Illinois, yet recommended the retention of Bishop Van de Velde at Chicago. The Bishop, who took part as a member of this august assembly, was selected by it as the bearer of its decrees to Rome for approval. This mission he undertook more readily, as it was already his intention to visit France and Belgium, and he now resolved to extend his journey to Rome, in order to prefer his petition for release to the Sovereign Pontiff in person. He arrived at the Holy City June 22, and was received most kindly by the Holy Father, Pius IX., from whom he received two audiences; which resulted in his obtaining a favorable answer to his petition. He was assured that he would be restored to the Society of Jesus, though in the quality of titular Bishop, and that he would be translated to a milder and more favorable climate. He left Rome September 16, visited portions of France, Germany, and Belgium, and whilst at Liege, assisted at the consecration of Mgr. de Montpellier. November 17, he embarked at Liverpool for New York, and arrived at the latter place on the 28th of the same month.

On returning to Chicago he resumed his labors as before, but they were interrupted by the return of his disease. As a relief to his sufferings, he paid a visit to the Fathers of the Holy Cross, at Notre Dame du Lac, in the diocese of Vincennes, where he spent eight or ten days. On his return he commenced the visitation of his diocese, which was resumed from time to time and continued till September. The accounts received of this journey awaken our surprise how one person could do and accomplish so much. He gave confirmation in thirty-three places, many of them at great distances apart, blessed five new churches, laid the corner-stones of five new ones, all of brick, and of good dimensions, while the foundations of three more were being laid, and arrangements were made for the commencement of several others in different locations. The increase in the number of Catholics during his administration at Chicago was very great, and at the time of this visitation was believed to have reached one hundred thousand. He had since Easter visited nearly every Catholic congregation or settlement in the State of Illinois, traveled over six thousand miles, given confirmation in more than fifty-eight places, and confirmed nearly three thousand six hundred persons. In the short space of four years he had commenced not less than seventy churches, to nearly all of which he contributed liberally from his own limited means; nearly sixty of these were ready, or nearly so, for divine service; fifty-three of them were built in places where before there was no church, and seventeen were built to replace old and small chapels removed. Most of these churches were of very respectable sizes, and several were one hundred and fifty feet long and sixty feet wide. Besides these churches, eleven others, which had been commenced and left unfinished before his accession, were completed by him. The whole number of churches in Illinois, in October, 1853, was one hundred and nineteen. Many other important establishments and works were commenced, and most of them completed by Bishop Van de Velde before his translation to Natchez.

It was during the visitation of his diocese that he received from Rome the brief transferring him to the vacant See of Natchez, agreeably to his own request. The transfer dates, in fact, from July 29, 1853. The refusal of Bishop Melcher to accept the new See of Quincy, to which was annexed the administration of the See of Chicago, upon the translation of Bishop Van de Velde, caused the Archbishop of St. Louis to request Bishop Van de Velde to accept the administration of those two dioceses, which he readily consented to do; thus, until Bishops could be established at Quincy and Chicago, assuming on his shoulders the burden of three dioceses. His great devotion to the cause of religion is signally shown in the zeal with which he labored up to the last moment for the two dioceses which he was on the eve of quitting. Not only in the diocese of Chicago were his labors unabated, but in the new See of Quincy he commenced the work, which most others would have left to the Bishop to be appointed for that post. Thus we see him purchasing a beautiful piece of land as a site for the future Cathedral of Quincy. Thus too we see him make arrangements to rebuild the frame church at Aurora, which had been blown down in a hurricane. Thus also we see him, on the eve of his departure, and while suffering with his disease, undertaking, in an unusually inclement season, even for that climate, the long, cold, and laborious journey by way of Waukegan to Mechanics' Settlement, in order to lay the corner-stone of a new church. The journey was made in a carriage hired for the purpose, through a cold and violent storm of snow and wind. One of the most respectable citizens of Waukegan claimed the honor of driving the Bishop's carriage. On arriving at the spot, the only preparation for the ceremony was a large hole dug for the cornerstone; but the corner-stone itself, which, lodged in a wagon, had accompanied the Bishop's party in that unpleasant journey from Chicago, had gone astray and had traveled out of the diocese to Kenosha. Telegrams and wagons were sent to arrest the wanderer, but in vain; and when all were assembled on the site of the future church, every countenance expressed disappointment except that of the Bishop, who, with a countenance unclouded by the storm, by his own sufferings, or by the common disappointment, coolly and cheerfully went to work. He immediately called for a tape-line or measure to lay off the dimensions of the church; as no measure could be procured, he deliberately stepped off the dimensions, had stakes driven in at the corners and along the sides, and the cross planted in the spot where the future altar was to be raised. He announced that Mass would begin, after Mass confirmation, and next and last the corner-stone would be laid, provided that wandering though inert mass should be arrested and brought back in time. The storm was still raging; Mass was celebrated under a shed by the Rev. Mr. Coyle, the pastor of the neighboring district, at which sixty persons received holy communion; a sermon also was preached, and after that the Bishop, coming forward, delivered a short exhortation, recited the prayer before confirmation, and then bestowed confirmation upon the sixty devout persons whose piety had so well sustained them in the midst of such a terrific conflict of the elements. While performing these ceremonies the Bishop stood under the shed with his priests and people; the intense cold hardened the sacred oils and stiffened the fingers of the ministering Bishop and priest, the leaves of the book had to be held down, and the Bishop was frequently seen to brush away the flakes of snow from the passages he was reciting from it. After all these labors and devotions, there were few in the pious assembly who regretted the non-arrival of the corner-stone. A cold ride of several miles through the storm was now encountered before a fire could be approached or their hunger relieved.

It was thus that Bishop Van de Velde continued to the last the great work of religion. He never rested from his labors, and, when he finally departed from Chicago for Natchez, there were few indeed, either of the clergy or laity, that did not sincerely regret the loss of such an apostolic Prelate to the Diocese of Chicago; that there should have been even a few, is one of the sad evidences of human weakness which the church has sometimes had occasion to lament.

Bishop Van de Velde departed for the South, November 3, 1853, and arrived at Natchez, November 23, where he was most joyfully received by all the clergy and people, who had so often heard of his great labors, noble sacrifices, and heroic services to religion. He proceeded on to New Orleans, assisted at the consecration of the Right Rev. Dr. Martin, Bishop of Natchitoches, made a spiritual retreat at Spring Hill College, near Mobile, and thence proceeded to Natchez and took possession of his See, December 18.

His administration of the Diocese of Natchez lasted but two years, but they were years of zealous labor. With renewed zeal he commenced his new work, and undertook and accomplished much for the extension of religion in Mississippi. One of his first acts was to make the visitation of his diocese, to investigate the condition of the various congregations and their necessities, and make every effort to supply them with good and zealous pastors. He founded two schools at Natchez, and took measures for completing its Cathedral. He also undertook the work of erecting a College, and purchased a fine property in the suburbs of the city for this purpose. His career of usefulness was suddenly cut short in the inscrutable designs of Providence.

His death was truly a painful and afflicting one, but at the same time it was a death which affords great instruction to the living, in giving an example how a Christian ought to die. On October 23, 1855, he met with a severe accident by falling down the stairway, breaking his leg in two places. The news of this misfortune soon spread abroad, and the Catholic population flocked around the episcopal residence to express their sorrow and to make every offer of sympathy and assistance to their beloved chief pastor. A fever which accompanied the inflammation of the leg soon partook of the nature of the prevailing epidemic; yellow fever seized the patient, and for several days he suffered from severe convulsions. The Bishop's patience during his agonizing illness was the admiration of his attendants; he was perfectly re signed to the will of Him who sent him, and calmly awaited the hour. He received the last rites and holy consolations of religion with great devotion. He died on November 13, 1855, the Feast of St. Stanislaus, in whose honor he had just finished a novena. His remains were deposited in a vault prepared for them under the sanctuary of St. Mary's Cathedral, Natchez, amid the fervent demonstrations of sorrow, veneration, and love of a devoted and afflicted flock.

RIGHT REV. BERNARD O'REILLEY, D.D.,

*Second Bishop of Hartford, A.D. 1850.**

THE life of Bishop O'Reilley, adorned as it was by conspicuous virtues and illustrated by the services he rendered to religion and humanity, has been made painfully interesting by the sudden and appalling tragedy in which he perished. The fate of the unfortunate steamer *Pacific*, engulfed with all her passengers in the waters of the ocean, is remembered with lively and heart-rending emotions by millions to this day. Sudden as was his fate, who is there in life so well prepared as was this good Christian Bishop, who at the time of his destruction was voyaging in the service of God, his flock, and his Church?

Bernard O'Reilley was born in the county of Longford, Ireland, in the year 1803. His family had long been distinguished in the land for their Catholic piety, for their patriotic devotion, and for their sufferings in the cause of their oppressed country. " Being in early years carefully instructed in piety," writes one who knew and loved him well, "and trained up in the way the child should go, he departed not therefrom during the rest of his life. In early youth he was conspicuous for that humility and dignity, sweetly blending, which ever afterwards ornamented himself, while they instructed and delighted all around. Some of his coevals even now love to testify, that even in boyhood's giddy season he displayed that

---

* Authorities: *Catholic Almanac*, 1857; cotemporaneous publications and original sources.

solid devotion and greatness of soul which endeared him when living to those who had the happiness of his society, and which, even in death, embalm his memory."

There were few young men of his day in Ireland more versed in the traditionary lore of his native land, or better grounded in classic literature than he. At the age of twenty-two years he disclosed to his good parents the fond aspiration of his soul, which was to serve God in the holy sanctuary, and be the minister of his graces and mercies to man. He expressed his willingness to remain and exercise the high functions of the priesthood amongst his own people, but declared his preference to embark at once for some more favored land, where a free altar and an untrammeled priesthood were guaranteed. His parents not only blessed, but rejoiced at, the high and noble choice their son had made, and freely gave their consent to sacrifice their son to the service of unknown souls in a foreign land. He embarked for America, January 17, 1825, and soon after landing entered the Ecclesiastical Seminary of Montreal, "where to this day his name remains in sweet odor for piety, talent, and dignified deportment." He afterwards continued his theological studies at St. Mary's College, Baltimore, was ordained in the holy priesthood October 13, 1831, in the city of New York, by Right Rev. Francis Patrick Kenrick, of Philadelphia, afterwards Archbishop of Baltimore. Archbishop Hughes preached the ordination sermon.

He at once commenced his career of charity and self-sacrifice. The community of New York now saw the fragrant flowers of religion which had heretofore bloomed and shed their fragrance in the secluded halls of the Seminary. Besides his labors in New York, he carried the consolations of religion to Brooklyn, that entire city being then wholly dependent on him for Mass once in the month. There were few that did not observe or experience and admire his zeal. To the young he was generous and winning, to the aged respectful and humble, to the afflicted sympathetic, to all charitable.

It was these noble tastes and pursuits which made him, from sympathy and high Christian inclinations, ever seek the field of duty, labor, and peril. The terrific visitation of the Asiatic Cholera to New York, in 1832, presented to him the field in which his heroic soul and stalwart frame would be of service to his fellow-men, and to this post of duty and exertion he immediately devoted himself. His untiring exertions by day and night to alleviate the sufferings of the diseased, to console, comfort, and bless the dying, to bury the dead, and to sustain the sinking courage and wasted energies of the living, have forever associated his name with the history of that awful visitation, and embalmed it in the hearts of many who we trust are in heaven, and of thousands who yet survive to recount his noble heroism. Twice stricken down with the epidemic himself, he each time arose from his bed of sickness but half restored, in order to devote himself to others more severely afflicted than himself. God seemed to preserve his life for others. After relief was vouchsafed to the pestilence-stricken city, and the foul plague had departed, leaving many a widow and orphan behind to weep over the graves of its victims, to these afflicted ones Father Bernard O'Reilley was truly a father, a friend, and protector. His exertions in behalf of the widows and orphans of 1832 were as generous and self-sacrificing as his labors for the sick and dying had been untiring and brave.

Seeking no rest after the labors and sufferings of the epidemic, we find this devoted priest at a new post of arduous duty and painful privations immediately afterwards. In December, 1832, he was appointed pastor of St. Patrick's Church in Rochester, where for many years he performed most extensive and fruitful labors in the ministry. The Catholics whom he had to attend were scattered from Auburn to Niagara Falls, and Father Bernard O'Reilley was the only missionary in this extensive country; indeed, he and Father Metz were the only priests in the vast region which afterwards became the Diocese of Buffalo. The widely-dispersed members of the flock had to be sought after by long and solitary journeys, performed frequently at night and in the midst of winter, and when found, had to be instructed in their religion and restored as lost sheep to the Church. Many of them were divided and estranged among themselves, even in the congregation at Rochester, and had to be reconciled through the mediating influences of the Church, the pastor, and the sacraments. The pastor, while thus engaged in seeking his own, had to encounter the bitter and deeply-rooted prejudices which prevailed in New England and Northern New York against Catholics and their Church—a difficult and delicate task for a strange priest to undertake in such a community, but one which Father O'Reilley performed with courage, ability, and success. The Church of St. Patrick had been built by Father Patrick Kelly twelve years previously, when Rochester was a small village. It was the foundation, however, upon which Father O'Reilley continued to build, and before long his mission foreshadowed the future and now developed and flourishing state of religion, not only in Rochester, but in the present Diocese of Buffalo. It is justly said by a Catholic historian,* that "in that city his zeal and labors were untiring; and most of the institutions there are due to his energy and devotedness."

The following friendly, but just tribute to Father O'Reilley, is from the pen of one who was intimately acquainted with his life and services:—" To the untiring exertions of Father Bernard O'Reilley, next to God, we must attribute the wonderful change wrought in favor of Catholics, and the triumphant victory which our holy faith achieved in Rochester and the surrounding country. The fortunate and grateful citizens of that place, seeing his stainless, steady, onward career, admired the man and honored the priesthood in his name. The Kearneys, Bradleys, Gallerys, and Tones, can best tell what fruit his labors produced during the nineteen years that he was pastor in Rochester, for they were witnesses from the beginning of his mission there; they saw with grief our divine religion as delicate as the solitary plant in the sand of the desert. They, too, saw it watered, and its rapid growth attended by the good husbandman; they lived to see that once weakly plant become the most majestic tree of the garden, and reposing to-day under the solemnity of its shade, they can and do say, ' God hath wrought this work. He is glorified in the zeal of His priest, who adorns the ministry by his virtues.' As flowers impregnate the surrounding atmosphere with their odor, so did he impart to the social order in Rochester the influence of his innate virtues: modesty with firmness, charity without ostentation, liberality without weakness, are virtues so discernible to-day in that

---

* Shea's *Catholic Church in the United States*, p. 484.

community, that one may say, 'Though dead, he still speaketh to them.'"

In October, 1847, Bishop Timon took possession of his newly-created See of Buffalo, and immediately appointed Father O'Reilley his Vicar-General, and invited him to take up his residence at the Episcopal mansion at Buffalo. It was with sincere sorrow and with many regrets that he obeyed, though cheerfully, for God's sake, the voice of his Superior and of his own conscience, in leaving his beloved flock, whom he had so long and so sedulously guided. He thenceforth devoted himself with untiring zeal and industry to the new duties imposed upon him of presiding over the new Seminary, and assisting in the affairs of the Diocese as the Bishop's Vicar-General. The saintly Bishop of Buffalo fully appreciated the co-laborer he possessed in his Vicar-General; and on many occasions, in private conversations, and oftentimes through the public press, bore the most earnest and grateful testimony to his Vicar's fidelity, ability, and zeal. To the clergy and people of the Diocese he was also endeared by a thousand ties, and by as many noble and generous kindnesses extended to them, in his modest and unpatronizing manner.

The hospital at Buffalo was one of Father O'Reilley's special cares, and its great success was chiefly due to his paternal solicitude. It was placed in charge of the Sisters of Charity, and in this, as in many other instances, their pure and holy lives, angelic charity, and unselfish devotion, caused many of their patients to recognize as the only true Spouse of Christ, that Church which alone has or can produce such fruits as these. It was not long before the Sectarians became jealous of the prosperity of this institution, and alarmed for their own communities; and one of them, over various anonymous signatures, commenced in one of the public journals a series of attacks against the hospital. The first of these was answered by Father O'Reilley, over his own name, who, assuming the aggressive now, so unsparingly and skillfully pressed his adversary in several replies to his attacks, that the enemy was compelled to unmask himself, and proved to be the "Rev. John C. Lord, D.D., Pastor of the Central Presbyterian Church." An extended public controversy between this individual and Father O'Reilley followed, which, extending far beyond the original scope of the discussion, embraced in its range the respective merits and doctrines of the Catholic and Presbyterian Churches. Father O'Reilley showed in his articles no inconsiderable power as a controversialist, historian, and theologian. He completely silenced his adversary, and gained great popularity and favor in the community for the assailed institution. He wound up the contest by publishing three articles of striking ability and spirit, respectively entitled, "Catholicity the Friend of Civil and Religious Liberty," "Presbyterianism the Enemy of Civil and Religious Liberty," "The Catholic Church, the Church of Christ."*

The Council which assembled at Baltimore, May 6th, 1849, nominated the Very Rev. Bernard O'Reilley to be Bishop of Hartford, as successor to Bishop Tyler. The proceedings of the Council, owing to the Roman revolution and the exile of the Holy Father, did not receive his approval until after his return to Rome, when the letter of appointment, dated August 9th,

* *Discussion Relative to the Buffalo Hospital of the Sisters of Charity*, between the Rev. John C. Lord and the Very Rev. B. O'Reilley. pp. 72. Buffalo. 1850.

1850, was transmitted. Bishop O'Reilley was consecrated in the Church of St. Patrick, Rochester, the scene of his long and faithful services to religion, in the presence of his former flock, whom he had so well guided in the way of salvation by his teachings, and edified by his virtues.

The new Bishop entered at once upon the duties of his high and difficult office. Few persons at the present time can realize the embarrassments and struggles of his position—embarrassments and struggles which had broken down the health of his worthy predecessor, and sent him to an early reward. Fortunately for Bishop O'Reilley and the Diocese, he possessed a robust constitution, and great physical activity and endurance, which went far to sustain his brave soul in the struggle. The minds of the people with whom he now went to reside were, from education and social training, thoroughly impregnated with Puritan bigotry and intolerance. His own people were comparatively few in numbers, and weak in social and worldly advantages. The Bishop displayed his rare qualities and talents in softening down the bitterness of his enemies, while he defended his own people with courage and resolution. His dignity of deportment, unaffected piety, and amiability of disposition, caused the former to see the Catholic religion exemplified, even to their own admiration; while his own flock gained courage from their Bishop, and from the increase of their churches, clergy, laity, and institutions. For over five years he devoted his energies to the great work of planting the faith in an uncongenial soil, and in demonstrating to an unwilling public mind the compatibility of the Catholic religion with free government and republican institutions. Religious and charitable institutions sprang up around him, and churches were erected in various parts of the diocese.

The providing of a sufficient and competent body of clergy for his diocese was one of the most earnest efforts of his life. His pastoral letters to his people on this important subject show how fervently and zealously he worked in this regard. In one of them he says:—

"The work in which I invite you to take a part is eminently the work of God: it embraces the extension of His empire on earth, through the increase of the priesthood. Through other means He might, did He so will it, provide for His Church; but in mercy He asks our co-operation, that we may participate in the blessings consequent on a work so holy. Let us then labor together in this great cause of God, that together we may rejoice in the triumph of our faith, and in season partake of the happiness to be awarded fidelity and zeal."

In another of these paternal epistles, he writes:— "When the chief Pastor, in his diocese, invokes the aid of his faithful people in behalf of some great diocesan object, their charitable contributions are made to God; and if they at any time stop to consider the aid they may have rendered, it is but with a view to express their gratitude for being in a position to take a part in a work promotive of the glory of God.

"The Bishop is burdened with the solicitude of his diocese: he must provide pastors for the faithful, and ever be prepared to meet every contingency that may possibly diminish the number of his priests.

"He conceives it to be his duty not only to provide the larger congregations with pastors, but to have seasonably afforded the consolations of religion to the smaller sections, and even, where it is possible, to isolated families.

All his anxieties are about his priests and people; for God and for them he lives and labors, and is prepared to exhaust himself in promoting their spiritual interest and happiness."

Bishop O'Reilley did not live to see his Ecclesiastical Seminary established on a permanent basis; but as an evidence of his efforts to secure priests for his people may be mentioned the fact, that before his death he had twenty-two young men studying in various ecclesiastical institutions, for the purpose of preparing for the holy ministry in his diocese.

In announcing the Jubilee of 1854 to his people, Bishop O'Reilley alludes in striking terms to the spirit and sentiment of the non-Catholic world towards the Church, and probably no Bishop in the United States had more reason to deplore the existence of such feelings towards the Catholic Church than Bishop O'Reilley and his estimable predecessor, Bishop Tyler. The Prelate thus alludes to the subject:—" The Church of the living God, as is usual where prejudice gets the better of reason, and passion alone is privileged to rule, is now visited with the most gross misrepresentations; doctrines which it abhors, and practices which it is occupied in repressing. are unblushingly attributed to it; its priests, occupied in their sacred calling and offering offence to none, are assailed with the lowest and grossest reviling, whilst its best and most devoted members are ungenerously pursued with calumny and hatred that know no bounds.

" Divine Charity, so essential to the peace and happiness of men, and so strongly and frequently enforced of God, is to a great extent ignored, and apparently eradicated from the hearts of great numbers. This amiable virtue will doubtless survive the shock it is receiving.

and yet comfort those who are systematically opposed to it."*

One of the most fruitful services rendered by Bishop O'Reilley to the States of Rhode Island and Connecticut was the introduction of the Sisters of Mercy, whose institutions of charity and education have multiplied in astonishing numbers, and have been the instruments of countless benefits and blessings. One of the severest trials of the good Bishop's life was in witnessing the anti-Catholic bigotry of the times and country arrayed against these innocent and angelic Sisters, at the very moment they were spending their lives in the service of their neighbor. In 1855, a mob arose in Providence and threatened the good Sisters with death and their house with destruction. In this emergency the Bishop felt that they looked to him as their protector, and God enabled him to shield his children. Scorning all temporizing policy, the Bishop stood before the brutal mob undaunted, and boldly announced to them: "The Sisters are in their home; they shall not leave it even for an hour. I shall protect them while I have life, and, if needs be, register their safety with my blood." The storm of bigotry and passion was dissipated by such courage and intrepidity, and the Almighty protected through His servant His own household.

Bishop O'Reilley's visitations of his diocese were frequent and laborious; his exertions and responsibilities in the erection of schools, asylums, and other institutions, almost appalling; his attendance at the Councils of Bal-

---

* The debates of this period in the Senate of the United States, in which the story of the Madiai family at Rome, and other calumnies against Catholics figured, present one out of many instances in which Catholics have been misrepresented in this country in high public and official places.

timore, his visits to Europe, his exertions to promote the cause of religion and education, and the many countless labors of the episcopal office, gave him but little rest. The necessary exertions to raise means to sustain his various undertakings were most onerous and embarrassing at times; but he undertook and carried them out with vigor and cheerfulness; and did not call upon his flock for a dollar for his own expenses. He increased the churches of his diocese to forty-six, besides thirty-seven stations; the number of his priests to forty-two, besides twenty-two clerical students; in addition to these he had two male and three female academies, and three orphan asylums; and the Catholic population was nearly if not quite seventy thousand before his death.

In order to complete his facilities for educating the rising and future generations of his flock, he paid his last and fatal visit to Europe, sailing December 5, 1855, undaunted by the terrors and dangers of the ocean voyage in mid-winter. A less courageous spirit would have deferred the voyage to a more propitious season, but to Bishop O'Reilley the necessities of his children always seemed to him pressing and indispensable, and he was a stranger to fear. His present object was to secure the services of a body of religious men in Europe to come to his diocese and take charge of the education of the male children. He had in a great measure succeeded in his efforts, and, as if guided by Providence to perform a last filial duty in visiting his parents in Ireland, he discharged this grateful task, and again in the midst of winter embarked, January 23, 1856, for his diocese, on board the ill-fated steamer *Pacific*. His flock were awaiting his return with anxious hope and with many prayers for his safety. But the Mother in Heaven, to whom he was greatly devoted, that Star of the Sea, was watching her pious son as a pilgrim to the celestial Jerusalem, and praying for his release from the trammels of earth and his admission to the ocean of endless bliss.

So quietly and unostentatiously did Bishop O'Reilley act in all his life, and in this instance particularly, that it was quite uncertain whether he was on board the *Pacific*. When her delay in arriving at her port of destination became the cause of general alarm on both sides of the ocean, it was then that inquiries were anxiously made whether the Bishop was on board the missing vessel. His name did not appear on any list of her passengers, and it was hoped and believed by many that a person of his standing and extended acquaintance could not have taken passage on an European steamer, and the fact remain unknown or even doubtful. But his more intimate friends knew that he was in the habit of traveling in this humble and retiring way, that he avoided display, and even the most ordinary discovery of himself, and that it was his general custom in traveling to enter his name on hotel registers as simply " Mr. O'Reilley." The very uncertainty of the case made the fears and sufferings of his friends and flock the more painful. Inquiries were finally made of his brother in Ireland, who had probably seen him off, and from him the sad truth was learned that the fate of the *Pacific* and her passengers must also be that of Bishop O'Reilley. It was not until the middle or last of April that the Bishop's fate was regarded as hopeless, when a deep and prolonged wail of sorrow broke forth from both sides of the Atlantic, and was fervently echoed and re-echoed from every portion of the Christian world. "At length," wrote the Bishop's reverend brother, "the alarming rumor of the loss of the *Pacific* spread through every corner of the land, and fear and hope, and joy and grief, in rapid succession, alternately affected the community at large. Every exertion was made, by land and sea, to aid or discover the missing vessel. Finally, the silence of any hopeful circumstance was so deep that all pronounced it the silence of death, and the death-knell of Bishop O'Reilley rang from Georgia to Maine, and echoed through the world. At that dark hour the grief of his widowed diocese was almost beyond control. Priests and people thronged to the altar of God to offer, or assist in offering, the all-atoning sacrifice for the repose of his soul. Many venerable Prelates and clergymen came from a distance to offer their prayers and sympathies for him, and even the illustrious John, of New York, was present, in his gentleness of heart, to share the sorrows of the bereavement."

Death to the good Christian is a blessing, for it is the end of this sad journey of life, and carries him through the portal of the eternal paradise. But when the victim of death is one in whose person centre the hopes, the dependence, and the guardianship of others,—some providential vocation on earth,—then it strikes us as a great public calamity. And when death is sudden, tragic, widespread, and devastating, whether by the fell swoop of pestilence on the land, or of storms or accidents on the sea, it becomes appalling, and human grief on such occasions is natural and approved both of man and God. Only the imagination can picture the horror and the sufferings of that awful moment, when the gallant and powerful ship plunged against the more impetuous and more ponderous and terrific mountain of ice, and instantly burst into fragments, and, with all on board, became engulfed in the fathomless depths of the ocean :—

> "Then rose from sea to sky the wild farewell,
>   Then shriek'd the timid, and stood still the brave,
> Then some leaped overboard with dreadful yell,
>   As eager to anticipate their grave ;
> And the sea yawn'd around her like a hell,
>   And down she suck'd with her the whirling wave,
> Like one who grapples with his enemy
> And strives to strangle him before he die.
>
> "And first one universal shriek there rush'd,
>   Louder than the loud ocean, like a crash
> Of echoing thunder ; and then all was hush'd,
>   Save the wild wind and the remorseless clash
> Of billows ; but at intervals there gushed,
>   Accompanied with a convulsive splash,
> A solitary shriek, the bubbling cry
> Of some strong swimmer in his agony."
>
> BYRON.

At Hartford and Providence solemn Requiem Masses were offered for the repose of the soul of Bishop O'Reilley, in June, 1856, in the presence of numerous Prelates and priests, and of an immense concourse of sorrowing people. The churches were crowded at five o'clock in the morning, many hours before the services commenced. The tragic character of the death they assembled to mourn, rendered the occasion more solemn and impressive, and the Church omitted no rite or invocation that could testify her love for her departed son. Archbishop Hughes pronounced, at the Requiem Mass at Providence, the funeral discourse on Bishop O'Reilley which was an eloquent tribute to, and a glowing eulogium on, the virtues, labors, and sacrifices of the deceased Prelate. An eye-witness thus alludes to that feature in the scene, *the empty catafalque*, while the mortal remains were far away; their only casket being the broken hull of the ship, their grave the depths of the ocean: "Now that all hope has ceased for the safety of the ill-fated *Pacific*, a solemn Requiem Mass was all that could be offered in memory of him who sank with her to rise no more in time. There is a melancholy in death,—nature loves itself, and the horror of death never becomes intense till ashes return to ashes, and dust is consigned to dust. But this becomes more bitter when the wail of sorrow is raised only above the empty bier or the decorated catafalque; when the burning tapers that surround it seem only to show that nothing but a symbol is there. How happy was the widow of Nain, that she had even the body of her only child—for then she became certain of a miracle from the instant our Blessed Saviour touched the bier. Poor widow! blessed was your sorrow. . . . . . But to-day widows and orphans crowd around an empty bier and a splendid catafalque. All the gorgeous pomp that love could give was bestowed, but it was empty— the mind could not rest on that splendid pageant of hollowness, but bounded from the glitter and the glare of that mournfully bright solemnity to the Atlantic ocean—to the steamer *Pacific* and her unfortunate passengers, and asked itself a thousand questions as to how they went down; till back to the catafalque, with its questions unanswered, it had to come; that *steamer* sank and the waters closed over her; the treacherous waves came smoothly together, no mark remained on their bosom to tell where she wounded them, and no mark can point to the spot or awake a prayer or a sigh from the passing traveler." *

---

* The *American Celt*, June, 1856.

"In the death of the venerable Bishop O'Reilley, the American Church lost one of her most faithful defenders, society one of its brightest ornaments; the entire inhabitants of the land, without distinction of creed or party, join in paying the tribute of esteem and veneration to his memory; while the Catholic community, in prayer and hope, bow down to the holy will of God, with that resignation which characterized the Bishop himself in life, and which, amid the perils of death, earned for him, we trust, that blessed invitation of God, 'Well done, good and faithful servant, enter into the joy of the Lord.'" *

---

* *Catholic Almanac*, 1857.

RIGHT REV. FRANCIS XAVIER GARTLAND, D.D.,

First Bishop of Savannah, A.D. 1850.

FRANCIS XAVIER GARTLAND was born in Dublin, Ireland, in the year 1805. He came to America while yet a child, and made his classical studies at Mt. St. Mary's College, Emmittsburg. Embracing the life of the sanctuary, he continued his studies with that view, and made a complete course of theology. He was ordained at Philadelphia, by Bishop Conwell, about the year 1831 or '32. When the Rev. John Hughes, afterwards Archbishop of New York, took possession of the new church of St. John at Philadelphia, in 1832, Father Gartland became his assistant, and was ever zealous in supporting Dr. Hughes in his energetic efforts for the good of the Church. An instance of his zeal in this regard is related as having occurred in 1835, when Dr. Hughes, embarrassed by the heavy debt contracted in building St. John's, and finding his efforts to raise means at home not wholly successful, announced to the congregation that he was about to go on a begging tour of five or six months through Mexico, in order to raise funds to pay off the church debt. At the conclusion of this announcement, Father Gartland, who was sitting in the sanctuary, and was then the celebrant of the late Mass, arose on the impulse of the moment, and without premeditation made an eloquent and forcible appeal to the congrega-

---

* Authorities: *Catholic Almanac*, 1855; *Life of Archbishop Hughes*, by John R. G. Hassard; *Catholic Almanacs, Magazines,* and *Metropolitans*, etc., etc.

tion, appealing to them generously to raise from their own resources the required funds, and thus save their pastor from the labors, fatigues, and dangers of such a journey. His appeal was a complete success; the necessary funds were raised by the pew-holders to pay the most pressing liabilities of the church, and the pastor of St. John's was relieved of his embarrassments and his journey. Dr. Hughes ever entertained for him a high regard and warm friendship, and after the removal to New York of the former, his letters to friends in Philadelphia were sure to contain some message of friendship for Father Gartland.

On the appointment of Dr. Hughes to the co-adjutorship of New York, Father Gartland succeeded him as pastor of St. John's, where he officiated, together with the late Dr. Francis Patrick Kenrick, then Bishop of Philadelphia, until his appointment to the bishopric of Savannah in 1850. In 1845 he was appointed by Bishop Kenrick his Vicar-General, an office which he held during the remainder of his residence in Philadelphia. His long missionary career in Philadelphia for nearly twenty years gained for him, by his zeal and untiring labors, the commendation of all. That he enjoyed the friendship and admiration of Dr. Kenrick, whose estimate of the sacerdotal character was high indeed, is a fact, which affords the best proof of his many virtues and useful services to religion. He was always much attached to the diocese of Philadelphia, where he had numerous and warm friends to the end of his life. Whenever his duties called him northward he loved to visit the scenes of his early labors, and take part in the works which constantly evinced the growth of the Church in that diocese. During his Vicar-Generalship he took an active part in assisting Bishop Kenrick, in his great efforts to extend the Church and to spread the benefits of religion throughout his extensive diocese. He laid the corner-stone of several new churches while with Bishop Kenrick, and amongst others, on May 4, 1845, that of the church at Reading, on which occasion he celebrated High Mass in the old church. In December, 1846, he dedicated the Church of St. Anne, Port Richmond, on which occasion Bishop Hughes 'preached the dedication sermon. On February 7, 1847, he dedicated the Church of St. Michael, at Kensington, on which occasion Bishop Kenrick preached the dedication sermon.

The Seventh Council of Baltimore, in May, 1849, proposed to the Holy See the erection of several new episcopal Sees, and amongst them was the See of Savannah, for the State of Georgia, embracing also all that portion of Florida which stretched east of the river Apalachicola, for which Dr. Gartland was nominated as Bishop. The Roman revolution retarded the examination of the acts of the Council. The Holy Father, Pius IX., re-entered Rome April 12, 1850; the Sacred Congregation resumed its functions soon after, and, by the letter of August 9, the Propaganda transmitted to Baltimore the Pontifical briefs, one of which constituted Dr. Gartland the Bishop of Savannah.

He was consecrated on Sunday, September 10, 1850, at St. John's Church, Philadelphia, by Archbishop Eccleston of Baltimore, assisted by Bishops Kenrick of Philadelphia, and O'Connor of Pittsburgh, in the presence of a large number of clergy, students of the Seminary of St. Charles Borromeo, and an immense and devout concourse of the laity. The consecration sermon was preached by the Very Rev. Dr. McCaffrey, President of Mount St. Mary's College, Emmittsburg, and was described at the time "as a magnificent tribute to the beauty, majesty, and worth of the Church of the living God." An eye-witness of this imposing scene, one who had long known Dr. Gartland as a priest at Philadelphia, thus expressed the sentiments of the Catholics of that city: "In a few weeks the Right Rev. Bishop Gartland will leave us ; tears and benedictions will mark the day of his departure; tears for his loss, for his separation from those whom, with not less zeal and ability than disinterestedness, he has served for the last eighteen years ; blessings, too, will accompany him, warmer and louder than those which were fervently whispered on every side as he passed down the crowded nave of St. John's on Sunday morning last, invoking God's blessing on his flock, on the stranger, and the children of Israel, and the adversaries of our faith who were there present." Having completed his business in Philadelphia, he departed amidst tears and blessings, to go to his new and destitute see, where poverty, labor, and self-sacrifice awaited him.

During his short episcopate of less than four years, Bishop Gartland did all that his extremely limited resources rendered possible to accomplish for the organization of the new diocese and the spread of religion therein. During this time he erected three new churches, and he enlarged, with an addition of twenty-five by sixty feet, the church, now Cathedral, of St. John the Baptist, and rededicated it on Sunday, June 26, 1853. In the first year of his episcopate he visited Europe, to gain some assistance for his sparse and needy flock, then composed of about five thousand five hundred Catholics, scattered over the State of Georgia and East Florida. While at Carlow College, in Ireland, in November, 1851, he engaged the services of Rev. Michael Cullinan, then a theological student, whom he afterwards ordained at Savannah in 1854. During his brief administration an Orphan Asylum for boys was established at Savannah, the Society of Our Lady Help of Christians, the Confraternity of the Rosary of the Blessed Virgin Mary, the Confraternity of St. John the Baptist for the prevention of intemperance, the Society of St. Vincent de Paul, Day Schools and Christian Doctrine Schools in various places, and at Augusta an Affiliation of the House of Our Lady of Mercy, the parent house of which had already been established at Savannah. The fact that the Catholic population of his diocese was nearly doubled in less than four years under Bishop Gartland, is a practical proof of his efficient and successful labors for the Church, and the flock committed by her to his pastoral care.

The glorious death of Bishop Gartland, which occurred at Savannah, September 20, 1854, was the crowning merit of his noble career. No higher eulogium could be pronounced on him than that "he fell a martyr to his holy zeal and fidelity." The yellow-fever, that scourge of the seaport towns and cities of the South, desolated Savannah in the summer and fall of 1854. The good Bishop devoted himself to his flock and to the pest-stricken people around him with heroic constancy, fidelity, and self-sacrifice. While the fever was raging in his own house, and all around him in the city, he passed from place to place, and from hospital to infirmary, from bed to bed, administering to the corporal relief and spiritual consolation of the people. The good Bishop

Barron was struck down with the fever in Bishop Gartland's residence, and received from him the most tender care and nursing. A hurricane, which swept over the city, added to the distress of the people, and the Bishop's residence was especially marked out for its violence. The roof was violently forced from the house, and the suffering inmates had to be removed elsewhere. Bishop Barron died on the 12th, and Bishop Gartland, who had been untiring and unflinching in the midst of the scourge, was himself stricken down, and, like a true shepherd, gave up his life for his flock on September 20th. He was immolated on the altar of Christian charity. His career of usefulness was cut short in the prime of his life and strength, for he was only in his forty-ninth year at the time of his death.

The loss of Bishop Gartland was severely felt and deeply lamented by the Church in America. The assembly of Prelates in Council at Baltimore the following year was sincerely grieved at his untimely end. A letter addressed by Archbishop Kendrick of Baltimore, in the name of the Council, to the Councils of the Work of the Propagation of the Faith, alluded most feelingly to this sad event. "Death," writes Archbishop Kenrick, "has deprived us of the valuable talents of the Bishop of Charleston, and the services of the zealous and indefatigable Bishop of Savannah; but the death, as well as the life, of these two Prelates has reflected great honor upon the Episcopacy. The Right Rev. Dr. Reynolds has worn himself out in the service of his church; more happy still the Right Rev. Dr. Gartland, of Savannah, in having fallen a victim to his charity. During the past summer, the yellow fever ravaged his episcopal town with unprecedented violence. Every one who had the means sought to escape by flight from the frightful and disastrous scourge; but this good pastor, ready to lay down his life for his flock, remained at his post, seeking after those whom the pest had attacked, and actuated solely by the desire of gaining souls to Heaven. Two of his priests (he had only three near him) were disabled by the fever; the Right Rev. Dr. Barron, ex-missionary Bishop of an African colony, and who was for the time stationed with Bishop Gartland to assist in attending the sick, died gloriously in the exercise of his duties; but the generous and heroic Prelate was only thereby inspired with greater zeal for the salvation of souls. At length the malady attacked him also, and he died calm and resigned, a true martyr of charity. His solicitude for the wants of his flock, as well as his unremitting labors, had doubtless, Gentlemen, already enfeebled and predisposed him for the attack of the disease; and there can be no doubt that Dr. Reynolds' death was accelerated by the same cause."

RIGHT REV. JOSEPH CRETIN, D.D.,

First Bishop of St. Paul, A.D. 1851.*

DR. CRETIN was one of those pioneer Bishops of the North-west, under whose missionary labors the Church made an almost incredible progress, and regained, in our own time, an immense territory, which, nearly two centuries ago, had been her own. Like Bishop Loras, of Dubuque, under whom he had served as a priest, he became a distinguished promoter of Western immigration ; and under his great efforts the Church kept pace with the impetuous and wide-spreading tide of population.

Joseph Cretin was born in Lyons, France, about the year 1800, and made his ecclesiastical studies in the splendid institutions of that diocese. There, too, he was ordained in the holy ministry. He dedicated himself to the foreign missions; and when Bishop Loras visited Lyons, in 1838, in search of laborers for his new and unorganized diocese, Father Cretin was one of the two priests who volunteered to accompany him to the wilds of America. He arrived with Bishop Loras at New York, in October, 1838, and at Dubuque, in April, 1839. He was a faithful counselor and untiring co-laborer of the Bishop of Dubuque for twelve years, and was one of the most active and successful missionary priests in this country. During these twelve years he

---

* **Aut**horities: *Catholic Almanacs*, from 1839 to 1858; *History of the Catholic Missions*, by J. G. Shea ; various Numbers of the *N. Y. Freeman's Journal, Metropolitan,* etc., etc.

was the Vicar-General of Dubuque, and during a considerable part of the time pastor of the Cathedral Church of St. Raphael. He made frequent and laborious excursions to scattered and distant Catholic stations and families. In 1843 he went upon the Indian Mission, and established his residence at Prairie-du-Chien, among the Winnebagoes. This tribe had been visited by the pioneer missionary, Father Mazzuchelli; and on the creation of the See of Dubuque they petitioned to Bishop Loras for a priest. It was only after renewed requests that a priest could be given them. Father Petiot was sent to them; but the Indian agent threw every obstacle in his way, and finally, by misrepresentations, induced the Governor of Iowa to dismiss him from the territory. The Indians renewed their petition, and caused their wishes to be laid before the President, and presented a new petition to Bishop Loras. It was now, in 1843, that Father Cretin became their pastor, and was requested by them to build a church and school-house.* Again his noble and holy work was interfered with. He was forbidden to have a school, or, if allowed, it was on terms wholly inadmissible. Yet with undaunted zeal he continued his labors, and it was not until 1848, when he was expelled by the Government officials from the mission, and the Winnebagoes removed to Long Prairie, that he returned to Dubuque. How unfortunate, alas! has been the Indian policy of our Government. The only means that could make Christians and peaceful subjects of the Indians were either rejected or allowed to be defeated by the local officer, and the sad alternative of war and extermination has been the result.

---

* Shea's *History of the Catholic Missions*, p. 399.

Father Cretin, on his return to Dubuque, in 1848, resumed his duties as Vicar-General of the Diocese and as pastor of the Cathedral. He also attended a French congregation at St. Joseph's, in Dubuque County.

The Seventh Council of Baltimore, which assembled in May, 1849, recommended to Rome the erection of a new See at St. Paul, for the Territory of Minnesota, and the appointment of Dr. Cretin as its first Bishop. The Propaganda, by letters of August 9, 1850, approved these suggestions, and transmitted the necessary documents to the Archbishop of Baltimore.

The first Catholic priest, and first of Europeans, who visited the vicinity of the new Episcopal See of St. Paul, was the famous Father Hennepin, who, in 1680, was a prisoner of the Sioux. He explored the Mississippi between the Illinois and the Falls, which he named in honor of St. Anthony of Padua, and of which he published a glowing description in 1683.

Bishop Loras, accompanied by Father Galtier, visited Mendota and St. Paul in 1839. Father Galtier went to establish a mission at Mendota, then the headquarters of the Indian trade above Prairie-du-Chien. The only progress in civilization made since the visit of Father Hennepin, nearly two centuries before, consisted in the new storehouses of the Fur Company, Mr. Sibley's fine stone dwelling, a group of log huts, and one or two neat white cots—all swarming with population. Such was Mendota. On the opposite side of the river, crowning the majestic bluff, stood Fort Snelling, and the stone houses of the Indian agent and interpreter. The original name of this settlement was *"Pig's Eye;"* but it was now destined to bear the more becoming name of St. Paul.

All beyond these early works of civilization was a wilderness, as unredeemed as when seen by Father Hennepin. Behind Mendota, and clustering in the valleys of the neighboring hills, were the lodges of the Sioux; the smoke was curling from their open summits, and within and around crowds of children and dogs, young Indians and squaws, were swarming, while the painted warriors were stretched upon their blankets before their scattered tents, which extended with picturesque effect to the banks of the Minnesota. The virgin wilderness beyond lay in gloomy and fearful silence.

The few French and Canadian attachés of the Fur Company welcomed the good missionary, whose ministry recalled the devotions and virtues of their early homes and altars. Mr. Scott Campbell, the interpreter, shared his residence with Father Galtier, and religious services were held there till 1841. In that year Mr. J. B. Farribault presented to the mission a log-house for a church; the cross soon surmounted this primitive temple of Minnesota; the Divine Lamb was offered upon its altar, and the new temple and parish were dedicated to the Almighty under the patronage of St. Peter. In the same year the first church on the opposite bluff was erected of logs also; it was placed under the invocation of St. Paul, and soon the whole settlement was named in honor of that apostle. In 1842 Father Cretin visited Mendota and St. Paul, accompanied by Father Ravoux. They established the Sioux mission. Father Ravoux remained to conduct it, while Father Cretin returned to the Winnebagoes about Prairie-du-Chien. The results of this mission were well described by a writer in the *St. Paul Pioneer*,* who saw what he so well chronicled:—

---

* Republished in the *New York Freeman's Journal*.

"The zeal and piety of Father Ravoux were exerted with benefit to the manners and morals of the settlers. A large number of the half-breeds, descendants of men who had forgotten the teachings of their youth, were gathered by him into the fold of the Church, and baptized in the faith of their fathers. Marriage was once more sanctified by religion. Birth began to be regarded as the inauguration of a soul, and death its resignation to a forgiving God. And over all the simple people of those days, in whose hearts the priest touched mysterious cords of awe, and love, and reverence, never touched before, he held the same sway of gentleness and goodness that Chatèaubriand attributes to the venerable missionary among the Indian tribes of Louisiana, where René sought for spiritual consolation in the recesses of the forest. The extent of their reclamation from the state of demoralization described by Col. Snelling, a few years before, was apparent in the state of society which prevailed here at the period of our Territorial organization. The sanctions of the Church were accepted by the people as social laws, and the sacredness of family ties and social thrift took the place of beastly and reckless dissoluteness of manners, which had before prevailed. Of a summer Sunday the little log church upon the hill was the central figure of a pleasant picture. Too small to hold the crowds that flocked to it, the reverent worshippers knelt in ranks upon the grass outside the window—the red-belted and moccasined voyageurs mingling with the tawny groups of children rescued by the Church from barbarity."

Father Ravoux officiated on alternate Sundays at St. Paul and Mendota, preaching in Sioux, English, and French. He extended his labors above the Falls of St.

Anthony, and established the mission of St. Francis Xavier; but this mission languished under the corrupting influences of the intercourse of the whites with the Indians, and was finally removed to Lake Pepin, where several Catholics had settled. This noble missionary was still conducting the mission of St. Paul in 1850, and in the following year had the happiness of welcoming the first Bishop of St. Paul to the joint field of their exalted labors.

The Bishop elect knew better than any one else the rude and uncultivated vineyard which God and his Church had assigned to him to cultivate. It required apostolic zeal and resources, and Heaven's sustaining power, to draw forth from the wilderness and create, as it were, an organized Church for the North-west. Not waiting for consecration, and without going to survey his spiritual domain, the scene of past services and of so much future labor and so many privations, he proceeded at once to his native France for the purpose of procuring priests for the new diocese. While there he had the consolation of receiving episcopal consecration, on the same Catholic soil on which he had received holy orders. He was consecrated in the domestic chapel of the Bishop of Belley, by the hands of that Prelate. assisted by the Coadjutor Bishop of Belley and the Bishop of Lausanne and Geneva, January 26, 1851. He immediately returned to the United States, accompanied by several clergymen whose services for the missions of Minnesota he had secured in France.

Arriving at the majestic bluff of St. Paul, in the summer of 1851, he commenced his work. He had seen and labored in Minnesota before. Her vast extent, her mighty rivers, her immense forests, her prairies, her lake-shore, her Indian tribes were all familiar to him. He had visited and announced the eternal word at St. Paul when it was merely a fort, with neither church nor priest. He was not discouraged when the voice of Rome made him the chief pastor of her vast domain, and her chief missionary. He accepted for his Cathedral a log chapel, whose dimensions were 45 × 18, and for his episcopal palace a log shanty 18 × 18. He was happy in the apostolic simplicity and poverty with which he inaugurated his episcopate. His clerical force consisted of three priests, whose ranks he immediately increased by the addition of six more whom he brought with him from France. Such was the Church of Minnesota only twenty years ago; such was the episcopal city of St. Paul. The first Bishop has gone to receive his eternal reward; the second is now zealously and ably prosecuting his work; and St. Paul, the capital of Minnesota, is a city of nearly fifty thousand inhabitants. A writer, in 1869, when its population was thirty thousand, says: "To-day one-half of the population is Catholic. We have in the city four churches, four schools, one academy, orphan asylum, hospital, House of the Good Shepherd, many benevolent societies; throughout the State forty-five secular, fifteen regular priests, and over one hundred churches. With the ever-increasing flow of immigration, new congregations are daily springing up in the wilderness, fresh priests are pushing Westward with the crowd, and the *old* pioneers are astonished to find themselves no more on the frontier, but in the very bosom of civilization." *

Before the end of the first year after his arrival Bishop

---

* *New York Freeman's Journal*, August 28, 1869.

Cretin had ten priests laboring in various parts of his diocese. The congregation at St. Paul was ministered to by himself and Father Moran. But the little log chapel was too small, and the Bishop obtained a large building of brick and stone, which was applied to the manifold purposes of a Church, a Seminary, and School, under the charge of Fathers Legendre and Peyrogrosse; and a residence for the Bishop and his clergy. He also secured a promise of a colony of the Sisters of St. Joseph, from St. Louis, to whom he intended to confide his schools. The arch-confraternity of Our Lady of Victories was also established at St. Paul and other parts of the diocese. The Theological Seminary commenced its exercises with two students, and a school for boys was opened in the basement, under the direction of Father Peyrogrosse and the tuition of Mr. Murrey. The episcopal residence could not have been a very favorable place for recollection, and for the quiet and systematic discharge of the important duties connected with the organization and government of so new and vast a diocese, for in one part of the building the services of the church were held, and the coming together and departure of the congregation were taking place; over the Bishop's head was the Ecclesiastical Seminary, and under him, in the basement, was a school for boys. He also commenced to make his plans for the erection of a suitable church, the future Cathedral of St. Paul. In two years the congregation of St. Paul numbered fifteen hundred souls, composed almost entirely of French Canadians, Irish, and Germans. In the same year his theological students were increased to six, four of whom were accommodated in other dioceses.

Bishop Cretin also organized, with astonishing rapidity,

Catholic parishes in every direction. So great was the influx of population, embracing large numbers of Irish Catholics, that flourishing congregations and substantial stone churches seemed to spring up on every side. His efforts were greatly promoted by a zealous and self-sacrificing body of priests, who shared the apostolic spirit and emulated the heroic example of their Bishop. Schools kept pace with the churches, and secular education became disseminated together with the saving truths of religion. The Bishop's resources were severely taxed by the urgent necessity for churches and schools. For his churches he of course asked nothing from the Legislature; but as the policy of making education a State affair had been adopted in Minnesota, under the Puritan traditions which an immense New England immigration had brought to the West, he thought it but just that he, who had been so great a promoter of education in Minnesota, should receive a fair proportion of the common school fund, raised by a general tax, for the support of his schools, and that Catholics should not be deprived of that liberty of conscience and equality before the law, of which the community was always boasting. As early as 1853 he commenced the agitation of this question. He did not meet with greater success than attended the efforts of Bishop Fitzpatrick, at Boston, and of Archbishop Hughes, at New York. The result of his efforts was described by the Bishop in the following plain and characteristic language:—

"The New Englanders, pretty numerous in St. Paul, have imported from their former home their narrow Eastern prejudices against liberty of conscience and the freedom of education. In the name of liberty, as understood by them, they disregarded last year numerous petitions on that subject, and defeated a bill claiming that each denomination should be authorized to have schools of their own, supported by the public funds, provided these schools be well conducted, and although religious instructions should be given there; they thought proper to compel parents to pay taxes for schools that their conscience and their pastors forbade them to profit by. There is no hope to obtain anything this year from our Legislature, neither from the School Commissioners, for our numerous schools. These gentlemen would do well to take some lessons of liberality from their neighbors in Dubuque and Galena."*

In 1853 Bishop Cretin introduced into his diocese the Sisters of St. Joseph, and established under their charge a fine academy for the education of young ladies. He secured for this purpose a commodious brick house, in a fine and healthy location on the highest point of the bank of the Mississippi, between the upper and lower town. Mother Seraphine, long Superior of the Sisters of St. Joseph at Carondelet, and founder of the colony at St. Paul, presided over this fine academy, which disseminated its blessings through the community. The Bishop in the same year acquired for the Sisters a large block of land, a donation for the most part of Mr. H. Price, and erected on it spacious stone buildings, designed for the charitable purposes of an Hospital and Orphan Asylum, and sufficiently large to accommodate a Novitiate for the Sisters. The good Sisters of St. Joseph are still conducting at St. Paul their Novitiate, Academy, Asylum, and Hospital, and are also teaching the parochial schools.

The Indian missions, during his missionary career in

---

* *Catholic Almanac*, 1854, p. 172.

the diocese of Dubuque, had been objects of Dr. Cretin's tender care and ardent zeal; under his episcopate they became especial favorites and cherished objects of his most paternal solicitude. Even while the influx of European population and the increase of congregations taxed his means and labors to so great an extent, he had time, zeal, and resources left for the promotion of the salvation of his Indian children. In the first year of his administration he had several Indian missions in successful operation. It has already been related how the Winnebagoes were removed in 1848 from Prairie-du-Chien to Long Prairie, beyond the supposed reach of missionaries, and how the mission was broken up. No sooner had he taken possession of his see than he revived the mission of the Winnebagoes at Long Prairie, and appointed the Rev. Francis de Vivaldi, Canon of Vintimil, its pastor. The mission was fruitful of most consoling results: a population of two hundred joyfully embraced and followed the sacred truths and holy practices of religion; a school of Indian children, at which the daily attendance was between sixty and ninety, was opened and successfully conducted. Three Sisters of St. Joseph taught these simple children and pupils of the Church, and by their zeal, piety, and charity trained their young hearts for Heaven. The Bishop succeeded in obtaining some assistance from the Federal Government, but soon this was neutralized by the refusal of the local official to deliver the money placed in his hands to pay the teacher and furnish the scholars with provisions and clothing. The Bishop was obliged to advance considerable sums of money in order to prevent the teacher and scholars from starving.

The Indian Mission at Pembina, the first post within

our territory, near the British possessions and the Selkirk Settlement, which had been established some years before by the indefatigable Father Joseph Bellecourt. was also cherished and promoted by Bishop Cretin. The church was dedicated to St. Joseph, and the congregation numbered fifteen hundred Catholics, mostly half-breeds. The mission also had a fine school under the direction of Sisters of the Propagation of the Faith. In the same mission was another church, that of the Assumption, twenty miles from Pembina, which was also attended by Father Bellecourt.

Missions for the Ojibways were also established at the following places: at *Crow Wing*, where there was a Catholic population of two hundred and fifty; at Mill Lake, which possessed a Catholic population of five or six hundred Indians; and at *Sandy Lake* and Sacrapids, all of which were attended by Father Pierz; and at Fond-du-Lac, on the St. Louis River, where a Catholic population of five hundred half-breeds and Indians were attended by Father Skolla.

Under the auspices of Bishop Cretin, the Brothers of the Holy Family were introduced into his diocese in 1855, and took charge of the schools for boys. The Bishop also made arrangements for a priest of the same Order to come to St. Paul City and found a novitiate for the reception and training of Brothers. These good Brothers, besides teaching the male schools, acted as sacristans, choristers, and catechists. The introduction of the Sisters of St. Joseph at St. Paul has already been mentioned; besides these, Bishop Cretin procured a colony of seven Sisters of the Propagation of the Faith, whom he stationed at Pembina. In their school they imparted a good practical education, and taught the English, French, and Indian languages. These pious Sisters subsequently extended their efforts to the sick and poor. The Bishop also established the Order of St. Benedict at St. Cloud, Stearns County, where a convent was founded and chartered, under Father Cornelius Wittman as prior; also a convent of Benedictine nuns, which commenced with four professed Sisters and three novices. Select and free schools, charitable and devotional societies, were established in many parts of the diocese. Indeed, Catholicity in the far West, under the indefatigable Bishop, and the zealous French and other clergymen who assisted him, bestowed graces and consolations upon her children as numerous and precious as were enjoyed in older and more favored lands.

Bishop Cretin was an earnest and untiring friend and promoter of westward immigration; not an immigration which looked only to the delving and material pursuits of men, but one that was designed and directed so as to build up communities of Christians, who with strong arms and brave hearts developed the riches bestowed upon a generous soil by the Creator, while their toil was sweetened and blessed in being presented as an offering in His honor, and its superabundant fruits expended in rearing churches and schools for the promotion of religion and education. He was ever ready to give the best and most conscientious counsel to poor immigrants arriving in our Atlantic cities, and to direct them to localities where success and blessings awaited their industry. Frequent applications were made to him for information and advice, from Europe and from our Eastern cities; so numerous were the letters he received on these subjects, that in 1853 he adopted the plan of publishing in the *New York Freeman's Journal,* and probably in other papers, a general answer to them all. The following is an extract from one of these interesting documents:—

"A residence of three years in the Territory, and the visits I have been obliged to make in many distant parts of it; the testimony of settlers quite disinterested in the matter, who have come from the East, from the South, and from the West, and who declare they prefer this to any country they have lived in; the fact of the extraordinary crop of all kinds yet standing; the nature of the soil, which does not lose its productive faculties either by the drought or by any excess of rain (it is a light, black, sandy gypsum soil, which absorbs the damp and the heat of the atmosphere); and, above all, the healthiness of the country (bilious fevers are unknown), have fully convinced me that in all the Union a better location could not be found for the emigrant. Millions of acres of fine prairies, bordered with timber and sprinkled with small clear lakes and streams, are not yet claimed by any one.

"But I would recommend the new-comers not to settle at too great a distance from a church; their children, particularly, would soon become like little savages.

"I can only mention some places where there is a church, or where a church will be soon erected, as valuable pieces of land have already been secured for that purpose. Those places are St. Paul, St. Peter, St. Anthony, Little Camden, Stillwater, Hastings, Le Sueur, Sauk Rapids, Cannon River, or Faribeau, Traverse des Sioux, Wabasha, on the Lake Pepin, and many new towns springing up. None of these places, although they are located on rivers, are exposed to overflow. The roads are generally very good.

"The winter season is pretty severe, but, according

to the judgment of many, it is the most agreeable, being the most healthy, and the weather constantly dry.

"Vegetation begins late, but it is so luxuriant that any one can perceive its progress from morning till evening. I have not yet met with a stranger who is not delighted with the aspect of the country, particularly of St. Paul. Without going out of the city, they may see in the gardens corn-stalks more than twelve feet high. I do not laugh any more at the prophecy of some of our statesmen, who declared in their public documents that before long it would be a new Stockholm or a new St. Petersburg.

"Believe me, sirs, that in these statements I have no other view but to give testimony to the truth itself, and to guide to a safe place the many destitute emigrants who are lingering on your shores, and perishing, body and soul, in your Babylon.

"The shortest and cheapest way to reach Minnesota is through the Lakes and Galena." *

The increase in the population of Minnesota, for several years succeeding 1853, was almost fabulous. But the facts are well authenticated. A statement of the Catholic statistics alone, for one year, based upon Bishop Cretin's own relation, will serve as a proof of this astonishing growth of our country and Church. In the single year 1856, the Catholic population of Minnesota was *doubled.* At the end of the year 1855 its numbers were twenty-five thousand, and at the end of the year 1856 they were fifty thousand. The Bishop had to meet this wonderful increase in so new a country, by providing churches and priests for their spiritual care and guidance; the task seemed impossible, especially in

---

* *N. Y. Freeman's Journal,* Sept. 3, 1853.

his already impoverished condition; but he spared no labor, and shrank from no sacrifice that could promote his success; the result will speak for itself. At the close of the year 1855 he had ten priests; at the end of 1856 he had increased the number to nineteen. A corresponding increase in churches, chapels, and stations was effected during the same time throughout his diocese. It has already been stated that when he was appointed Bishop, in 1850, he had one log church and three priests. In the short period of three years, during which he administered this young diocese, he increased the number of the places of divine worship to twenty-nine churches and thirty-five stations, and the number of his priests to twenty.

In the midst of his great labors, Bishop Cretin found time for improving the condition of his congregations and schools, and for providing them with better accommodations and improved facilities. He also undertook and carried forward the erection of the new Cathedral of St. Paul, a fine and massive structure, one hundred and seventy-two feet long, seventy feet wide, forty-two feet from floor to ceiling, and surmounted with a fine tower. This temple is remarkable for its tasteful simplicity. Bishop Cretin estimated its cost at seventy thousand dollars.

The long and exhausting labors of Bishop Cretin, both as a priest and as a Bishop, the hardships and privations of his missionary career, and the unceasing exertions of mind and body which his episcopate entailed upon him, had now exhausted his health. Apoplexy struck him down in the midst of his labors, and in the fulness of his success. He died February 22, 1857, in the fifty-seventh year of his age. He is justly regarded as one of the most apostolic and saintly Prelates of the American Church.

RIGHT REV. JOHN NEPOMUCENE NEU-
MANN, D.D., C.SS.R.,

*Fourth Bishop of Philadelphia, A.D. 1852.**

THE trying periods of internal dissension and of cruel persecution through which the Church of Philadelphia had passed during the episcopates of Bishops Egan, Conwell, and Kenrick, requiring, as they did, the exercise of the sterner qualities of head and heart, as well as the full exertion of the episcopal powers, were followed by the calm and prosperous administration of Bishop Neumann. His gentle virtues beautifully illustrated the pastoral office. His meekness and apostolic zeal for the good of his flock came in the appropriate order of God's mercy to his Church, and accomplished results not inferior to the achievements of others, whose careers were more stirring and brilliant in the sight of men. While the splendid talents and dazzling genius of a Bishop England at the South, and the unquailing championship of an Archbishop Hughes at the North, were admirably adapted for the spheres assigned to those distinguished Prelates, there was an equal fitness and a commensurate good accomplished in his time and place by the humble, zealous, learned, and saintly Bishop Neumann. His attainments in the languages, sciences, and sacred studies were the handmaids of his apostleship. He

---

* Authorities: Original Documents supplied by the Redemptorists; *Funeral Obsequies of Right Rev. John Nepomucene Neumann*; *The Metropolitan*, Vols. II., III., IV., V., and VI.; *Catholic Almanac*; *New York Freeman's Journal*, etc., etc.

acquired various languages in order that he might hear the confessions of the humble emigrants flocking to our shores from the nations of Europe. Through the physical sciences he rendered an homage to the God of all science. His profound knowledge of ecclesiastical sciences enabled him to train the young Redemptorists of this country for their noble mission, to excel in guiding and instructing a numerous body of clergy, and in exploring the devious paths leading to the conversion of the infidel and the sinner. Whether he stood at the altar of the Cathedral, in the councils of the Church, or in the cell of the condemned criminal, he was ever the same humble and zealous servant of God. His position in the history of our Hierarchy is amply vindicated by the monuments of his great services and success, and the tradition of his virtues and sanctity will be an ever precious legacy in the Church of America.

Bishop Neumann was the third of six children, and the first son of Philip Neumann, of Obersburg, Bavaria, and of Agnes Lebis. He was born in Srachatic, a town of Bohemia, where his parents were settled, and where his father conducted a large stocking-weaving factory, on Good Friday, March 20, 1811. He was baptized on the day of his birth in the Church of St. James the Great, and his god-father, John Mack, the Mayor of the town, bestowed upon him the name of John Nepomucene, the glorious patron of Bohemia. His parents were most devout children of the Church, and most scrupulous in the duties of their state. The religious training of their children especially engaged their attention, and their piety and zeal in this regard were signally rewarded by vocations for a religious life bestowed upon one-half of their children; for besides the call of John

Nepomucene to the sacred ministry, two of their daughters joined the Sisters of St. Charles in their native country. While the father was engaged all day with his factory, the mother of this exemplary family was occupied in the service of God and the education of her children. "Our education," said Bishop Neumann, "was according to the ancient mode." From this good mother he learned the beauties of the way of God. She attended early Mass during the week, frequently approached the sacraments, added many fasting days of her own observance to those appointed by the Church, was constant in practising the devotion of the way of the cross, and sanctified her home as a temple of religion by family prayers, the recitation of the rosary, and other devotions. In these pious practices she accustomed her children to accompany her, and in her attendance at church she had always some of them at her side. Bishop Neumann related, as an anecdote of himself, that his mother trained him to go with her to the church from his tenderest years, and even before he had arrived at sufficient discretion to appreciate fully such acts of piety; and that it frequently required the promise of a penny to induce him to go. His regular attendance, however, gave occasion to the mothers of other little children to cite his example for their imitation, when one of them, a playmate of John Nepomucene, replied, "Give me a penny every day and I will follow his example."

The good effects of the pious example and religious training he received in his youth were strikingly manifested in his conduct as he grew older, and indeed throughout his life. In proof of this it may be stated that he was found worthy to receive the sacrament of confirmation when eight years old, and when the older children were preparing for their first communion he was also examined in Christian doctrine, and, though only nine years old, was found prepared to approach with his seniors. He retained through life a lively remembrance of his first confession, of his confirmation, and of his first communion, and could, when a Bishop, recall the most minute details of those sacred events.

He inherited from his father an inquiring intellect and an insatiable love of books. He commenced attending school on the feast of All Saints, 1818, his seventh year; he was always at the head of his class, a circumstance which he modestly attributed to the desire of the teachers to please his father, who was a man of influence, and always an incumbent of some one of the municipal offices; but his success was better accounted for by his own untiring application; for while his companions were at play he was at his studies. He read all the books he could get his hands on, and in his classes was not content with committing his tasks to memory, but insisted on knowing and understanding the reason and causes of things as well as their effects. One day he surprised his teacher by asking "how it was that the globe stood in space without support?" He frequently puzzled his mother by his inquiries, and she was under the necessity of recommending him to postpone his researches for maturer years. But such were his faith and devotion, that he was in the habit of referring the phenomena of the physical world and the mysteries of creation to God, and thus practically solved the most difficult problems in the physical sciences. Although he could not comprehend how the spheres were held together by invisible bonds, and moved in harmony at such immeasurable distances, he well knew that God alone could accomplish such wonders, and he venerated them as external manifestations of God's glory, and of His wisdom, and of His mercy to man.

The holy ministry was so exalted a state, and was reserved for only a small number comparatively of the applicants, that young Neumann did not presume to aspire to it. But in spite of the apparently insuperable barriers which separated him from the priesthood, his piety was extraordinary, and his young life showed signs of a future vocation. Not content with serving his pastor's Mass every morning, he had constructed a little altar of brass, which he surrounded with lights, flowers, and pictures, and these became the miniature shrine of his youthful devotions, and developed in him that love for the altar of God and His sanctuary, for the beautifying and adornment of which he in after-life considered no treasures too rich, no expenditures too lavish. One day, as he was about to commence his meal, he said grace, signing himself by mistake with a Latin cross instead of the three crosses on the forehead, mouth, and breast; a maidservant of the family, who was remarkable for her sanctity, on observing him do this, uttered a prophetic exclamation, referring to his evident vocation to the sacred ministry. His mother was delighted at this; she frequently related the circumstance in his presence, and by every word and action endeavored to cherish in him an aspiration for holy orders. The thought of becoming a priest now frequently passed through his mind, and though his prospects in that regard were slight, he consulted his parents on the subject when eleven years old, and with their consent went every evening to his pastor's residence to study the rudiments of Latin. In 1823, at the age of twelve years, he left home on All Saints' Day, a day which he seems to have frequently selected for the important acts of his life, and went to Budweis to continue his studies under the Fathers of the Pious Schools. Here he was so far in advance of his class that he had little studying to do, and spent his time in devouring the contents of nearly all the books in the library. This circumstance of his having but little to do in the way of regular studies in order to keep up with his class together with some irregularities in the school, caused him to become almost disgusted with collegiate studies and to think of abandoning them, but his mother's persuasions corrected his impetuous haste in the pursuit of learning and controlled his action in this regard. As he advanced into the studies which suited his talents, he became enraptured with them. The humanities and higher classics delighted him. He next became engrossed with philosophy, and at the same time gave full scope to his love of the natural sciences. As he became advanced in years and studies, he became a master of natural history, physics, geology, and astronomy; and although he had formed a dislike for algebra, geometry, and trigonometry, he now prosecuted those branches with avidity. He formed a little circle with eight of his companions, who communicated to each other their acquisitions and observations in the various studies they pursued. These latter studies were prosecuted under the priests of the Cistercian Order, to whom he ever cherished a lively gratitude. Under their pious guidance he also made great progress in piety, went frequently to the sacraments, and what was rare in a college-boy, usually so giddy and inconsiderate, he remarked that he strove to save his parents unnecessary expense for his tuition and board, and for this purpose chose to occupy a room with two other students.

At the age of twenty he returned home a thorough scholar. During the vacation of 1831, he and his parents were greatly concerned about the choice of a profession. Theology, Law, or Medicine was to be selected, and all were surrounded with barriers unknown in this country. Theology, especially, seemed beyond his reach, since he had learned that out of ninety postulants only twenty were to be selected, and in order to gain acceptance the strongest testimonials and recommendations were necessary. His father consented to give him the medical course at Prague, though accompanied with great expense, and he accepted this offer. But his mother still held before his view the exalted office of the priesthood, and in answer to the many obstacles stated to her, and in the face of them, she insisted on making the effort to secure his admission to a theological school. At her instance young Neumann prepared a petition for that purpose, and forwarded it to the Episcopal Consistory of Budweis, in order more to comply with her wishes than with any hope of success. Her constancy and his virtue were rewarded by a favorable answer from Budweis, and admission to the Theological Seminary of that city was accorded to him. He commenced his theological studies in that institution on All Saints' Day, 1831.

The earnestness and industry, with which he had prosecuted his studies at the College of Budweis, were now redoubled in the classes of the Seminary. The progress he made during the first year in Sacred Scriptures, the Hebrew language, and in Church history, elicited high encomiums from his Professors. He received tonsure and minor orders July 21, 1832. His second year was crowned with still greater success in more advanced studies. He distinguished himself in canon law. It was also during this time that he began to read the journals of the Leopoldine Society, in which he was particularly interested in the letters of Father Baraga, afterwards Bishop of Marquette. From this moment the resolution of devoting himself to the American mission took possession of his mind and heart. He communicated his views to a few only of his companions, and endeavored to inspire them with the same holy purpose. Being desirous of studying French and English, as a preparation for his future labors in America, he applied for and obtained admission into the University of Prague. Here, though disappointed in his hopes of learning those languages, he prosecuted his studies with extraordinary zeal, and while he perceived that several of the Professors were tainted with prevailing errors, his own superior judgment and correct studies enabled him to detect and reject all doubtful teachings. He finished his course at Prague with distinction, and in August, 1835, he returned to Budweis.

His ordination was delayed by the extreme old age and feebleness of the Bishop of Budweis, and he resolved to make his way to America without waiting for that event. His father was at first loath to consent, but his mother generously seconded his exalted purpose and self-sacrifice. His Bishop, the clergy, and his father now applauded his choice, and though numerous obstacles opposed his plans, he was unshaken. The funds to defray his traveling expenses were raised partly by collections in the parishes of Budweis, and partly by a contribution from one of the societies in aid of the foreign missions. He applied first for acceptance by Dr. Kenrick into the diocese of Philadelphia, but was disappointed by that Prelate's withdrawal of his call for missionaries just at that time. His next application was to Bishop Bruté, of Vincennes, and again he was not accepted. Finally he applied to Bishop Dubois, of New York. He resolved, however, not to await the result of his last petition, but leaving home February 8, 1836, he reached Paris after encountering many difficulties, and, finding his funds greatly reduced, bought his ticket for America by the Havre vessel without further delay. The diligence from Paris started without him, and all his efforts to procure a conveyance to overtake it failed; he set forth on foot. When he arrived at St. Germain he was drenched with rain, and presented so moving a spectacle to a benevolent gentleman, to whom he related his adventures, that his new acquaintance procured him a conveyance, so that he arrived at Havre in time. He secured his passage for eighty francs, but had to carry his own provisions along. He sailed in the *Europe*, an American vessel, April 20, 1836. During the voyage, which lasted till Trinity Sunday, his life was providentially saved in a most signal manner, the particulars of which he has himself related.

On his arrival at New York, he was received with great cordiality by Bishop Dubois, who was in want of German priests, and who was particularly rejoiced at the acquisition of one who brought such high testimonials for learning and zeal. While awaiting ordination, he was intrusted with the preparation of the German children in New York for their first communion. He was made sub-deacon June 19, 1836, deacon on the 24th, and was ordained priest on the 25th, by Bishop Dubois, in St. Patrick's Cathedral. On the following day, which was Sunday, he celebrated High Mass at the Church of St. Nicholas, and administered their first communion to the children whom he had prepared.

Having been already destined by Bishop Dubois for the Mission at Williamsville, Erie County, he started immediately for that place, remaining a few days at the Bishop's request at Buffalo. St. Joseph's Church at Buffalo not having been finished, he officiated at St. Patrick's, in which he preached twice on the Sunday he spent there, heard confessions, and administered baptism, all for the first time. It was during his journey that he met and conversed with the first Redemptorist he ever saw, Father Prost, whose edifying conversation and society detained him for a day longer at Buffalo. Father Pax, of Eden, near Buffalo, accompanied the young missionary to Williamsville. Besides Williamsville he attended the mission at Northwood, Lancaster, and other places. His missionary labors extended over a wide field. In addition to these duties, having had occasion to dismiss the teacher at Williamsville, he discharged the laborious duties of teacher for seven months, rather than allow his parishioners, who were poor, to be burdened with the teacher's salary. So zealous were his efforts for the good of his people, and so unsparing his labors, that his zeal required to be checked, and he has himself said, "Father Pax thought that I worked rather hard in my first fervor, and consequently I received from him frequent admonitions." The Redemptorists at this time were few, and their Order not organized in this country. Father Prost, their Superior, was singularly attracted by the zeal and virtues of Father Neumann, and used his utmost efforts to draw him to the Congregation of Our

Most Holy Redeemer. He endeavored to persuade Bishop Dubois to transfer the mission at Williamsville to the Redemptorists, and to induce Father Neumann to continue the mission as a member of the Congregation. But neither the Bishop nor the priest was prepared for such a change. The Mission of Father Neumann at Williamsville was for a time interrupted by his appointment as temporary pastor at Rochester, where he witnessed the wonderful fruits of the zeal and labors of the Redemptorists. He was particularly pleased with the fraternity of Mount Carmel, introduced by Father Prost at Rochester, and he petitioned also for its establishment at Williamsville. His mission at the latter place was enlarged so as to embrace other stations, and extended over two hundred miles. With the exception of small congregations at Williamsville, Northwood, and Lancaster, the Catholic population was composed of scattered families living at great distances apart. He traveled many miles to carry the sacraments to an individual or family, and was frequently engaged the entire day in going from one house to another. In these journeys he suffered exhausting fatigues and the pangs of hunger for long periods of time. He went upon his errands of mercy and benediction in all weathers; no companion shared his travels or privations. He carried his vestments and other altar service with him, and after an early journey of many miles and great exhaustion, his greatest consolation and refreshment consisted in arriving at some house or village in time to renovate his being with the bread of life and the blood of the Lamb. Four years were thus spent by this young and devoted missionary in the arduous but consoling labors of his extensive mission.

During these missionary years he exerted every effort with which a heavenly zeal inspired him, to awaken an exalted sense of religion and a burning love of God in the hearts of his flock. He frequently grieved over the neglect of men to accept the graces offered to them, and their attachment to the follies and indulgences of the world. He often felt a desire to retire from the world and commune with Heaven. He had several times been thrown in contact with pious and zealous members of the Redemptorist Order, and had admired their holiness and wondered at the remarkable success attending their labors. In the spring of 1840 he was prostrated with an exhausting fever, and during his convalescence visited the Redemptorist Father Landale, at Rochester, for several days. But as yet he did not feel convinced of his vocation, and he has himself remarked "that neither Father Landale nor myself spoke or even thought of my entering the Congregation of the Most Holy Redeemer." He attributes his vocation not to the conversations or suggestions of any of the Redemptorists he met, for they failed during four years to convince him, but to a "supernatural desire," with which God inspired him during the fall of 1840. He then applied to Bishop Hughes, and requested him to transfer the mission of Williamsville to the Redemptorists. Receiving no answer from that Prelate, in consequence of his absence from New York, he applied to Father Prost, and was readily received into Redemptorist Order. He left the mission, which he so faithfully served for four years and a half, October 9, 1840, and made a long and painful journey to Pittsburgh, where he met with a cordial welcome from Father Tschenhens the Superior there, at whose request he celebrated High Mass on the day of his arrival, which was Sunday. The early departure of Father Tschenhens for Baltimore, and the constant engagements of Father Chackert on missions, devolved upon him at once the entire duties of the congregation at Pittsburgh. He was invested with the habit of the Congregation of Our Most Holy Redeemer by Father Prost, the Provincial, on the feast of St. Andrew. At this time the Redemptorists had neither novitiate nor master of novices; they were composed entirely of the first members of their Order who had come to America, and were kept incessantly at work in administering to the spiritual necessities of the German Catholics, principally in the States of Pennsylvania, Maryland, Ohio, and New York. Father Neumann was successively sent to Baltimore, then to St. Nicholas' Church in New York, where he remained only a fortnight, then to Rochester, where he remained two months, and next to Norwalk, Ohio, where he remained till November, 1841. These changes were necessitated by the emergencies of the missions, and Father Neumann, ever ready as he was to serve, rendered invaluable services at all of these places. He was now recalled by his Superior to Baltimore to make his noviceship, which he had already made several attempts to accomplish in the midst of his labors. Receiving permission to give missions on his journey to Baltimore, his travels were full of exhausting labors on the way, and were interrupted by a serious illness. At Canton, Ohio, he met the Most Rev. Archbishop Purcell and his Vicar-General, who, in consequence of a report which was then current, that the Redemptorist Order in America was about to be dissolved, invited Father Neumann to Cincinnati. He preferred to return to Baltimore and share the counsels and fortunes of his brethren. At the request of Bishop Purcell, however, he went to Randolph, where the church had been burned by a band of bigots three years before, and where a priest had not officiated since. He gave a mission to the German Catholics of this place, who flocked in great numbers to his sermons and to the sacraments. Continuing his journey, he arrived at Baltimore on the feast of the Immaculate Conception, and immediately commenced his noviceship for the third or fourth time. Such was the need of his services, and such his progress in spirituality, that his novitiate was extremely brief, for at the end of two weeks he made his vows under the direction of Father Alexander, at St. James' Church, January 16, 1842. This was the first profession of a Redemptorist in America. Though he had scarcely made a novitiate at all, and had been too constantly engaged in active missionary duties to have time or opportunity for ascetic studies or exercises, he was a master of the interior and contemplative life, and a true religious.

Immediately after his profession he was appointed assistant to Rev. Father Fay, at St. James' Church, where he zealously labored, and where he took particular charge of the religious training of the children. A more extensive and arduous duty was also devolved upon him—that of giving missions in various cities. Thus he frequently visited Cumberland, Harper's Ferry, Martinsburgh, Richmond, Frederick, York, Columbia, Strasburg, and many other places in the States of Virginia, Maryland, and Pennsylvania. He assisted at the laying of the corner-stone of St. Alphonsus' Church, Baltimore, May 1st, 1842. His labors in this extensive and fruitful field continued until March 5, 1844, when Father Alexander, his Superior, who had thus witnessed and admired his truly religious zeal, appointed him Superior of the Redemptorist Convent at Pittsburgh. His three years at this place were years of untiring service and most beneficial results. His predecessor, Father Carteyvels, had already laid the corner-stone of St. Philomena's Church. Father Neumann now enlarged the plan, built the church, and made it a most beautiful temple. He remained its pastor until January 25, 1847, and during his administration of the Convent and Church a vast amount of good was accomplished. Among the German-speaking population especially, his labors produced the most abundant fruit, and won the highest encomiums of Dr. O'Connor, then Bishop of Pittsburgh, for his zeal and capacity. He was now recalled to Baltimore in January, and in February, 1847, he was appointed by Rev. Father Held, Provincial of the Redemptorists in Belgium, the Provincial of the Order in America, a position which he held with eminent success and usefulness for a little over four years. He was appointed the first pastor of the splendid Church of St. Alphonsus, Baltimore, April 1, 1851. His services in the Order, of which he was an ornament, were particularly useful in leading the youths of the Novitiate and Seminary in the ways of St. Alphonsus, and in preparing them for future usefulness in the Church. At Pittsburgh and Baltimore he was remarkably successful in founding and nourishing pious confraternities, schools, asylums, and various benevolent and devotional societies. Though not an orator in the estimate of the world, he was a most effective preacher. His preaching was as untiring as his other labors. His exhortations were simple but learned, unostentatious but eloquent in the power of truth and in the spirit of faith. Although he was one of the humblest of men, he was ever ready to appeal to the human soul, relying not upon his own powers, but upon the Holy Ghost, and moved by the single motive of doing good. His attendance at the confessional was most assiduous; and it is related that he was gifted with a supernatural faculty of guiding souls in the tribunal of penance. The motive which actuated all his efforts was the salvation of souls. His extraordinary attainments and abilities were not displayed before the world. Among those who knew and appreciated his high merits, outside of his own Order, may be mentioned Dr. O'Connor, late Bishop of Pittsburgh, who knew him intimately, and the late Archbishop Kenrick, of Baltimore, who said that he was greatly influenced in nominating Dr. Neumann to succeed himself in the See of Philadelphia, by the high commendations of Dr. O'Connor—commendations not designed to influence or affect that appointment, but intended only to do justice to a priest of his "eminent merit."*

On the translation of Dr. Kenrick from the See of Philadelphia to the Archiepiscopal See of Baltimore, that Prelate nominated Father Neumann as second on the list of divines sent by him to Rome, from whom a successor to himself was to be chosen. But although he was not placed first on the list, the Holy See deemed the humble Redemptorist the most worthy, and sent his appointment forward to the Archbishop of Baltimore. It is not the least significant part of the honor involved in this appointment that the Holy See, already aware of his humility, and anticipating his refusal, accompanied the documents, in the first instance, with a strict injunction of obedience on the part of Father Neumann. This was a

---

* *Funeral Sermon* of Dr. Kenrick on *Bishop Neumann.*

severe blow to his humility; but his spirit of obedience, not less than his humble resignation to the will of superiors, left him no room for hesitation. On receiving his appointment he exclaimed, "Tu autem Domine, miserere nobis!" and immediately added, in the spirit of joyful obedience, "Deo gracias et Mariæ!" Never, perhaps, was man affected less by so great a change in his position; for it was remarkable in the episcopate of Bishop Neumann that he was the same humble servant of a crucified Master, who had announced the Word, in 1837, near the Falls of Niagara, and had carried the cross of the Redemptorists at his side in his ministry among the German Catholics of Pittsburgh and Baltimore. In alluding to his acceptance of the mitre, Archbishop Kenrick, while preaching the funeral sermon of Bishop Neumann, made the following remarks:—"The sacrifice of his feelings in this circumstance can only be esteemed by those who knew his deep humility and great love of the religious state. He felt as if he was torn from his loved retreat, and from the society of his brethren, to be exposed to the gaze of a proud world, likely to scorn the lowliness of his appearance and the simplicity of his manners. He dreaded the responsibility of governing a flock so vast, and of managing interests so complicated, for which his previous retired habits had ill prepared him. He feared lest the difference of nationalities might impede and embarrass his efforts, if not wholly defeat them. But as he had not sought or desired the post, he went forward, relying not on himself, but on God, who strengthens the weak, and effects His high counsels by the instruments of His own choice, to show forth His power and mercy."

Bishop Neumann was consecrated by Archbishop

Kenrick, at St. Alphonsus' Church, Baltimore, on Passion Sunday, 1852, which, by a remarkable coincidence, fell in that year on March 20, the birth-day of the newly-consecrated Bishop. The day of his consecration was a proud day for the Redemptorist Order, for the Catholic German population of Baltimore, and for all, except the humble recipient of the honors of that brilliant occasion. The immense procession, the numerous banners, the splendid music, and rich decorations of St. Alphonsus, the meetings and congratulations of the German Catholics of the city, and their handsome presents, were but so many tributes to humble virtue; so many evidences of the popular appreciation of sanctity. The laity in a body called on the Bishop at his residence, adjoining St. Alphonsus', and presented him with an address of congratulation, handsomely framed; they also presented to him a golden chalice and pectoral cross and chain, together with a set of episcopal vestments; and in the evening he was serenaded by a full military band, and the German societies. The good Bishop's reply to the address was brief and appropriate, and, as everything he did or said was designed for the good of others, replete with good advice. His mind was, from the beginning, occupied with measures designed for the beenfit of his new flock, and before he even reached his See, he was taking steps for providing his diocese with Catholic schools, and protecting his people from the injurious influences of the non-Catholic education by which they were surrounded.

He took possession of his see March 28, but he went quietly to work: one of the very first acts of his ministry in Philadelphia, one so characteristic of this servant of God, and one replete with honor before Heaven, was to visit the prison of the county, and sit for a long time with two condemned malefactors, the brothers Skupinski, who were to suffer death for the murder of the boy Lehman; his ministry in their regard was blessed, and the unfortunate prisoners consented to prepare their souls for their impending summons before the judgment-seat of the Most High, and to accept the services of Father Etthoffer, whom the Bishop sent to them as their spiritual director.

The first few days after his arrival he spent in visiting the religious houses and institutions of Philadelphia, at which he was received with every demonstration of joy and reverence. On the following Sunday, Palm Sunday, he blessed the palms at St. John's; in the afternoon administered confirmation at St. Patrick's, and in the evening delivered an admirable discourse at St. Joseph's, selecting for his subject the devotion to St. Joseph. Of this sermon the following remarks were made by one of his hearers: " In his instruction on devotion to St. Joseph, it seemed to us that we could see the idea and plan of one great part of the work that he is resolved with God's help to accomplish in Philadelphia. The gentleness, the love, and yet the firmness, with which he insisted on the necessity of parents having their children brought up as Catholics, not in the Church only, but at home in the family, and also in *schools under the care of the Church*, is a full guarantee that the day is not distant when there will be no church in Philadelphia without its schools adequate to the reception and instruction of the entire Catholic youth."

It was thus that Bishop Neumann commenced his episcopate; it was thus that he labored incessantly to the end of its duration. His first pastoral to his flock was issued in Easter week, 1854. It breathes the true apostolic spirit, and is replete with admirable instruction. In it he also announces the jubilee proclaimed by Pope Pius IX., in 1854; makes a powerful appeal to the people to provide the means for completing the new Cathedral of Saints Peter and Paul, and introduces to their notice the necessity and importance of providing Catholic schools; these were measures for which he never ceased to labor during his administration. He shortly afterwards issued a special circular in relation to the new Cathedral, and presented a plan of organized contributions. The work upon this splendid temple of religion was prosecuted by him with characteristic energy and success; in 1854 he called and presided over a mass meeting of the Catholics of Philadelphia, at which a new stimulus was given to the work; in 1857 he erected a fine chapel to the Cathedral, to answer as a place of worship until the Cathedral should be completed, and so constructed as to be turned over to school purposes afterwards; in 1859 he had the work so far progressed as to enable him to see the first cross erected on its summit; and before his death the Cathedral was nearly completed.

The parochial schools of the Diocese of Philadelphia, and especially of the city, increased wonderfully in numbers, attendance of scholars, and in efficiency, during his administration, and became a crowning glory of his work. The boys' schools he confided to the Christian Brothers, and those of the girls to the Sisters of St. Joseph, Sisters of Charity, Sisters of Notre Dame, and other female religious Orders. The daily attendance at the schools of a single parish in Philadelphia, in 1859, was one thousand. There were but two parochial schools in Philadelphia when he arrived there, in 1852, and at the time of his death, in 1860, he had increased the number to nearly one hundred. These were the nurseries of Catholic society, in which good citizens of the world were trained, because their chief training was aimed at making them citizens of heaven.

Bishop Neumann was devoted to the interests of the whole Church, and was ever useful in her councils by his learning, and still more by the benign influence of his gentle virtues and sanctity. In 1852, shortly after his installation as Bishop of Philadelphia, he attended the first National Council of Baltimore, and so anxious was he that its deliberations and decrees might be inspired by the Holy Ghost and useful to the American Church, that in his Pastoral he made special mention of it, and directed particular prayers to be offered at the Mass by his clergy, and in all religious houses, to this end, until after the adjournment of the Council. He was also one of those American Bishops invited by our Holy Father, Pius IX., to assemble at Rome in 1854, on the occasion of the definition of the dogma of the Immaculate Conception. He was remarkable for his devotion to St. Joseph, and for that to the Blessed Virgin. The first sermon he preached in his diocese, as early as 1852, was on the devotion to St. Joseph, and had he lived to our times he would have ardently united with us on earth, as he now no doubt unites with the choirs of heaven, in honoring St. Joseph with the new title of Patron of the Universal Church—a glorious title bestowed upon the Foster Father by that same saintly Pontiff who proclaimed the glorious title of the Mother, *Conceived without Sin.*

On the eve of his departure for Rome, in 1854, Bishop Neumann issued a beautiful Pastoral, announcing the

Jubilee of the Immaculate Conception, proclaiming his faith in and adherence to the expected dogma, and exhorting all to cultivate the devotion to Mary Conceived without Sin. An extract from this admirable Pastoral will serve to illustrate the pious and devout life and character of Bishop Neumann:—

"As the long-wished-for day approaches, let us pray still more fervently, attentive to the invitation of the Church we often hear, *Sursum Corda! Let us lift up our hearts* in frequent, earnest prayer, that the decision may be such as will redound to the praise of the adorable Trinity, the salvation of men, and to the honor of her who, next to God, is indeed the

>Æterna Cœli Gloria,
>Beata Spes Mortalium.

The eternal joy and glory of the heavens; the ever-blessed hope of fallen man. If such be the will of God, and your piety deserves it, before the close of this year we may hear again the voice of Peter, as when the days of Pentecost were accomplished, making known by the lips of Pius IX., to the assembled representatives of every nation under heaven, that from henceforth and forever all generations of true believers shall invoke Mary, Mother of God, as the EVER IMMACULATE VIRGIN, CONCEIVED WITHOUT STAIN OF ORIGINAL SIN."

Bishop Neumann sailed for Europe from New York, October 21, 1854, and soon joined his colleagues around the throne of Pius IX. Amidst the august assembly of illustrious Prelates then assembled at Rome, Bishop Neumann attracted the notice of the Sovereign Pontiff, by whom he was promoted, on account of his learning and piety, to a high honor in the Papal jurisdiction.

Right Rev. John N. Neumann, D.D., C.SS.R. 453

There was no Prelate in that sacred assembly who experienced greater joy or more heart-felt devotion at the proclamation of the dogma of the Immaculate Conception than did Bishop Neumann. His joy and devotion on this ever-memorable event found full and eloquent expression in the second Pastoral on this subject which he addressed to his diocese on his return.

From Rome he went to visit his native country and town, and his venerable father, who was also living at the Bishop's death. The following account of this event in his life is too interesting to be omitted :—

" The Bishop arrived at his native place, Srachatic, at eleven o'clock A.M., whither the Prelate was conveyed on a sled drawn by four horses, as is customary in those countries, and which the people out of respect and love for him obliged him to accept, that he might thus accelerate his journey, because of the intense cold. At a distance of two miles from the aforesaid town, the guard civic, and a large number of people, went to meet the respected dignitary, and thus to conduct him in a long train to town, and before all to the temple of the Most High God, at whose entrance the beloved Prelate was received by the Dean and numerous clergy of the place and its environs, and an immensely large number of people, comprising at the same time all the civic officers of the place and vicinity. The Dean congratulated the Right Rev. Prelate in a short but very appropriate address, comparing him to St. Paul, apostle of the nations, requesting of him, as the greatest favor of the moment, his apostolical blessing.

" In his reply the Right Rev. Bishop expressed the most affectionate and cordial thanks to the reverend speaker and the surrounding crowds for their kind reception, alluding, among other things, to the following particulars: that it was just on the very day, 3d of February, nineteen years ago, since he left his home for the missions in North America.

"After the usual thanksgiving in the temple of the Most High for his safe arrival, the Right Rev. Prelate was thence conducted in a splendid carriage, and in the midst of innumerable crowds of people of every kind and description, to his father's residence, where, at the principal entrance, a venerable old man, nearly ninety years of age, stood in the greatest expectation, scarcely believing in the reality of what was going on before his own sight, bathed in tears of joy and of consolation, distrusting as it were his own conviction that the Prelate whom he was to receive in his trembling arms, and to see another 'Joseph's face,' should be his own son, thus escorted with cries of jubilation and hosanna by the crowds prostrated on the ground in order to receive the American apostle's blessing; a most touching and impressive scene for all spectators."*

It was in the active and fruitful work of the Church that Bishop Neumann chiefly distinguished his administration: in continuing and increasing the work of his predecessors; in new and important undertakings of his own: in the providing of new churches for the rapidly increasing population of his diocese; in supplying them with priests; in founding and supporting schools and religious and educational institutions and religious houses, and in promoting piety and faith amongst his people. In the first five years of his administration he solemnly blessed and dedicated over fifty new churches; and such

---

* *Catholic Instructor* and *The Metropolitan*, 1855.

was the fervor of his flock, that no sooner were twenty or twenty-five Catholic families settled together in any interior town or village than they petitioned the Bishop for a church, and frequently he, in his prudence, had to restrain their zeal or postpone their generous undertakings. He established in his diocese the Devotion of the Forty Hours, and was thus instrumental in its being adopted in other dioceses. He was distinguished for the exactness and precision with which he carried out all the details of the ritual and ceremonial of the Church. He exacted the same precision from the clergy, and to this end he enacted several practical statutes in his Diocesan Synods. He required that everything around the altar and sanctuary should be neat, and that the sacred vessels and vestments should be kept in appropriate cases and places. He induced a mechanic in Philadelphia to manufacture a leather box or capsule, after a design of his own, for the preservation of the holy oils This case has since been adopted into general use in most, if not all, of the dioceses of this country. He gave to the Ecclesiastical Seminary of St. Charles Borromeo a prosperity it had never known before; and founded in 1849 a Preparatory Seminary in connection with it, which has to this day proved a blessing to the diocese, and now educates about forty students, candidates for the priesthood. He greatly increased the number of his clergy, and was to all of them a kind and indulgent father. He was most generous to the poor, and preferred to be surrounded by them rather than by the rich. He, with his brothers and sisters, united in bestowing their patrimony, consisting of the extensive family residence and grounds, upon their native town, for a hospital for the poor. The visitations he made of his diocese were incessant, and not a year passed that he was not thus engaged; and so ardently did he labor amongst his people that he might be regarded as not only the chief, but even as the actual pastor of each congregation. He usually spent in every visitation about three days with each congregation, preaching, hearing confessions, acting in special cases, enrolling members in various religious confraternities, and arousing the zeal and piety of the people. Frequently he thus visited between fifty and sixty congregations during a single visitation, and would sometimes confer confirmation on over five thousand persons within a few weeks. Among the means he adopted to promote the salvation of his people were the Missions, which he induced his former brethren of the Redemptorist Order to give amongst them; and Archbishop Kenrick has related that " The preaching of the Divine Word by those zealous missionaries, with various exercises of piety during one or two weeks, in various parishes of Philadelphia and in the diocese, have brought thousands upon thousands of neglectful souls to the sacraments, after years of delinquency." The conferences and synods he held with his clergy enabled them to participate in the vast ecclesiastical learning he possessed, and they were frequently astonished at his wonderful attainments. He was a model for their imitation. No priest in his diocese spent more time in the confessional, and he studied and acquired numerous modern languages in order to hear the confessions of poor emigrants. He even acquired the Irish language, in order that he might hear the confessions of a few of the old Irish Catholics who had been accustomed at home to go to confession in that language, and could not express themselves in any other. To his clergy he gave annual retreats, in which he was an example to them of every virtue. His success in the administration of this important diocese may be estimated from the great increase which took place in the number of the clergy. When he went to Philadelphia in 1852 the diocese possessed about one hundred priests, and in eight years he increased the number to one hundred and fifty-two, besides sixty clerical students. In 1860 the diocese possessed two hundred and twenty-two churches, chapels, and stations. Besides the parochial schools he established, industrial schools were founded and numerous religious institutions, colleges, academies, orphan asylums, and hospitals. It was said of him by one of his own priests that in eight years he accomplished the work of twenty.

Bishop Neumann was one of the most learned men in the United States, and had few equals in this or any country. He was a master of the ancient languages; he spoke fluently all the dialects of Austria; he could converse freely in at least twelve modern languages. He was a profound theologian, and could readily settle any disputed point which might be referred to his decision without reference to books. He was versed, too, in the exact sciences, and possessed an extraordinary memory. An evidence of this was related, showing his acquaintance with the science of botany, which he had not studied or perhaps thought of for many years. He was paying a visit to the Academy of the Sacred Heart, at Eden Hall; the ladies of the school were unable to classify a certain flower which had just been cut; their botanical text-books failed to enable them to decide the question; when the Bishop entered the room he looked at the flower, and immediately informed them to what species and class it belonged. "He had, indeed," said Archbishop Kenrick, "great natural aptitude for learning, and his literary taste manifested itself not merely in theological pursuits, but in astronomy, botany, chemistry, and various sciences directed to improve and delight the mind. The treasures of learning, concealed under his humble exterior, are scarcely credible to those who did not know him intimately. We prize him, however, for his piety and devotion far more than for his literary and scientific endowments, and value more the humility of his deportment, the purity of his life, the zeal with which he sought the salvation of souls, than the honors which crowned his studies in the university, or the admiration caused by his knowledge of twelve or more languages." Yet such was his humility that he several times tendered his resignation, under the sense of his own unworthiness and insufficiency. He discharged every duty of his office, and was ever tenacious of its rights under a sense of loyalty to the Church. Yet he fled from its honors, courted retirement, still loved the cloister, and would at any time have gladly exchanged his fine episcopal city for the mission of any small town or village. The sanctity of his life was such as is rarely met with, even in the most favorable retirement and seclusion of the cloister, and was the more extraordinary in one who was actively and successfully engaged in the government of a large and populous diocese, and oppressed with many cares and solicitudes, not for himself nor for this world, but for his Church and flock, and for the interests of Heaven. His life demonstrates the compatibility of a high state of spiritual perfection with the discharge of laborious and useful duties in the world. He was possessed of a powerful frame and constitution, and these alone, with the strength he drew from above, enabled him to perform such untiring and unsparing labors. Enjoying robust health, he yet made every day's exercises a preparation for death. "He lived by faith and walked with God. Each year of his life he passed ten days in retreat, preparing for death; each month he observed a day of special recollection in spirit; each morning he meditated on heavenly things; each hour, and almost each moment, his soul communed with God."

The following anecdote is related of Bishop Neumann by Eliza Allen Starr, in her interesting work on *Patron Saints*: "The late Bishop Neumann, of Philadelphia, a most holy man, some years before his death, lost, in an unaccountable way, not only a very choice collection of theological books, but a great number of precious relics. The good Prelate was very much grieved, especially for the loss of the relics, and immediately began a novena to St. Anthony of Padua. He also promised, that if these treasures were found he would have a picture painted in honor of St. Anthony. Hardly were the nine Tuesdays of the novena over, when the books and relics were restored to him as mysteriously as they had disappeared. The Bishop, who knew how to be grateful for favors as well as how to ask for them, kept to the end of his life an affectionate devotion to St. Anthony, and I have still one of the pictures of our Saint which he brought himself from Padua."

The biography of Bishop Neumann would be incomplete without some account of the Genoa ivory crucifix—that superb work of art and touching object of devotion, which he purchased at considerable cost, and which, when once acquired, he prized above all price.

It was the workmanship of an inspired monk at Genoa.

Carlo Antonio Pesenti was born of parents belonging to the peasantry inhabiting the beautiful valley Brembano, about fifty miles from the cathedral city of Milan, February 22, 1801. His piety found expression in his youth in carving in common wood, and with a rude knife, images of the Blessed Virgin and of his patron saints, St. Charles and St. Anthony. His only models were the statues in the shrines of the Madonna on the wayside, and the figures of the saints that stood in the village church. As he approached manhood he resolved to devote himself exclusively to God, and with a heart as simple as a child's, yet wrapped in the love and devotion of the ages of faith, he started from home on a pilgrimage to the tomb of the Apostles at Rome. Political disturbances prevented at that time all strangers from entering the Papal States, and young Carlo sought and obtained hospitality at the ancient Convent of St. Nicholas of Tolentino, a venerable pile situated outside of the wall of Carbonara, and standing like a coronal upon one of the lofty hills which overlook " Genoa the superb." The sacred cloisters had been desecrated by Napoleon, who turned them into barracks for his troops; but they were now again restored to the devout service of God. Here young Pesenti humbly begged to be received as a lay-brother, made his noviceship, and was received as such into the convent. For fifteen years he was unknown save to his convent, by whose inmates he was venerated for his many virtues; to the poor, the sick, and the ignorant in the neighborhood he was known by his offices of charity; and in Heaven he was known by the incense of his fervent prayers, offered in atonement for the sins of a wicked world. He continued still to carve in his rude manner the images of the saints, studying their lives and characteristics from the books in the convent library, and imitating the pictures of them in the illuminated manuscripts he there found. During these years of contemplation and seclusion he often meditated on the passion and death of Our Lord; this sublime subject began more and more to absorb his thoughts and to kindle his sympathies into a flame, and his devotion to *Jesus Crucified* gave a seraphic expression to his countenance. One day the humble monk of St. Nicholas was seated in his cell, when the all-absorbing subject of the passion took possession of his soul and of all his faculties; he saw the appalling drama of Calvary; he ascended the mountain in company with the three Marys and the friends of Jesus; the turbulent and blood-thirsty crowd was there; he heard the murmur of their passions, the uproar of their derisive laughter, the exultation of their fancied triumph; but in the midst of all, the figure of the Man-God soon claimed his exclusive gaze, until he saw it hanging lifeless on the cross; the light of the sun was obscured, and by the lurid blaze of lightning, arrested and fixed against the dark background of angry clouds, all objects, save the Cross and the Crucified, faded from his view, and there he stood alone and gazed:—

> Pro peccatis suæ gentis,
> Vidit Jesum in tormentis
> Et flagellis subditum.

The vision was about to pass away, but the pious monk prayed that the divine image might remain fixed in his soul and durable in his memory; his prayer was heard. "The monk looked up; a ray of light shone on the countenance of a Saviour dead; life had flown at the same instant that the light returned. Suffering had been there, it was now gone; the departing agony had left a mark upon the brow, as if for testimony that it had been there; yet over the features a smile of sweetness ineffable calmly rested. It was a smile of agony lighted by love divine, though unrequited. The glory brightened as the monk, with pity sublimed by love, gazed upon the features of the dead who conquered death. These heaven-illumined features were portrayed upon his heart, while a voice within his soul commanded him to fix that look on some imperishable substance."*

Returning to the external world, Fra Carlo found himself stretched upon the ground in an attitude of adoration, sympathy, and love; he had seen the crucifixion of the Man-God; he was bathed in tears. His anxious soul, ere the gush of overpowering sentiments had passed into the calmer recollection of the vision, was troubled as well as electrified over the appointed task, long sought by him, now Heaven-imposed. How could he perform his cherished work? How could he fix that form, those features, that expression, on some imperishable substance? In his perplexity he had recourse to Mary, *Mater Dolorosa*, and to her he addressed those sublime words of the Poet-Pontiff:

> Santa Mater | istud agas,
> Crucifixi fige plagas
> Cordi meo valide:

and the picture became daguerreotyped upon his own soul.

In an old store-room of the Convent of St. Nicholas

---

* *Funeral Obsequies of Right Rev. John Nepomucene Neumann*, etc., p. 34.

was a huge piece of ivory, measuring in length over three feet, and fourteen inches in diameter; it had remained there for ages, neglected and almost forgotten, save when some inquiry elicited the response that it was supposed to be the tusk of some huge monster of antediluvian date, and had probably been brought to Genoa in remote ages from the East by some Genoese ship. No piece of modern ivory could compare with it in size or appearance. No sooner had the monk, Fra Carlo, composed his thoughts and repeated his prayer when he thought of the monster piece of ivory in the store, which he had often seen and passed unnoticed, but in which he now beheld the means of perpetuating those divine features, suffused with a mingled expression of pain, love, majesty, and resignation, which were stamped upon his heart. His vision was related to his brother monks, permission was obtained, and the mass of ivory was carried from the store-room to the cell of Fra Carlo. For four years he labored at his task; the exterior decayed and porous parts of dull gray had to be removed; next the parts of denser and mottled brown; then the hard black layer of flinty substance; and then there remained the hard pure ivory, of yellowish creamy tint, too hard to cut, but not too hard for the inspired sculptor to work into the image of the Crucified. His work was mingled with prayers, and the shapeless mass began to give forth the expression of divinity in death. The good monk wept again over the sufferings he again saw, and supplicated Heaven for strength and guidance to the accomplishment of the work of mingled love and penance. He frequently wrought at the ivory figure before him for twenty-four and even thirty hours consecutively, with barely food enough to sustain life, and through the still hours of the night, until the dawning light of day looked into his cell. His mind sometimes became distracted with thoughts of the outer world, and his heart oppressed with gloom and despondency; but then he would prostrate himself before his developing image of the Savior, and gain new strength and energy through the prayers he then addressed to the glorified Savior in Heaven. He often invoked the aid of the Blessed Virgin in obtaining for him the gift of perseverance and final success. As the work progressed towards completion, its extraordinary merit, its perfection far beyond the standard of human art, and the interesting history of the work and the workman, were wafted by fame far and near, and distinguished artists, connoisseurs, and public functionaries visited his secluded cell; and still without vanity, and solely from motives of devotion, the humble monk worked on. Towards the close of the year 1843, Mr. E. Lester, the United States Consul at Genoa, visited the Convent of St. Nicholas, and against the wishes of Fra Carlo saw the image. In the enthusiasm of his admiration he made every effort to become its possessor, and finally the monk, influenced by the motive of relieving and benefiting his convent, accepted the liberal price offered for it, and it was transferred to the consular residence. The monk continued his work on the image for six months, visiting, by permission of his superiors, the Consul's house, and thus this wonderful work received its finishing touches from the hands of the untutored artist. When completed it was attached to a cross of ornamental colored wood, which was well calculated to set off the beauties and perfection of the image, and was then exhibited at the Academy of Fine Arts at Genoa. The world of art and taste turned out to visit it, and all were enraptured with its exquisite beauty and its artistic perfection. Artists were unbounded in their praises of it. Celebrated anatomists scrutinized it rigidly, and pronounced it a miracle of anatomical accuracy. All were puzzled at the production of such a work of art by a simple lay-brother, uninstructed in art, and at such a perfect delineation of the human form, in which every vein, every muscle, and every detail was perfect, by one who had never learned anatomy. The hanging body, the drooping head, and above all the expression of the divine countenance, were regarded universally as unequaled by any other representation of the same subject. The crucifix was then carried to Florence, at the suggestion of Mr. Powers, the American sculptor. He fancied he could improve a portion of the eyebrow, but at the end of the ten days, during which it was left with him for that purpose, he frankly admitted that it could not in any particular be improved, in his opinion, by any artist on earth, and, he added, "certainly not by me." Of it he subsequently wrote to Mr. Lester: "It is the largest work I have ever seen in ivory, and I doubt if another could be found of so great a size, executed in the same material. But this, though of considerable importance, is the least of its recommendations. There is an expression of calmness and dignity about it, which I conceive to be quite characteristic of our Saviour, and which I have never seen before in any similar work."

This exquisite work was exhibited in several cities of Europe and America; it was purchased from Mr. Lester by a gentleman, who sold it to the Cosmopolitan Art Association for ten thousand dollars; it passed next into the hands of a citizen of Pennsylvania, and from him to Bishop Neumann.

Bishop Neumann regarded it not so much as a work of art, as one of heavenly inspiration; as a powerful though silent appeal to the religious sensibilities of the human heart. He did not agree with the secular press in regarding it as an effort of mere human genius; but he believed it to be *inspired*, in reward for the piety and devotion of the humble monk, and he resolved to place it in his Cathedral chapel, and finally in the new Cathedral. It stood above the remains of Bishop Neumann as they lay in state at the Cathedral chapel, mute but touching emblem of redemption, a warning of the universal fate of man, and an invitation of hope for all who, through the Cross, were struggling for life everlasting.

Bishop Neumann's death was sudden to the world, but to him, who lived in constant preparation, it was neither "a sudden nor an unprovided death." It occurred January 5, 1860. As he lived, he died, in the service of his Church. He went from his residence in Philadelphia to attend to some business for the benefit of religion; had just finished the execution and acknowledgment of a paper, crossed the street and was returning home, when suddenly he sat down upon the steps of a house, fell over and expired. He was honored by Prelates, priests, and laymen as a saint. Every honor was paid to his memory, and it was remarked by one of the pulpit orators, who took part in the funeral ceremonies, that his mortal remains, after five days, showed no signs of decay, "for he thought that God thereby testified his approval of the holiness of the life of the deceased Prelate." At the request of the Redemptorists, his remains were interred at their Church of St. Peter, and not at St. John's, as was at first intended. Archbishop Kenrick, who preached his eulogium in terms of unbounded praise, said of Bishop Neumann: "His soul now communes with the Ambroses, the Augustines, the Gregorys, and especially the sainted Alphonsus, whom he imitated so diligently. With them he praises God for the multitude of His mercies, and gives Him homage."

RIGHT REV. FREDERIC BARAGA, D.D.,

First Bishop of Marquette and Saut St. Mary, A.D. 1853.*

AT the then distant Falls of St. Mary the heroic Jesuits had planted the cross and announced the "Prayer," years, says Bancroft, before Elliot had preached to the Algonquins, whose camp-fires were burning within ten miles of Boston. There the generous martyr, Father Jogues, and afterwards the illustrious Marquette, had offered sacrifice, and dispensed the sacraments among the tribes whom they had won to the faith. Two centuries afterwards the saintly Baraga renewed their noble work; and the Church, ever fond of glorious traditions, associated her Hierarchy with the names that had grown venerable in her missionary history. The See of Marquette and Saut Sainte Mary was appropriately presided over by the devoted and untiring successor of Raymbaut, Jogues, Marquette, and Menard. The life and labors of Bishop Baraga should be precious to us, for they connect our age with that of the great pioneer missionaries of the North-west, who centuries ago commenced the great work which he so successfully renewed and followed up in our own day. They show that the Church, fruitful mother of saints, is still producing holy and apostolic men, and that the spirit of a Xavier is not extinguished:

---

* *Life and Services of the Right Rev. Frederic Baraga, First Bishop of Marquette and Saut St. Mary*, by Father Jacker, V.G., delivered at St. Peter's Cathedral, Marquette, and published in the *Catholic Telegraph*, February 19 and 26, 1868; *The Metropolitan*, Vols. I., II., III., IV., V.; De Courcy and Shea's *Hist. Catholic Church in the United States*; *The Catholic Almanac*, 1848; Shea's *History of the Catholic Missions*, &c. &c.

"But still, Our Lord, the Crucified! hath warriors brave and true,
And noble deeds of Christian might even at this hour they do ;
On many a far-off barbarous coast, on many a foreign strand,
'Neath the wasting heat of southern isles—and in our own free land.
Well may we dwell on Christ's own words—' Earth is the harvest-field,'
And souls His priceless love redeem'd, the harvest it doth yield."

Frederic Baraga was born June 29 (the feast of Saints Peter and Paul), in the year 1797. His birthplace was the town of Treffen, in Carniola, which formed the northern part of the kingdom of Illyria, in the south of the Austrian Empire. His family, though not related to the imperial house of the Hapsburgs, as has been frequently asserted, ranked among the first of the province, and were in affluent circumstances. They owned and resided in one of those mediæval feudal castles which Germany had inherited from the past, the former strongholds of the baronial nobility of the middle ages. Though not possessed of a patent of nobility from any worldly prince or government, "the nobility of Frederic's parents consisted in their integrity, their virtues, and their strong and enlightened attachment to the faith of their ancestors, than which a nobler inheritance they could not leave him." It was in this ancient castle, and in the society of these virtuous parents, that Frederic spent the first nine years of his life. His first instruction was received from a private teacher, under the parental roof. His character was formed from his tenderest years by his fond but judicious parents, to habits of virtue, industry, and piety. The society and scenery by which he was surrounded also contributed to ennoble, to purify, and to elevate his mind and soul. Carniola enjoyed an almost Italian sky, was traversed by branches of the noble Alps, and was noted for three great natural curiosities: the quicksilver mines of Idria, the lake of Kirknitz, and the Grotto of Adelsberg. He belonged to the pure Sclavonic race, and his native tongue was the Illyrian, one of the most melodious of the Sclavonic dialects. The Carniolians, like the Tyrolese and inhabitants of the mountainous regions, were hardy, industrious, pure-minded, truthful, frugal, and neat. The simplicity of ancient manners prevailed there, and the people were well instructed in the duties of Christian life. Young Baraga, under these influences, grew up with a strong, energetic, and single-minded character; and such were his early habits of order and neatness that they were never relaxed, even in the midst of savage life in the wilderness, nor amidst the labors, hurry, and fatigues of an Indian mission, nor even in those rapid and exciting fishing and hunting excursions in which he accompanied the Indians, in order, like an angel guardian, to calm their passions, suggest the prayer of penance or thanksgiving, or sanctify the journey with sacrifice and sacraments. The noble character and exact devotion to duty which were impressed upon him in the ancestral castle of Treffen, were remarkable throughout his career amidst the barbarous tribes of our country; while "eating and sleeping in their wigwams, and traveling with them in the woods and on the great lakes of this continent."

When nine years old he commenced his regular studies at the College of Leibac, the capital of his native province. Here his solid and earnest traits of character were exemplified under trying circumstances for a student. Europe was shaken to its centre by those unparalleled military convulsions which signalized the career of the first Napoleon. Provinces and kingdoms were wrested from their hereditary princes by the victorious sword of

Napoleon, and dynasties and empires were remodeled by his imperious will. Battles of gigantic proportions, decisive of the fate of nations, were fought; and rumors of battles, of treaties, of conquests and reconquests, and of stunning events of every kind, were rife; to-day's rumors of peace were silenced in the din of bloody strife on the morrow; and the public mind was kept in a state of indescribable ferment and excitement. Leibac was situated on the high road between Italy and Vienna, and felt every vibration and shock of those stirring times. In the midst of these disturbances, so unfavorable to study, the mind of young Baraga was solely and calmly intent upon his books. That passing events did not escape his notice, and that he drew from them treasures of wisdom and experience, was often manifested in his after-life, by the profound observations he made on men and governments in the society of his friends. But his mind was never distracted with politics. His classics and mathematics preoccupied his mind, and his love of duty and religion engaged the attention of his soul. The kingdom of Illyria was wrested from Austria by the sword of Napoleon; its institutions and laws yielded somewhat to those of the conqueror, and the French language was introduced into the schools. Gifted with a talent for the acquisition of languages, Frederic readily acquired the French, and gave signs of that peculiar ability which, while he was seeking other fruits, rendered his name famous in the scientific world. He became a thorough Latin and Greek scholar, and, among modern tongues, he added, with comparative ease, the German and the Italian to the French and his native Sclavonic. He was distinguished amongst his fellow-students not only for these acquirements, but also for his application to and proficiency in his general academic studies.

In 1816, having finished these courses, he commenced the study of the law at the celebrated University of Vienna. Access to the bar was no easy thing in Austria; a thorough course of five years' study in jurisprudence, civil law, and the kindred branches, was required for admission to the legal profession, or to any of the government offices. The acute and subtle intellect of Frederic was at ease in these pursuits, and he accomplished the course, and graduated in 1821, with distinguished success. His meditations during these years of study were not exclusively given to the civil law, but they turned chiefly on God, eternity, salvation. His favorite motto was, "*Unum est necessarium.*" With the bright prospects which the world spread before him, his companions were astonished when he announced his intention of abandoning all, and of devoting himself exclusively to the Almighty in the sacred ministry. He entered the Ecclesiastical Seminary of Leibac; and such was the kindred preparation he had received at the law school of the University, and such his earnest application, that he accomplished his theology in two years. He was ordained in the priesthood September 21, 1823, when in his twenty-sixth year. The love of God and of his neighbor had induced him to embrace this career; and now a holy zeal for God's glory and the salvation of souls impelled him onward in every act and undertaking of his life. To him the holy ministry was a sacred, a sublime, an awful calling—inconsistent with leisure, idleness, self-gratification, ambition, or vain-glory. His life was an illustration of all this. Happy in being admitted into the sacred vineyard, he resolved to devote himself exclusively to its cultivation, and in doing so he courted labor, privation, fatigue, self-sacrifice, and the denial of human consolation.

For seven years he exercised the holy ministry in Carniola with great zeal and edification, presenting an instructive example in the different positions he filled. The name of "*Father Frederic*" became a household word, because the people saw in him the virtues, the labors, and the sanctity of the Lord's anointed. He was never idle. In the intervals between his parochial occupations, he employed himself in preparing books of devotion for the people. In doing this he also endeavored to elevate and improve his native Sclavonic, then greatly neglected; and by his correct taste and classic cultivation he greatly contributed to its present improved condition. His style was admirably suited for the preparation of works of popular devotion. Free from overstrained effort, but direct in purpose, simple in style, and sound in doctrine, his little works had the happy facility of conveying to the mind the sublime truths of religion, and to the heart the most fervent sentiments of piety, by means at once judicious and unpretending. His "*Spiritual Pasture*" was particularly efficacious, and is still found in the hands of many a pious worshiper in his native country.

In his personal devotions he was very exemplary. Knowing how recollected and circumspect a minister of the Most High should be, he kept up through life the practice of devoting the first one or two hours of every day to devout meditation, as a preparation for the encounters, the difficulties, and surprises of the day. He arose at four o'clock, and frequently at three o'clock in the morning, and gave that time until five to his accustomed meditation. Whether in his own quiet and simple room at Treffen, or in the forests of our own Northwest, in a crowded hotel, or in the bewildering din of the wigwam, on the broad lakes, in the midst of a journey or in a storm, he was ever faithful to this salutary practice. However late at night he arrived at his place of rest after a fatiguing journey, he arose at the usual hour, and on his knees commenced the day in communion with his Creator.

His paternal inheritance was held as a trust for the poor, and as far as available had been applied to their relief. Indeed he divested himself finally of all worldly goods, transferring his portion to his brothers and sisters, and reserving to himself the small pittance of three hundred dollars a year, and even this he afterwards abandoned to others. So that when he resolved to devote himself to the salvation of the unenlightened and heathen tribes of our country, he was obliged to avail himself of the noble generosity of the "Leopoldine Society," which was similar in its objects to the "Association for the Propagation of the Faith," and which had been organized under the patronage of members of the imperial family of Austria, and received its name from the Archduchess Leopoldine. He offered his services for the Indian Mission, and after protracted and wearisome negotiations with the civil and ecclesiastical authorities, all was arranged, and he welcomed the happy hour when he was permitted to offer up home, friends, comforts, and family, as a sacrifice to the Lord. Sailing from Havre, December 1, 1830, being thirty-three years of age, he arrived in New York on the last day of the month and of the year. Auspicious, indeed, was the new year that ushered in a missionary career of so much usefulness and benediction to our land ! " My heart is full of gratitude," he writes, after his arrival in New York, to his favorite sister Amelia, "towards a kind Providence that has lovingly guided me thus far. Such were the feelings with which I set my foot on the soil of the New World—this great but little cultivated part of the Lord's vineyard, where so much labor is to be done for the salvation of innumerable thousands that as yet do not know their Creator in Truth." Pushing westward without delay towards the cherished objects of his zeal and charity, " like his predecessor in the same field, René Menard, two hundred years before, he too went forth trusting in the Providence which feeds the little birds of the desert and clothes the wild flowers of the forest."

> "Redeemer of a fallen race !
> Most merciful of kings !
> Thy hallowed words have clothed with power
> Those frail and beauteous things.
> All taught by Thee, they yearly speak
> Their message of deep love,
> Bidding us fix, for life and death,
> Our hearts and hopes above."

He arrived at Cincinnati January 18, 1831, and was cordially received by the venerable and apostolic Bishop Fenwick, who was delighted to find that his desire was not to remain in the more comfortable mission of the City, but to seek the rude and comfortless castles of the barbarian. Detained by the inclemency of the season, he devoted his time to missionary duties in Cincinnati, preaching in German, hearing confessions, visiting the sick, and instructing the children. It is said that while in Cincinnati, he heard confessions in all the modern languages which he understood, except his own. Here he studied English with great success; and with his heart intent on his Indian mission, he found time and opportunity, amidst his many occupations, to begin the study of the Ottawa dialect. He commenced his journey northward in April; and his progress is described as one continued mission. Gathering together the few Catholics he found in any place, he preached to them, renewing their faith and reviving their piety; instructing and administering the sacraments. His hearers were frequently composed more of Protestants than of Catholics, and of them he wrote, "They were well pleased with the doctrine I preached; but a tree will not fall at the first stroke." From Miamisburg he journeyed six miles into the woods to visit one Catholic family, and nine miles in order to prepare for his final journey a poor Irishman almost deaf and blind, then over eighty years of age, and who had not seen a priest for fifty years. What a blessing, what a joy to this aged but straying member of the fold! What a consolation to both priest and penitent! What charity could be superior to this? At Dayton he found a few lukewarm Catholics; his happiness in serving their souls, and the needy condition in which he found them, tempted him to ask the Bishop, whom he met there, permission to remain and labor in their midst, and devote himself to the noble work of going throughout that immense diocese in search of neglected and wandering members of the fold of Christ. But Providence still guided his steps northward to the storm-beaten shores of the lakes, the scenes of his future exalted labors, struggles, and victories. He made the journey to Detroit with Bishop Fenwick, and remained there five days, hearing confessions and preaching. Navigation having now opened, he set out, May 20, for Arbre Croche, the place of his destination, and arrived there on the 28th of the month.

Arbre Croche, or Waganakisid, was a village of the Ottawa Indians, of considerable size, and was situated on Lake Michigan, in the northwestern part of the Lower Peninsula of Michigan, then an almost unbroken wilderness, inhabited by Indians and a few trappers and explorers. The Jesuit missionaries of the seventeenth century had consecrated the place by the presence of the sacred offices, and by their own prayers, labors, sacrifices, and lives. But the vicissitudes of their Order, and the struggles of States for dominion, had nearly obliterated their traces. But Christian traditions still remained, and a Belgian missionary, Father Dejean, had revived these and reopened the mission only two years before the arrival of Father Baraga. But he had returned to Europe, and the mission was discontinued before the arrival of this saintly Prelate and apostolic priest. The neophytes now hailed with joy the arrival of their Bishop, in 1831, and received the father whom he bestowed upon them, and whose first appearance among them gained their hearts, with every demonstration of gratitude. Though they had erected a church, presbytery, and school-house, whose only covering was of bark, these were out of repair, for they had been without a pastor. Well did Father Baraga write, not only for himself, but still more for the poor Ottawas, "Happy day, which first placed me in the midst of the savages, among whom I now shall live until I draw my last breath, if such is the holy will of God." And again, "My desire is now accomplished; I now live in the midst of the poor savages, the greater number of whom are still pagans, and a field, immeasurably great, is open to cultivation before my eyes. There are none but savages in my mission; I am the only white man far or near." He thus humorously describes his residence: "When it rains I have to spread my cloak over my table to save my books and papers from a deluge. Above my couch I extend the umbrella to keep it dry; as for my own person, I retire to that corner of my room where the drops fall less thickly."

We now behold with what zeal and devotion the good missionary, who had longed to be with his savages and now rejoiced in their society, addressed himself to his cherished work. Under his pious guidance the community entered at once upon the public practice of a Christian life. At five o'clock in the morning the "Angelus" bell summoned the Christian population to the house of prayer, where the chief of the band recited the morning exercises. The holy sacrifice was then offered up by the pastor, in a remote Indian village, and in the presence of newly-converted Christians, whose numbers and devotion might be an example to the populous congregations of our large cities. The day was spent in instructing the children and visiting the families, both Christian and pagan. To such of the latter as evinced a disposition to yield to the sweet and gentle yoke of Christ, he showed especial attention. The missionary's life was so frugal and mortified, his wants so few and simple, that he had the whole of his time to bestow upon his flock. No hour of the day passed without its good deed. At evening the vesper bell again summoned the people to church, where they recited the evening prayers, and received catechetical instructions from their devoted pastor. He was assisted by an interpreter, a pious aged lady assigned to that work by Bishop Fenwick, and who was familiar with the English, French, and Indian languages. On Sundays, in addition to these exercises, a sermon was given at High Mass, and an instruction after Vespers. Arbre Croche soon became a well regulated Christian community. Scarcely a day passed that some of the Indians did not approach the sacraments, and on Sundays and festivals crowds knelt at the sacred table. The orgies of paganism became not only avoided, but despised and ridiculed; the bags and charms of the medicine-men were brought together and burned amidst the acclamations of the people; and the Great Spirit became the object of their supreme adoration, and His minister their only "Manitou." For the good and well-disposed he always had a word of kindness and encouragement; he was severe in his exposure and denunciation of crime, superstition, and deception, and at the same time ever ready to embrace with forgiveness and joy the converted pagan and the repentant sinner. When Bishop Fenwick again visited Arbre Croche, in 1832, he was delighted at the success of Father Baraga's mission. In little over a year he had baptized two hundred and sixty-six Indians, and at his little church of St. Peter's there were seven hundred Christian Indians. There were now two schools for the children. The Bishop confirmed one hundred and thirty-seven of the flock, by whose fervor and piety he was greatly consoled. Father Baraga had extended his labors as far as the Castor Islands, and beyond Lake Michigan, where he had erected several churches. A school had been erected at St. Joseph's, and another at Green Bay, and the church at the latter place was nearly finished. His own report of his missionary expeditions, made July 1, 1832, will be read with interest: " As soon as my parishioners had performed their Easter devotion, I set out to announce the word of God to others of those children of nature who had never heard it from the mouth of a Catholic priest. First I visited a very pleasant island in Lake Michigan, situated at such a distance that, seen from the shore, it appeared only as a misty streak, scarcely visible. This island is rather large, about four leagues in circumference, and is called Beaver Island. Last winter an Indian of that place had come to Arbre Croche in order to be baptized. He had conversed with some Christians, who had made him acquainted with their religion and instructed him in its tenets; now he is himself an excellent Christian. This good man, having received baptism, returned to his island, and by him I sent word to the inhabitants that in the spring I would come and preach the word of God to them, for the neophyte assured me that the Beaver Island Indians would be happy to see a messenger of the faith in their midst. It is true there were persons who did not share my pleasant hopes, and had strong doubts about the success of my undertaking; still I went, trusting in the Lord, who has promised to be with his servants at all times, even to the end of the world."

"My heart beat when we approached the island. I use to carry a white flag, traversed by a red cross, which I unfurl when I approach a mission, so as to make the mission boat recognizable. When we neared the island we were sailing with a fine breeze; pleasantly the ensign of peace waved in the air, and carried before us the tidings that the servant of the Crucified was coming. The Indians, having, with their wonderfully keen sight, perceived and recognized it at a great distance, the chief at once ordered his own to be hoisted on the top of his hut. My native companion instantly knew the chief's flag, and as they interpreted this as a favorable omen, my apprehensions were calmed. When we finally came closer to the island, I saw a number of savages hasten to the shore. Almost all the inhabitants collected there to welcome us. The men gave two rifle volleys to signify their joy at the missionary's arrival. Scarcely had I stepped ashore when all the men came forward and saluted me with a hearty shaking of hands; then they conducted me into their village, which means a cluster of huts built of bark. I first entered the chief's habitation, where quite a number of those poor savages collected, and would not be satiated beholding the priest, a thing they had never seen before.

"In conversing with the pagan natives a certain ceremonial is to be observed. Accordingly, I did not at once break the proper object of my coming, but spoke of divers matters, and finally requested the chief to call a grand council for the following day, as I had to speak with him on serious matters. So they assembled on the next day, and I made a speech, briefly and energetically explaining the necessity and advantage of the Christian religion, and finally requested the chief to give me an answer. He did so by his speaker, saying that they considered themselves happy to see a priest on their island, and that they frequently desired to adopt the Christian religion. The joy with which such an answer filled the missionary's heart can be imagined! I remained with them some time and instructed them, and the 11th of May was the happy day on which I baptized twenty-two of these savages."

Auspicious as was the commencement of this island

mission, the joy of the missionary and the conversion of the islanders were not unattended with alloy and opposition. As usual, the trouble arose from the medicine-men, who saw in the conversion of their deluded subjects the ruin of their own cause. Opposition was raised to the erection of a church on the island, but liberal and frequently repeated presents of trinkets and tobacco allayed the trouble. Subsequent renewals of the persecution induced the Christians to emigrate and go to Arbre Croche. Appreciating the strength of the faith which nerved these Christians so recently converted to sacrifice their homes for God, Father Baraga received them with paternal kindness into his flock. The missionary extended his excursions, during this and the following summers, to other and more distant islands, amongst which were Little Detroit, Grand Traverse, Manistee, and Grand River, the last of which was two hundred miles from his mission. At these places he instructed and baptized numbers of Ottawa Indians, and, wherever it was practicable, erected a little bark church for their devotions. Having thoroughly acquired the Ottawa language, he prepared his Ottawa prayer and hymn book and catechism, which he had printed at Detroit in August, 1832, while the Indians were on their annual trip to Canada to receive their bounties from the government. This was the first of a series of works in the Indian languages, which evince his zeal and industry, and which have greatly added to his fame. A priest who met him at Detroit, thus appropriately wrote his impressions of the indefatigable missionary: "Father Baraga is very poor and lives like a Trappist, but his happiness is immeasurably great."

So far his career was full of consolations, but now we

are to see him struggling with opposition and dangers. In the spring of 1833 he had visited Grand River, near the present site of Grand Rapids, and had there baptized nearly a hundred Indians. His observation of the deplorable condition of the inhabitants of that region only stimulated his zeal to labor for their regeneration. In the autumn of this year he secured a successor for his mission at Arbre Croche, Father Saenderl, C.SS.R., and proceeded to Grand River. A sectarian missionary had resided there nine years, and had secured about a dozen converts; these raised an opposition to Father Baraga's entrance into the field. Disregarding their evil disposition, he pressed forward to his work, but only to encounter more serious troubles. The vicinity of the whites, and especially of the traders frequenting Grand River, demoralized the poor Indians with liquor, as one of the appliances of their trade. In vain would be their conversion to the religion of the white man, if the vices of the latter paralyzed the action of grace in their souls. A difficult field was thus presented to our good missionary, but he advanced to his work with courage and ardor. His sermons, his instructions to the children, his excursions in quest of souls, and his efforts especially to extirpate the vice of intemperance, while attended with great success, drew down upon him the malice of the liquor dealers and of their unfortunate victims. His zeal and his devotion to the cause of their regeneration increased with their malice, until his life was not safe in his own house. His life was saved on one occasion, from the fury of a howling and murderous band of drunken savages, by the strength of the bolts upon his door. His patience was untiring under these difficulties. He undertook another journey to Detroit, partly on foot and partly on horseback, to obtain mechanics to assist him in the erection of a substantial church, presbytery, and school-house. He encountered and overcame the appalling difficulties of the roads, and narrowly escaped starvation. He baptized during his entire stay at this mission one hundred and seventy Indians, and, but for the drunkenness introduced by Europeans, would have reaped a much more abundant harvest. Finding that personal danger did not drive him from his post, his enemies petitioned the government for his removal; and although the Governor of Michigan wrote in his favor, he was finally compelled to seek other fields of labor. After sixteen months spent at Grand River, he turned over that mission to the Hungarian missionary, Father Viszeczky and, with a heart burning for the conversion of souls, and especially of those numerous heathens on the south shore of Lake Superior, who were plunged in utter ignorance of the faith, and whom he had been long anxious to evangelize, he proceeded to his next mission, at Lapointe.

The mission among the Chippewas had been sanctified by the visit and death of Father Menard, who, in 1661, lost his life in the woods of Upper Michigan. Here, too, the illustrious Allouez and Marquette had labored; and the Jesuit mission was continued until the suppression of the Society, towards the close of the eighteenth century. Intercourse with the Canadian traders and the " *Courriers des bois,*" most of whom intermarried with the tribe, kept up a remembrance of Christian traditions; and a considerable population of half-breeds only needed a missionary to induce them to a Christian life. Detained by the closed condition of navigation at St. Clair River, our zealous missionary devoted his time to the spiritual wants of the European settlers there. Souls were to him so precious that his whole heart became absorbed in the service of even one, wherever he chanced to be. At St. Clair River he thus poured forth in a letter the burning sentiments of his heart:—

"It appears strange to me to be in a congregation of whites. I live here in peace, and am much more comfortable than among my Indians; but I feel like a fish thrown on dry land. The Indian mission is my life. Now, having learned the language tolerably well, and being in hopes that I will perfect myself in it still more, I am firmly resolved to spend the remainder of my life in the Indian mission, if it is the will of God. I am longing for the moment of my departure for Lake Superior. Many, I hope, will be converted there to the religion of Christ, and find in it their eternal salvation. Oh! how the thought elevates me! Would that I had wings to fly over our ice-bound lakes, so as to be sooner among the pagans! But what did I say? Many will be converted! Oh, no! If only one or two are converted and saved, it would be worth the while to go there and preach the gospel! But God, in his infinite goodness, always gives more than we expect."

Father Baraga arrived at Lapointe du Saint Esprit (which in our day has unfortunately lost its dedication to the Holy Ghost) in August, 1835. Henceforth, for eighteen years, his labors were among the Chippewas bordering on Lake Superior. His mission was a religious wilderness, without priest or chapel, on his arrival there; his exertions under Providence made it a Christian settlement. By overcoming difficulties, enduring hardships and privations, and struggling against poverty, opposition, and trials which were almost incredible, he succeeded in opening and establishing a mission, and in erecting a church of considerable dimensions, the work of seven days. He also erected a dwelling for the missionary, and a number of houses for the converted Indians. But for the assistance he received from the Leopoldine Society in his native country (and this was not great, owing to the numerous calls made upon their generosity), it is difficult to see how he could have accomplished anything in so remote and abandoned a field. He went to Detroit in 1836 to receive a box of goods, church furniture, and little presents for the Indians, which had just arrived from Vienna. When he set out, on the 8th of June, from Detroit, on his homeward journey, he had just money enough to carry him to Lake Superior. "With this," says his Vicar-General, Father Jacker, "he thought himself rich." A steamboat conveyed him in to Mackinaw, and, after visiting his children at Arbre Croche, he proceeded to Saut St. Mary; a tedious voyage of eighteen days brought him to Lapointe du St. Esprit on the 27th of July. The gratifying result of his labors in the short space of two months enabled him to write to the Leopoldine Society: "Thanks to God, a thousand thanks! Already a great number of pagans have been received in the fold of the Holy Church, namely, one hundred and forty-eight. May God grant that all these neophytes, or at least the greater part of them, once enter heaven; what a consolation would this afford to me on the day of judgment." Towards the end of the year the baptisms numbered one hundred and eighty-four. His labors were untiring, and his enterprise in the pursuit of the souls so precious to him was unceasing. He seemed to seek always to extend the area of his efforts, extensive as it was. The Indians at Fond-du-Lac, about seventy miles distant from Lapointe du St. Esprit, near the site of the present Superior City, were represented to him as favorably inclined to the faith; he lost no time in going to visit them, and made that point one of his missionary stations, which he regularly visited. Also the Indians at Bad River, about seventeen miles to the south, were embraced within his apostolical ministry. The roving and wild life of the Indians rendered it exceedingly difficult and laborious to conduct a mission amongst them. They spent their days in fishing and hunting, returning to their wigwams only at night; thus, during the unusually severe winter of 1836–7, he was obliged to travel six miles every day, in order to instruct them at night after their return from the woods and waterside. He continued this arduous course until all were sufficiently instructed to receive baptism.

Father Baraga's efforts were always directed to the permanency of results, and to secure the lasting redemption of the Indians from paganism and barbarism to Christianity and civilization. Hence he commenced the study of the Ottawa language during his first detention at Cincinnati, and lost no time in producing his Ottawa prayer and hymn book. During the winter of 1836-7, when his evenings were devoted to evangelizing the Indians, he employed the leisure of his days in the composition of devotional works for his children. *The Ogibway Prayer and Hymn Book and Catechism;* the *Extracts of the History of the Old and New Testaments, with the Gospels of the Year*, in the same language; his *Treatise on the History, Character, Manners, and Customs of the North American Indians*, in German;

and a popular devotional work in the Sclavonic language, were the fruits of this winter's literary labors, in addition to his missionary duties. The latter would have been sufficient for most men to accomplish, but Father Baraga accomplished all with apparent ease. Destitute of means, he was compelled to await the arrival of funds from Vienna.*

One of the most striking and admirable circumstances in the history of Father Baraga was his extreme poverty; striking when contrasted with all that he accomplished in spite of it; and admirable, in being voluntary and courted; for he abandoned every comfort in his native country to share the poverty and hardships of savage life. His whole treasury this season consisted of three dollars. His food was only bread and fish, and seldom both together; his clothing was simple and scant, and it required the utmost care and the most timely reparation to preserve it. His only regret was for his flock; and he endured the sorrow of beholding the children of his neophytes going without clothes in the severe winter of Lake Superior, and whole families re-

---

* The following list of Bishop Baraga's works is given in Mr. J. G. Shea's *History of the Catholic Missions* ;—

1. *Anamie Misinaigan.* (A Prayer and Hymn Book, and Catechism.) First edition. Detroit, 1832. Three others since.
2. *Gaie Dibadjimowin, Gaie Jesus, Obimadisiwin oma Aking.* (Bible Extracts, Life of Christ, Epistles and Gospels.) Laibach, 1837. Detroit, 1837. Second edition, 1846.
3. *Kawlik Enamiad o Nanagatawendamowinan.* (Instructions and Meditations on all the Doctrines of the Catholic Church.) 712 pages. Detroit, 1849.
4. *Chippeway Grammar.* 576 pages. Detroit, 1849.
5. *Chippeway Dictionary.* 662 pages. Cincinnati, 1852.
6. *History, Character, and Habits of the North American Indians.* Laibach, 1837. (Paris, 1837.)

It has been also remarked, that "no missionary of whom we have had occasion to speak has published more works in Indian dialects, or treatises on them, or issued more frequent editions."

duced to starvation, without his being able to relieve them. His solicitude was not that of an ordinary pastor for his people; besides the great labors he performed for their spiritual assistance, he was also compelled to provide houses for them to live in, to instruct them in the modes and economies of civilized life, and to originate the means of elevating and improving their physical as well as their moral condition.

In 1837 the long-expected succor arrived from Vienna, and thus the excellent missionary was enabled to carry on the grand work he had so generously begun. He was always, however, provident of the future, and saw the necessity of securing more ample means for putting his mission upon a solid foundation. By great economy, he saved sufficient funds from those sent over in 1837 to enable him to go to Europe and plead the cause of his impoverished but hopeful church. He accordingly visited Europe in the fall of that year, and was thus enabled to have his Indian books printed in Paris. He also continued, everywhere he went, his labors for the salvation of souls, and preached in Paris for the German population of that city. In his native country he was received with distinguished attention, and Cornialia especially felt proud of her saintly son. He preached to immense audiences, and availed himself of every opportunity to draw the souls of men to God. In the following spring he returned to his beloved children on the shores of Lake Superior. For eight years he continued his glorious endeavors to extend the Church among the Indians of this missionary field. His life now assumed a more regular course, and he was able to follow out his plan of operations with more regularity and system. Every year he added conquests to the dominion of

Christ, and brought into the Christian fold, by conversions and baptisms, over seven hundred souls, Indians and half-breeds. A gentleman, who made a tour of exploration through the mineral regions of Lake Superior, thus describes his visit to Lapointe du St. Esprit and its pastor:—

"I did not become acquainted with Rev. Mr. Baraga until I reached Lapointe. On my arrival there I called upon him and introduced myself. I found an humble priest, I should judge something above forty years of age, a little broken by hardships and exposures, under a rigorous climate, to great privations; but cheerful, communicative, and stored with all that kind of information which I wanted, and which he freely gave me. Mr. Baraga is a great linguist; besides a knowledge of all the languages that are taught in Catholic Seminaries of Europe, he speaks with great correctness the English and French, and is a perfect master of the Ojibawa dialect. He preaches to his congregation in that language, into which he has translated the Life of Christ (*Jesus obimadisiwin oma aking*), and a book of hymns and canticles from the Latin and French. I am indebted to him for a copy of his Life of Christ (*Jesus Oma*).

"On the 15th of August, the day of the festival of the Assumption of the Blessed Virgin Mary, I attended divine service in the chapel of Lapointe. On entering the chapel I was pleased with the simple neatness of the place, and struck with the much more than tolerable altar-piece, representing St. Joseph at work as a carpenter, the Blessed Virgin sitting in a graceful posture intent upon her sewing, whilst the infant Christ, with a really angelic countenance, seems as if occupied alternately at looking upon the work going on before him and then up to Heaven—

a sort of double expression which I fancied the painter had succeeded in imparting to the Christ, though I cannot describe how he did it. The perspective, too, of the background of the picture is in much better keeping than is usually seen in altar-pieces destined for chapels built in the wilderness. The figures are pretty well drawn. The fault of the picture is in the profusion of colors; for, though not unpleasantly intermixed, they are too glaring, and too many.

"The Mass was celebrated by the Rev. Mr. Baraga with great unction, and responded to by the congregation, composed principally of half-breeds, with much apparent devotion. The Mass was served by two youths, and its principal responses sung in Latin by three male half-breeds. During the Mass, two canticles of the Blessed Virgin were introduced, which were sung in French by the same voices. Mr. Baraga's sermon was couched in plain, intelligible language—in French—and explained the Catholic doctrine of the Assumption as distinguished from the Ascension. The reason why the story of Martha and Mary was introduced into the gospel of the day was also explained in a manner that made it, even to most ordinary apprehensions, a striking and appropriate exordium to the mysteries of the incarnation. It was a good sermon, which affected me by its touching simplicity. At the afternoon service some of the psalms were sung in Latin, and an address was delivered by Mr. Baraga in the Ojibawa language.

"The chapel at Lapointe is also one of Mr. Baraga's *buildings.* It is, to say the least of it, *conspicuous;* for whether one approaches or recedes from the post, its two belfries are the most prominent objects. Seen from the 'Détour,' amidst the beautiful group of islands known collectively as the 'Twelve Apostles,' so called, because their first Christian observers—the Jesuits—supposed them not to exceed that number; whereas it is now ascertained that there are twenty-three, of which nineteen have been named. They always present a grateful beacon to the 'voyageur.'"

In 1843 Father Baraga, having placed the mission of Lapointe du St. Esprit in a flourishing and secure state of progress, confided its care to the Rev. Father Scolla, and went in pursuit of new and equally glorious conquests and victories. His next mission was the "Ance," an anciently established trading-post of the American Fur Company, between Pointe Abbaye and Keweenaw Point. When he first visited the Ance, in 1843, he saw at once the advantages of its central location as the headquarters of missions which might be established among a number of scattered Indians who were well disposed to the faith. Hence he transferred his residence from Lapointe du St. Esprit to the Ance. He encountered great difficulties at first, for he found the Indian settlement steeped in idolatry and intemperance. The few con verts made by the Methodist mission resisted his coming to reside there, and serious threats were made against him. Not discouraged by his first reverses, he persevered till he won the souls of the children. With them he already had a congregation of angels, and the work began to prosper. A medicine-man was next converted, and this gave an impetus to religion. With great labor and cost he erected a church and parsonage, and about thirty comfortable houses for the converted Indians. These were located on a large tract of land purchased by him for the Indians, with the view, by providing for them a permanent home, with altar, firesides, and priest, to reclaim them not only to God, but also to civilization. The effect of his ministry was wonderful. Superstition, drunkenness, and all other vices began rapidly to disappear. In 1849 his village contained forty-two Christian families, and in 1850 not a pagan was left. The population were sober, industrious, comfortable, and happy. These reformations produced not only the regeneration of their souls, but a great improvement in their physical health. So salubrious had the Ance become, that in over fourteen months prior to August, 1850, not one death occurred at the mission. So impressed were the Indians far and near with the wonderful benefits of Father Baraga's system, that numerous families from Vieux Lac du Flambeau, and other even more distant points, came flocking into the new mission. A regular school for Indian children, both boys and girls, was established, and the good missionary became their teacher. Under such exertions and management the reclamation of our Indians seemed a certain result, if the means were only adopted; but, alas! how different is the history of the aborigines, whose fate is foretold in a single word — *extermination.*

The writer last quoted thus describes his visit to the Ance:—" On our arrival, as our boat bore the American flag, we were saluted by a volley of musketry from the Indians; and a similar salute was given to us on the next afternoon, upon reaching the settlement on the opposite shore. It is this settlement that owes its present condition to the Rev. Mr. Baraga. It is called the parish of St. Jesus, and numbers about one hundred and fifty resident Indians, who are all Catholics, and perhaps fifty more who worship here though living at the Saut, where there is a Protestant mission under the charge of a very amiable gentleman, Mr. Pitzell, and a government agency. There is in Mr. Baraga's settlement a fine chapel, which I may say he has built with his own hands. It is on a commanding situation, a short distance in the rear of a row of lodges, built of logs, floored, and divided into convenient apartments to accommodate a family decently. There are twenty-one of these lodges at present finished and occupied; some few others are in progress of construction, or nearly finished. . . . . There is also a school-house, a store, and other buildings scattered over the grounds, so as to make in all twenty-seven buildings. The site of this settlement was selected by the reverend gentleman, whose name I have now frequently mentioned, not only for the beauty of its position, that commands an extensive water view, and for its healthfulness, but because the lands adjoining it, and extending northerly for ten or fifteen miles, have an excellent soil, affording natural meadows that supply an abundance of grass, fine groves of sugar-maple, elms, and evergreens, and, when cleared, yields plentifully in potatoes and corn, as well as most of the useful vegetables. In the wild state, strawberry-vines, raspberries, currants, whortleberries, and gooseberry bushes literally mat the hill-sides. There are also springs of deliciously cool water at the temperature of forty-eight degrees, and which become a luxury in the summer season, when the waters of the lake along the shore are not agreeably potable. As the reverend missionary was absent when we visited the parish, I had no means of getting the most authentic information of his progress in Christianizing his flock, but I had abundant evidence in the 'talk,' at which I was present, with the Indian agent and his interpreter, of the great veneration and esteem in which he is held by his parishioners; for while they seemed disposed to complain, with or without reason, that they did not receive that assistance from the government officers who reside on the other side, namely the carpenter, farmer, and blacksmith, which they had been promised, they at the same time ascribed their apparent improvement to the counsel and exertions of their pastor. Owing also to his absence, I had not an opportunity of attending divine service, or of witnessing any religious ceremony, to form an idea of their devotional bearing when in the chapel, which is tastefully arranged; but in the progress of my voyage up the lake, after leaving the Ance, I had occasion to observe, in the midst, it is true, of some levity, a general observance of the forms required by our Church, such as crossing one's self before meals, kneeling to pray, &c.; and once, when traveling on a Sunday, I noticed a young Indian of very decent appearance, and who could read, devoutly engaged on his knees in the forward of the boat, reading over the service of the Mass. In the afternoon the whole boat-crew joined him, singing, in the Chippeway language, canticles to the air of some of our French canticles, with which I was sufficiently acquainted to join in with them, to their evident satisfaction. On inquiring of *Urgens*, for so he called himself, whether he had not been taught them by Mr. Baraga, he seemed to be pleased to hear the name, and replied in the affirmative."

Father Baraga's resources were greatly increased by an extraordinary, and, to him, unexpected augmentation of his white congregations, which will be mentioned hereafter. These resources enabled him to build up the Indian village at the Ance, and provide houses and a church for them. His Indian books were sought for in every direction, and his means now enabled him to supply the demand, by printing new editions. He also prepared a new and more comprehensive work for the instruction of his converts, and for the conversion of the Pagans. It was in his only little room adjoining the Church of the Ance, and not long before his consecration, that he produced "his masterly philological works, an invaluable grammar and dictionary of the Otchipwe (Chippeway) language—works not surpassed, if equaled, by any similar attempts in philological science, *i.e.*, the conquest for the scientific world of a hitherto uncultivated language of savages." These works were dispensed by the generous missionary throughout the immense regions of his missions, which extended from Grand River, on the Eastern shore of Lake Michigan, to stations beyond the head of Lake Superior, a distance of six hundred miles. Such was the inspiring influence of Father Baraga's labors, and such the good effects of presenting the truths and devotions of the Christian religion to the Indians in their native tongue, that applications for the books came from the far-off wilderness of Lower Canada, and from the prairies of Minnesota.

About the year 1845 the celebrated copper mines of the Upper Peninsula of Michigan began to attract attention; the spirit of enterprise undertook their development, and a large population from the States, Canada, Ireland, Germany, and other nations, began to pour into the country. They were scattered around and among the Indian missions of Father Baraga, over a region of from twenty-five to a hundred miles. A large proportion of them were Catholics, and were utterly unprovided with any of the comforts or conveniences of their religion. The labors already performed by Father

Baraga were enough to employ the time and energies of any pastor, but this immense increase in the demands upon his care and attention only aroused the indefatigable missionary to still more extraordinary exertions. He commenced at once to visit the mining locations both in the District of Keweenaw Point and the Ontonagan District. At first his efforts reached every want, and carried the appropriate remedy to every soul in that busy and teeming scene. But the increase of the Catholic population soon became so great, that he found it imperatively necessary to secure the services of more priests. In one of his letters in 1853, written after his consecration, he mentions, as an evidence of the rapid increase of the Catholic population there, the fact that in his former visits he usually baptized from twelve to fifteen children, whereas in the visit now made to them he baptized no less than fifty-six new-born infants. In the same letter in which he gives an account of his first labors as Vicar-Apostolic, he writes:—

"What a pity to see so many Catholics destitute of almost all spiritual help and comfort! When I saw that, I was touched to tears, and thanked the kind Providence of God Almighty, who affords me now a fair opportunity to remedy such depressing wants of the poor Catholics of Upper Michigan. On this last missionary visit I pointed out several places, and secured lots for the building of churches, school-houses, and dwelling-houses in the different prospering mines of the Upper Peninsula, especially at Ontonagan village, at the Minnesota mine, at Norwich mine, at Eagle Harbor, at the South Cliff, and in the iron-mining region of Père Marquette. Some of these churches are almost finished, and others are in a way of progress. The church at Ontonagan village is nearly completed, and will be dedicated next spring to God Almighty, under the name of St. Patrick, who will be the patron saint of this principal church on Lake Superior. It is seventy-six feet long, thirty feet wide, and twenty feet high outside. The steeple is built in a particular manner; it is both beautiful and strong, and about sixty feet high."

In March, 1853, Father Baraga was on his way to Cincinnati to see about the publication of his works; and while crossing Lake Michigan in a sleigh with eight other persons, the ice broke, and the entire party narrowly escaped with their lives, but not until they had suffered much from extreme cold and exposure. At Cincinnati he gave a glowing account of the mineral wealth of that region, and dwelt with yet greater fervor upon the still more precious treasures which he sought and found in that country of future hope and promise.

Father Jacker pays the following eloquent tribute to the labors and services of his lamented friend and Bishop:—

"Catholics were living in almost every one of them (the mining settlements), and he was the only priest living within hundreds of miles. This is enough to prove, to the satisfaction of any one who knows how manifold and frequent are the claims of the Catholic people upon their pastor's services, that Father Baraga had no easy times during his ten years' stay in L'Ance. Many of my hearers know it. But to draw a picture of the devoted priest's labors and hardships in visiting this part of his flock, whether in sudden cases of sickness or at regular intervals, several times in the year, ready to start at any moment, and always present at the appointed hour in spite of the most fearful obstacles; traveling by water and land, in the heat of summer, among the swarms of mosquitoes, or in winter walking in snowshoes for days and weeks, now through the almost pathless woods, now on the frozen surface of the lakes, in the icy blast of the north wind, and blinded by the whirling snow, often bending under the burden of his books and Mass utensils; frequently camping in the forest, or seeking rest under the cover of a snow-drift; refusing at the same time all the usual gratifications of exhausted nature in the form of fermented drinks, but satisfied with a cup of water or a little cheese, and going without food, if need be; to describe his indefatigable zeal in announcing the word of God to those simple people in their respective languages, late in the night and early in the morning combating their abuses, but also defending them against unjust oppression, and all this not for the sake of lucre, for all his savings belonged to the poor, but driven by that heavenly charity of which his heart was overflowing; to speak of his candor, his kindness and comity in conversing with all; of his condescension to the ignorant, and of his fearlessness in reproving the proud offender—to portray these and all the other virtues of a Christian and a priest, by which Father Baraga, during his missionary career among the mining population, edified all and won their love, or at least commanded their respect and admiration, and how, by doing so, he gained for our Holy Church the lasting good-will of many of the most influential outside of her fold; this is a task which, if it could ever be accomplished, must at least not be attempted within the narrow compass of one hour's reading."*

---

* *Eulogy on Bishop Baraga*, by Father Jacker, in the Cathedral of Marquette.

We have already, in some measure, anticipated the labors of the Bishop in our account of the missionary priest. The National Council, which assembled under the Presidency of Archbishop Kenrick, at Baltimore, May 9, 1852, amongst its acts requested the erection of a Vicariate-Apostolic in Upper Michigan. The Holy Father approved this measure by his apostolic letter of July 29, 1853, and Father Baraga was consecrated Bishop of Amyzonia *in partibus*, and made Vicar-Apostolic of Upper Michigan, November 1 of the same year. His missionary labors, after his consecration, continued as before. Now the arduous task of providing pastors for the rapidly increasing flock that was rising up around him, was added to his already immense labors. To provide priests for his vast missions now engaged his serious attention, and for this purpose he visited Europe in 1854, and returned, in June of that year, with twelve new co-laborers for the field. In May, 1855, he attended the Provincial Council of Cincinnati. He also introduced into his Vicariate the Brothers and Sisters of the Third Order of St. Francis, whom he found invaluable assistants in instructing the Indians and in leading their devotions. His visitations of his extended diocese, the administration of the sacrament of confirmation, his effortsto provide churches for the new settlements, and his own personal missionary labors, now occupied his time and attention faithfully for several years. At one time we hear of his presence at Arbre Croche, among his former congregation, confirming their faith, and renewing their piety; at another, we read of his arriving at Little Traverse Bay at Christmas, where he celebrated Pontifical Mass at midnight, and again in the forenoon, confirming and giving first communion to numbers of his children, and on the same occasion, at Vespers, the office was sung alternately by the Sisters of the Third Order of St. Francis and the Indians, accompanied by the melodeon; and again we find him at Cincinnati, appealing to the more favored Catholics of that city in behalf of his Indian missions. From these scenes he passes to others, equally interesting and fruitful of good, and thus he spent his time in building up the Church of God in that interesting part of our country. In 1856 an episcopal see was erected at the Saut St. Mary, and the Right Rev. Dr. Baraga was made the Bishop of that diocese on the 9th of January, 1857. It embraced his former Vicariate-Apostolic. From his humble episcopal residence at the Saut, he governed and cherished the churches which he had spent so many years in creating. During the periods of his residence there, between his visitations of the diocese and missionary labors elsewhere, he performed all the parochial and missionary duties of the place for the Indians of the neighborhood, and was always the same humble, patient, zealous, and charitable minister of God that he had been at Arbre Croche and the Ance. The weight of his episcopal cares, anxieties, and difficulties bore more heavily upon him than his more active labors; but the hardships and exposures of the latter had already enfeebled a once hardy and enduring frame, and rendered the man, worn out in the service of God, less powerful to endure the former. In 1865 the episcopal see was transferred to Marquette, and Bishop Baraga was created Bishop of Marquette and Saut St. Mary, October 15, 1865. In spite of his exhausted health he continued his career of labor, hardship, and exposure. He never slept on a bed, but always on the floor or on a bench, even on the occasion of his visits to Bishop Lefevre, of Detroit; he walked forty miles per day on snow-shoes over the northern snows, and slept, like the Indians, under the snow at night. His duties called him to go in the face of terrific storms and intolerable cold, and he was never known to shrink from any encounter, however severe, when there was a prospect of doing good. These hardships and exposures finally cost him, and the Church in the United States, his invaluable life.

About the year 1861–62 the good Bishop had started from his ice-bound and storm-beaten home to meet his colleagues in council. He had to travel a distance of over a hundred and fifty miles through snows, storms, and ice, partly in snow-shoes and partly in open sleighs. When he arrived at Thunder Bay, on the western shore of Lake Huron, he was almost frozen, and quite ill. His health never recovered from this exposure. In the early part of 1866 he perceived signs of the palsy manifesting themselves, and the danger was the more distressing, as he knew this to have been an hereditary disease in his family. "The hand," says his reverend and eloquent eulogist,* " which had so often been raised in paternal love to impart blessings—that hand which had been the instrument of his signal services in the cause of religion, when composing his excellent works, written in divers tongues, that laborious hand refused to do its duty and to execute the orders of his still active mind. In the month of September, of the same year, he made his last entry in the journal which he had kept for many years. About the same time he preached his last sermons, in three languages, in St. Ann's Church, at Han-

---

* Father Jacker's *Eulogy of Bishop Baraga.*

cock, and he said so to himself, for he felt that his voice too was failing." With the unrelaxing grip of death upon him, he continued cheerfully and earnestly to discharge his work, as far as his bodily strength would permit him to do so. When he received from Archbishop Spalding the invitation to attend the National Council at Baltimore, in October, 1866, whose convocation had been delayed by the war, he did not think of his infirmities, but proceeded on the long journey to his post of duty. While in attendance on the Council, he was stricken down by apoplexy on the steps of the archiepiscopal residence. He fell upon the cross suspended from his neck, the cross which he had followed in faith and in deed, the cross which, like his Divine Model, he bore upon his shoulder, the cross which was found stained with his blood, as the Cross of Calvary was stained with the most precious blood of his Savior!

In the midst of danger and suffering his thoughts reverted to his far-off children on the lake-shore, and declining many kind invitations, and that especially to spend his remaining days in repose with one of his episcopal brethren, he gathered up his remaining strength and returned to his distant diocese. His condition sufficiently improved to enable him to perform missionary duties once more, but only for a short time. For four weeks he performed the ministerial duties of the post, and during the absence of the pastor paid the sick-calls to those less ill than himself, administered baptism, and attended the confessional. But his strength soon failed to such an extent, that he was only able to leave his room to attend the Holy Sacrifice on Sundays and holydays. Though the body was almost lifeless, his mind was clear, and he devoted his remaining days to communion with God, spending his whole time in meditation. "Sitting on a chair, with the head sunk deeply on the breast, he reviewed in mind his many years of service in the Lord's vineyard; in the valleys of his sunny home, on the shores of Lake Michigan, and in the dreary woods of this Upper Peninsula. And what was the result of his silent musings? That he was nothing but a useless servant, and had nothing whereon to rest his hopes for eternity, than the great mercy of his Redeemer and the power of forgiveness of sins granted by Christ to His Holy Church."

On the night before the feast of the Epiphany, the good and saintly Bishop felt the presence of death, and immediately fortified himself with the sacraments. He was calm, resigned, and hopeful only in the mercies of his Lord. To the service of God he had devoted his life; to the forgiveness and compassion of that same Master he now resigned his soul. On the night of the 6th of January, 1868, he calmly and fervently breathed his last, leaving behind him a name that will be cherished and venerated as long as there is a Church in America to reap the fruits of his labors, and treasure the traditions of his virtues and services as a precious legacy and a noble example for his children. "He will never be forgotten, as long as a Christian soul shall be living on Lake Superior; and many will bless his memory, for to them he was a benefactor, a messenger of peace, a teacher, a guide, and loving father."

RIGHT REV. GEORGE ALOYSIUS CAR-RELL, D.D.,

*First Bishop of Covington, A.D. 1853.**

GEORGE ALOYSIUS CARRELL was born at Philadelphia, June 13, 1803. His grandfather, Timothy Carrell, was a native of Ireland, and came to this country before the Revolutionary War. He established himself as a grocer on Water Street, Philadelphia, where success attended on a life of industry and integrity. His father, John Carrell, was a native of Philadelphia, and his mother, Mary Julia Moore, was a native of Lancaster, Pennsylvania. A large family, four boys and four girls, were reared by these excellent parents in piety and rectitude. The Bishop was the seventh child. The house occupied by his parents, and in which he was born, was the old mansion of William Penn, at the corner of Market Street and Letitia Court. Having received elementary instruction in the schools of his native city, he was sent, in 1813, when only ten years old, to Mt. St. Mary's College, Emmittsburg, Maryland, where he spent three years. In 1816 he entered Georgetown College, where he pursued his collegiate course for four years. He next entered the novitiate of the Society of Jesus, at White Marsh, Maryland, and was remarkably earnest and sedulous in the study and practice of a spiritual life. At the end of two years thus spent he returned to his

---

* Authorities: *New York Freeman's Journal*, October 10 and 24, 1868; *The Metropolitan*, 1853 and 1854; *Catholic Almanacs*, etc., etc.

family, with whom, however, he spent but a short time.
He did not lose sight of his chosen vocation, and soon
afterward entered the Theological Seminary of St. Mary's,
Baltimore. Here he was a schoolmate of several who
afterwards became distinguished in our ecclesiastical
history, amongst whom was Archbishop Eccleston. He
again entered Mt. St. Mary's College, where he continued his theological studies under the learned and pious
Dr. Bruté. Having completed his studies, he was ordained in the holy priesthood in 1829, in St. Augustine's
Church, Philadelphia by Bishop Conwell.

For six years he labored earnestly on the mission, and
was assistant-pastor of St. Augustine's Church, and at
the same time attended the mission at the Furnace, in
New Jersey. He was next appointed pastor of the
Holy Trinity Church, Philadelphia. His next mission
was at Wilmington, Delaware, from which place he also
attended Westchester, Pennsylvania, and Newcastle,
Delaware. In all these positions he proved himself a
laborious priest and a good pastor, winning for himself
not only the high esteem and friendship of Bishop Kenrick, but also the kind regard of the entire population,
including great numbers of other denominations, especially of the Society of Friends at Philadelphia. At
Wilmington his ministry was especially useful. Here
he established two excellent schools—one a boarding
and day school for young ladies, in charge of the Sisters of Charity, now a flourishing institution, with its
three hundred pupils. The other was a fine school for
boys, which is still in successful operation, and accomplishing much good. After these six years' experience
of missionary life, he felt a renewal of his early desire
for the retirement, and for the regular and devotional

Right Rev. George Aloysius Carrell, D.D.   507

life of a religious order, and resolved to join the Society of Jesus, in which he had so profitably spent two years of noviceship in his youth. Before doing so, however, he spent some weeks in assisting the pastors of St. Augustine's, Philadelphia, and St. Paul's, Pittsburgh. Bishop Kenrick was greatly grieved at losing so good a priest; and many regrets were expressed by the Catholics and Protestants of the communities in which he had labored. The prayers and blessings of all accompanied him on his departure.

Father Carrell had applied for and received admission into the Society of Jesus, in the Province of St. Louis— first as a novice at Florissant, where he renewed the chastening exercises and studies of St. Ignatius, and two years afterwards as a scholastic at St. Louis. He was soon appointed a professor in St. Louis University, and afterwards, in succession, pastor of the College Church of St. Francis Xavier in 1837, Rector of the St. Louis University from 1845 to 1848, and President of Purcell Mansion College for young boys, near Cincinnati, Ohio, from 1851 to 1853. In all these positions of responsibility and care he won distinction by his attention to duty, his administrative talents, his learning, and dignified deportment.

The First National Council of Baltimore, which met May 9, 1852, recommended the erection of the See of Covington, embracing the eastern portion of Kentucky— until then forming part of the diocese of Louisville—and proposed as its first Bishop Dr. Carrell. The Holy See, by apostolic letter of July 29, 1853, approved these recommendations, and decreed accordingly. Dr. Carrell was consecrated Bishop of Covington, at Cincinnati, on the Feast of All Saints, November 1, 1853. The new diocese was an extensive one, bounded on the north by the Ohio river, on the south by the State of Tennessee, on the east by Virginia, and on the west by the Kentucky river. It contained, at the time of Bishop Carrell's consecration, only ten churches and seven priests. The Bishop immediately commenced the erection of his new Cathedral Church of St. Mary's, which in a year was ready for divine service. Churches and schools began to spring up in various parts of his diocese, and it was a matter of remark how rapid were the strides made by religion and education during his administration. At the commencement of his episcopate his diocese was without any of those great aids and promoters of religion and education, the religious Orders of the Church. He gave special encouragement to their introduction and development, and had the happiness of seeing his diocese blessed with the presence and labors of the Sisters of the Poor of St. Francis, the Sisters of Charity of Nazareth, the Monks and Nuns of St. Benedict, the Sisters of the Visitation, and the Ursuline Nuns, all of which had under their charge, in various parts of the diocese, fine academies, schools, and benevolent institutions for both sexes. It was with satisfaction and gratitude to God that Bishop Carrell could point to his two male and twelve female religious institutions, to his hospital, two orphan asylums, and an infant foundling asylum.

Bishop Carrell's name is intimately associated with the cause of education in Kentucky and Ohio. The various literary and collegiate institutions in which he was professor, or over which he presided, turned out, from year to year, many educated gentlemen from various parts of the country, and even from foreign lands, who ever afterwards cherished a warm sense of gratitude and affection for Dr. Carrell. It was no uncommon occurrence for persons of eminence in their various States, and even from Mexico and Canada, to travel hundreds of miles out of their way, in order to see and reverence in Bishop Carrell the instructor of their youth, the early preceptor of their hearts in the way of virtue, and of their minds in learning. Though retired, and even ascetic in his life and tastes, Bishop Carrell's society was much sought after by the good, the pious, and the learned; for in him they found at once the Christian gentleman and scholar, the self-denying man of God, and the genial companion. A distinguished Protestant civilian of Kentucky once said, "I regard Bishop Carrell as my *beau ideal* of a Christian Bishop."

As an educator of his own people Bishop Carrell was indefatigable. He gave special attention to the parochial schools of his diocese, which he placed in the most competent hands, both for secular and religious training. He was also zealous and laborious in the sacred calling of his ministry, and never spared himself in the great work of doing good to others. Remarkable as he was for his fine personal appearance, this was lost sight of in the pleasure afforded by his refined manners, cultivated conversation, and innocence of character. His interior life was ascetic, self-denying, and devout; his exterior life was modest, affable, and simple. He was particularly tender to the poor, the sick, and the afflicted; and while to all he was a good pastor, to these he was a considerate parent. Such were his simplicity of life and voluntary poverty, that he would accept no salary from his Cathedral, or even regular tribute from his diocese, and limited his income to a few voluntary gifts from the people as he made the visitation of his diocese, and these he restricted in many years to the trifling sum of one hundred and fifty dollars, and never allowed them to exceed four hundred and fifty dollars. All above this he returned to the donors, whom he knew not to be in affluent or even easy circumstances. The poverty of his Cathedral and other congregations affected him so much, that he resolved to allow them to contribute nothing to him. It is said that even from his meagre resources he found it possible to spare something for alms to the poor, whom he never forgot, even in the midst of his own poverty.

The life of retirement from the world which Bishop Carrell led, especially when not engaged in the active works of his ministry, led some even of his own flock to suppose that he was reserved, and without sympathy for his people. Nothing could have been more erroneous. His poverty, voluntarily embraced in order that he might be like the poor, and in order that he might relieve their sufferings, would be a refutation of this impression. His labors for his flock, and his services in promoting the spread and facilities of religion and education throughout his diocese, are inconsistent with this view. We have seen how few were the churches and priests of his diocese when he assumed its administration. He had the consolation of seeing the number of his churches and stations increased to nearly ninety, and the number of his priests increased to thirty-three, besides eleven clerical students. He not only took delight in promoting these strides of the Church in his diocese, but also in presenting her offices and ceremonies to his flock with imposing and edifying effect. An extract from a cotemporaneous non-Catholic account of one of the public ceremonials in his diocese, in 1860, will be given to show

how truly united he was with his flock, and how he sympathized with them in their joys and pleasures:—" The ceremony of laying the corner-stone of St. Anne's Church, in West Covington, was conducted on such a scale as to transfer the solemn festivities from all the Catholic churches of Covington and Newport to the public highways, and to cast over the whole of those cities an air of public rejoicing, which was just sufficiently subdued by the quiet and solemn manner of the numerous societies which were out, to preserve the idea of the religious character of the day. The parade of splendid banners, and the long lines and orderly ranks of neatly decorated members of the various benevolent associations and religious societies, were truly imposing, especially as they passed around and up the beautiful hills of West Covington. On reaching the site of the church, which is a beautiful ridge commanding an extensive view of the three sister cities, and a great stretch of river scenery, both above and below, we found the masonry of the church in an advanced stage, surmounted by a convenient platform for the speaking. The Right Rev. Bishop Carrell, with some twenty priests, and young clerks in white and shining robes, advanced from a neighboring dwelling, and commenced the dedication by chanting various prayers and hymns. The Right Rev. Bishop then preached, in his clear and distinct manner, a sermon of forty minutes. The discourse was explanatory, historical, and hortatory; was exceedingly happy in its tone and expression, and was filled with passages of striking elegance and eloquence. He was followed by Rev. Father Stanislaus, of Birmingham, Pennsylvania, in the German language. His manner was forcible, clear, and interesting. The scene from the spot on which the church will stand was one of the most lively and brilliant we have ever beheld on any public occasion. In the centre the platform, crowded by the clergy in their robes, and surmounted by the flag of our country and the solemn emblem of Christian faith, the cross; immediately around were ranged in order some twenty exceedingly fine banners, then in widening circles the various societies, and beyond the multitude of some four thousand upturned faces; then buggies and carriages, and farther up the surrounding shady slopes numerous groups were seated—even to the distance of half a mile were many such parties and family gatherings, seeming to enjoy in all its fulness the poetry of the scene, with its sights and sounds. We learn that John Slevin, Esq., of Cincinnati, is the donor of the ground for the church, which, in compliment to his lady, will be called the Church of St. Anne. We cannot close this notice without expressing our admiration of the general conduct of the large gathering on this occasion. All seemed imbued with the proper spirit for such a ceremony. During its continuance and after its close all was quiet, not even a momentary interruption having marred the religious joy of this gorgeous and unusual but yet solemn mode of Sabbath worship."*

Bishop Carrell was a fine preacher, and possessed a natural eloquence, heightened by classic taste and learning, and intensified by his earnest, sincere, and truthful character. In this respect his preaching was an illustration of his life and character, which were remarkable for directness, a love of truth, a high sense of honor, punctuality in all engagements, and devotion to duty. He was ever sensitive to all human sufferings, and depre-

---

* The Cincinnati *Daily Inquirer*; *N. Y. Freeman's Journal*, June 16, 1860.

cated the prevalence of war among men. The recitals of battle, carnage, and death, during our own late civil war, deeply affected his sensitive nature, and he invariably requested his friends to spare him the pain of listening to them. His health, for some time before his death, began to fail, and his friends saw the effects which the anxieties and cares of his office, and probably his self-denials, had caused on him. He was several times in danger of death from a complication of diseases under which he suffered. During this long period of suffering, and especially during his last days of pain and final dissolution, he displayed patience, resignation, and cheerfulness, and illustrated in his own person the gospel he had so well announced to others. He died September 25, 1868, in the sixty-sixth year of his age.

RIGHT REV. JOSUE MARIA YOUNG, D.D.,

Second Bishop of Erie, A.D. 1854. *

THE original name of Bishop Young was Josue Moody Young; during his Catholic life it was changed to Josue Maria, in honor of the Blessed Virgin Mary. He was born in Shapleigh, Maine, October 29, 1808, of Protestant parents. The town of Shapleigh has since been divided, and that part of it which is now called Acton was the birthplace of the Bishop. His father, Jonathan Young, was born at Barrington, New Hampshire, in 1773, was a graduate of Harvard University in 1798, an Universalist in religion and a farmer by occupation. His paternal grandfather was Peter Young, a native of England, who settled in Dover, and belonged to the sect of Congregationalists.

His mother's maiden name was Mehetable Moody, daughter of William Pepperell Moody, of Saco, Maine, and through her he was descended from one of the oldest, most talented, and respectable families in New England. They belonged to the Congregationalist, then the prevailing sect of New England, and many of them were eminent ministers or teachers in their day. His father and mother were married in 1799.

The first of his maternal ancestors in this country was William Moody, who came from Essex, England, about 1634, with his three sons, Samuel, Joshua, and Caleb.

---

* Authorities: *Catholic Almanac*, 1867; De Courcy and Shea's *Catholic Church in the United States*; the Baltimore *Metropolitan*, Vols. I., II., and L, N. S. · Allen's *Biographical Dictionary*, etc., etc., and original sources.

His son Caleb was settled in Newbury, and the son of Caleb, the Rev. Samuel Moody, was the most eminent of the family. He was a graduate of Harvard in 1697, and was ordained December 29, 1700. He was regarded as a most efficient minister in his church, was greatly respected for his talents, his labors, and his charities, and was so eloquent that, we are told, "the people hung upon his lips." He never accepted any salary, and, during his long career as minister, lived entirely upon the voluntary offerings of his people. So confident was his reliance upon this source, that he frequently took no forethought for providing the day's meal for his family; and it is related that on one occasion his wife came and informed him that the dinner-table was set, but there was no dinner to put upon it; he had scarcely given his usual answer, that Providence would take care of that, when a rap was heard at the door announcing the arrival of a complete dinner from one of his neighbors. He was said to be irritable, and sometimes harsh, in his efforts to correct the vices of his people, and it is related that one day, as he was passing a tavern and gambling-house, he suddenly entered, and finding one of his parishioners there, caught him forcibly by the neck and expelled him from the door. One of his most remarkable and long-remembered sermons was on this theme: "When you know not what to do, you must not do you know not what." He left behind him a tract on "The doleful state of the damned, especially of such as go to hell from under the gospel;" another on "Judas hung up in chains;" an "Election Sermon;" and a "Life of Joseph Quasson, an Indian." He died in 1747, aged seventy-two years.

A son of the above, the Rev. Joseph Moody, was

minister of the North Church of York, and subsequently Register of Deeds and Judge of one of the courts. Still later he organized a new Church, of which he was minister. He was much respected by his people, in spite of his marked eccentricities. He possessed great native wit. of which several instances were recorded. While boarding with the deacon of his church, Deacon Bragdon, the latter came to him one day and requested his prayers for one of his neighbors, charged with some serious fault, and who, as the deacon said, "had got terribly out of the way." The minister asked if the deacon himself did also take part in the offence. "No, no, no," said the deacon, "if I thought I did I would take my horse and ride fifty miles on end." "Ah," replied Mr. Moody, "I believe, Deacon Bragdon, it would take a pretty good horse to outride the devil." He also published during his day several religious tracts.

Samuel Moody, a son of Rev. Joseph Moody, a graduate of Harvard, was one of the most celebrated teachers that New England ever produced. After many previous years of teaching in other schools, he was for thirty years the principal of the academy at Newbury, founded by Governor Dummer, and so great was his reputation that pupils flocked to him from a great distance. Many of the most eminent men of the Revolutionary era in New England had been his pupils. His infirmities alone compelled him to stop teaching, and all of his people said of him that "he was conscientious, faithful; a man of piety and religion."

The Rev. Joshua Moody, an eminent teacher and minister of Newburyport, was of the same family. He was for a long time minister at Isle of Shoals, and it is related that on the loss of a fishing shallop in a north-east storm at Ipswick Bay, he endeavored to impress the religious reflections suggested by the event upon his seafaring hearers at the Shoals in this way: "Suppose, my brethren, any of you should be overtaken in the bay in a north-east storm, your hearts trembling with fear, and nothing but death before you—whither would your thoughts turn, and what would you do?"—"What would I do?" replied one of the hardy seamen present, "I would instantly hoist the foresail, and scud away for Squam!"

We have accounts of several other members of Bishop Young's maternal family, who were distinguished graduates of Harvard, and eminent as ministers or teachers. One of them published a sermon on the death of General Washington. Scarcely a family history in New England could be better selected to illustrate the characteristic views, manners, and traditions of that part of our country before the Revolution. Bishop Young inherited to some extent the stern character of his Puritan ancestors, but in him it was finely tempered by the true faith. Though he did not enjoy, as most of them had done, the benefits of an university education, he did not permit this disadvantage to prevent him from developing fine natural abilities in a higher and holier sphere, nor from rising to an eminence superior to them all. He has been justly ranked among the "self-made men" of distinction in America.

His early education was probably nothing more than could be procured at a country free-school in New England. In such schools the Bible, or selections from it, formed a prominent part of the exercises in reading, and it was not unlikely that from reading and hearing such lessons read by others, he acquired that knowledge which made him so familiar with the language of Scripture, evinced by his ready quotations in after life, before and after his entrance into the Catholic ministry. At the age of eight years he went to live with his uncle, Samuel Moody, at Saco, and was there baptized and educated in the Congregational faith. He spent most of his time here at school, and employed his leisure in assisting his uncle, who was a baker. In 1823 he was an apprentice to the printing trade in the office of the *Eastern Argus*, at Portland, and for about a year after his apprenticeship he edited *The Maine Democrat*, which was published at Saco. During his apprenticeship he evinced a great passion for reading. After his return from his uncle's family to that of his father, he abandoned Congregationalism, and became an Universalist like his father. While working at the office of the *Argus*, Providence threw in his way a young Catholic boy named John Crease, who worked in the same office. The young Universalist was not backward in opening his batteries on his "deluded" companion, and the latter was not unprepared or unwilling for the attack. The Universalist champion, however, was both willing and anxious to read, and eagerly devoured the contents of several Catholic books which his fellow-apprentice lent him. His first impressions were surprise at the misrepresentations against Catholics, which he had from his infancy received from his teachers; and at finding how differently Catholic doctrines, morals, and traditions were set forth in Catholic books, from the accounts he had read and heard in all other quarters. The barriers of prejudice having been thus removed, the profound truths, exalted morals, inspiring traditions, and winning devotions of the Catholic Church, as good seed cast into a generous soil, took root in his heart. In the summer of 1827, the venerable Bishop Fenwick, of Boston, made his first episcopal visitation to Maine, then comprising a part of his diocese. Josue Young at this time disclosed to his friend, John Crease,* his own conviction of the truth of the Catholic faith, and was by him introduced to Bishop Fenwick. Those who remember the paternal kindness and the apostolic zeal and dignity of Bishop Fenwick, may well imagine how affectionately he embraced this young inquirer after truth, and how deeply his eloquent and fervid words were impressed upon the soul of the earnest listener. The following anecdote is related of this portion of his life: Some one asked him what part of the doctrine of Transubstantiation he considered the most mysterious; he immediately replied: "Not how the blood can be present under the appearance of bread, but how the body can be present under the appearance of wine."

In October or November, 1828, he publicly received conditional baptism at the hand of Rev. C. D. Ffrench, the first Catholic pastor of Portland, being then about nineteen years old; and in the following year he made his first communion, under that pioneer priest. He attained his majority in October, 1829, and continued his labors at the printing business until towards the close of 1830. He was now advised by physicians that the

---

* John Crease was a native of Boston. He used to read the Mass prayers for the few Catholics of Portland, Maine, when the priest happened to be absent on Sundays. This was forty years ago. He followed the Rev. Mr. Young to Lancaster, Ohio, and resided with him till the elevation of the latter to the See of Erie; he then followed the Bishop, by his invitation, to Erie, and resided with him till the Bishop's death; the room he occupied was one of the sacristies attached to the sanctuary of St. Patrick's Church, Erie. He was greatly venerated for his many virtues.

climate of the West would be more congenial with his health. Having resolved to devote himself to the enlightenment and conversion of others, who, like himself, with a desire to know the truth, had yet been reared in ignorance and error, he saw that the ecclesiastical state was his vocation. Guided by the counsels of Bishop Fenwick, of Boston, he corresponded with Bishop Rosati, of St. Louis, and Bishop Fenwick, of Cincinnati, from both of whom he received letters of encouragement. By the advice of the Bishop of Boston, he finally decided to attach himself to the Diocese of Cincinnati, for which city he departed in the fall of 1830. He made something of a tour through several Western States, and spent some time in Kentucky, working as a journeyman printer. After his arrival in Cincinnati he continued to work at his trade, and received employment in the office of the *Catholic Telegraph*. His zeal in teaching catechism and in promoting the cause of religion in every way in his power, while thus an humble layman, was a source of edification to all who saw him.

It was not long after the arrival of Bishop Purcell at Cincinnati, that that Prelate discovered the high order of talents and many fine traits of character possessed by this earnest young man; and it was under the Bishop that he commenced his studies for the sacred ministry.

The Bishop shortly afterwards sent him to Mt. St. Mary's College, at Emmittsburg, to complete his studies and prepare for his high vocation. In 1837 he was ordained priest, and entered at once upon the arduous and self-sacrificing duties of a .Western missionary. For seven years he labored earnestly, unremittingly, and successfully in this difficult and laborious field, and was, during a portion of that time, connected with the Academy at Cincinnati, which has since expanded into St. Francis Xavier's College. During the greater portion of these years he was the devoted and indefatigable pastor of St. Mary's Church at Lancaster, Ohio. He also made monthly visits to Logan and other missionary stations, and was commended as a laborious, humble, and zealous laborer for the spread of the gospel and the salvation of souls.

The Holy See, in confirmation of the recommendations of the National Council which assembled at Baltimore, in May, 1852, by an apostolic letter of July 29, 1853, carved a new episcopal see out of the diocese of Pittsburgh, and located it at Erie. It embraced within its jurisdiction the ten north-western counties of Pennsylvania. The name of Rev. Josue M. Young was first on the list of nominations for the new bishopric. But Bishop O'Connor, in his solicitude for that portion of his flock which had just been separated from Pittsburgh at his suggestion, and in order that he might more effectually carry out his views in proposing the division of his diocese, recommended to Rome that himself should be transferred to the new See of Erie. Accordingly the Holy See transferred Bishop O'Connor to the See of Erie, and appointed Dr. Young to succeed him in the bishopric of Pittsburgh. The humility of the latter made him shrink from the elevation designed for him, and he solicited permission to decline the appointment. In the mean time Bishop O'Connor took possession of the See of Erie and commenced its organization. When, however, Bishop O'Connor's removal from Pittsburgh became known, his former diocesans remonstrated against the change, and the other Bishops gave their advice against it, this arrangement not having been treated of in the Council, or anticipated by them. Dr. Young earnestly seconded their views. The Holy See acted in accordance with these suggestions, and transferred Bishop O'Connor back to Pittsburgh. Dr. Young, while released from the appointment to Pittsburgh, received that of Erie.

The City of Erie occupies the site of the old French fort Presqu'ile. It has been stated that this place was pointed out for the future seat of a bishopric by the venerable Bishop Flaget, as early as 1836.* From the time of the French, who established missions among the Erie Indians, the holy sacrifice of the Mass had at intervals been offered there. Father Luke Collet, a Recollect, had been chaplain at fort Presqu'ile in 1755. In the beginning of the present century Irish immigrants began to settle there, and the missionary, Rev. Father Whelan, visited them in 1807. "We know of no other missionary there," writes Mr. Shea,† "till Father William O'Brien, a native of Maryland, and a pupil of Georgetown, who had been ordained in 1808, repaired thither in 1815. The Rev. Charles B. McGuire, of Pittsburgh, held some stations there in 1816 and 1817, after whom Rev. Terrence McGirr came to Erie three times from 1818 to 1821 to administer the sacraments. The Rev. Patrick O'Neil was then appointed to serve Erie at long intervals, and his last visit took place in 1830. The Rev. Francis Masquelet, an Alsatian priest, showed himself several times at Erie from 1834 to 1836, and the Rev. Patrick Rafferty, the author of a small history of the Protestant Reformation, was there in 1837, and till this period the city was too unimportant, and the missionaries

---

* *Annals of the Propagation of the Faith*, xxii., 341.
† De Courcy & Shea's *History of the Catholic Missions in the United States*, 310.

in the State of Pennsylvania too few, to enable Erie to have one permanently stationed there. The Rev. Mr. McCabe resided there from 1838 to 1840, and the following year Father J. Lewis, of the Order of St. Francis, was appointed to take charge of the German population who had begun to settle in Erie. This was the epoch of the erection of the two little wooden churches, one for the American and Irish, the other for the German Catholics. Since then both have been rebuilt of brick." One of these afterwards became St. Patrick's Cathedral. There were Catholic families at Erie of great piety and zeal for religion, conspicuous among whom were the Dicksons, who gave largely of their means to sustain the cause of Catholicity in Western Pennsylvania, and with whom the missionary always found hospitality and support.

Bishop Young was consecrated by Archbishop Purcell at the Cathedral of Cincinnati, on Low Sunday, April 23, 1854. He returned to Lancaster to settle up his affairs, and bid farewell to his congregation whom he had served so well and long. As a testimony of their attachment to him and a proof of their zeal for religion, his congregation of St. Mary's gave him a handsome donation to aid him in the arduous work of organizing his new diocese, and in establishing the Church in that extensive and needy region. He very soon afterwards repaired to Erie and took possession of his see. One of his first acts was the announcement of the jubilee, in an earnest and stirring pastoral letter. Almost immediately afterwards he made a visitation of his diocese, and commenced those untiring labors which distinguished his career in the Church, and which continued during his entire episcopate. " With a sparse population, slender means, and a rough field of labor, he accomplished a great deal, and left behind him a reputation for earnestness, eloquence, and zeal, of which the Catholics of Erie diocese may well feel proud. A New Englander by birth, he retained to the last, while exhibiting on all occasions the most uncompromising opposition to religious error, many of those peculiarities for which his countrymen are distinguished, thus affording in his own person perhaps the best illustration of the thoroughness with which the Church Catholicises the convert, without compelling him to renounce those traits of character which serve to individualize the man, indicate his origin, or reflect the school of thought in which he has been trained."* Firmly persuaded and deeply convinced of the truth of the religion which after careful study and earnest prayer he had embraced, he did not hesitate in plain terms, sometimes, perhaps, in the opinion even of his friends, in terms too plain, to warn sectarians of the danger to their eternal salvation to which they exposed themselves, by remaining without the one fold of Christ. Still, if he spoke the truth plainly, it was from motives of charity, and from a solicitude for the 'dearest interests of mankind.

He was rigid to himself, and lived in the practice of strict mortification. He loved retirement, was an excellent economist of time, spent the few leisure moments he could get from severe labor in study, and had acquired a fund of varied and useful learning. He was an early riser, and usually offered the holy sacrifice of the Mass on the mornings of the week at six o'clock. He was also usually engaged late at night in the confessional.

---

* *The Pittsburgh Catholic.*

He was a devout client of the Blessed Virgin. He was disinterested in his nature, and he devoted all to the service of God and his neighbor. Hospitality to the clergy and to all others in need, was often mentioned by his friends as one of his prominent virtues. Not only did the homeless or suffering priest find in his house an asylum of sympathy and relief, but also the friendless orphan found there a home, until provision could be made for his reception into some institution provided for his permanent relief. Destitute wayfarers never called in vain at his door for food, or the means of reaching their destination, for he remembered that in olden times there were those who, "in practising hospitality, ministered to angels." He established an hospital for the sick at Erie, and, though the institution was subsequently removed to Meadville, the building still continues under the care of an edifying female religious community, and is now used as a house for destitute orphans. Bishop Young made great efforts for the education of the Catholic youth of his diocese. He erected a commodious and handsome building for gratuitous educational purposes, which were partially carried into effect during his lifetime, and since his death the male department has been placed under the care of the Brothers of St. Francis, and the female department under that of the Sisters of St. Joseph. This institution is now achieving great good.

The numerous churches built and good works accomplished, and others commenced by Bishop Young, remain now as so many monuments of his energy and devotion. In the first year of his administration there were twenty-eight churches in the diocese of Erie; these he increased to more than fifty; there were fourteen clergymen, and he left fifty-one. The Bishop had also a number of students preparing for the ministry, and several youths engaged in their classical studies, who purposed qualifying themselves for the same holy service. The academies and schools of the diocese, orphan asylums, infirmary, and hospital, are amongst the benefits he conferred upon his flock. His episcopal visitations were frequent and laborious. His sermons were earnest, strong, and sometimes eloquent, and were listened to with great attention by Protestants. Rapid and great as was the march of population and material development in the diocese of Erie during his episcopate, the progress of religion and of the Church have been still more remarkable and successful.

Though Bishop Young's health had for some time been such as to warn him and his friends of his liability to sudden death, he continued with unabated activity and energy to discharge his arduous duties. Missionary labors over a wide and uncultivated field were constantly added to those of his episcopal office. His priests found him an excellent example of self-sacrifice, labor, and zeal. His death occurred suddenly on the evening of September 18, 1866, at his residence in Erie, from disease of the heart. No perceptible change in his health occurred during the day; he arose at his accustomed early hour and offered the daily Mass. In the afternoon a Benedictine Father, then visiting his brethren at Erie, called on the Bishop, who conversed with him long and freely. In the evening, Rev. Mr. Carroll, pastor of St. Patrick's, a young clergyman just ordained, and two other persons, were in the Bishop's office; they heard suddenly an unusual noise in his apartment adjoining; Father Carroll hastened thither and found him in the agonies of death. He recognized the priest, received from him the final absolution, and the sacrament of Extreme Unction. He survived only a few minutes. Simultaneously with his death, the Bishop of Cleveland, accompanied by the Very Rev. William Caron, arrived at the episcopal residence on a visit. The presence of one so familiar with Bishop Young as Bishop Rappe, must have been at that sad moment a great consolation to the afflicted church of Erie, mourning over the loss of its chief pastor.

Bishop Young was one of a family of ten children, all of whom, influenced by his example, became Catholics, except one sister, who was, however, married to a Catholic. While he was a missionary at Lancaster he visited his home in New England, and it is said that he was greatly wounded by the cold reserve of many of his relatives, who were Congregationalists, and who greatly resented the adherence of their nephew to the "Babylon of Sin," and still more his becoming a "Romish priest." He also returned to Portland, Maine, during his episcopate, and visited the newspaper office in which he had been employed as a printer when a youth; he took a compositor's place and set up in type a small paragraph for the paper, in which he announced his own arrival in town, and stated that the person who set the types was the Catholic Bishop of Erie, and the same person that had been an apprentice in that office twenty years before. The passage appeared in the paper.

The funeral service over Bishop Young was performed on Friday, September 21, at the Cathedral, and was attended by Bishop Rappe, of Cleveland, who celebrated the Requiem Mass; by Bishop Domenec, of Pittsburgh, who delivered an impressive funeral sermon; by several of the clergy, numerous religious and charitable societies, and by a large concourse of the people. At the Month's Mind, on October 25, which was also largely attended by the clergy and laity, the Solemn Mass was celebrated by Bishop Verot, then of Savannah, now of St. Augustine, who pronounced a warm eulogy on the deceased Prelate. Bishop Young's remains were interred in a vault prepared for their reception in the cemetery, about two miles from the episcopal residence.

RIGHT REV. HENRY DAMIAN JUNCKER, D.D.,

First Bishop of Alton, A.D., 1857.*

THIS Prelate, who was distinguished for the sanctity of his life and the devotedness of his missionary labors, was a native of Fenetrange, Diocese of Nancy, Lorraine. He came to this country when young, attached himself to the Diocese of Cincinnati, made his ecclesiastical studies in that city, and was during this period a most zealous teacher of catechism and instructor of youth, as well as a diligent and edifying student. He was ordained by Bishop Purcell as deacon on Sunday, March 9, 1834, and as priest on March 16, Passion Sunday, 1834, at Cincinnati, and was the first priest ordained by that Prelate. His first mission was as pastor of the Church of the Holy Trinity, the first German Catholic congregation formed in Cincinnati. There he served with zeal for two years. He was next stationed at Canton, where he was pastor of St. Mary's, from which central station he also served Circleville, Waverly, the German Catholics at Portsmouth, Zanesville, Somerset, and St. Joseph's. He was engaged in these laborious missions nearly ten years, when, in 1846, he was appointed pastor of the Church of Emanuel, at Dayton. While thus engaged he also attended Urbana, Bellefontaine, West Liberty, Springfield, Xenia, Lebanon, Miamisburgh, and a number of German settlements.

The See of Quincy, Illinois, was, by decree of January

---

* Compiled from current periodicals and newspapers, particularly the *New York Freeman's Journal.*

9, 1857, transferred and annexed to the new See of Alton which latter See embraced not only the south-eastern portion of Illinois, which constituted the late See of Quincy, but also the counties of Adams, Brown, Cass, Menard, Sangamon, Macon, Moultrie, Coles, and Edgar in that State.

Father Juncker, who had spent twenty-three years of missionary labor in the priesthood, was appointed first Bishop of Alton. He was consecrated by Archbishop Purcell on Sunday, April 26, 1857, in St. Peter's Cathedral, Cincinnati. The assistant Prelates were Bishop Henni, of Milwaukee, and Bishop Young, of Erie. There were also present Bishops Miles, Lefevre, Spalding, De St. Palais, and Carrell.

He lost no time in commencing the labors of his episcopate, and soon discovered how inadequate to the real wants of so extensive and needy a diocese were the eighteen priests, then engaged in the sacred ministry within it. He labored with great zeal to supply this want. He went to Europe in the first year after his consecration, to provide for many necessary wants of his diocese. He celebrated his return in July, 1858, by ordaining four young priests, Messrs. Brennon, Kollop, Petit, and Carroll. It is worthy of remark, that during little over a year, at the commencement of his episcopate, he held four ordinations, and in that short time he increased the number of his priests from eighteen to forty-two. Eight new churches were erected in the first year of his episcopate. In the second year he had the happiness of finishing his fine stone Cathedral of Saints Peter and Paul; it was designed after some of Mr. Pugin's examples, and is one of the best churches in the country. The fine altar-piece is an old painting of great beauty and value, and had for years adorned a church of the Franciscans in Mexico. It was saved from the fire which destroyed that church by being cut from the frame, but not until after it had been seriously injured by the fire, and was sent as a present from the Franciscan Fathers, after the Mexican war, by a Protestant soldier, who was also the bearer of a letter from the Fathers to the Bishop. The injuries to the painting were repaired by Mr. Hahne, the artist, of Cincinnati, who also embellished the walls and ceilings of the Cathedral. The edifice was consecrated on Sunday, April 19, 1859, by Archbishops Kenrick, of St. Louis, and Purcell, of Cincinnati, assisted by Bishops Duggan, Luers, Whelan, and Juncker.

The work to be accomplished by Bishop Juncker in a new and rapidly growing country, then but imperfectly supplied with priests, churches, and schools, was arduous and difficult. He spared no effort to build up the Church around him, and to supply his flock with the blessings of religion and education. His visitations of his diocese were long and severe journeys, and laborious missions among the people, in which the Bishop performed every office of the priesthood. An account of one or two of these visitations will serve to illustrate the character of the labors and services he performed during every year of his episcopate. The visitation in the fall of 1858 has been chronicled as follows:—

"Notwithstanding the severity of the weather, the Right Rev. Bishop of Alton has endeavored to visit a large portion of his diocese during the last few weeks. On the 21st of November he arrived at O'Hara's Settlement, Randolph County. After having celebrated Mass on that day, he announced to the congregation the commencement of the Jubilee, and gave, every day of his sojourn there, an instruction suitable for this purpose, and together with the pastor of this place, Rev. J. W. Gifford, heard the confessions of the people. On Tuesday, the 23d of November, he dedicated the beautiful brick church of St. Patrick. It is sixty-five feet long and forty feet wide, and almost out of debt. On the following Sunday he administered the sacrament of confirmation to forty-five persons, of whom several were adults. After Mass, the congregation went in procession to the graveyard, which was then blessed by the Right Rev. Bishop. In his last sermon he admonished the people most earnestly to establish a Catholic school among themselves, that their children might not grow up without the proper and most necessary instruction in the faith of their forefathers. The congregation corresponded willingly to the wish of their Bishop, and promised to use all their efforts to erect a school in the next year. The Catholics are mostly Americans of Irish descent.

"On Tuesday there came a deputation from a small place called Red Bud, about seven miles distant from O'Hara's Settlement, to invite the Bishop to come thither and give the Catholics an opportunity to gain the graces of the Jubilee, since a priest had never been amongst them. They were mostly Germans, and it was not known to the Bishop that there were any Catholics living in this place. Many of them had not made their confessions or received communion for five, ten, and twelve years, being so far away from a priest that could understand them. The Right Rev. Bishop arrived there on Thursday afternoon and stayed with them till Saturday, hearing their confessions and giving them instructions. Over one thousand persons were reconciled with their God and received communion. Many shed tears of joy for the happiness they had experienced and the blessings they had received. Previous to the Bishop's departure he was waited upon by Mr. Crozier, a wealthy Protestant citizen of the place, who made a donation of a beautiful block in the town (172 feet by 300 feet) for church purposes, and the congregation subscribed $1,500 towards the erection of a church. Their Protestant brethren, seeing their zeal and knowing their circumstances, have also promised to contribute liberally for the same purpose.

"From there the Bishop went to the old French settlement, Kaskaskia, at which place they have no priest, but have testified their zeal by erecting a neat brick church, although they number no more than fifty Catholic families. The Bishop stayed with them a few days, and promised to reward their zeal by sending them a priest as soon as possible."*

In the fall of 1859, Bishop Juncker made a visitation of the southern portion of his diocese, an account of which is here copied, as illustrative of the labors of our Bishops, and of the manner in which the foundations of the Church have been laid in our country:—

"The retreat at Cape Girardeau being concluded, the Right Rev. Bishop of Alton proceeded to Cairo, and, after a short stay, from thence to Shawneetown. This place, although one of the oldest in the State of Illinois, has not as yet a Catholic church; a want mostly owing to the circumstance that for a long time, if ever, there has not been a priest residing there. The Bishop celebrated Mass in the house of Mr. Stout. The room in

---

* *Western Banner; New York Freeman's Journal*, January 8, 1859.

which the holy sacrifice was offered proved too small for the number of worshippers, hence a great many of them had to assist outside. The Bishop, seeing the necessity of having a church at this place, caused arrangements to be made for building one as soon as possible. A subscription was opened, and the proceeds give well-grounded hopes that good success may shortly be expected. Mr. Stout has donated to the Right Rev. Bishop four acres of land for a cemetery, to be handsomely laid out at the expense of the donor. The Rev. Mr. Jacque has been appointed to take charge of this mission. Afterwards the Right Rev. Bishop started for Pond Settlement, where there is a log church, in which Mass was celebrated by the Bishop. The little church was crowded, and the hearts of all present were filled with gladness to see their Bishop in their midst—a happiness they never had experienced before. A number of the Catholics from Equality, a town not far from there, waited on the Bishop to obtain his permission to build a church in their place, in which a great many Catholics reside. Their request was readily granted, and, judging from their good-will, we may expect also to see a church in that place in a short time."

The visits of the Bishop to various of the most scattered parts of his diocese are next noticed, and the account concludes as follows :—

"After a fatiguing journey of three weeks, he arrived at Alton on the 17th inst. (September). We have every reason to hope, that this visit to the southern part of the diocese will be very advantageous to the cause of Catholicity, in this hitherto neglected portion of Illinois."

The statistics of the diocese of Alton, in 1868, contain

the proudest eulogy on Bishop Juncker and his work. The number of priests in his diocese were increased to one hundred, besides twenty-five clerical students; the churches to one hundred and twenty-three; and the parochial schools to fifty-six, many of which were attended before his death by from four to six hundred children. He bequeathed to his diocese also two colleges for boys, six academies for girls, two hospitals, and an orphan asylum. He also erected near his Cathedral a fine episcopal residence, designed at the same time to serve as his Ecclesiastical Seminary.

After a long and severe illness, Bishop Juncker died at his residence, in Alton, on the Feast of the Guardian Angels, October 2, 1868.

RIGHT REV. CLEMENT SMYTH, D.D.,

Second Bishop of Dubuque, A.D. 1857.*

MOST of the religious orders of the Church have contributed from time to time some of their members to the American Hierarchy. Though recently established in our country, and few in numbers, the Cistercian Order of our Lady of La Trappe gave its founder, a true son of St. Bernard, to be the second Bishop of Iowa. Clement Smyth was born at Finlea, near Killaloe, County of Clare, Ireland, January 24, 1810. Born on the Feast of St. Timothy, the name of that Apostle was also conferred on him in baptism. Reared amidst the lakes and mountains of classic and picturesque Killaloe, second only in beauty and historic interest to the lakes of Killarney, the mind of young Smyth sought and reveled in the contemplation of nature and loved retirement. The inspiring scenery of his native place, and the meditative habits acquired in the constant admiration and love of God in his external works, produced a marked effect upon his life and character, and moulded the career of the future Trappist. A mind thus accustomed to reflect upon elevating and ennobling subjects, when brought in contact with the books of the school, with teachers and comrades, was startled with the new and engaging world thus introduced to its acquaintance; the heroic in history, the sublime and beautiful in literature, the mysteries of science, and the variety of lan-

---

* *Catholic Almanacs*, 1854, 1858, 1859, and 1866; *The Metropolitan*, 1858; *Freeman's Journal*, 1859 and '60, etc., etc.

guages, ancient and modern, captivated his soul and fed his intellect. There are few students who do not recall with pleasure the recollection of these first delights of education. To one who possessed the brightness of intellect and earnestness of character for which young Smyth was distinguished, these pleasure were peculiarly attractive, and while they thus impressed, they did not change the aspirations of our student. The following account of his school-days will be read with interest:—

"After passing through the limited course of studies at his village-school, the young aspirant after knowledge sought in the city of Limerick what his native village could not afford him, the rudiments of a classical education. It might be said of him with propriety that it was here, while diverted from other purposes, giving his mind solely, so far as study was concerned, to the classics of Greece and Rome, that the character was formed which influenced his after-life. What wonder is it that a youth from an Irish country village, going among strangers at the period of which we write, shut in to a great extent from the world around him, and occupying his mind with the sublimities of the Iliad and the classic beauties of Virgil and Horace, should, when the time came to choose a position in life, become a recluse? We all know from man's experience in every age, that our position, our professions, trades, business, and employments, and especially what is called our vocation, is, so far as our will has any influence over our conduct, influenced, and, we may say, controlled, by circumstances in that period of our lives which is known as youth. Sometimes we are the creatures, the subjects of these circumstances, while in other cases we control or use circumstances as we will. Having acquired such a mastery of the classics as the rigorous rules of Trinity College, Dublin, require of an aspirant to that seat of learning before he can be entered among its pupils, young Smyth became a student of that celebrated abode of learning. Here he perfected himself in those studies, especially in Latin and mathematics, which qualified him for the profession of which he afterwards made choice. Having completed his college studies, the time arrived when he must determine, so far as it depended on him, the choice of a state of life. It is at this period of his life that we should look for something characteristic of the man. Naturally we will expect to find him, an educated youth, just stepping on the threshold of manhood, ambitious, if not for fame, at least of entering a profession in which he may acquire wealth and worldly honor. We are mistaken. His ambition leads him in quite another direction. He does not even aspire to the priesthood."

Clement Smyth, having now arrived at manhood, felt the strongest inclination to a religious life. His humility was conspicuous in this event of his life. Instead of aspiring to the honor and dignity of offering sacrifice on the altar, he sought rather the more humble but truly honorable office of serving in the sanctuary and the Church. He joined a community of lay brothers—the Brothers of the Presentation—at Youghal, near Cork, as a postulant. He remained but a short time in the Presentation Order; he had modeled his life and aspirations after the examples of the holy recluses and hermits of God, whose history he had studied; and he longed for the more rigid and strict seclusion and discipline of the cloister.

With such sentiments, it is not surprising that in deciding his vocation he selected the Trappists, the most rigid, penitential, and ascetic Order in the Church. In Waterford County, Ireland, in a bleak and rocky region, existed the venerable and celebrated Monastery of the Cistercian Order of Our Lady of La Trappe. He was well aware of the life of the Trappists; he had carefully studied their institute; and what, in a worldly view, would be repulsive to our nature, to him was most attractive. Turning his steps towards the sacred precincts of the Abbey of Melleray, he was received as a choir brother, and in due time as a professed religious. The following account of the Trappists is from an address delivered at the Agricultural Festival of St. Cier-Lalande, by Cardinal Donnet, Archbishop of Bordeaux: *—

"What is a Trappist, then? Well, he is a man like all the rest of us, with the exception, however, that he is a little more humble, a little more abstemious, loses less time in sleep, and for these reasons is considerably our superior.

" Sleep indulged to excess, otherwise called *sloth*, the pleasures of the table, and an unbridled tongue, have caused a troop of miseries in this world. It needs not an initiation in the science of Hippocrates to divine that. Yes, there is danger in sleeping too much, in eating too much, and in talking too much. Now, the Trappist sleeps little, eats little, and does not talk at all. It is for this reason that he is not only a saint, but also a skilful farmer; and that is why I wish to propose him to you as a model in all that is susceptible of your imitation. I wish also to prove to the man of agricultural pursuits, whose life is often one of privations, that there exist men who might have procured themselves in the world all

---

* *The Metropolitan*, 1854.

the enjoyments of life, and who condemn themselves, by voluntary choice, to eat less, to sleep less, to labor more, than the workmen of our cities, or the inhabitants of our country districts.

"The Trappist rises every morning at two o'clock, on Sundays at one, and on great festivals at midnight. Prayer and the labor of his hands divide between them all his time till eight o'clock in the evening, his hour of retiring to rest.

"From Easter till the 4th of September the Trappist eats two meals a day, the first at half-past eleven A.M., the second at six in the evening; all the rest of the year he makes but one repast, which he takes at half-past two o'clock P.M., and in Lent at four; and he devotes but one half-hour to this only meal.

"I had the happiness of passing at La Trappe the eight days preceding my episcopal consecration, in 1835. On those days, as at all times, the fare consisted of a pea-soup, a dish of beans seasoned only with salt, and water. A pear or other fruit formed the dessert of each one. The Trappist knows neither meat, nor fish, nor butter, nor eggs.

"Will you say that to go on in this way is self-murder; that it is to bury one's self alive, and render one's self useless to society? But how many farmers, how many workmen of all trades, never make use of either flesh, meat, or fish?

"Why reproach the Trappists for doing, in the spirit of penance, what others do from necessity? Be assured of it, not only intemperance but good cheer has destroyed many virtues, engendered many evils; the lovers of gourmandizing are commonly unchaste and ungenerous; they are selfish and devoid of energy.

Trust not the countries which produce, which foster them.

"Reckon, then, if you can, the services rendered to society by the houses of La Trappe. Count the fields cleared and improved; the wild heaths and uncultivated wastes now covered with rich crops. Reckon the poor clothed and fed, the sick and infirm succored, the orphans harbored and educated. The Trappists, then, may be called the benefactors of humanity, the Providence of all around them.

"A colony of Trappists is a village containing every kind of business. Besides the farming Trappist, there are seen the miller, the blacksmith, the carpenter, the joiner, the mechanic; and all these men labor from the rising to the setting of the sun. How could I recount all they have done at Melleray, Montague, Port au Salut, Valsainte, Augne Belle, Briquebec, Font Gombaut, Sepfont, Staoueli! there may be seen the prodigies operated by faith, love of God, and a desire of serving our neighbor.

"Thirty years ago I visited one of the places which, at a later period, was chosen as the abode of one of these religious colonies. The land was covered with thorns, rocks, and moving bogs. No horseman could cross this district, on account of the quicksands occurring in every part. At the present day these marshes and wastes are replaced by fields of an admirable fertility; the rocks have, for the most part, disappeared under a stratum of vegetable earth, and the scythe moves fearlessly over the rich meadows created by these cenobites. Canals, skilfully distributed, maintain a perpetual verdure over these now luxuriant groves; drains, dug under ground to the depth of three or four feet, receive the waters of the wet lands, and pour them into a pond, which is made to feed several mills. It appears to me that these works, begun and completed by the Monks of La Trappe, are sufficient proofs of a patient and active intelligence, and of a most profound knowledge of agriculture."

The life of the Trappist is not without its consolations, even such as are appreciated in the world. A barren waste, under their skilful and untiring husbandry, becomes a smiling and fruitful garden, an oasis in a desert of rock or swamp, and around them arise the thrift, abundance, and activity of religious civilization. Their abundance, the fruit of their own sweat and toil, enables them to dispense a bountiful charity to the poor, while they practise themselves the most rigid self-denial. Their voices are tuned alone to the praises of the God who gave them, and those who sing not have the silence of their lives broken only to listen to the hymns of adoration to the only perfect One. So far from losing their love for and sympathy with their fellow-men, these sentiments are fostered and developed by the love of God and the ascetic study of human nature. The life of Father Smyth is a fine illustration of these truths.

Gifted with a good voice and musical talents, he was selected, while a brother of La Trappe, to lead the choir of the Monastery of Melleray, a task which he performed with sincere devotion and pious ardor. So earnestly did he devote himself to the grateful duty assigned to him by his Abbot, that his voice, once powerful and melodious, lost its strength under the too great exercise and exertion imposed upon it. He was compelled to give much time and pains to its restoration.

The country around the venerable monastery of Melleray was poor, and but little reclaimed by its indigent inhabitants. A consequence of this general poverty was the want of schools for the education and Christian instruction of the children of the district. Touched with charity for their necessities, Brother Clement Smyth conceived the project of establishing under the auspices of the Monastery a school for the education of these poor children. He proposed his plan to his Superior, who cordially approved it, and as Brother Clement was admirably qualified by his fine education and varied accomplishments, as well as by his zeal for the task, the good Abbot appointed him to conduct and direct the school. This good work succeeded admirably; the school became celebrated throughout Europe, and now numbers its students above five hundred. Here we have again a practical refutation of the charge against the Trappists, that they are drones and useless members of the Church and of society.

In addition to the arduous duties thus devolved upon him, Brother Clement continued to perform his usual and regular duties as a member of the community, and was regarded with admiration for the noble example and holy life he exhibited. His learning, attainments in many useful and scientific departments, and holiness of life, marked him out to his superiors for elevation to the holy priesthood. He never aspired to this rank or dignity, and it was only in compliance with the express wishes of his superiors that he commenced those studies which are the immediate preparation for Holy Orders. Having completed his ecclesiastical studies, he was ordained a priest in the year 1844. Henceforth the life of Father Smyth was a model of strict observance of the rules, discipline, and austerities of his Order; a life which has been described in the following words:—"We of the world know but little of the hidden life of the Cistercian. Unbroken silence for months and years, except in prayer and praise to God; austerities, compared to which the ordinary fasts of Christians are luxuries; vigils, which task not only the physical nature of man, but subject his supernatural qualities to an almost unendurable ordeal; —such was the life spent by our late Bishop for fourteen long years, with scarcely an intermission. No wonder that he had so well studied the nature of man as to sympathize with his fellow-beings in affliction; that his long and sacred communion with his Creator had fitted him to counsel the doubtful, to comfort the sorrowful, to strengthen the timid, to reprove with Christian indignation the transgressor, not only of the laws of God, but of the law of civil order."

From the products of their own labor the monks of Melleray gave generously to the poor. So little did they think of saving anything from their estate, that in 1848, when the famine devastated Ireland, the monks of La Trappe were among the poorest of the poor and the greatest sufferers. While helping to relieve the sufferers in their afflicted district they were themselves suffering the tortures of famine. They were even driven to the necessity of sending out a portion of their community to America, to seek upon our hospitable shores the means of subsistence. Father Smyth was selected for this trying task; and he, accompanied by Brother Ambrose Byrnes, landed at New York early in the spring of 1849. They visited several localities in the United States and Canada, for the purpose of securing a suitable location for a new Cistercian Monastery. Not succeeding in their efforts, they directed their course to the

"Far West," and were kindly and generously received by Bishop Loras, of Dubuque. The good Bishop gave them several hundred acres of land in a rich locality, in Vernon Township, Dubuque County, Iowa, not far from Dubuque. By their own efforts, more land was acquired, and they finally secured about sixteen hundred acres. By good management, the toil of their own hands, and the blessing of Heaven, they brought their lands under fine cultivation and to a state of productiveness. Like others they experienced pecuniary embarrassments, but they overcame these as well as every other difficulty. Thus was founded by Father Smyth the Monastery of New Melleray, of which he was the prior.

But these good monks did not confine themselves to the cultivation of their estate; the good of their neighbors became an early object of their solicitude and zeal. Father Smyth and his brethren, with the approbation of Bishop Loras, organized a congregation of the Catholics in the vicinity of their convent; three priests of the Order attended to the parochial duties, and the Trappists erected a fine church sixty feet long, at their own expense, to accommodate the congregation thus formed under the shadow of New Melleray. So great was their success, that the church became too small for the increasing numbers of the devout worshippers who attended. The Trappist Fathers were sedulous in their attendance at the altar, in the confessional, and in the pulpit; large numbers of communicants gathered around the communion rail every Sunday; and several converts were brought back to the fold.

Encouraged by these evidences of Divine favor, Father Smyth, here as at old Melleray, established a school for the gratuitous education of the children of the neighborhood, without distinction of religious denomination; and had the consolation of seeing a flourishing school conducted by his brethren, who devoted themselves with great energy and generosity to this good work.

Father Smyth had around him a large and exemplary community of Trappists, numbering forty-seven members, before he left the monastery for St. Paul, in 1856. The community, in 1855, possessed thirteen choir members, of whom seven were priests, thirty-two professed laybrothers, and two novices. The Trappists of New Melleray are now erecting a new abbey.

The health of Bishop Loras, of Dubuque, which had been failing for some time, became so infirm in 1856 as to require the appointment of a coadjutor. While the Bishop, his clergy, and his flock, were earnestly desirous that one might be chosen who would not only be a suitable person to bear a portion of the episcopal burden, but would also be worthy to succeed Bishop Loras, it was with a singular unanimity that the eyes of all were turned to the Abbey of New Melleray, and to its able and zealous prior. It was thus that the choice, which fell upon Dr. Clement Smyth, was received with universal approbation and joy throughout the diocese. His able administration of the affairs of New Melleray, and his experience in ecclesiastical government, marked him out as a fit successor to the good and laborious Bishop Loras. He was consecrated at St. Louis, by Archbishop Kenrick, May 3, 1857, under the title of Bishop of Thanasis *in partibus;* and was appointed also administrator of the vacant see of Chicago.

He devoted himself to the new duties of his position with the same zeal with which he had filled every position occupied by him. He succeeded in lightening the burden of Bishop Loras, and in carrying out his measures with signal success. The prosecution of the work on the new Cathedral became an especial object of his efforts. The financial troubles which soon followed did not deter him from his undertaking; and while the general derangement of the country cut off the supply of means, he sought elsewhere and obtained the means necessary to enable him to carry on the building to a state of completion sufficient to permit its use for divine service, although unfinished in its details and ornaments.

The death of Bishop Loras, in February, 1858, devolved upon Bishop Smyth the entire duties and responsibilities of the episcopal office, as well as the title of Bishop of Dubuque. Though the cloister and the monastic life had been his vocation for so many years, he at once advanced into the vast field of missionary labor now devolved upon him, with the energy and zeal of an old missionary. His visitations of his diocese were performed with apostolic labor, and were productive of great fruit. Although Bishop Smyth could not be called an orator, he was one of the most effective speakers in the Church, and one of her most useful Prelates. He did not address himself to the imagination or fancy of his hearers, but to their intellects, to which he brought conviction, and to their hearts, in which he awakened true piety and devotion. Scenes have been described during his journeys through Iowa, in which the churches were crowded with persons of all denominations eager to hear him speak, and whom he addressed with such pathos and effective eloquence that every eye was flowing with tears. His exertions in the midst of his poverty to supply the many rising and increasing congregations in his diocese with churches and priests were untiring. He regarded a church, however humble, as a great point gained in the development of faith and religion amongst the people, and in order to gain this point he commenced usually with the erection of a log church, which was not long afterwards supplanted with a large and handsome brick one. To supply pastors to his flock also taxed his exertions severely, but he succeeded wonderfully in meeting both these important requirements. Thus during his short episcopate he increased the number of his churches from fifty to seventy-nine churches, eight chapels, and twenty stations, and the number of his priests from thirty-seven to sixty-three. This is certainly an astonishing increase in the development of the Church; one which kept pace with the rapidly increasing Catholic population of the State, which was doubled during his administration. Schools increased in every direction, as did also the religious communities of the Sisters of Charity, and the Abbey of New Melleray almost doubled its pious and useful members. Besides the greatly augmented number of priests he left in the diocese at his death, there were then twenty-five clerical students preparing still further to recruit the ranks of the clergy of Iowa.

Charity was the crowning virtue of Bishop Smyth. His efforts for the education of the poor, at the Abbeys of Melleray in Ireland, and of New Melleray in Iowa, prove that this heavenly virtue was well cultivated by him as a monk of La Trappe; and his efforts in the same direction, and still more his endeavors and sacrifices to relieve the poor and provide for the orphan, while a Bishop, show that in assuming the mitre he became a true father to his people. It has been well said of him that

Right Rev. Clement Smyth, D.D. 549

"kindness of heart, nay, tenderness of heart, was the source, the fountain, whence flowed succor to the needy, the visit to the sick, consolation to the distressed, the benignant smile of recognition to those who would slyly pass him by." He projected the Orphan Asylum for the destitute children of his diocese, and this became a cherished object; one which he sustained through life, and did not forget to think of and bless during his last moments. During the severe winter of 1859 and '60, his paternal heart was grieved at the sufferings of his people. He was most active in his efforts to relieve the families brought to sickness and hunger by the fearful cold and the pangs of hunger. For this purpose he organized Conferences of the Society of St. Vincent de Paul, and from the pulpit eloquently and effectively pleaded their cause. He cherished the societies and the sodalities with especial care, attending their meetings, instructing their members in the perfection of the gospel, and in encouraging their generous and devotional practices. Many converts were brought to the faith by his zealous exertions, and when he administered confirmation, it was usual to see some adults, who were just becoming reconciled to the Church, advancing to the altar to be anointed in the faith. In the city of Dubuque alone he administered confirmation to as many as seven hundred persons in eighteen months, and to fourteen hundred within the State during the same period of time.

Bishop Symth seldom left his diocese, and then only on business connected with its best interests. He visited Europe in 1862, for the accomplishment of objects affecting the good of the Church in his diocese. While abroad he visited the venerable Abbey of Melleray in

Ireland, where he had made his monastic vows, had accomplished so much good, and where his name was held in veneration. He was received there with every demonstration of respect and honor; the inmates turned out to welcome him, and the students of the Seminary he had founded presented to him an address of congratulation and of thanks for the benefits he had conferred upon them and the institution.

The death of this excellent Prelate, which took place September 23, 1865, was in keeping with the holy life he had led. He was in the prime of life, and in the midst of useful plans for the good of his flock. But he, who, as an humble brother of the Presentation, and as a lay-brother of La Trappe, had learned to obey the remotest wish of his superior, was now ready to obey the call of his Creator with resignation and joy. He repeated constantly, during his last sickness, the words, "Thy will be done, O Lord!" During those trying moments he maintained a characteristic firmness and courage, and infused it into those who surrounded his death-bed. Perceiving one of his priests affected to tears, he said to him, "Be a man, sir; be a Christian!" His illness was short, but painful; the good Bishop welcomed his sufferings with gratitude, and calmly resigned his life into the hands of his Creator, at the age of about fifty-five years.

RIGHT REV. JOHN BARRY, D.D.,

Second Bishop of Savannah, A.D. 1857.*

BISHOP BARRY was born in the Barony of Forth, County of Wexford, Ireland, about the year 1799. He dedicated himself to God at an early age, and while an ecclesiastical student in Ireland, attached himself to the diocese of Charleston, then governed by Bishop England. He continued his studies at Charleston in the Theological Seminary established there by Dr. England, by whom he was ordained in the Cathedral of St. Finbar, September 24, 1825. He celebrated his first Mass in the same church, on Sunday, October 2. The assistant priest, deacon, and all others who attended at the altar, six in number, were promoted and ordained within the diocese of Charleston, and this was the first occasion on which all the clergy celebrating at St. Finbar's were students of the diocese and ordained within it.

He was sent by Bishop England to Augusta, Georgia, where he was pastor of the Church of the Holy Trinity until the death of Bishop Gartland, in 1854. In 1839 he was appointed the Vicar of Bishop England for Georgia. In 1844, under Bishop Reynolds, he was appointed Vicar-General of the Diocese of Charleston, First Assistant in the Cathedral of St. Finbar, and Superior of the Theological Seminary. He still retained charge of the church at Augusta, which he visited on the fourth Sunday of every month. He established the first Catho-

---

* Compiled from *Catholic Almanacs* from 1833 to 1860; cotemporaneous journals, etc.

lic day-school in the State of Georgia, at Savannah, and immediately saw it well attended by Catholic children. Heroic charity was the crowning virtue of the character and life of Dr. Barry. Thus, in 1832, we behold him giving up his own house as a Cholera Hospital, and afterward turning it into an asylum for the orphans made by the pestilence. In 1846 he attended the Sixth Council of Baltimore, as Theologian to Bishop Reynolds. In 1853 he was appointed Vicar-General of the Diocese of Savannah, under Bishop Gartland. In December, 1853, he formed an *Affiliation of the House of Our Lady of Mercy* at Augusta, and continued for some time to act as its Director. His zeal was conspicuous in every good work. During the prevalence of the yellow-fever at Savannah, in 1853, he volunteered to go to the scene of danger and death, while others were flying from it. There, in union with Bishop Reynolds and his clergy, and Bishop Barron, he devoted himself to the sick and dying. He witnessed the deaths of two priests and two Bishops from the pestilence, and still, with unfaltering courage and true Catholic zeal, he remained active and untiring at the post of duty and of danger.

On the death of Bishop Gartland from yellow-fever, Dr. Barry was appointed Administrator of the diocese. As such he attended the Eighth Council of Baltimore, in May, 1855. He continued to administer the Diocese of Savannah, after Bishop Gartland's death, till 1857, when he was appointed by the Holy See to the vacant See. He was consecrated in the Cathedral at Baltimore by Archbishop Kenrick, on Sunday, August 2, 1857. The assistant Prelates were Bishops Neumann, of Philadelphia, and Portier, of Mobile; and Bishop McGill, of Richmond, preached the consecration sermon.

Returning to the South, Bishop Barry took upon himself the government of the Diocese of Savannah, in which he had for so many years been a zealous and untiring laborer. The cotemporary notices of his episcopal career give a most favorable account of his efforts for the good of his flock. His episcopal visitations were prosecuted with great energy and with great results for his diocese. The following notice of one of his visitations, which were like harvest-times to the gatherer and gleaner, is from a non-Catholic cotemporaneous print, the *Atlanta Examiner:*

"The high character for learning which is awarded to this distinguished Prelate throughout the State, his active benevolence, patriotism, and piety have long since conferred upon him a popularity which but few divines of any denomination can claim to possess. We were glad, therefore, to hear of his visit to his flock in Atlanta, and trust that in future we may all become as familiar with his face, virtues, and usefulness as was Augusta, where for so many years he 'practised what he preached,' and Savannah, in which city he now resides. Confirmation was also administered by the same Right Rev. Prelate at Savannah, on the 28th of November, to 150 persons, several of whom were converts. A new church, commenced last summer at Augusta, is advancing rapidly to completion. At this city, as well as at Macon and Columbus, confirmation was administered shortly before Christmas."

Dr. Barry governed the Diocese of Savannah two years as Administrator, and three years as Bishop. His arduous duties were discharged under the pressure of ill-health, contracted by his long and untiring labors, during thirty-six years of missionary life, and especially by the severe campaign of charity and love, which he went through during the prevalence of the yellow-fever at Savannah in 1855.

Bishop Barry was compelled to seek restoration of health by a visit to Europe. He sailed from New York, July 2, 1859. But his vital powers were entirely spent in the service of God, his Church, and his flock, and he yielded at last to a languishing disease, which prostrated him at the Convent of the Brothers Hospitalers of St. John of God, at Paris, where he had been staying a month previous to his death. During his last illness he received the most tender and affectionate care and attention from the pious Brotherhood of St. John, and was visited by Mgr. Marlot, the Cardinal Archbishop of Paris, who, two days before his death, went to offer consolation and assistance to the dying Prelate. His last days were illustrated by his characteristic virtues, resignation and devotion. He died November 19, 1859, at about the age of sixty years.

RIGHT REV. JOHN HENRY LUERS, D.D.,

First Bishop of Fort Wayne, A.D. 1858.*

THE wisdom with which the Church selects from her children those who are to fill the highest ecclesiastical offices and dignities, has often been regarded as one of the marks of her divine inspiration. At one time we see her selecting from the noblest and wealthiest, and at another from among the sons of her humblest and poorest. She elevates to the episcopacy and cardinalate a Charles Borromeo, a Francis de Sales, from families little removed from royalty; and she bestows like dignities upon a Wolsey, a Thomas of Canterbury, who sprang from the humblest peasantry. Our Saviour, too, gathered around him apostles and disciples from every walk of life, conspicuous amongst whom were the fishermen, whom he called to be the fishers of men. To all alike he said: "Follow thou me." The Church, in like manner, when she selects a successor to the Apostles, simply asks, "Is he worthy?"

It was thus with that worthy Prelate whom the widowed church of Northern Indiana has come to mourn, after our work had been prepared for the press; one who sprang from the humblest sphere, but proved himself worthy of the best ages of the Church.

John Henry Luers was born near the city of Münster,

---

* Compiled chiefly from original material furnished by Archbishop Purcell, and by Rev. E. P. Walters, and from the following authorities: *The Catholic Magazine*, 1846; *The Metropolitan*, 1858; *The New York Freeman's Journal*, 1858 to 1871; *The Ave Maria*, July 15, 1871; *Catholic Telegraph*, July 6, 1871, &c., &c.

Westphalia, a province of Lower Germany, September 29, 1819. His parents, though poor in the goods of this world, were possessed of a generous faith, and well endowed with the graces of religion. They were particularly solicitous for the moral and religious welfare of their children. In 1833 this pious family, urged by poverty, emigrated from their native country, and after a tedious voyage in an emigrant ship, landed at New York, June 7, of the same year, friendless and almost alone. John was then in his fourteenth year. The father of the family, with the characteristic thoughtfulness of his race, lost no time in fruitless efforts to make a livelihood in our Atlantic cities, but pushed onwards towards the West. Ohio was at that time the pioneer State in industry, enterprise, and development, and was particularly attractive for Catholics. The saintly Bishop Edward Fenwick had traversed it from one extremity to another; he had wished to place a priest in every thriving mission or village, but when this was impossible, he girded himself for the work of saving souls, and gave to the poorest hamlets the consolation of his own apostolic ministry. Thus, while struggling to build up his own diocese, he was laying the foundations of the three flourishing Sees of Cincinnati, Cleveland, and Columbus.

Religious training was what the father of this good family mainly desired for his children. Piqua was at that time prominently mentioned as likely to outstrip Cincinnati itself in growth; and located as it was on the Miami River, and being the terminus of the Miami Canal, it connected Cincinnati, on the Ohio River, with Toledo on the Lakes. Here the emigrants determined to settle. Locating themselves upon a farm in the neighborhood of the town, the boys united their labors with those of their father in supporting the family. But John was placed as clerk and assistant salesman in the store of a Protestant merchant in Piqua, where his strict integrity and attention to business won for him the respect and confidence of his employer and all who saw him. But alas! while gaining the encomiums of men, he was losing grace with God. Without deviating from the moral lessons of his youth, he was fast neglecting and forgetting his religion. Upon one occasion, when the young clerk returned home for a short vacation, it fell to his lot in turn to recite the night prayers for the assembled family. To the amazement of the father, his son could not remember a word of his prayers. The Bishop often afterwards jocosely said, whilst reciting this incident, " The subsequent interview between my father and myself was of such a *striking* nature that I received sufficient reasons to promise to relearn what I had forgotten. It was a *sore* lesson, but one which I never forgot."

A most effectual change now manifested itself in his thoughts and feelings. The things of God now greatly engrossed his mind. He began to perceive that those who labor for the salvation of souls were the favored ones of heaven. He even began to sigh to become one of the dwellers in the sanctuary. But how could he acquire the education required for this exalted station, or even cherish a hope of ever attaining it? Events, however, showed that heaven had marked him out for one of its own. It was not long afterwards that Archbishop Purcell, the successor of the saintly Fenwick, visited the vicinity of Piqua, in order to confer confirmation. On the roadside, as he was riding along, he overtook a lad trudging right manfully in the same direction. Impressed with the boy's appearance, the Prelate reined up his horse, and the following conversation ensued :—" Where are you going, my son?" asked the Archbishop. "I am going to Mass, sir," answered the youth. "It is a long way to walk, my boy, and you may get up behind one of these gentlemen," replied the Archbishop, pointing to a priest who was riding by his side. "Thus," said the Archbishop, in preaching the funeral sermon of Bishop Luers, "did I become acquainted with your Bishop thirty-six years ago." The conversation which followed disclosed the young man's religious aspirations, but in his situation there seemed to be no hope of attaining the object of his desire. But the Archbishop inspired him with hope, and remarked to him, "Fear not, my son; if God has destined you for the sanctuary, and has given you a vocation, He will in His wisdom provide the means. But you must pray that God's will may be done." From that moment the desire of devoting himself exclusively to God's service took possession of the heart of young Luers. He became fond of study, and was rarely afterwards seen by the companions of his sports. General M. D. Morrison, then one of his companions, now a Member of Congress from Indiana, has related, since the Bishop's death: "Bishop Luers, when quite a boy with us in Piqua, suddenly stopped playing with the boys, and this being something unusual, we often asked, 'What has become of John Luers? He never comes around with us any more.' The reply given was: 'Why, he's got hold of some old Latin books, and he is studying them; he is going to be a Catholic priest.' The next thing I heard of him was, that he had gone off somewhere to school."

The old Seminary of St. Francis Xavier, in Brown's County, Ohio, conducted by the Lazarists, a religious congregation distinguished for training young men for the ministry, was the only Alma Mater of Bishop Luers. To its classes and privileges he was introduced by Archbishop Purcell, to whom he applied to be received as a candidate for the priesthood. He could not have fallen into the hands of better masters for worldly science, and above all for the science of the saints. It was at the feet of the good sons of St. Vincent that his natural qualities were developed by study and sanctified by grace, until he became a fit instrument in announcing the word of God, and in performing His divine ministry. During his seminary life none gave more evident marks of a sacred vocation, none was more edifying in conduct, none more proficient in study. Bishop Luers did not possess what would be called a quick or brilliant mind, but what was far better, a profound mind. He thoroughly understood the sciences he applied himself to, and mastered them in all their depths and ramifications. His good memory enabled him to treasure up all he acquired, and to draw upon his well-stored mind with aptness and facility. The reports sent by the superiors of the Seminary to Archbishop Purcell, from time to time, were of the most satisfactory character. To a close application to study he united solid piety, ardent zeal, and a generous desire to devote himself to the service of God and the good of his neighbor. Having been found worthy of the exalted office to which he aspired, he was ordained subdeacon by Archbishop Purcell, in the Cathedral of Cincinnati, on All Saints' Day, 1846; deacon on the Feast of St. Charles Borromeo; and on the Feast of St. Martin, November 11, in the twenty-fifth year of his age, he was elevated to the holy priesthood. He was the last priest ordained from the old Seminary in Brown's County, which is now succeeded by the Ursuline Convent of St. Martin.

He zealously embraced the new career of usefulness and labor now opened to him. Archbishop Purcell exhibited great discernment in selecting him, though so young a priest, for one of the most important posts in his diocese. The congregation of St. Joseph's was struggling to erect a church, the walls of which were half up, but a heavy debt was hanging over them and paralyzing every effort. In this emergency Archbishop Purcell appointed the young priest pastor of the new and struggling congregation. From that moment new life was infused into the enterprise, and it was not long before the Archbishop had the consolation of dedicating to the service of God that first fruit of his labors. Not only was the church of St. Joseph finished, but it was also cleared of all encumbrances. But his work was really now only begun. He realized in his own person a remark which he frequently addressed to his own clergy when he was Bishop: "I have somewhere read that more men rust out than wear out; a piece of mechanism is more apt to get out of repair when not employed than when performing its accustomed labor." He took a census of the children of his parish, and discovered one thousand young ones needing instruction. He also found that many parents could only be reached through their children. It was chiefly through the rising generation that the faith could be preserved in a city like Cincinnati, where infidelity and irreligion stalked abroad in the open day, spreading moral poison through all the walks of life, showing contempt for Christianity by devoting the Lord's day to frivolity, self-indulgence, and amusement, and in throwing open the places of dissipation to both sexes and to all ages and conditions. Catholic schools were the weapons he used against these evils. Soon a substantial school-house arose, and the children were gathered in numbers under its roof. He thus had the happiness of seeing those whom he had baptized now reared in the faith, and in a pure and holy life. He made it a rule, while in Cincinnati, to visit the schools every day. How acceptable must have been the atonement for the sins of that city, when from the hearts of so many innocent children arose the prayer of faith and love on high, "May Jesus Christ be beloved!"

"Under his active, zealous care, this large church was rapidly finished," says a recent publication,* "and the large debt as rapidly paid. It soon became, under his pastoral guidance, one of the largest and most important German congregations in the city. In labor, Bishop Luers, during the years of his priesthood, was indefatigable. At St. Joseph's he has left a most eloquent testimony to his great worth. Though he parted from the scenes of his early labors years ago, his former parishioners treasure, in undimmed remembrance, his name and good works, and speak of him as if he were still walking reverent among them. Several whom he baptized and prepared for their first communion, are now worthy priests of the dioceses of Cincinnati and Fort Wayne."

Twelve years of zealous pastoral labor and devotion to the good of his flock rolled around, during which Father Luers won the esteem of his Bishop and the love of his people. In the mean time great changes were being wrought in the Catholic Church of America.

---

* *Catholic Telegraph*, July 6, 1871.

When he was appointed pastor of St. Joseph's, the three States of Ohio, Kentucky, and Indiana, were under the spiritual rule of one Bishop. Catholics were few in numbers, except in the large cities and towns, and did not usually belong to the wealthy classes. Their ranks had been increased to some extent by conversions from the sects. But during the years 1847, 1848, and 1849, causes were at work in Europe which greatly affected the growth in population of the United States, and more than a corresponding increase in the Catholic population. The tide of immigration poured its masses into the United States, and in the three States of Ohio, Kentucky, and Indiana, twenty thousand Catholics were added to our people annually. A multiplication of Catholic dioceses resulted from these causes. Northern Ohio was erected into a separate episcopal see, located at Cleveland. In 1853 Kentucky felt the swelling tide, and the eastern part of the State was formed into the diocese of Covington. Indiana had not yet increased her Catholic population to the same extent, owing in part to the location and physical formation of the State. Her shape is long and narrow, being two hundred and seventy-five miles long, and about one hundred and seventy-five miles wide. A traveler from Ohio, on reaching the Wabash, would imagine himself in a different country. The southern part of the State, in which Vincennes is located, is high, hilly, and rolling; that portion which lies north of the Wabash is level, flat, and, in 1846, was marshy, requiring a vast expenditure of labor and money before it could be rendered available for cultivation. Besides the more favorable condition of Southern Indiana, in respect to soil and topographical formation, it was thrifty and prosperous, and was readily and conveniently reached by immigrants following the Ohio, then the great highway of travel. But Northern Indiana was the route to the great North-west; railroads were constructed across her bosom, ditches were opened at the public expense, and competition of travel enlivened and enriched her territory; and what had been regarded as a vast morass now became a blooming garden. The University of Notre Dame, located at South Bend, contributed its share in changing the face of the country; Fort Wayne, at the junction of the St. Mary's and St. Joseph's rivers, suddenly became a place of importance, as did also Logansport, Lafayette, Laporte, and other flourishing towns, in which churches had been erected and schools established. It was under these circumstances of progress and development, added to the remoteness of the northern half of the State of Indiana from Vincennes, that the Right Rev. Bishop de St. Palais proposed its erection into a separate diocese. The military highway, known as the National Road, which divided the State in two, was chosen as the dividing line; the Provincial Council adopted the suggestion, and Rome ratified the action of the Council. It was thus that the diocese of Fort Wayne was created in 1857.

The wisdom of the Council was still further manifested in the selection of Father Luers as the first Bishop of Fort Wayne, a result least anticipated by himself and by the congregation of St. Joseph's. He humbly bowed his head to the mandate of the Holy Ghost, expressed through Rome and the Council, exclaiming, "Behol ! thy servant, O Lord!" He was consecrated in the Cathedral of Cincinnati, the same temple that had witnessed his ordination as a priest, by Archbishop Purcell

January 10, 1858. The assistant Prelates were the Right Rev. Maurice de St. Palais, Bishop of Vincennes, and the Right Rev. George Aloysius Carrell, Bishop of Covington. The assistants in the Pontifical Mass were the Very Rev. E. T. Collins, Vicar-General, Archdeacon, and the Rev. Messrs. J. Abrinck, of Pomeroy, and C. H. Borgess, of Columbus, now Bishop of Detroit, deacon and subdeacon. The solemnity of the occasion was increased by the presence of the representatives of many religious orders, amongst whom was the Right. Rev. Boniface Wimmer, mitred Abbot of the Benedictine Convent of St. Vincent at Latrobe, Pennsylvania. The consecration sermon was preached by Dr. Spalding, the present Archbishop of Baltimore.

But on the same day with his consecration a tribute was rendered to the newly consecrated Bishop, which was a striking evidence of his recognized worth and services, and of the pious gratitude of his devoted flock. The entire congregation of St. Joseph's came forth in the afternoon of January 10, to testify their love for the pastor whom they were about to lose, their appreciation for his labors, and their admiration for his virtues. The new Bishop was requested to meet them at the altar of St. Joseph's, the scene of his long and faithful missionary career. "The sanctuary was brilliantly illumined, the church thronged to overflowing. A framework erected in the sanctuary bore, in the midst of light, appropriate texts of Scripture; the choir commenced the proceedings with a hymn. The Rev. Mr. Stehle, aided by the Rev. Mr. Somers, who were afterwards charged with the care of the congregation, arranged rich offerings appertaining to the episcopal capelle and office on a credence table, and an address was read to the new Bishop. The little boys and girls of the school, handsomely dressed, the girls in white and wearing bright crowns, the young unmarried men and ladies, the fathers and mothers of families, the officers of religious societies, and all the German Catholics of Cincinnati, through their able representative Father Otto, had a word and a gift for their Right. Rev. friend, the delivery of which was interspersed with music from the choir. It was a heart-offering from all present to the merit and virtues of the faithful pastor now leaving them. The Archbishop, and the Right Rev. Bishops of Vincennes and Covington, who were in the sanctuary, were deeply affected by this exhibition of an entire people's gratitude and faith." * A large delegation of both Catholics and Protestants from Fort Wayne met the congregation of St. Joseph at Cincinnati, and thus voices of gratitude, benediction, and farewell were mingled with those of future joy, loyalty, and promise. Bishop Luers took leave of St. Joseph's congregation in the afternoon. Another witness of these impressive scenes has thus written: "It was a touching sight to see St. Joseph's congregation on last Sunday afternoon, when the Bishop of Fort Wayne came to say 'Farewell.' Not a dry eye could be seen in the crowded edifice, and sobs were frequently heard breaking the solemn stillness of the church. After the exercises were over in the church the newly consecrated Prelate visited the schools, and here, to see and hear the tokens of sorrow everywhere visible, became perfectly painful; and it was only after repeated assurances that he would often visit them could their grief be restrained. Kneeling to receive his blessing, with a thousand wishes for his welfare, the impressive scene closed."

---

* *Catholic Telegraph*, 1858.

In a day or two afterwards Bishop Luers departed for his new home, and lost no time in taking possession of his see, and in commencing the exalted and arduous work before him. He arrived towards evening, alone and unannounced, carrying his traveling-bag in his hand, at the door of the residence of Very Rev. Father Benoit. A day or two afterwards, when the gentlemen who had in charge the preparations for extending to the Bishop a public and honorable reception at Fort Wayne, came to the house to inquire when he was expected to arrive, great was their surprise when the Bishop opened the door for them and answered their inquiries in person. Their disappointment was lost sight of in their admiration for his humility, while the Bishop enjoyed himself mirthfully at their expense.

Bishop Luers found his diocese poorer than he even expected. A small frame church, which had grown almost dilapidated in the service, was his only Cathedral. A neat brick building, erected by the Rev. A. Bessonies during an absence of Father Benoit in Louisiana, was the episcopal residence. Father Benoit, whom he appointed his Vicar-General, was a veteran missionary of nearly a quarter of a century of zealous labor; he had traversed the length and breadth of the diocese in its service, and thoroughly understood its history, its condition, and its necessities. In him the Bishop found a zealous and invaluable vicar and co-laborer. The diocese of Fort Wayne embraced a territory one hundred and twenty miles long and one hundred and seventy miles wide, comprising thirty-eight counties, with a scattered Catholic population of twenty thousand souls, whose spiritual wants were supplied by eleven secular priests and three priests of the Congregation of the

Holy Cross, engaged on the mission. These twenty churches, if such they could be called, were mostly of the poorest description, and wholly unable to accommodate one-half of the congregations. Many places were destitute of both churches and priests. The Bishop seemed to possess the faculty of ubiquity in his efforts to supply their necessities himself. He was from this circumstance seldom at home, and it might be said that his episcopal palace was a railroad car. On one day he would be in a remote corner of his diocese, and in a day or two afterwards he would be heard of in quite an opposite quarter, preaching, offering Mass, and administering the sacraments. His answer to the many petitions he received for resident priests, was a generous effort to bestow upon the congregations the efforts of his own ministry. He fervently prayed for the advent of more priests to his diocese; and within the first year of his episcopate two priests were ordained for the diocese, and he welcomed them as messengers sent from Heaven in answer to his prayers. So earnest were his efforts in this regard that in two years he could point to eight more clergymen ordained by himself. He had also eight ecclesiastical students in preparation for the sacred office in various seminaries. This supply scarcely diminished the demand for priests, for in the same short period his Catholic flock was increased by more than twenty-five thousand.

Bishop Luers gave his early attention to the work of erecting a Cathedral worthy of his Diocese. Father Benoit had already matured plans for that purpose, and in the spring of 1859 the present Cathedral—a Gothic building one hundred and eighty feet long by eighty feet wide, with two towers in front—was undertaken. The corner-stone was laid by Archbishop Purcell on Trinity Sunday of that year, and such was the energy of the Bishop and his Vicar-General, that it was under roof before winter. It was thrown open to the thousands who crowded to see its graceful proportions, and to attend a grand fair held within its unfinished walls, in order to defray the expense of its completion. Other places soon emulated Fort Wayne in the erection of fine churches, in which they were warmly encouraged by the Bishop, who had the happiness every year of laying the corner-stone of two or three fine churches, ranging in value from fifteen to forty thousand dollars. In these works he was warmly seconded by his zealous clergy, most of whom had been educated in the diocese, and under his eye, and were devoted to him as he was to them. He was remarkable for his affection for his priests. The same interest he manifested in them while they were students of the Diocese continued and increased when he recognized in them the laborers in the Lord's vine yard. It was remarked that he never spoke disparagingly of any of them, but delighted in commending and encouraging their labors, and in speaking of them in praise. He also took pleasure in assisting them, and in sharing with them the labors of the mission. He would frequently travel all night, at great inconvenience, in order to arrive at an early hour at places where he was announced or expected. On his arrival he would repair to the confessional, and hear the confessions of the people until his time for saying Mass arrived. He was devoted to the celebration of the holy sacrifice, esteeming it the greatest privilege of his life. It made no difference at what hour of the night or morning he arrived at a place, he was found at the altar at the early hour of six. He used to say: "God derives more glory from the celebration of one Mass than from the praise of all the angels in heaven. Ought not priests to give God that glory, at no matter what personal inconvenience?" This love of the holy sacrifice sometimes brought him in contact with strange characters and amusing occurrences. On one occasion he arrived at the house of a priest at an early hour; the priest was ill, and was attended by an odd, though well-meaning yet impetuous, character as a nurse, who, on hearing loud knocks at the door, threw up the window and addressed the intruder as follows:— "Be off to . . . . out of that! Don't you know his reverence is sick, and can't go on sick-calls? A pretty time of the day you are calling." The window closed amid a shower of abuse on the unknown Bishop. He quietly walked, valise in hand, to the convent, where he met with a cordial reception. He said, "There was a man down at Father . . . .'s house who ordered me to rather warm quarters, but I thought it better to come and say Mass." The visit was well timed, for the good nuns had not enjoyed the consolation of Mass in their community for some time.

Bishop Luers was prompt, and at the same time prudent, in checking and correcting any irregularities he observed in the management of ecclesiastical interests. A custom prevailed in many of the congregations of having one or more laymen to aid the pastor in providing and managing the temporalities of the churches. Bishop Luers discovered that this custom, in several cases, led to encroachments upon the rights of the pastor, and savored somewhat of lay-trusteeism, which had been fruitful of such serious evils in other dioceses. He resolved to arrest the evil at once. He availed himself of the first retreat of the clergy, and of the synod following it, to apply the correction. He was in the habit of holding a biennial retreat for the clergy; he now made arrangements for holding these spiritual exercises at the University of Notre Dame, an accommodation which resulted in great advantage to the clergy and diocese of Fort Wayne. He gave notice that the next retreat would be held at the University of Notre Dame, on August 18, 1863; its exercises were conducted by the gifted Father Smarius, S.J., and after the retreat followed the Diocesan Synod. At this assembly Bishop Luers, in a few well-timed remarks, exposed the evil he desired to correct; statutes were enacted for that purpose, regulating the temporalities of the churches, the relations of the clergy and laity to the temporalities, and defining the duties of all. The result was the ultimate withdrawal of laymen from all control over church temporalities, and the establishment of peace and good understanding throughout the diocese.

Bishop Luers was distinguished for his devotion to the Holy See. He had long desired to go in person to visit the shrine of the Apostles, to inhale the religious and inspiring air of the Eternal City, to manifest his loyalty to the Vicar of Christ on earth, and to receive the blessing of our Holy Father Pius IX. He had a profound appreciation for the grand and symbolical services of the Church, and had ever endeavored to present them to his people, in his own chaste but modest Cathedral, with becoming beauty and solemnity. To visit the grand basilicas of Rome became a cherished object with him, and especially that mighty pile in which the genius of religion became enshrined under the magic touch of Michael Angelo, and in which,

"From each carved nook, and fretted bend,
Cornice and gallery seemed to send
Tones that with Seraph's hymns might blend."

He started upon his pilgrimage to Rome May 22, 1864, accompanied by his chaplain, Rev. A. Oechtering, leaving the administration of his diocese in the hands of Father Benoit. His European tour was most gratifying to him, and at the same time most beneficial to his diocese. He visited Louvain, that old Catholic monument of learning, and by his earnest appeals and winning manners, secured the services of four young levites for the diocese of Fort Wayne. At Rome he was received with great kindness and affectionate regard by the Holy Father, who conferred on him a mark of his confidence and esteem, in empowering him to draw up a Constitution and Rules for the Community of Sisters of the Holy Cross in America, as an independent organization from the mother-house of the same Order in France. These good Sisters had struggled through difficulties for years; it was impossible for the Order in France to understand the position and requirements of the community in the young and growing West, and nothing but embarrassment grew out of the relation. The Holy See, after long but prudent delays, confided their interests to Bishop Luers, who on his return, with the assistance of Father Sourin, Priest of the Holy Cross, and of Mother Angela, Sister of the Holy Cross, prepared a new Constitution and Rule for the Order in America. His work was approved by the Sovereign Pontiff, and under their new institute the good Sisters have advanced in prosperity and usefulness a hundred-fold.

Bishop Luers found in the Order of the Holy Cross, with its priests, brothers, and sisters, most valuable auxiliaries in the great and good work he achieved for his diocese. He honored and cherished these holy colaborers with paternal affection and encouragement; and they, in their turn, have enriched his diocese with the fine University of Notre Dame; have taken charge of eleven female academies, an orphan asylum, six religious institutions, and forty parish schools. Such has been the growth of the Order of the Holy Cross in the diocese of Fort Wayne, that they have been able to carry the blessings of their institute to many other dioceses. They numbered at the time of Bishop Luers's death twenty-one priests in the diocese, six scholastics, ninety-one professed brothers, fifty-two novices, and ten postulants. Besides these were the excellent Sisters of Providence, introduced at Fort Wayne by Father Benoit, while it was embraced in the diocese of Vincennes. These Sisters established, under Bishop Luers, the Academy of St. Ignatius at Lafayette. Under Bishop Luers's administration were also introduced into the diocese of Fort Wayne the Sisters of the Precious Blood, who have charge of St. Mary's Home, in Jay County.

In his visitations of his diocese, and in his labors among his flock, Bishop Luers was untiring. He frequently went through his diocese, visiting one town or village after another, instructing the people, conferring confirmation and first communion after having first prepared the recipients of these sacraments in many instances himself, hearing confessions, laying the cornerstones of new churches, dedicating and consecrating new temples of the faith already finished, projecting and providing sites for others, founding parish schools, and placing them under the care of the Brothers and Sisters of the Holy Cross, and performing every work of the holy ministry and every deed of Christian charity. In all these labors he took pains to present the ceremonies of the Church to the public eye with imposing splendor and touching effect. He preached frequently, and with great impression upon his hearers. Although he commenced his studies late in life, it was remarked of him, that in his discourses he gave proof of a thoroughly trained and educated intellect. The progress made by religion in his diocese, during his administration, attests his zeal, his energy, and his labor. Fifty churches and ten chapels were erected in the diocese of Fort Wayne during his episcopate, in addition to the rebuilding of the Cathedral and other churches, and six new churches were in course of erection at the time of his death. The whole number of the clergy at the commencement of his administration was twenty; at his death he left over twenty-one regular priests, forty-eight seculars, and ten clerical students. Houses of charity and education were multiplied, and the Catholic population of the diocese was more than doubled during the thirteen years that he governed it. His metropolitan, Archbishop Purcell, under whose eye his studies as a candidate and missionary labors as a priest were performed, has said that he presided over the See and diocese of Fort Wayne "with marked ability and zeal." The Catholic journals and statistics of the last thirteen years show that his career was a most active, laborious, and useful one, and that his death inflicted a serious loss on the Church in this country.

Bishop Luers was remarkable for his charity to the poor, and to the orphans especially he was a provident father and most tender and solicitous guardian. His heart was pierced with grief at the sight of the many orphans who were left destitute by our late civil war. Many of them were Catholics, and while the State felt great sympathy for them, it was but too clear that their greatest danger consisted in the public provision which was about to be made for their support, and which, while it generously provided for their temporal wants, would expose them to the greatest misfortunes in eternity, the loss of their faith. Bishop Luers resolved to devote himself to this good work with all the energy and zeal of his character. He purchased a tract of land in the suburbs of Fort Wayne, in the spring of 1865, as the site of his orphan asylum, and Father Benoit and his successor, the Rev. E. P. Walters, undertook to solicit subscriptions for the erection of the necessary buildings. In the fall of 1865, a solemn Jubilee was proclaimed by our Holy Father, Pope Pius IX., and among the conditions for gaining the indulgence was that of bestowing alms upon some object of charity designated by the ordinary of the diocese. Bishop Luers gladly availed himself of this opportunity, by designating the orphan asylum as the object of their charity on this occasion. He addressed several earnest and eloquent pastorals to his flock on this subject; the following extracts from that which he issued on the feast of the Assumption, 1866, will illustrate his zeal and efforts in this good work :—

"In our day, many sympathize as little with poor Jesus as did the Jews of old, who only longed for a rich Messiah. They seek Him to this day without finding Him, as Christ Himself told them. The promises of God in regard to the poor are disregarded, because the baneful vices of avarice and pride have taken possession of their hearts, as was the case with the Jews, and their imitators in all ages. The spirit of religion and the love of neighbor impelled our forefathers to erect magnificent churches, schools, orphan asylums, hospitals, universities, and other like institutions, to give learned men and saints to the land. Within these institutions men were trained for the object of their existence, and while the *Te Deum* resounds within those time-honored walls, it is re-echoed by the saints above, who erected those buildings."

Bishop Luers intended to commence the erection of the asylum in the fall of 1866, but unavoidable delays occurred in carrying out his plans. In the mean time, he learned that a large tract of land in Jasper County, affording a more suitable site for the proposed establishment, was offered for sale. At the spiritual retreat of the clergy held at the University of Notre Dame, in 1867, he announced the proposed change of location to the pastors, who cordially approved his views and pledged themselves to their support. Immediately after the close of the retreat, Bishop Luers issued an admirable address on the subject of this cherished work, from which the following extracts are taken:—

"Dearly Beloved in Christ: The number of orphans has lately increased to such an extent, that the erection of an asylum for them has become an imperative necessity. It is a holy duty, incumbent upon us all, to take care of the spiritual and bodily wants of those who have no longer father and mother to do it for them, and who like strangers now wander over God's wide earth imploring our pity, mercy, and love.

"A year ago I purchased twenty-five acres of land adjoining this city, for the purpose of building such an asylum upon it, but as yet it has not been commenced.

"On this all-important matter I consulted with the clergy lately assembled in spiritual retreat at Notre Dame, and as building materials and labor are yet very high, the building to be erected would cost from $30,000 to $35,000, which amount would have to be on hand immediately. To obtain this seems to be a matter of impossibility. It was therefore unanimously agreed to accept the favorable offer of the Spilter Farm at Rensellaer for $18,000.

"This place contains nine hundred and thirty-three acres; six hundred and fifty of which are under fence, two hundred under cultivation, two hundred wood, the balance prairie. There are on it two dwelling-houses, one of which contains twelve rooms, affording accommodation for forty or fifty orphans.

"Experience teaches that not a few of those who have been raised in the asylums of our large cities, for want of suitable employment and from other unavoidable causes, have not realized the expectations, considering the extraordinary care and attention bestowed upon them. Here, upon the farm selected, the children can have employment suitable to their age and strength, and growing up with industrious habits, they can become men who will be an honor to the institution and a source of consolation to their benefactors."

In drawing a picture of the wants and privations which emigrants experience in coming to America, the good Bishop must have recalled his own sufferings, and was thus well qualified by observation to place himself in the position of the orphan in making the appeal:—"Who amongst immigrants," he writes, "has not more or less experienced the feelings of the orphan? when the storm raged on the ocean and the end seemed nigh, far away from home, from father, mother, kindred, and friends, an indescribable longing after home weighed down the anxious heart, and a sense of utter loneliness stole over the whole being. Friend, have you forgotten the journey? With the grace of God you safely reached your destination, America. But here again strange faces; strange manners and customs, a strange language perhaps, like so many insurmountable barriers, rose up before you. You felt alone, discouraged, forsaken, in short, an orphan. A longing after the lately abandoned fireside and friends almost overpowered you, and in the long, long hours of anguish and desolation, silently and unseen, many a scalding tear trickled down your cheek. How happy were you when meeting a true friend who took an interest in you, and by word and deed came to your aid, one who supplied the place of father and mother in your regard in that trying hour. This raised you up, made you what you are, secured you the place and position in society which you now occupy, and of which you are justly proud. Had you not met with such a friend, what might have become of you? What in all probability would you not be? This kindness and love, which in your poverty and misery you received from others, bestow in turn upon the orphan."

Having purchased the Spilter Farm, Bishop Luers appointed Rev. George Steiner, Rev. J. Mayer, Rev. P. P. Cooney, and Rev. E. P. Walter to solicit contributions throughout the diocese, and to prepare the buildings for the reception of the orphans. Rev. Joseph Stephens was placed in charge of the property and of the immediate preparation for the orphans. The Bishop struggled through many discouragements, and overcame almost despair. In September, 1868, he had the happiness of seeing the Sisters of the Holy Cross welcoming to the farm-houses thirty-five destitute orphans. Soon the number increased to sixty. He gave a considerable portion of his time and personal attention to the improvement of the farm, in seeing it fenced, drained, and cultivated. On the approach of Christmas, 1869, he issued the following circular on this subject so dear to his heart:—

FORT WAYNE, December 10, 1869.

To the Clergy and Laity of the Diocese :—

We shall soon celebrate the Festival which commemorates the Birth of the Redeemer of the world, and presents to our view the Divine Babe lying in the manger of Bethlehem.

The recurrence of this Festival is an occasion of great joy, especially to those families whose members habitually fulfil their religious duties; and if in some there is negligence in the service of God during the year, Christmas is a time of reconciliation; all may, therefore, participate in the joy of this Festival.

In these days of rejoicing, when you give thanks to God for the birth of your Saviour, and for all the spiritual gifts that flow therefrom, as well as the comforts of life which you have received from His bountiful hand, remember the poor and the orphans who appeal to you to help them in their need, to clothe them and give them shelter from the frost and rain, and to prevent them from perishing with hunger.

As God has given you the fruits of this world, lay up for yourselves a treasure in heaven, by giving of your abundance to those who are in want. Do not be grudge a couple of dollars to the orphans. Be more manly, more *human* and more generous than to make a wry face over a small portion of your abundance given to the poor. God loves a cheerful giver. Do not, then, part with a few dollars as if so many sound teeth were being pulled out of your head. Open wide your purse, give with a generous heart; avoid the stigma of stinginess, that mark of little souls and sordid hearts. Have a laudable respect for yourselves as men occupying respectable positions in society, as Christians professing to be followers of our Lord, who loved the poor, and do not give merely twenty-five cents when you could give four times that amount; do not place ten cents upon the collection-plate when you could give at least half that number of dollars.

That you may all have an opportunity of fulfilling your duty of giving alms, we hereby direct that on Christmas day the usual collection be made in all the churches and stations, for the benefit of the Orphan Asylum, in which you should all take the greatest interest.

Invoking upon you the abundant graces which the Infant Jesus desires to bestow upon you all, and most particularly wishing that your hearts may be touched by compassion for God's suffering poor, we commend you all to the Sacred Heart of Jesus and to the patronage of Our Lady of the Sacred Heart.

The alms given on the occasion of the Jubilee should be forwarded to us without delay.

In the stations the collection for the orphans should be made as soon as possible after the Festival.

Pastors are requested to read this letter to their parishioners, as has hitherto been the custom, and to urge upon them the necessity of contributing liberally for the support of the orphans.

Given at Fort Wayne, the 10th day of December, Feast of the Translation of the House of Nazareth.

✠ JOHN HENRY,
Bishop of Fort Wayne.

The Asylum of St. Joseph soon became self-sustaining. It was placed under the government of a body of priests of the diocese selected by the Bishop, and became an incorporated institution. He frequently visited the Asylum, and was never so happy as when surrounded by these innocent children. He used to mark out some special work for them on the farm, and then superintend its performance. He took part in their devotions and in their sports. He rewarded them with presents for good conduct, and frequently acted as arbiter in their disputes. On one occasion he proposed to take the vote of the orphans, whether he should present them with one large foot-ball or a dozen hand-balls. The little group soon became warmly divided in sentiment on the question, and no village election could have been conducted with more spirit and excitement. For two days the discussion and contest waged, and the vote stood equally divided, when a little deaf mute, who seemed as much excited over the question as if he had heard and taken part in the debate, came forward and gave the deciding vote in favor of the foot-ballers. A loud shout announced the result, and the Bishop, who had exceedingly enjoyed the scene, not only threw the coveted toy in their midst, but remained to see the game. He was ever the most welcome visitor to St. Joseph's, and his visits were hailed with joy and announced by every tongue. He never allowed a Christmas to pass without an appeal and a collection in their favor. After his death, it was discovered that he had had his life insured for $10,000 for their benefit.

His affection for his clergy has already been mentioned. He felt a deep interest in all that concerned them, and especially in providing for their support in old age. He earnestly favored the plan of providing for the support of aged priests throughout the United States, and called the attention of the Second Plenary Council of Baltimore to this important subject. In the absence of any general provision on this point, he adopted a plan for his own diocese, and encouraged the formation of the Catholic Clerical Benevolent Association of the Diocese of Fort Wayne. This society became incorporated for the period of twelve years, by which time funds enough will have accumulated to give an annual pension of five hundred dollars to each member.

Bishop Luers on many occasions became a public champion and defender of the faith. In the northern portions of his diocese the German population predominated among the Catholics, and German pastors' were given to them. The sectarian ministers took an ungenerous advantage of this circumstance by challenging these pastors to public controversy, knowing their inability to conduct a discussion in English on anything like fair terms. In the case of the Rev. Father Oshtering, who had received a good English education in this country, these tricky controversialists met with a great surprise and an overwhelming and silencing defeat. But in many cases no such champion was at hand; but Bishop Luers, who watched the interests of his whole flock, was ever ready to go to their defence. On such occasions he managed to have business at the place where the attack was made, and by his sermons and lectures completely silenced the assailants. On another occasion, the election of a Catholic citizen on the School-Board at Lafayette gave occasion to the most bitter and insulting attacks upon the Church and her ministers, from the press and the pulpit. Bishop Luers went to this town to administer confirmation, and he availed himself of the opportunity of reminding Catholics of their duties in regard to the Catholic education of their children; and illustrated his remarks by alluding to the Commune of Paris, which he regarded as a result of Atheistic education. On the following day he was violently attacked by the secular press, and his remarks were greatly misrepresented. He replied in a card, from which the following extract is taken:—

"It is with me a matter of sincere regret that our non-Catholic friends will not understand the Catholic position upon the so-called public school question. We do not object to Protestants sending their children to the public schools, nor to their supporting them by a tax or in any other way they may deem fit. We have not the slightest intention of interfering with their existence. They may, perhaps, think they are well adapted to the wants of those who patronize them, but Catholic parents, who realize the sacred obligations of preparing their children not only for this life but for the life to come, prefer to see their children in schools where religious instruction and moral discipline go hand in hand with secular education. Many Catholics regard it a hardship that they should be taxed to support a school system that they do not and cannot approve; but in Indiana it is the creature of the State Constitution, and until that instrument is changed or amended in this particular, Catholics as law-abiding citizens must continue to bear their share of the burden, as well as assume their share of the responsibility."

Bishop Luers attended the Provincial Councils of Cincinnati, and sat in the Second Plenary Council of Baltimore, which assembled on the first Sunday of October, 1866. He was one of the Prelates excused from attending the Œcumenical Council of the Vatican, convened by our Holy Father Pius IX., on account of the pressing necessities of his own diocese, and in order that he might also exercise the functions of the episcopal office in favor of other and neighboring dioceses. He afterwards expressed his regret that he was not present in that august assembly, to testify his homage to the Vice-Gerent of Christ, and to record his *Credo* on the sublime truths therein defined, and especially in favor of the dogma of Papal Infallibility. He, however, rendered important services to religion in his own and in other dioceses whose Bishops were at Rome. He was most of the time absent from home, laboring for the good of souls, and the amount of work accomplished by him was extraordinary. He administered confirmation in almost every county of three States, and holy orders in most of the ecclesiastical seminaries. His services were greatly sought after, because he was ever ready to do good, and because of his simplicity of character, indifference to attentions, and his easy, gentle, and paternal manners. It was while rendering services in another diocese that he was stricken down in death, with his armor on, and in the fresh odor of many good deeds and saintly virtues.

At the request of Very Rev. Edward Hannin, Administrator of the Diocese of Cleveland, Bishop Luers went to that city, where he arrived on the evening of June 28, 1871, to administer holy orders to some of the ecclesiastical students of the Seminary. On the following morning he said Mass at half-past five, and then gave minor orders to three seminarians, and deaconship to another. After breakfast he started on foot, satchel in hand, to take the train for another diocese, where he intended to perform a similar service, intending to call on the way at the episcopal residence at Cleveland. A carriage had been ordered to the Seminary for him, but as he felt so well he preferred walking. When within a few rods of the Bishop's house, he fell, on the corner of Bond and St. Clair streets, from apoplexy and the bursting of a blood-vessel. Those who ran to his aid, perceiving that he was an ecclesiastic, carried him to the Bishop's house, where he received absolution, extreme unction, and the last indulgence. He expired in fifteen or twenty minutes after the fall. His remains were carried, in a funeral train draped in mourning, from Cleveland to Fort Wayne, escorted by clergymen and laymen from both dioceses; other delegations joined the sad and solemn funeral at various points on the way, and on arriving at Cleveland every honor which veneration, love, and religion could suggest was paid to his memory. A delegation from St. Joseph's Church, Cincinnati, went to pay their last tribute of love and gratitude to their former pastor. His funeral took place at the Cathedral of Fort Wayne, on July 4, and was attended by Archbishop Purcell, Bishops De St. Palais, O'Hara, Toebbe, McCloskey, of Louisville, and Borgess; by the Very Rev. Edward Hannin, of Cleveland, and by a large concourse of the clergy and laity. Archbishop Purcell delivered a glowing eulogy on the virtues and services of the deceased. His remains were deposited in a vault immediately in front of the altar, under the floor of the sanctuary in the Cathedral.

RIGHT REV. PETER JOSEPH LAVIALLE, D.D.,

*Third Bishop of Louisville, A.D. 1865.**

PETER JOSEPH LAVIALLE was born in the village of his own name, Lavialle, near Mauriac, Province of Auvergne, France, in 1820. He enjoyed the fine advantages of early religious and secular education, in which his native province abounded. He dedicated himself and his all to the service of the Almighty. From the time of his first communion he made choice of his vocation. He was trained in theology by those learned and devout men, the Fathers of St. Sulpice. It was from such preceptors as Fathers Olier, Odin, Garnier, and Duclot, that he not only imbibed theological learning, but also that distinguishing trait of strict regularity in all spiritual concerns for which he was remarkable. He was a student of theology in France, in 1842, when his relative, the Right Rev. Guy Ignatius Chabrât, then Coadjutor Bishop of Louisville, invited him to join that diocese. Arriving at Louisville, he continued his studies in· the diocesan Seminary, and was ordained in the holy ministry in 1844. He was then selected to assist in the pastoral and parochial duties at the Cathedral, a position which he filled with zeal and fidelity for about five years. In 1849 he was appointed professor of theology in the Seminary of St. Thomas, which had been founded by Bishop David, and built up to eminent usefulness by his efforts and example. Such was his ability for the dis-

---

* Compiled chiefly from a *Notice of Bishop Lavialle* by Hon. B. J. Webb, and from cotemporaneous publications.

charge of duties connected with teaching and governing institutions of learning, that after having been seven years professor at St. Thomas' Seminary, he was appointed in 1856 president of St. Mary's College, and continued to discharge the duties of that responsible position. During the life of the venerable Bishop Flaget, a warm and holy friendship existed between him and Bishop Lavialle.

In 1865, when Dr. Spalding was transferred from the See of Louisville to the Archiepiscopal See of Baltimore, the Rev. Mr. Lavialle was selected as his successor.* More than once before had the episcopal dignity been tendered to him and declined; and in 1860 he returned the bulls appointing him to Louisiana. No longer able to resist the wishes of Rome, he accepted the See of Louisville, and was consecrated September 24, 1865. With all his energies, and with truly apostolic zeal, he continued the glorious work in Kentucky, which had been commenced and prosecuted by Bishops Flaget, David, and Spalding. He visited his diocese several times during his short episcopate, and bestowed especial attention upon every part of it. It has well been remarked of him, that " Not even the smallest congregation of his diocese has failed to receive the benefits of his personal labors in their midst; and not a religious house is there under the jurisdiction of the See that he has not frequently visited, and where his presence has not brought renewed spiritual life." New churches arose

---

* Bishop David was not Bishop of Louisville in the order of succession, but only Coadjutor Bishop; so also was the Right Rev. G. I. Chabrât, who resigned in consequence of his loss of sight, and is now living in retirement in France. The Second Bishop of Louisville, in the order of succession, was Bishop Spalding, who, on his translation to the Archiepiscopal See of Baltimore, was succeeded by the Right Rev. Dr. Lavialle, as Third Bishop of Louisville.

in various parts of the diocese under his inspiring labors and exertions; and it may be mentioned as an example of his successful and untiring endeavors, that besides the new churches erected elsewhere, he built in his episcopal city of Louisville, during his short episcopate of two years, no less than four new churches. "It would seem," says the notice from which this memoir is chiefly compiled, "as if he had taken for his motto the words of his blessed Master, as recorded by St. John, 'I must work the works of Him that sent me while it is day; the night cometh, when no man can work.'"

His physical strength was unequal to the labors and fatigues which his energy and zeal imposed upon him. He allowed himself no relaxation or repose from "the works of Him that sent" him. His feeble health yielded under the struggle, and it became necessary for him to retire for a time, in the hope of renewing his strength for further labors. He retired for several weeks to St. Joseph's Infirmary of the Sisters of Charity, and next went to Nazareth, near Bardstown, where for a time he seemed to improve under the tender and careful nursing of the good Sisters. His disease, however, was too deeply seated in his constitution to yield to treatment; his strength gradually failed, and his body gradually sank, until May 11, 1867, when he calmly and resignedly expired, manifesting to the last the exalted virtues which had illustrated his whole life. His untimely death was deeply lamented by his flock, who gratefully appreciated his virtues and were much attached to his person.

A distinguished member of his flock has appropriately said of his lamented friend and Bishop:—

"The evidences of one's vocation are generally of

easy recognition. In the case of our late Bishop, they were so apparent as to have been frequently remarked upon by those who had opportunities to observe his manner of life. He appeared to be at all times duly impressed with the responsibilities he had assumed; and more particularly was this the case after he became a Bishop in the Church of God. In him, heart and mind, body and soul, were as holocausts freely offered to the Divine Head of the Church for his own sanctification and for that of his people. The Bishop had proposed before the end of the present month (May, 1867), to visit Rome in company with a number of his episcopal brothers. For twenty years he had not seen any member of his immediate family. A friend, some time ago, had informed him of the preparations which his aged mother had been making for the reception of her honored son and expected guest. He was heard on several occasions to speak of the pleasure he anticipated in once more seeing and conversing with her. In this world they will meet no more; but we must trust that they have already met in the mansion of their Father in heaven. While the dews of death were gathering on his face, the news arrived that she had preceded him to the eternal home, where there shall be no more parting of loved ones—having passed from earth on Passion Sunday."*

The death of Bishop Lavialle was a severe blow to the Church of Kentucky, which he had faithfully served for twenty-five years, and was received with unfeigned grief by his devoted flock. A delegation of two hundred gentlemen of Louisville went to Nazareth to escort

---

* *Reminiscences*, etc., by Hon. B. J. Webb.

the remains of the deceased Prelate to his Cathedral. Twenty priests chanting the appropriate hymns, sixty Sisters of Charity, with over two hundred of their pupils, united with the Louisville delegation in following the deceased to the depot, and on arriving at Louisville, the procession was augmented by three thousand members of the various societies of that city. After a preliminary burial service by the Very Rev. B. J. Spalding, and a sermon by the Rev. Father Schacht, the afflicted and bereaved flock poured into the Cathedral, to gaze for the last time upon the countenance of their beloved father and Bishop. On the following day a solemn Requiem Mass was offered for the repose of the soul of the deceased, in the presence of the children of the parochial schools, who filled the Cathedral. The third day's services consisted of the closing funeral service, a solemn Requiem, attended by three Archbishops : the Most Rev. Dr. Spalding, of Baltimore, the Most Rev. Dr. Purcell, of Cincinnati, and the Most Rev. Dr. P. R. Kenrick, of St. Louis ; by five Bishops: the Right Rev. Doctors de St Palais, of Vincennes, Luers, of Fort Wayne, Carrell, of Covington, Rosecrans, of Cincinnati, and Feehan, of Nashville, and by sixty-two priests and a thronged congregation. After the close of the solemn Mass of Requiem, the Most Rev. Archbishop Spalding pronounced a glowing eulogy of his deceased colleague, and eloquently dwelt upon his many virtues and his great services to the Church of the West.

The following tribute to the virtues and labors of Bishop Lavialle is taken from a cotemporary non-Catholic print: * " The news of the death of the above-named pious Prelate of the Roman Catholic Church reached

---

* *Louisville Daily Courier.*

Louisville early on yesterday (Sunday) morning. For weeks the physicians and friends attending upon him had despaired of his life, and consequently the intelligence of his death was not unexpected, either by his own people or by the general community. He died calmly as an infant lulled to its rest, at half-past nine o'clock, on the evening of Saturday last, May 11, at the residence of the Ecclesiastical Superior of the Nazareth Community of Sisters of Charity, near Bardstown, Kentucky. During his entire illness he had been cared for by the good Sisters with the most affectionate tenderness. His case, however, proved to be beyond the reach either of medical skill or careful nursing of those whose vocation it is to wait upon the sick. Several of his clergy were present, and nearly all of them had, at one time or another, since his condition was pronounced dangerous, visited him and received his blessing.

"Among the members of his flock, Bishop Lavialle bore an exalted reputation for holiness of life and zeal in the discharge of the duties laid upon him by his position in the Church. He is regarded by his entire people as having actually sacrificed his life for what he esteemed to be their good. Of a naturally delicate physical constitution, it is not at all wonderful that the labors he imposed upon himself should have proved too great for any long-continued endurance. It is not yet two years since he was raised to the episcopate, and yet there is scarcely a single mission in his whole diocese that he has not visited at least once, and many of them frequently. These episcopal visitations, in the Catholic Church of this country, involve an amount of labor and fatigue of which few persons, not conversant with the facts, have any proper conception. With a man of

Bishop Lavialle's strict ideas in regard to the awful responsibilities of the episcopal office, it may well be conceived that he not only divided with the subordinate clergy the labors incident to these visitations, such as preaching, catechising the children, and hearing confessions, but that he too frequently insisted on doing more than was his proper share of this arduous work. The seeds of the disease that undermined his health, and finally led to his death, there can be no doubt, were implanted in his system by the labors and exposures which he underwent during his last visitation of the diocese.

"Though of an exceedingly retiring disposition, this quality did not serve to hide the natural amiability of his character. He was thoroughly loved and venerated by his clergy, as well as by the people, the result more of his eminent virtues than of his social qualities. He was by no means a brilliant speaker, but there was that earnestness about the man, and a certain unction in his discourses, which ever told with powerful effect upon his hearers, whether these were learned or simple. He appeared at these times to have divested himself of that which was merely human, and indeed, 'put on the Lord Jesus Christ.' Such was the man, on account of whose removal from their midst the Catholics of Kentucky are to-day mourning. They have our sincerest sympathy."

APPENDIX.

APPENDIX.

I.

RIGHT REV. EDWARD BARRON, D.D.,

Bishop of Constantine and Vicar-Apostolic of both Guineas, Africa.*

THE name of Bishop Barron is associated with the generous efforts of the Church to convert to the faith the Africans, on their own soil, by means of missionaries sent from the United States, and with our own missions at home, and is distinguished in our annals by the zeal of an apostle and by the heroic death of a martyr.

The Right Rev. Edward Barron was born in Ireland in 1801, and was brother to Sir Henry Winton Barron, of Waterford. He made his ecclesiastical studies at the College of the Propaganda, in Rome, and there received his diploma as Doctor of Divinity. Returning to Ireland, he performed missionary duties there for several years, and then came to the United States, to whose missions he proposed to devote his services. He attached himself to the diocese of Philadelphia. In that city he was pastor of St. Mary's Church, President of the Theological Seminary of St. Charles Borromeo, and Vicar-General of the diocese. The Holy See, in 1840,

---

* Authorities: *Catholic Almanac*, 1855; *New York Freeman's Journal*, 1854 and 1855; *Catholic Magazine*; *The Metropolitan*; *The Catholic Church in the United States*, by De Courcy and Shea, etc., etc.

communicated to the Bishops of New York and Philadelphia the desire that two missionaries, one from each of these dioceses, should be selected to go to Liberia and labor for the conversion of the Africans. The field was uninviting in a worldly view, for the climate was deadly; but still *there* was a glorious work. Two apostolic men and holy priests, not waiting for official appointment, volunteered for the service; these were Dr. Barron, of Philadelphia, and Rev. John Kelly, of the diocese of New York. They embarked, together with Dennis Pindar, a lay Catechist from Baltimore, December 21, 1841, for Cape Mesurado, and thence proceeded to Cape Palmas. On February 10, 1842, Dr. Barron offered up the Holy Sacrifice for the first time in that region since the Jesuit Mission of Sierra Leone, established under Father Bareira, in 1604, when a native prince and many of his people were converted to the faith. The work of the mission under Dr. Barron was commenced with great zeal. The missionaries preached to the natives the word of God by means of interpreters, and the first fruit of their labors was the observance of the Lord's day by the Grebos nation. Encouraged by his first efforts, and desirous of obtaining the necessary means and missionaries to place his mission upon a firm foundation, Dr. Barron returned to the United States, and thence to Ireland, in order to realize from his hereditary estate the resources he needed for this good work. He next proceeded to Rome to make a report of his progress, and to place at the feet of the Sovereign Pontiff his offering of a new conquest for the faith, and his hopes for its success. The Holy See, fruitful mother of new missions, was not behindhand in the work it had inaugurated, and, in order to give power and organization to the work, raised the country into a Vicariate Apostolic, and placed it under the government of Dr. Barron, as Bishop of Constantine and Vicar-Apostolic of the two Guineas. The new Bishop of Africa succeeded in obtaining as laborers for his mission, seven priests of the Society of the Sacred Heart of Jesus, and three lay-brothers of the same Order. This little band of apostles sailed from Bordeaux in September, 1843, and arrived at Cape Palmas November 30, 1843. These generous sons of the Church were Father John Remi Bessieur, from the diocese of Montpellier, afterwards Bishop of Gallipolis and Vicar-Apostolic of the Guineas ; Father De Regnier, who nobly yielded his life for his mission in December, 1843 ; Father John Louis Rousset, of Amiens, who gloriously followed him to join the martyr band of Heaven; Father Francis Bouchet, of the diocese of Annecy, who yielded up his soul in the same exalted cause, May 28, 1844, at sea, while accompanying Bishop Barron from Assinée to Toal; Father Audibert, who died at Great Bassan, and Father Laval, who died at Assinée, in the summer of 1844, victims to the climate and martyrs to their zeal; and Father John M. Maurice, now pastor at Greece, New York. Dennis Pindar, the Catechist, after two years of heroic labor and saintly zeal, yielded at last to the deadly climate, January 1, 1844, but not until he had, under God, saved the lives of Bishop Barron and Father Kelly from the attacks of fever, which prostrated them also in the midst of their sublime exertions.

Thus was the modern Church of Africa founded, by the sufferings and deaths of heroic sons of the faith. But it was impossible to continue the good work under such devastation ; the Bishop, after witnessing the deaths of most of his priests, and finding himself and the other survivors prostrated by the climate, again proceeded to Rome to report the condition of his charge, and to concert measures for relieving the mission and continuing the work. It was wisely determined at Rome that the African mission should be confided to an Order of priests expressly organized and trained for the conversion of the colored race, such as the Society of Father Leibermann. Bishop Barron accordingly resigned his Vicariate in 1845, returned to the United States, and devoted himself, as before, to the American mission. Father Kelly, who had been his devoted and zealous co-laborer, by instructions from Rome, accompanied Bishop Barron back to the United States.

A diocese in the United States was several times offered to Bishop Barron, and as often declined. The good Prelate preferred the humbler work of the missionary priest, and first at Philadelphia, then at St. Louis, and finally in Florida, though with impaired health and a broken constitution, he labored for the good of souls with untiring energy. Whilst thus engaged he assisted also in the work of the episcopate, in order to lighten the burden of the Bishop in whose diocese he was, by administering confirmation, and such other episcopal functions as he might be requested by the ordinary of the diocese to perform. But the work of the mission was his chosen task, and in each of these dioceses he left memorials of his zeal and labors.

In the summer of 1854, while serving in Florida, he was forced to go to the North, in order to save his already impaired health from the effects of the excessive heat prevailing at the South. But the saddening accounts he received of the ravages of the yellow fever in the South, induced him to return too soon to scenes of suffering and death, from which so many others were flying. Arriving at Savannah, he united his feeble strength but heroic zeal to those of Bishop Gartland and his priests, and for two weeks he spared not himself in the heavenly work of visiting and serving the sick and dying, and in carrying to them the consolations of religion. Exhausted by disease of the lungs, under which he labored, and still more by his untiring exertions day and night, he was himself attacked by the yellow fever. At the residence of Bishop Gartland the prostrate Prelate received every office of tenderness, gratitude, and Christian sympathy. He who had spent himself for others received even now a reward on earth, in the overflowing kindness and lavish services of the noble Bishop of Savannah, for whom he was so soon to lead the way to Heaven. But even now an ordeal of suffering, the regimen of pain that precedes the blissful reward, was reserved for him; while in his severest sufferings, a violent storm tore the roof from the house in which he lay, and exposed the heroic sufferer to the fury of the elements. Removed in haste to the hospitable house of a pious Catholic citizen of Savannah, where everything was done that Christian love and charity could suggest, death soon closed out from his view all earthly scenes of pestilence and woe, and at the same moment opened to his enraptured soul the heavenly vision. Bishop Barron, "a martyr to his charity," died September 12, 1854. He was soon followed by his noble friend and peer in Christian heroism, the heroic Bishop Gartland. The remains of the two Prelates lay side by side for years. But the ravages of the recent war disturbed their resting-place, and left it open and unguarded. The Sisters of

Mercy, kindred spirits with the noble dead, removed their remains to a temporary place of interment at their convent. In 1867, the remains of Bishops Gartland, Barron, and Barry were reinterred together in the Catholic Cemetery, of Savannah, with the most solemn and imposing ceremonies. The inscription on the tomb of Bishop Barron is as follows:—

EDWARD BARRON, Bishop of Africa,
Where he lost his health, returned to America,
and died in Savannah during the epidemic,
September 12, 1854.

"I most gladly will spend and will be spent myself for your souls."— 2 Cor. xii. 15.

II.
RIGHT REV. CHARLES AUGUSTUS MARY JOSEPH DE FAUBIN-JANSON, D.D.,

*Bishop of Nancy, France.**

THIS distinguished Prelate employed the exile, which he suffered for political reasons, in performing missionary labors in the United States, and his name is held in grateful remembrance in our midst. He was born at Paris, in 1785, and embarked in secular pursuits, which he abandoned for no lack of success, for he had attained to the office of an Auditor in the Council of State at the age of twenty-one. He resolved now to forsake the world and devote himself to the work of heaven. He entered the Seminary of St. Sulpice, and was raised to the holy priesthood at Chambery, in 1811. During the political convulsions of this period, his extraordinary energy and ability were restrained in their efforts; he remained at Savoy until the restoration of the Bourbons in France, and then, returning to his native country, he devoted himself with his wonted zeal to the founding of missions. Of a truly pious and devout nature, his ardent zeal and devotional sentiments found vent in a fervid and effective eloquence, which through every part of France drew crowds to repentance and grace. The house of the Missionaries of Mt. Valerian, founded by

---

* Authorities: *The Catholic Church in the United States*, by De Courcy and Shea; *N. Y. Freeman's Journal*; *The Catholic Magazine*; *The Metropolitan*, etc., etc.

him, is a monument of his services to the cause of religion. With the ardor and devotion of former and better days, he made a pilgrimage to the Holy Land, and here, after doing homage to God in the scenes of His earthly career, and venerating the sacred places, he addressed himself to the labor of doing good. The temples of the East, like those of France, echoed with his eloquence, and his labors were fruitful in many conversions to the faith, especially at Smyrna. The Holy See, appreciating his splendid gifts and valuable services, raised him to the episcopal office, and appointed him Bishop of Nancy. Political intrigues hampered his freedom, curtailed his usefulness by restraining his labors, and he was finally forced into exile. He took refuge in the United States, in 1839. He did not allow his place of refuge to become a haven of rest or inactivity. He visited many of the dioceses of the United States and Canada, in all of which he rendered valuable services to the cause of religion. Canada, Louisiana, and New York were the principal theatres of his missionary exertions, and in all these places he has built up monuments which attest his goodness and his labors. In Canada his missionary services yielded extraordinary fruits, and his charities have brought many blessings on his name. Among the monuments of his zeal in that country is the colossal cross, one hundred feet high, which he planted on the mountain of Belœil, "whence the august sign of salvation casts its protecting shadow over the surrounding fields and villages." In Louisiana and other parts of America he distinguished himself by the organization of ecclesiastical retreats for the clergy, and missions among the people. In 1841 Bishop Faubin-Janson was in New York, and did much by his eloquence and fervor in arousing the spirit of religion amongst the people, and especially among the French inhabitants of that city. The latter flocked in crowds to hear his sermons, and the spiritual retreat which he opened in St. Peter's Church, in 1841, was attended with immense success. In a sermon which he preached April 10, 1841, he appealed to the French inhabitants of New York to erect a church for themselves, in which they would be addressed in their own tongue. He told them that the Germans had been provided with a German church, under the care of the Redemptorists, and even the Huguenot French had a church of their own; and that, by such means, many French Catholics had been drawn into a practical abandonment of their own altars. His eloquent appeal had the desired effect: on the following day the French Catholics held a meeting and resolved to build a church; the site was purchased, and Mr. de la Forêt, the French Consul, laid the cornerstone, October 11, 1841; the generous Bishop of Nancy made a loan of six thousand dollars for the erection of the church, and subsequently made a donation of the principal in the diocese. The Rev. Annet Lafont, of the Society of the Fathers of Mercy, was appointed pastor in 1842, and continues to this day the noble work com menced by the Bishop of Nancy.

The Fourth Provincial Council of Baltimore, which assembled May 17, 1840, unanimously invited the zealous and distinguished Bishop Faubin-Janson to assist in their deliberations, as a testimonial of their appreciation and gratitude for his great services to religion in the United States, and as a mark of honor and sympathy for so noble a confessor of the faith. He returned to France in 1842, and in the same year he visited Rome, and was received by the Pope with great distinction. In several long and interesting interviews which he had with the Holy Father, he gave a full account of the missions in the United States, and received from the Pope, as an acknowledgment of his zeal and services, a fine medallion portrait set in gold. Having returned to France, he devoted the remainder of his life to works of benevolence and religious enterprise, the principal amongst which was the founding of the Society of Holy Childhood, for the salvation of Chinese infants. He died at Provence, full of years and merits before God and man, July 12, 1844.

III.
CARDINAL CAGETAN BEDINI,
*Apostolic Nuncio.**

CARDINAL BEDINI was born in Sinigaglia, May 15 1806. Devoted from early life to the ecclesiastical state, he enjoyed all the advantages of mental and moral culture which the splendid institutions of Rome afforded. After his ordination he was appointed secretary of the Prince, afterwards Cardinal, Altieri, Nuncio at the Court of Vienna, a position which he filled for several years with energy and ability. The distinction he acquired in this office secured for him the appointment of Inter-Nuncio to the Imperial Court of Brazil. While in Rio de Janeiro, Monsignore Bedini gained eminence both by his vigorous discharge of duty and by his talents as a diplomatist. He extended a firm and noble protection to a number of German immigrants, with whose wrongs he ardently sympathized and whose rights he ably defended.

Monsignore Bedini returned from his Brazilian mission to Rome during the revolutionary period of 1848 and 1849, when Garibaldi and his infidel co-conspirators were struggling to overturn all legitimate and stable government, to destroy the Church, and to suppress religion. The four Legations, Bologna, Ferrara, Forli, and Ravenna, forming part of the Pontifical States, were

---

* Authorities: *The Catholic Church in the United States*, by De Courcy and Shea; *The Roman Almanac*; Contemporary Publications, etc., etc.

involved in the prevailing anarchy and violence of the times. The Holy Father Pius IX., who had himself signalized his reign as temporal sovereign by inaugurating the most mild and generous measures of civil government, and who received from the wicked and unscrupulous agitators and revolutionists of the day nothing but ingratitude and treachery, was indebted to the arms of Austria for the restoration of the four Legations to the mild sceptre of their legitimate sovereign. He conferred upon Monsignore Bedini, then recently returned to Rome with the laurels of his Brazilian service, the Archiepiscopal dignity, under the title of Archbishop of Thebes, and the appointment of Pro-Legate, or Papal Governor, of the four provinces named, an office which was by no means attractive to an ecclesiastic in such distracted times, and which there were few willing to accept. The Pro-Legate at once established himself at Bologna, and, instead of acting upon the maxim, *Silent leges inter arma*, he signalized his advent by proclaiming, March 26, 1849, the restoration of the ordinary and constitutional tribunals of justice, with whose proceedings and sentences he and his assistants in the administration could not and wished not to interfere. But owing to the obstinate and perverse resistance of the Garibaldians, the Austrian military authorities, May 17, declared Bologna to be in a state of siege, thus substituting martial law and the military courts for the recently restored laws and tribunals of peace. This state of things was afterwards extended to all four Legations. Thus the peaceful mission of the representative of the Holy See was suspended, all his powers of government practically superseded, and all power concentrated in the Austrian military governor. A number of prisoners were captured by the Austrians in the flight of Garibaldi, many of whom were charged with various crimes, and with violations of the laws of war,—were tried by the military courts, condemned and executed. Conspicuous among the prisoners thus captured and executed was Ugo Bassi, an ex-Barnabite priest, who had fallen from his holy calling, was an officer in Garibaldi's service, and was captured in arms against the Holy See. He was tried and executed in great haste and secrecy by the military authorities of Austria, and without the knowledge of Monsignore Bedini. The Rev. Agostino Ricci, parish priest of Santa Maria della Carita, Bologna, received but an hour's notice to visit the condemned before his execution, and immediately sent three clergymen to attend him in his last moments. He was completely changed by the grace of God, repented of his unpriestly conduct, and made an earnest retraction of all his offences against the Church and against religion. His retraction was as follows: "If there is ever found in any writing of mine, any word, proposition, or maxim whatever offensive to piety, propriety, or religion, I intend and wish it retracted in the most positive and efficacious manner; and so, too, I intend of any word or speech made in public or private, wishing to repair every scandal I may have given, and aid in the spiritual good of all, because I desire and wish to die a true Roman Catholic." At the place of execution, fixing his eyes on the sanctuary of San Luca, he said, before giving up his soul: "I beg pardon of all; I pardon all. I recommend fidelity to religion, and rejoice to be able to expire in peace, under the protection of the Blessed Virgin of San Luca." Monsignore Bedini, Cardinal Oppizoni, and the Superior of the Barnabites made every effort to have his retraction published, but this was not permitted by the Austrian military authorities. The person captured and executed with him was Giovanni Sirraghi, an Austrian deserter, then an officer of Garibaldi's army. The remaining persons condemned and executed were criminals of every grade of crime, from the bandit and thief to the murderer and ravisher. Not only was Monsignore Bedini powerless to condemn or to save, but it may be judged how fully his functions as civil ruler were suspended during these events, from the fact that he could not even secure permission to publish the retraction of Ugo Bassi.

These particulars are given in consequence of the claim made by the Revolutionists and Garibaldians that these persons were martyrs of liberty and victims of ecclesiastical cruelty; and because these false accusations were the cause of the cruel and brutal persecution which Monsignore Bedini was doomed to endure in our country, and led to his becoming, on our soil and in our midst, a confessor of the faith.

After the return of peace, Monsignore Bedini, as Pro-Legate of the four Legations, governed those provinces of the Church with great ability, eminent usefulness, and characteristic mildness. It was during his administration at Bologna, that the celebrated Madonna in the Church of Santa Chiara, at Rimini, several times miraculously moved the eyes. Pleased with his public services, and appreciating his fine talents for affairs, Pope Pius IX., in the spring of 1853, appointed him Nuncio to the Imperial Court of Brazil.

It was while engaged in examining and approving the proceedings of the First National Council of Baltimore, held in 1852, that the Holy Father, deeply interested in our country and in all that concerns its temporal and eternal welfare, and more than ever attracted towards us by the splendid exhibit of the Church made in that august assembly, resolved, while despatching Monsignore Bedini to his mission at Rio de Janeiro, to charge him also with a complimentary mission to the government and people of the United States, and the duty of investigating the state of religion therein. The American Chargé at Rome, to whom this intention of the Holy Father was communicated, expressed in behalf of our government the greatest pleasure at the proposed mission, and the assurance that "a most distinguished reception" awaited the arrival of the Papal Envoy in the United States, and also advised the government at Washington of the approaching visit. He arrived on our shores, visited the principal cities of the East, and at Washington presented to President Pierce the autograph letter of the Holy Father. He also commenced the discharge of his other duty, that of investigating the state of the Church and the condition of religion in the United States. Accompanied by Archbishop Hughes, he visited the West as far as Milwaukee, stopping in the various dioceses and consulting with their Bishops, visiting numerous colleges, convents, and other religious and charitable institutions; and doing all in his power to encourage and promote religion and education in our midst. All who saw him recognized in him the exalted character of the Christian Prelate, and the benevolence and magnanimity of the Christian gentleman and scholar. This event attracted no unusual attention at the time, certainly no displeasure on the part of Protestants in this country, who never entertained a thought that there was anything in this expression of good wishes and friendly regard, which was calculated to arouse suspicion or engender sectarian fears and animosities. Our countrymen were indebted to emissaries from abroad, and to foreign infidels in our midst, for the suggestion that Protestantism and the religious liberty of Protestants were endangered by such an event.

In the secret meetings of the Carbonari of Europe, a plot was formed to revenge on Archbishop Bedini, while the guest of our country, the pretended offences against their co-conspirators against law, order, and religion, charged against him while Pro-Legate at Bologna, and to defeat his peaceful mission to the United States. For this purpose the notorious Gavazzi, an ex-Barnabite, left London for our shores, and in concert with his con federates here raised the slanderous voice of malicious hatred and fiendish persecution against the Envoy of the Holy Father. The organ of these conspirators, and their mouth-piece, Gavazzi, while declaiming against the Holy See and the Church, and announcing to Protestants the most absurd tales about Popish intrigues and designs against American liberty, attacked the personal character of Archbishop Bedini, accusing him of every crime against humanity, calling him the "butcher of Bologna," "the Roman hyena," and applying to him the most insulting and opprobrious abuse and falsehood. There were not wanting newspapers in America to echo the base calumnies of these perfidious men, and one of these, the *New York Express*, distinguished itself in this respect, and published a list of fifty alleged victims of Archbishop Bedini's cruelty, including the case of Ugo Bassi, whom the Carbonari still claimed as a martyr to their cause, notwithstanding his retraction and sincere submission to the Church before his execution.

The whole non-Catholic and Protestant press of the country resounded with the falsehoods and calumnies that were manufactured in secret infidel and red-republican lodges in Europe. There was scarcely a voice raised in behalf of the persecuted Prelate. The *National Intelligencer*, at Washington, finally published a calm statement and full refutation of the charges, prepared by a Catholic citizen of Washington, and the Catholic press of the country triumphantly vindicated the exalted character of the Archbishop from the foul calumnies heaped upon it. But all in vain. It was supposed that Protestantism, while claiming to be a Christian church, would be promoted by vilifying the most august ministers and most ancient institutions of Christianity itself. Not only did the press enter blindly into the work of the Carbonari, but the pulpit and the rostrum resounded with calumnies against the Pope, the Nuncio, and the Church. Gavazzi followed the illustrious visitor from city to city, and dogged him at every turn, appealing all the time to the passions of the mob, the frenzy of the bigot, and the malice of the wicked. The Archbishop's life was in danger at every step; yet in the midst of such persecutions he deigned not to defend himself before such a self-constituted tribunal, or to enter the lists of controversy with such opponents. He continued his works of prayer, benevolence, and benediction. The extent to which these foreign infidels, who in their exile accepted our hospitality only to abuse it, proceeded, may be judged from what followed. A Sardinian frigate landed on our shores, in the summer of 1853, eighty-three Italians, said to be political exiles from Rome and Lombardy, but many of whom were transported criminals. These pretended champions of liberty entered into a conspiracy at New

York for the assassination of the Archbishop, and were about to execute their horrible purpose, when remorse seized upon the conscience of Sassi, one of their number, who warned the Prelate of his danger; but poor Sassi's heart received at the hands of his late associates the stroke of the assassin's dagger which was intended for the servant of God. The latter, who was then in Canada, on hearing of these appalling events wrote to his friends in New York the following words, so worthy of a follower of a crucified Saviour:—"I beg you to take no steps on my behalf with the authorities as to the affair of poor Sassi. It is not in the least my desire to pursue any one whomsoever with the sword of justice. My life is in the hands of God far more than in those of men. My ministry is one of peace and pardon, and my heart can only love those who hate me. Continue to comfort the hearts of the poor Italians, who, after all, cannot but be ever exasperated by the sufferings of exile. Poor people! they are indeed to be pitied. Rest assured that I will recommend them especially to God's mercy; and unable to extend my hand to relieve them, since I do not know them, I extend it gladly over them to bless them all—be they who they may."

After concluding his engagements in Canada, which consisted in laborious and exalted services to religion and to the cause of education, Archbishop Bedini returned to the United States, where he devoted himself in like manner to every work of religious zeal and charity. " Without regard to fatigue, he was seen in turn dedicating cathedrals, celebrating ordinations, giving the veil to religious, receiving the abjurations of Protestants, opening ecclesiastical retreats, presiding at college exhibitions, visiting convents and hospitals, consoling the sick, and blessing the orphans—everywhere welcomed as an envoy of mercy, and everywhere leaving piety, edification, and devotedness to the Holy See. . . . . The grandest ceremony of all was the consecration of the Bishops of Burlington, Brooklyn, and Newark, which took place in the Cathedral at New York, on Sunday, the 30th of October, 1853, by the hands of Archbishop Bedini." *

The silence of the illustrious Archbishop, under the atrocious calumnies uttered and published against him,—a silence broken only by words of prayer for his bitterest enemies and of blessings upon them,—began at last to open the eyes and touch the hearts of intelligent and well-disposed people. The contrast between his mildness and charity and the malice and injustice of his enemies was so great, that a reaction in his favor began to set in. An article in the *Courier and Enquirer* first raised the voice of reason, justice, and fairness, and soon the entire press of the country resounded with vindications and praises of Archbishop Bedini. The Mayor of New York invited him to visit the public establishments and benevolent institutions of the city; the excursion took place November 10, 1853, and was followed by a sumptuous banquet given in his honor by the Commissioners of Emigration. Archbishop Bedini was eminent not only for his ecclesiastical and diplomatic attainments, but also for his social and private virtues, his elegant manners, his magnanimity, his enlightened views, and his commanding appearance. All who now saw him were deeply impressed with his exalted virtues and character, and the honor of the country seemed at last vindi-

---

* *The Catholic Church in the United States.*

cated by the people themselves. But his Italian enemies were implacable.

In the following month of December, Archbishop Bedini started on a tour to the West. At Pittsburgh he was received with enthusiastic demonstrations by the Catholics; but the joyous occasion was marred by insults from some fanatical persons in the crowd. At Cincinnati the Italian Reds, unable to enlist Americans on their side, found willing colleagues in the infidel Germans, and a German newspaper published brutal insults against him, and incited the desperadoes to deeds of violence and blood. On the evening of December 24th, while the Archbishop was resting after the fatiguing religious ceremonies and duties of the day, the mob marched forth with arms and torches to the number of five hundred, headed by the editor of the same German newspaper, and, desecrating the sacred name of Freedom by proclaiming themselves members of the *Society of Freemen*, took the most direct road to the residence where their intended victim was sojourning. The policemen nobly resisted the advancing multitude, arms were discharged, eighteen persons fell in the struggle, and the Germans were dispersed, leaving seventy prisoners in the hands of the police. They now again began to appeal to Protestant bigotry, by representing themselves as the victims of triumphant Popery; they thus gained many adherents, their numbers were recruited, the policemen, who had so nobly done their duty, were dismissed, Cincinnati rang with the noisy and blasphemous demonstrations of the infidels, and they had the satisfaction of burning the Archbishop in effigy without molestation. The good and fearless Archbishop was not deterred, however, from remaining, as he intended, the entire week, visiting the Catholic churches and institutions of the city, celebrating Mass in several German Catholic Churches, and receiving everywhere among Catholics the most reverential attentions and heartfelt sympathies. He himself exclaimed, "Oh! how many reciprocal consolations! how many blessings given and received with a heart moved, but trusting in Providence!"

Returning to Washington, Archbishop Bedini availed himself of a short repose, after the excitements and persecutions through which he had recently passed. He was the guest of the French Minister, Count de Sartiges, and during his sojourn he received every mark of respect and honor from the representative of France, from eminent Catholic families, and from Catholic Institutions. At Georgetown College and other establishments ovations were celebrated in his honor. In the United States Senate the cause of the Nuncio was fully and ably debated, and every voice but one was raised in his vindication, thus supplying in some measure the apathy and indifference of the State Department under Mr. Marcy, in whose archives it was not even possible to find the correspondence of our Chargé at Rome, announcing the approaching mission of the Papal Envoy. The Archbishop had his final interview with the President, and his visit was about drawing to a close. In the mean time, the country was kept in a state of excitement and religious agitation by the infidel and sectarian press. Several fanatical street-preachers fanned the flame of bigotry by declaiming at the corners and in the public squares against the Church; conspicuous amongst whom were a porter named Parsons, in New York, and a madman named Orr, who assumed the name of the *Angel Gabriel*.

and whose incendiary harangues in this country were tending rapidly to the repetition of those scenes of fire and blood which had attended his career in other countries. In the city of New York, so great was the commotion, that the militia were called out to preserve order, a measure, however, rendered unnecessary by the magnanimous conduct of the Catholics, who, under the advice of Archbishop Hughes, refrained from approaching the scenes of excitement, and bore unmeasured insult and abuse without complaint, though several of their number fell victims to this unjust persecution.

The steps of Archbishop Bedini were now beset with assassins; his life was in constant danger. His movements were watched and telegraphed from city to city, and in several cities crowds assembled at the wharves on the departure of every steamer, ready to rush upon the Nuncio as soon as he appeared. The cities through which he passed abandoned all efforts at suppressing these riots, and even in those cities whose authorities had paid him public honors the same authorities now recommended the Nuncio to remain concealed, to shorten his stay, and to embark for Europe secretly. In whatever light we regard this sad chapter in our history, it must have demonstrated to the world the glories of the Catholic Church, her championship of Christianity and true civilization against infidelity and disorder, her persecution by infidels and anarchists, and the supernatural virtues of her children under calumnies and injustice. Deeply as we may feel the disgrace thus brought upon our country, there is a consolation in knowing that the Church in our midst has had her persecution for justice's sake, and has possessed on our soil so illustrious a confessor of the faith. A touching evidence of the sublime sentiments of Archbishop Bedini in the midst of such injuries, of his forgiveness of wrongs, and of his gratitude for the consolations received in the midst of his afflictions, is to be found in the beautiful memorial of his visit, which he left with the Catholics of the United States. While in New York, preparing for his departure, early in 1854, he had engraved a copy of the Madonna of Rimini, the same that gave miraculous signs during his administration at Bologna, and sent it for distribution among the various dioceses of the country. The picture bore the arms of the Prelate and the following inscription:—

To the Catholics
Of the United States and Canada,
C. Bedini, Archbishop of Thebes, Apostolic Nuncio,
Edified and Grateful,
Presents this Picture
Of the Blessed Virgin Mary, Mother of God.

On his return to Rome he received every mark of confidence and sympathy from the Holy See. He was made Bishop of Viterbo and Joseanella. The Holy Father made him a Cardinal Priest of the Holy Roman Church, under the title of S. Maria Sopra Minerva; his creation and publication as such took place in Consistory of September 27, 1861. He continued for the remainder of his life to discharge his episcopal duties at Viterbo, and those of Cardinal at Rome. He died at Viterbo, September 6, 1864, and was buried in his Cathedral in that city.

ANALYTICAL INDEX.

A.

Abell, Rev. Mr., II. 34.
Adams, Prest., I. 170, 171.
African Mission, II. 596.
Alemany, Most Rev. J. S., I. 541.
Altham, Father, I. 42.
Alton, Bishop of: Juncker, II. 529.
Anger, Rev. R., I. 329.
Appendix, II. 595.
Arbre Croche, I. 345, 348, 350.
Arundel, Lord, I. 37.
Ashton, Rev. J., I. 39.
Asturiano, Father, I. 26.
Augustinians, I. 102, 188.

B.

Badin, Father, I. 330.
Baltimore: Archbishops of, I. 5, 6, 32; Carroll, 32; Neale, 116; Maréchal, 239; Whitfield, 456; Eccleston, 525; Kenrick, 473; Spalding, 162, 375, 416, 451, 523; Cathedral of, 249, 467, 542; Primacy of Honor, 503.
Baraga, Right Rev. F.: His Life, II. 468; Youth and Education, 469–472; Studies Law, 472; Theology, id.; Mission in Austria, 473; Comes to America, 474; in the West, 475; Among the Indians, 477–487; His Works, 487, 488; His Poverty, id.; In Europe, 489; Again among the Indians, 489–496; The Copper Mines, 496; Vicar-Apostolic, 501; Bishop of Marquette and Saut St. Mary, id.; His Labors, 502; Death, 504.
Barber Family, I. 386, 391, 397, II. 273–277.
Bardstown, Bishops of, I. 5, 104: Flaget, 144; David, 256.
Barron, Right Rev. E.; His Life, 595.
Barry, Commodore J., I. 187.
Barry, Right Rev. J.: His Life, II. 551; Labors, id.; Administrator of Savannah, 552; Bishop, id.; Episcopal Labors, 553; His Death, 554.
Bayley, Bishop, II. 613.
Bazin, Right Rev. J. S.: His Life, II. 370; His Priesthood, id.; Bishop of Vincennes, 371; His Death, id.
Bedini, Cardinal: His Life, II. 605.
Benoit, Father, II. 565.
Bessonies, Rev. A., II. 565.
Bishops, American, their Labors and Trials, I. 8.
Blanc, Most Rev. A.: His Life, II. 58; Comes to America, id.; At Vincennes, 59; At New Orleans, 60; Consecration, id.; His Labors, 61–63, 65, 68, 71; Schism, 63–65; Archbishop, 66; At Rome, 67; Immaculate Conception, id.; Death, 71.
Bohemia, School at, in Maryland, I. 34.
Boarman, Rev. S., I. 39.
Boisnantier, Abbé, I. 73.
Bolton, Rev. J., I. 39. 124.
Boone, Rev. J., I. 39.
Boone's Chapel, I. 39.
Boston, Bishops of: Cheverus, I. 164; Fenwick, 375; Fitzpatrick, II. 310; Williams, 331; Bishop Caroll in, I. 82; See erected, 104; Ursulines, 175; Convent burned, 405.
Breen, Rev. J., II. 258.
Breckenridge, Rev. J., II. 84.
Brennan, Rev. C., I. 199.
Brent, Robert, I. 34; Capt. Geo., 40.
Brothers of St. Patrick, II. 529.
Brownson, Dr., I. 413.
Bruté, Right Rev. S. G.: His Life, II. 7; Youth and Education, 8–10; French Revolution, 10–16; Studies Medicine, 16–19; Joins the Sulpitians, 19; Ordina-

tion, 20; In America, 21; at St. Mary's, 22; Emmittsburg, 23-31; Sisters of Charity, 23-28, 33; Bishop of Vincennes, 31; Indiana, 32, 33; At Vincennes, 34; His Labors, 35-39; Poverty and Virtues, 39; His Death, 42.
Buffalo, Bishop of: T'mon, II. 337.
Bulger, Rev. R., I. 199, 203.
Byrne, Right Rev. A.: His Life, II. 264; Labors in Carolina, 265; In New York, *id.*; Church of Nativity, 266; Bishop of Little Rock, 267; His Labors, *id.*; His Death, 270.

C.

Cabeza de Vaca, I. 24, 30.
California, II. 158-165.
Canada, Embassy to, I. 43.
Carr, Rev. Dr. M., I. 188.
Carrell, Right Rev. G. A.: His Life, II. 505; Among the Jesuits, *id.*; Mt. St. Mary's, 506; Ordained, *id.*; At Philadelphia, *id.*; In the West, 507; Joins the Jesuits, *id.*; Bishop of Covington, *id.*; His Episcopate, 508-512; His Death, 513.
Carroll, Charles, of Carrollton, I. 34, 43, 47, 57, 428, 530.
Carroll, Daniel, I. 5, 7.
Carroll, Most Rev. J.: His Life, I. 32; Birth, 33; Character, 32, 106; At School in Maryland, 34; With the Jesuits in Europe, 35; Ordained, *id.*; Travels, 36; In England, 37; Maryland, 38; Mission, 40-48; In Canada, 44; Dr. Franklin, 47, 63; Patriotism, 32, 48, 100, 112; Correspondence, 47, 67, 68, 82; Controversies, 51; Gen. Washington, 56, 99, 100, 112; Holy See, 61; Superior of the Clergy, 63-65; Elected Bishop, 67; Appointed by Rome, 68; The Pope and the Republic, 69; Consecrated, 74; Installed, 76; Visitations, 82, 101; Coadjutor, 90; Honors, 93; Death of his Mother, *id.*; Indians, 84; Synod, 89; Institutions, 94; Pastorals, 98; Bonaparte Marriage, 101; His Labors, 102, 103; Made Archbishop, 104; His Virtues, 108; Death, 110.
Carroll's Chapel, I. 38.
Cass, Gen., I. 156.
Causse, Father, II. 127.

Chabrat, Bishop, I. 151, 222.
Chalon, Father, I. 454, II. 237.
Chanche, Right Rev. J. M. J.: His Life, II. 166; Ordained, 167; President of St. Mary's College, *id.*; Bishop of Natchez, 169; History of the Church at Natchez 170-177; His Labors, 178-189.
Charles I., I. 116.
Charles X., I. 181, 182, 451.
Charleston, Bishops of: England, I. 271; Clancy, II. 44; Reynolds, 291; Schism, 388.
Chase, Hon. S., I. 43, 47.
Cheverus, Cardinal, I. 87, 104; His Life, 164; College of Louis le Grand, 165; Sorbonne, 166; In England, 167; At Boston, 169; Indians, 170; Yellow Fever at Boston, *id.*; Labors, 172-176; Mother Seton, *id.*; Bishop of Boston, 173; Ursuline Convent, 175; Montauban, 177; Bordeaux, 180; Cardinal, 182; His Virtues, 183; Death, 184.
Chicago, Bishops of: Quarter, II. 240; Van de Velde, 372.
Christian Brothers, I. 536, 537, II. 68, 200, 269.
Church, Growth of in U. S., I. 6; Antiquity, 18.
Churches in U. S., I. 6.
Cincinnati, I. 6, 332: First Church in, 336; Poor Clares, 344; Bishops of: Fenwick, 328; Purcell, 516, II. 573; Cathedral, 342, 542.
Ciquard, Rev. Mr., I. 87, 241.
Clancy, Right Rev. W.: His life, II. 44; Coadjutor of Charleston, 44; Washington Irving, 46-56; Transferred to Demerara, 57; Return to Ireland, *id.*; Death, *id.*
Clark, Col. G. R., I. 147.
Clerical Association, Fort Wayne, II. 581.
Clergy, Associated, of Md., I. 40, 123.
Clergymen in U. S., I. 6, 59; In Md., 38; In Penna., 39.
Clinton, De Witt, I. 378.
Cloriviere, Father, I. 285.
Clowry, Father, II. 258.
College of Holy Cross, I. 407, 412.
Colored Sisters, I. 371, 458.
Columbus, I. 21, 22.
Concanen, Right Rev. L., I. 104: Life of,

Analytical Index.

140; At Lorraine, *id.*; At the Minerva, 141; St. Clement's, *id.*, 141; Declines Bishopric of Kilmacduagh, *id.*; Bishop of New York, 142; A Prisoner, 143; Death, *id.*
Conroy, Rev. J., I. 199.
Consecrations: Eric, I. 17; Juarez, 27; Carroll, 74; Penalver y Cardenas, 115; Porro, 139; Neale, 131; Concanen, 140; Flaget, 150; Cheverus, 173; Egan, 189; Connelly, 193; Dubourg, 221; Maréchal, 245; David, 265; Kelly, 268; England, 282; Conwell, 310; Fenwick of Cincinnati, 336; Rosati, 362; Fenwick of Boston, 390; Dubois, 428; Portier, 443; Whitfield, 460; Kenrick, F. P., 483; De Neckere, 522; Eccleston, 518; Bruté, II. 34; Clancy, 44; Blanc, 60; Hughes, 87; Loras, 129; Miles, 149; Diego y Moreno, 164; Chanche, 169; Lefevre, 193; Odin, 214; Quarter, 257; Byrne, 267; Tyler, 283; Reynolds, 296; Fitzpatrick, 320; Timon, 353; Bazin, 371; Van de Velde, 378; O'Reilly, 398; Gartland, 410; Cretin, 420; Neumann, 447; Baraga, 500; Carrell, 507; Young, 523; Juncker, 530; Smyth, 546; Barry, 552; Luers, 563; Lavialle, 586.
Congress, I. 43-46, 62, 187.
Cortez, I. 23, 24.
Corkery, Rev. Mr., I. 286.
Councils of Baltimore, I. 304, 346, 367, 463, 468, 503, 504, 505, 518, 534, 536, 540, 541.
Covington, Bishop of: Carrell, II. 505.
Crease, John, II. 519.
Cretin, Right Rev. J.: His Life, II. 415; At Dubuque, 416; Bishop of St. Paul, 417; His Labors, 420, 430; Growth of the Church, 429; His Death, 430.
Crucifix, the Genoa Ivory, II. 459-466.

D.

Darnal, Eleanor, I. 33.
David, Right Rev. J. B.: His Life, I. 256; With the Oratorians, 257; Seminary of Nantes, *id.*; A Tutor, *id.*; At Issy, *id.*; Ordained, 258; Professor at Angers, *id.*; French Revolution, *id.*; At Baltimore, 259; Mission, *id.*; Introduces Retreats in United States, *id.*; At G. T. College, 260; St. Mary's, *id.*; Sisters of Charity, 261; Mother Seton, *id.*; In Kentucky, 264; Declines the Bishopric of Philadelphia, 265; Coadjutor of Bardstown, *id.*; Poverty and Labors, 266; Death, 267.
De Andreis, Father, I. 321, 354, 359.
De Barth, Father, I. 188, 311, 312.
Decalogue, I. 415.
De Goesbriand, II. 61-63.
Dejean, Father, I. 348.
Delille, Abbé, I. 415.
Demerara, I. 121, II. 46, 57.
De Neckere, Right Rev. L. R.: His Life, I. 518; At the Barrens, 519; In Europe, 520; Miraculous recovery, 521; Bishop of New Orleans, 522, 524; His Death, *id.*
De St. Palais, Bishop, II. 590.
Desmoulins, I. 415.
Detroit, I. 346.
Devereux, J. C., I. 200.
Devlin, Daniel, II. 121.
Diderick, Rev. B., I. 39.
Diego y Moreno, Right Rev. F. G.: His Life, II. 157; In Mexico, *id.*; In California, 158; Indian Missions, 158-165.
Diggs, Rev. T., I. 39.
Dioceses, Number of, I. 6.
Dittoe, Peter, I. 334.
Divorce, I. 535.
Domenec, Bishop, I. 516; II. 346.
Dominicans: In Ohio, I. 102, 334, 336; In Kentucky, 330.
Donaghue, Rev. T. C., II. 133.
Donnelly, Terence, II. 121.
Doyne, Rev. J., I. 39.
Dubois, Right Rev. J.: His Life, I. 414, College of Louis Le Grand, 415; Remarkable Schoolmates, *id.*; St. Magloire, 416; Sorbonne, *id.*; Ordained, 417; French Revolution, *id.*; Comes to America, *id.*; At Norfolk, *id.*; James Monroe and Patrick Henry, 418; At Richmond, *id.*; At Frederick, *id.*; His Labors, 419, 422, 424, 431; Emmittsburg, 421; A Sulpitian, *id.*; Mount St. Mary's, 422-424; Devotion to Mary, 425; Sisters of Charity, *id.*; Bishop of New York, 428, 429; Trusteeism, 430; "Little Bonaparte," 431; In Europe, 432; College for New York, 433; Incendiarism,

id.; Churches, 434; Persecution, 435, 436; Coadjutor, *id.;* Death, 437.
Dubourg, Most Rev. W. L.: His Life, I. 205; Joins the Sulpitians, 207; President of G. T. College, *id.;* At Havana, *id.;* At New Orleans, 208; St. Mary's, Baltimore, *id.;* Cathedral, 211; Sisters of Charity, 212; Champion of the Faith, 215; Administrator of New Orleans, 217; War of 1812, 220; Patriotism, *id.;* General Jackson, 219; At Rome, 220; Bishop of New Orleans, 221; Journey to St. Louis, 221, 222; Labors, 223, 233; At St. Louis, 224, 232; Association for the Propagation of the Faith, 225; The Barrens, 230; University St. Louis, *id.;* Jesuits in the West, *id.;* Monroe and Calhoun, 231; Sisters of Loretto, *id.;* Sacred Heart, *id.;* At New Orleans, 233; Coadjutor, *id.;* College at New Orleans, *id.;* Bishop of Montauban, 234; Services in France, 236, 237; Archbishop of Besançon, *id.;* Death, *id.;* Character, 238.
Dubuque, Bishops of: Loras, 126; Smyth, 536.
Dunnin, Archbishop of Posen, I. 535.
Duval, Abbé Le Gris, I, 416.

E.

Eccleston, Most Rev. S.: His Life, I. 525; Ordained, 526; St. Mary's College, 527; Archbishop, 528; Labors, *id.,* 542; Labor School, 529; Redemptorists, *id.;* Churches, 530; Councils, 532, 536, 541, 545; Christian Brothers, 536; Pius IX., 540; Cathedral, 542; His Death, 543; Character, 544-546.
Egan, Right Rev. M., I. 104, 106; His Life, 185; A Franciscan, *id.;* In Pennsylvania, *id.;* Pastor of St. Mary's, Philadelphia, *id.;* Bishop of Philadelphia, 189; Schism, 190; Sisters of Charity, 191; Death, *id.*
Elder, Bishop, II. 69.
Emery, V. Rev. Mr., I. 91.
Emmittsburg, I. 95, 215, 421, 426; Mt. St. Mary's College, 422; Sisters of Charity, 425.
England, Right Rev. J.: His Life, I. 271; "The Little Papist," 273; Theology, 274; At Carlow 275; Ordained, *id.;* Labors, 276; Prisons, *id.;* Patriotism, 278, O'Connell, 279; Clerical Labors, 280; At Bandon, 280, 281; Bishop of Charleston, 282; Difficulties, 285; Labors, 286, 288, 294, 297, 305; School and Seminary, 287; Poverty, 289; Anti-Duelling Association, *id.;* Sermon in U. S. Capitol, 290; Adopted Country, 291; *Catholic Miscellany,* 292; At Cincinnati, 294; Yellow Fever, 295; Colored Population, 296; Ursuline Nuns, 299; Sisters of Mercy, *id.;* Eloquence, 302; Courage, 304; Councils, 305; Europe, *id.;* Hayti, *id.;* "Steam Bishops," 306; Health and Labors, 307; Last Address, *id.;* Death, 308; His Works, II. 306.
Enriquez, Cantador, I. 26.
Eric, Bishop, I. 13-18.
Erie, Bishop of: Young, II. 514; History of, 522.

F.

Farmer, Rev. F., I. 34, 39, 47, 187.
Faubin, Janson, Bishop: His Life, II. 602.
Feehan, Bishop, II. 590.
Fenwick, Rev. E., I. 249.
Fenwick, Right Rev. B. J.: His Life, I. 375; At G. T. College, *id.;* At St. Mary's, 376; Joins the Jesuits, 377; In New York, *id.;* New York Literary Institution, 378; Tom Paine, 379; Administrator of New York, 385; Labors, *id.,* 395, 400; The Quakeress, 386; Converts, *id.;* Cathedral of New York, 387; Vicar-General of New York, *id.;* President of G. T. College, *id.;* At Charleston, S. C., 388; G. T. College, 389; Bishop of Boston, 390, 392; Ursuline Convent, *id.;* His Mother, 404; Burning of the Convent, 405; College of Holy Cross, 407; His Coadjutor, 406; His Labors, *id.;* Character, 408; His Death, 411.
Fenwick, Right Rev. E. D.: His Life, I. 328; At Boonheim, 329; In Kentucky, 330; Apostle of Ohio, 331; His Labors, 333, 343-349; Dominicans, 335; Bishop of Cincinnati, 336; Poverty, 337; At Rome, 338-343; Cathedral, 343; Council, 346; Cholera, 349; Death, 351; Character, 352.
Fesch, Cardinal, I. 342.

Analytical Index.

Ffrench, Rev. C., II. 199, 398, 399.
Fitzpatrick, Right Rev. J. B.: His Life, II. 310; His Youth and Education, 311; At Montreal, 313; At Paris, 315; Ordained, 317; Mission at Boston, 318; Coadjutor, 319; Bishop of Boston, 321; Trials, 321-324; School Question, 324-329; Labors, 329, 330; His Virtues, 332-334; Death, 335.
Fitzsimmons, Rev. T., I. 57, 187.
Flaget, Right Rev. B. J., I. 104: His Life, 144; At Clermont, 145; Joins the Sulpitians, 145; Ordained, *id.*; At Nantes, *id.*; French Revolution, 146; Comes to America, *id.*; At Vincennes, *id.*; At Baltimore, 148; At G. T. College, *id.*; Gen. Washington, *id.*; At Havana, 149; Louis Philippe, *id.*; At St. Mary's College, *id.*; Wants to join the Trappists, *id.*; Bishop of Bardstown, 150; Consecrated, *id.*; Poverty, *id.*; Labors, 152; Cardinal Litta, 154; At Detroit, 155; Coadjutor, *id.*; Jubilee, 157; Dr. Kenrick, *id.*; Wants to resign, 162; At Louisville, *id.*; His Death, 163.
Fleming, Father, I. 124, 188.
Florida, I. 23, 25-27, 31, 362, 438, 442, 443.
Fort Wayne, Bishop of: Luers, II. 555; See of, 562-564; Clerical Association, 581.
Fourth of July, I. 545.
Framback, Rev. J., I. 39, 42.

G.

Gallipolis, O., I. 73.
Gallitzin, Rev. D. A., I. 491.
Galtier, Father, II. 130, 417.
Garda, I. 19, 20.
Gartland, Right Rev. S. X.: His Life, II. 408; At Philadelphia, *id.*; Pastor of St. John's, 409; Bishop of Savannah, 410; Labors, 411; Death, 413.
Garnier, Rev. F., I. 376.
Gaston, Judge, I. 375.
Gavazzi, II. 610.
Gensoul, Mother, I. 231.
Georgetown College, I. 76, 90, 92, 99, 130.
Georgia, I. 283.
Gettysburgh, Battle of, I. 514, 515.
Good Shepherd, Sisters of, I. 497, II. 69.
Greaton, Father, I. 128, 187.

Greene, Dr. I. 400.
Gregory XVI., I. 538.
Greenland, I. 15.
Gregorian Chant, I. 266.

H.

Harold, Rev. W. V., I. 189, 191, 313, 318, 320, 321.
Harrison, Gen., I. 153.
Hartford, Bishops of: Tyler, II. 272; O'Reilly, 391.
Hayti, I. 370.
Hennepin, Father, II. 417.
Henni, Bishop, I. 535, II. 297.
Henrietta Maria, Queen, I. 116.
Henrion, I. 230.
Heyden, Rev. Thomas, I. 318, 320.
Hierarchy, I. 5, 60, 66.
Hill, Rev. J. A., I. 344.
Hitzelberger, Rev. Mr., II. 34.
Hogan, Rev. Mr., I. 312-317.
Hoguet, H. L., II. 125.
Holy Cross, Order of, II. 571, 572.
Hudson, Father, I. 34.
Hunter, Rev. George, I. 38, 42.
Huronia, I. 22.
Hughes, Most Rev. J.: His Life, II. 74; In Ireland, 74; In America, 75; Mt. St. Mary's, 76; Ordained, 78; At Philadelphia, 78-86; Controversies, 78, 84, 114; *Catholic Herald*, 84; Coadjutor of New York, 87; Trusteeism, 88-90, 92; Labors, 88, 90-92, 118; Administrator of New York, 93; In Europe, 94; Daniel O'Connell, 95, 113; School Controversy, 95-110; St. John's College, 110; Know-Nothingism, 110-112; Sermons, 114, 119; Writings, 115, 119; Archbishop of New York, 116; At Rome, *id.*; Cardinal Bedini, 117; Immaculate Conception, 118; Cathedral, 120; Holy Father, 122; Mission to Europe, 123; Anti-Conscription Riot, 124; Illness, *id.*; Death, 125; Character, 74, 125.
Hynes, Rev. J. T., I. 344.

I.

Iberville, I. 114.
Illinois, II. 253-256.
Immaculate Conception, I. 506, 541, II. 67.

Indiana, II. 32, 33, 56a.
Infidel, Death of an, I. 379.
Indians, I. 6, 22-26, 84-87, 340, 345, 347, 348, 398, 399, II. 416, 477-501.
Inglesi, I. 234.
Intolerance, I. 38, 45, 52, 271, 276, 278, 280, 283, 328, 346, 433, 435, 436, 498-500.
Irish Brigade, I. 187.
Ironsides, Rev. Mr., I. 386.
Ireland, Persecution in, I. 171, 276, 278.
Irving, Washington, II. 46-56.

J.

Jackson, Gen., I. 219, 322-324.
James II., I. 33, 40.
Jesuits, I. 34-39, 98, 101, 111, 120, 194; In the West, 230, 364; In Massachusetts, 407; In Alabama 448; Indian Missions, 469, In Philadelphia, 496; In Baltimore, 505; In New Orleans, II. 62; In New York, I. 377-385, II. 110.
Juarez, Bishop, I. 21-31.
Juigné, M. de, I. 416, 417.
Joubert, Rev. Mr., I. 210, 371.
Juncker, Right Rev., H. D.: His Life, II. 529; Missions, id.; Bishop of Alton, 530; Labors, 530-534; Cathedral, 530; Visitations, 531, 534; Growth of the Church, 535; His Death, id.

K.

Kaskaskia, II. 382.
Kelly, Rev. J., II. 596.
Kelly, Rev. P., I. 199.
Kelly, Right Rev. P.: Life of, I. 268; President of Birchfield College, id.; Bishop of Richmond, id.; At Norfolk, id.; Poverty, 269; Teaches School, id.; Labors, id.; Translated, 270; Death, id.
Kenrick, Most Rev. F. P.: His Life, I. 473; Character, 474, 494, 507-510; Propaganda, 475-478; Ordained, 475; In Kentucky, 476-478; Jubilee, 479, 480; Coadjutor of Philadelphia, 483; Schism, 484-488; Pittsburg, 490; Seminary, 485, 493; Labors, 490; St. Charles Borromeo, 495; Institutions, 495, 497, 501, 502, 505; Philadelphia riots, 498-500, 502; Cathedral, id.; Archbishop of Baltimore, 503; National Council, id.; At Rome, 506; His Writings, 510-513; Death, 515, 516 Epitaph, 517.
Kentucky, Clergy in, I. 87.
Kewley, Rev. Mr., I. 386.
Kinsella, Rev. Mr., II. 258.
Kohlman, Rev. A., In New York, I. 377; Tom Paine, 279; Administrator in New York, 385.
Know-Nothingism, I. 495-500, II. 110-112

L.

Lafont, Rev. A., II. 603.
Lalor, Alice, I. 127-129, 131, 134.
Lalumiere, Rev. Mr., II. 34.
Lamy, Bishop, I. 541.
Langhill, Rev. A., I. 199.
Las Casas, I. 22.
Lavialle, Right Rev. J.: His Life, II. 586; Priesthood, id.; Bishop of Louisville 587; Death, 588; Character. 589.
Lazarists, I. 353, 358, 364, 530, II. 62, 204, 339-351.
Lee, Ex-Governor of Maryland, I. 419.
Lefevre, Right Rev. P. P.: His Life, II. 191; In Missouri, 192, 193; In Europe, 193; Coadjutor Bishop of Detroit, id., St. Ann's Church, 194; Cathedral, 195; Labors, 196-202; American College of Louvain, 199; Education, id., 200; Death, 202.
Legendre, Father, II. 422.
Levadoux, Rev. Mr., I. 87.
Levins, Rev. Mr., I. 435.
Lewis, Rev. Mr., I. 59, 123.
Liberia, I. 469, II. 595.
Liege, I. 35, 37.
Litta, Cardinal, I. 316.
Little Rock, Byrne, Bishop of, II. 264.
Loras, Right Rev. M.: His Life, II. 126; Education and Ordination, 127; At Mobile, 128; Bishop of Dubuque, 129; In Europe, id.; His Labors, 129-144; Immigration, 134; Indians, 136; Catholic Education, 138; Trappists, 139; In Europe again, 140; His Character, 144; Death, 146.
Loughlin, Bishop, I. 516, II. 125, 613.
Louis Philippe, I. 182, 236.
Louvain, American College of, II. 199.
Loyola College, I. 93, 505.

Analytical Index. 625

Lucas, Rev. J., I. 39.
Luers, Right Rev. J. H.: His Life, II. 555; An Emigrant, 556; At Seminary in Ohio, 558; Ordained, 559; Mission in Cincinnati, 560, 561; Bishop of Fort Wayne, 563; His Labors, 567, 572, 581, 583; Cathedral, *id.*; At Rome, 570; Orphans, 573–581; His Death, 584.
Lulworth Castle, I. 74, 76.
Luzerne, Marquis de la, I. 187.
Lynch, Bishop, II. 68.
Lynch, Dominick, I. 57, 199.

M.

McAleer, Rev. M., II. 154.
McCaffrey, V. Rev. Dr., II. 7–42, 411.
McCarthy, Abbé, I. 416.
McCloskey, Most Rev. J., I. 516, 536, II. 112, 121, 125.
McGill, Bishop, I. 161, 541, 544, II. 552.
McElroy, Father, II. 124.
Mackinaw, I. 345.
McNeirny, Rev. F., II. 125.
Madison, Prot. Ep. Bishop, I. 76.
Maine, Indians of, I. 84, 87.
Malou, Rev. P., I. 194.
Manners, Rev. M., I. 34, 39.
Marcy, Mr., II. 216.
Maréchal, Most Rev. A.: His Life, I. 239; A Lawyer, 240; French Revolution, *id.*; A Sulpitian Priest, 241; Flight to America, *id.*; Missionary, 242; At St. Mary's and G. T. Colleges, *id.*; In France, *id.*, 243; Returns to Baltimore, 244; Declines Bishopric of Philadelphia, *id.*; Coadjutor of Baltimore, *id.*; Archbishop, 245; Troubles, 246; Pastoral, 247; Cathedral, 248; At Rome, 249; In Canada, 250; Death, *id.*; Character, 251–253.
Marquette and Saut St. Mary, Bishop of, 468.
Mary, B. V., I. 81, 90, 536, 538, II. 67, 452.
Maryland, I. 34, 38, 40, 45, 65, 117, 120, 259, 374, 506.
Martinez, Father, II. 161.
Matthews, V. Rev. W., I. 311, 312, 321; Rev. Ignatius, 120.
Mathew, Rev. Theobold, I. 495.
Matignon, Abbé, I. 87, 175, 241.
Martyrs, I. 18, 93, 31, 350, 398, 524, II. 308, 525.

Martins, Father, I. 23.
Maurice, Rev. J. M., II. 597.
Mazzuchelli, Father, II. 129, 416.
Mercy, Fathers of, I. 448; Sisters of, 299, 306, 505.
Meurin, Father, II. 380.
Miles, Right Rev. R. P.: His Life, II. 147; Missions, 148; Convent of St. Catharine, *id.*; Bishop of Nashville, 149; Labors, 150–155; Cathedral, 154; Death, 155.
Minnesota, II. 429.
Mississippi, Valley of, I. 22.
Missouri, I. 360.
Mobile, Bay of, I. 29; See of, II. 603, 446–455; Bishops of: Portier, I. 438; Quinlan, II. 67.
Mollyneux, Father, I. 47, 90, 98, 131.
Moni, Abbé, I. 446.
Moranvillé, Abbé, I. 178.
Morris, Rev. P., I. 39.
Mosely, Rev. J., I. 39.
Mt. Carmel, Congregation of Our Lord of, II. 69.
Mt. St. Mary's College, I. 422–424.
Moylan, Col. S., I. 187.
Mullanphy, John, I. 364.
Mullon, Rev. J., I. 343, 344.

N.

Nagot, Rev. Mr., I. 206.
Narragansett Bay, I. 16, 17.
Narvaez, Pamphilo, I. 25–30.
Nashville, Bishops of: Miles, II. 147; Whelan, 155; Feehan, II. 590.
Natchez, Bishops of: Chanche, II. 166, Van de Velde, 372; Elder, 69; History of the Church at, 170–177; Cathedral, 179; Sisters of Charity, 186–188; In Europe, 187; At Baltimore, 189; Death, *id.*
Nauvoo, II. 381.
Neale, Capt. James, I. 116.
Neale, Most Rev. L.: His Life, I. 116; At St. Omers, 117; Bruges, 119; Liége, *id.*; Suppression of S. J., 120; In England, *id.*; Demerara, 121; In Maryland, 122, 123; In Philadelphia, 124; Yellow Fever, *id.*; Visitation Order, 127, 131–136; President of G. T. College, 129; Coadjutor of Baltimore, 130; Consecration, 131; Archbishop, 134; Administration, 134–138; Death, *id.*

Neale, Rev. Benedict, I. 39.
Nerinckx, Rev. C., I. 152, 154, 376.
Neumann, Right Rev. J. N.: His Life, II. 431; His Youth, 432–437; Theology, 437; In New York, 439; Ordained, *id.*; Missions, 440–442; Redemptorist, 442–445; Bishop of Philadelphia, 446; His Labors, 448–451, 454–459; At Rome, 451, 452; Immaculate Conception, *id.*; Crucifix, 459–466; His Death, 466.
New Melleray, II. 140.
New Orleans, Bishops of, I. 5, 6; Archbishopric, 542; Penalvery Cardenas, 114; Porro, 139; Dubourg, 205; De Neckere, 518; Blanc, II. 58; Odin, 203; Perché, 236.
Newport, I. 18.
New York, Bishops of: Concanen, I. 140; Egan, 185; Dubois, 414; Hughes, II. 73; McCloskey, 112; Yellow Fever, 902; Cathedral, 387.
Norridgewalk, Massacre, I. 401.
North Carolina, I. 283.
Northmen in America, I. 13, 15, 19.
Nott, Rev. Dr., II. 98.

O.

Oath of Bishops, I. 549.
O'Connell, Daniel, I. 279.
O'Connor, S. J., Dr. M., I. 501, 506, 512, 514, 515, 536, 544, II. 521.
Odin, Most Rev. J. M.: His Life, II. 203; A Lazarist, 204; In Missouri, 205; Ordained, *id.*; Missions, 206–210; In Texas, 210–214; V. A. of Texas, 214; History of Church in Texas, *id.*; Labors, 219–226; Archbishop of New Orleans, 226–239; In Rome, 234; His Services, 235; Council of Vatican, 236; His Death, 237.
O'Gallagher, Father, I. 285, 286.
O'Gorman, Rev. M., I. 193, 197, 199, 203.
Ohio, I. 73, 331, 334, 340.
Oliver, Father, I. 443.
Olivier, Rev. Mr., I. 97.
O'Meally, Rev. T., I. 317.
Orders, Religious, I. 26, 127, 300, 364, 497, 505, 528, 529, 536.
Oregon, I. 6.
O'Reilly, Rev. E. J., II. 252.
O'Reilly, Right Rev. B.: His Life, II. 391; Ordained, 392; Labors at New York, 392, 393; Rochester, 394–396; Buffalo, 396; Bishop of Hartford, 397; Labors 398–402; in Europe, 402; Died at Sea, 402–407.
Orr (Angel Gabriel), II. 615.
Otto, Father, II. 565.

P.

Paine, Thomas, I. 379.
Paraguay, I. 22.
Paresce, Father, I. 93.
Paulmeyer, Abbé, I. 227.
Pelamourgues, II. 129, 132.
Pellents, Rev. J., I. 39.
Penn, Wm., I. 185.
Pennsylvania, Catholics in, I. 65; Clergy, 38, 65, 87; Toleration under Penn, 185, Intolerance under William III., 186.
Pensacola, I. 442.
Perché, Archbishop, II. 225, 236.
Petiot, Father, II. 129.
Petit, Rev. Mr., II. 34.
Peyri, Father, II. 161.
Peyrogrosse, Father, II. 422.
Phelan, Father, I. 88.
Philadelphia, See of, I. 5, 104; During the Revolution, 187; Riots, 186, 498–500; Bishops of: Egan, 185; Conwell, 310; Kenrick, 473; Neumann, II. 431; Wood, 516; Proposed for first Bishopric, I. 73, 188; Father Greaton in, 176; Schism, 189, 190, 312, 322, 484, 488.
Philodemic Society, II. 153.
Pilgrims, Catholic, of Maryland, I. 374.
Pius IX., I. 538–540.
Plowden, Rev. Mr., I. 74.
Plunket, Father, I. 91.
Poor Clares, I. 131, 133.
Porro, Right Rev. F., I. 139.
Portier, Right Rev. M.: His Life, 438; Seminary at Lyons, 439; Volunteers for the Mission of Louisiana, 439; At Baltimore, 440; Ordained at St. Louis, *id.*; Labors, 441, 442; Yellow fever, *id.*; New Orleans, *id.*; Vicar Apostolic of Florida, *id.*; Consecration, 443; Poverty and Labors, 444, 445, 449, 451; Europe, 446; Bishop of Mobile, 447; Spring Hill College, 448; Visitation Nuns, 450; Cathedral, 451; Institutions, *id.*; Brothers of

Christian Instruction, 452; Councils, 453; Death, 454; Character and Writings, 455.
Power, Rev. Dr., I. 435; II. 100, 267.
Powis, Lord, I. 33.
Propagation of the Faith, Association for, I. 203, 225, 233.
Proyart, Abbé, I. 415.
Purcell, Archbishop, I. 161, II. 68, 296, 516, 557, 573.
Penalver y Cardenas. I. 114,

Q.

Quarter, Right Rev. W.: His Life, II. 240; His youth, 241-245; Mt. St. Mary's, 245; In New York, 247; Ordained, 248; Cholera, 249; St. Mary's Church, 250; Bishop of Chicago, 257; Consecrated, *id.*; at Chicago, *id.*; Education, 258; Cathedral, 259; Seminary, 259-262; Death, 263.
Quincy, Ills., II. 387.
Quincy, Josiah, Jr., I. 410.
Quinn, Rev. W., II. 124.

R.

Rale, Father, I. 22, 298, 398, 400, 401.
Rappe, Bishop, I. 536.
Ravoux, Father, II. 130, 132, 136, 419.
Redemptorists, I. 529, II. 62, 199, 442, 445.
Religious Liberty, I. 40, 52, 55, 117, 374, 375.
Republic, Catholics and the, I. 50, 53, 55, 56, 187.
Retreats, first introduced in United States, I. 259.
Revolution, American, I. 37, 42, 187, 272.
Revolution in Italy, II. 605.
Reynolds, Right Rev. I. A.: His Life, II. 291; At Bardstown, 292; At St. Mary's, *id.*; Ordained, *id.*; Labors in Kentucky, 293-295; In Europe, 294; Bishop of Charleston, 296; Pastorals, 296, 297, 301, 307; Labors, 299; Cathedral, 204; Bishop England's Works, 306; His Death, 308.
Richard, Rev. Mr., I. 87, 145, 241, 346, 350.
Richmond, Bishops of: Kelly, I. 268; Whelan, 516, 535, 541, II. 155; McGill, I. 161, 541, 544, II. 552.

Rio de las Palmas, I. 23, 26.
Rivet, Rev. Mr., I. 87.
Robespierre, I. 416.
Rock Creek, I. 38.
Roels, Rev. L., I. 39, 124.
Rome, I. 7, 36, 353, 474.
Romagné, Rev. Mr., I. 87, 401.
Rosati, Right Rev. J.: His Life, I. 353; Joins the Lazarists, *id.*; Father de Andreis, 354; Ordained, *id.*; Prophecy, 355; Joins Bishop Dubourg, 365; At St. Louis, 358; The Barrens, *id.*; Missionary, 359, 361; Superior of Lazarists, *id.*; Coadjutor of New Orleans, 362; Bishop of St. Louis, *id.*; Labors, 363, 367; Jesuits, 364; A mutual Benediction, 366; Cathedral, *id.*; Councils, 367; Pastorals, *id.*; At Boston, 368; Canada, 369; At Rome, 370; Hayti, *id.*, 372, 373; Coadjutor, 370; Returns to Rome, 373; Death, *id.*
Rosecrans, Bishop, II. 590.
Russia, Jesuits in, I. 98.
Ryan, Father, I. 320, 321.

S.

Sacred Heart, Sisters of, I. 364, 496, II. 110, 200.
St. Agnes' Convent, II. 149.
St. Catharine's Convent, II. 148, 153.
St. Charles Borromeo, Seminary of, I. 485, 493, 494.
St. Charles College, I. 530.
St. Domingo, Negro Insurrection, I. 209.
St. John's College, II. 110.
St. Joseph's College, Philadelphia, I. 496.
St. Louis, See of, I. 6, 362; Population, 361; Bishop Rosati, 362; University, 363, II. 377; Hospital, I. 365; Cathedral, 366.
St. Mary's College and Seminary, Baltimore, I. 76, 91, 208, 527.
St. Mary's of the Lake, University, II. 258.
St. Omers, I. 34, 36.
St. Paul, Bishops of: Cretin, II. 415; Grace, 149; Father Hennepin, 417; History of, 417-420.
St. Rose's Convent, I. 330.
St. Sulpice, II. 315.

St. Vincent de Paul, Society of, I. 211, II. 549.
Sanchez, Father, II. 161.
San Francisco, I. 6.
Sarria, Father, II. 162.
Savannah, Bishops of: Gartland, II. 408; Barry, 551.
Scandinavian Relics, I. 18, 19.
Schneller, Father, I. 435, II. 100.
Schools, Catholic, I. 469, 528, 530, II. 95-110, 324.
Scott, M., I. 332.
Seton, Mother, I. 94, 95, 193, 212, 261, 364.
Sewall, Rev. C., I. 39.
Seward, Governor, II. 98-100, 105-108.
Shanahan, Father, I. 195, 197, 199, 204.
Shaeffer, Rev. Mr., I. 222.
Shipwreck, II. 405.
Sisters of Charity, I. 94, 364, 396, II. 69, 333, 186-188, 200, 298, 356.
Sisters of Immaculate Heart of Mary, II. 200.
Sisters of Mercy, I. 110, 299, 306, 505, II. 259, 269.
Sisters of St. Joseph, I. 364, 396, II. 422, 424.
Slevin, John, II. 512.
Smarius, Father, 570.
Smith, Buckingham, I. 24, 30.
Smyth, Right Rev. C.: His Life, II. 536; His youth, 537; Trinity College, 538; Brother of the Presentation, *id.*; A Trappist, 539; Melleray, 542; A Priest, 543; In America, 544; New Melleray, 545; Coadjutor of Dubuque, 546; Bishop of Dubuque, 547; His Labors, 547-549; In Europe, 549; His Death, 550.
Somers, Rev. William, II. 563.
Sourin, Father, II. 571.
South Carolina, I. 283.
Spalding, Archbishop, I. 162, 373, 452, 416, 523.
Spring Hill College, I. 448.
Starrs, V. Rev. W., II. 125.
Stehle, Rev. Mr., II. 563.
Synod, First, I. 83, 89.

T.

Taylor, Rev. Dr., I. 391, 429.
Temporal Power of the Popes, I. 542.

Tessier, Rev. J., I. 210.
Texas, II. 214.
Thorpe, Father, I. 63.
Timon, Right Rev. J.: His Life, II. 337; His youth, 338; Joins the Lazarists, 339; Ordained, 341; Labors, 341, 346, 354, 363, 364; In France, 345; Texas, 345-351; Bishop of Buffalo, 352; Installed, 353; St. Louis Church, 355; Sisters of Charity, 356; Institutions, 357-359; In Mexico, 359; In Europe, *id.*; Pastoral, 363; Virtues, 366; His Death, 369.
Tompkins, Governor, I. 378.
Tornatori, Rev. J. B., I. 363.
Torres, Francisco, I. 369.
Torquemada, I. 24, 26.
Trappists: In New York, I. 378; In Iowa, 139, II. 539-542, 544.
Troy Seminary, II. 123.
Trusteeism, I. 98, 197, 315-322, 430, 484-490; II. 63, 194.
Tuite, Rev. W. R., I. 329.
Tyler, Right Rev. W.: His Life, II. 273; His Youth, 274-281; Ordained, 282; Mission at Boston, *id.*; Bishop of Hartford, 283; His Episcopate, 283-287; His Death, 289.

U.

Ugo Bassi, II. 607.
Ursulines: At Boston, I. 175, 392, 405; At New Orleans, 232; At Charleston, S. C., 299, 302, 306, II. 298.

V.

Van de Velde, Right Rev. J. O.: His Life, II. 372; His Youth, 373; In America, 375; Joins the Jesuits, *id.*; Ordained, 376; Mission in Maryland, *id.*; Goes to the West, 377; Rome, *id.*; Bishop of Chicago, 378; His Labors, 379-387; In Europe, 385; Transferred to Natchez, 387-390; His Death, 390.
Van Quickenborn, Father, I. 443.
Varela, Father, I. 435.
Vatican Council, I. 511.
Villanova College, I. 496.
Vincennes, I. 147; Bishops of: Bruté, II. 7; Hailandiere, 371; Bazin, 570; De St. Palais, II. 590.

Analytical Index.

Vinland, I. 16-18.
Virginia, Catholics in, I. 40; The Churches in, 268.
Vischering, Bishop of Cologne, I. 534.
Visitation Order, I. 94, 127, 131, 136, 364, 459, 497, 529, 543.

W.

Wallace, Rev. Dr., I. 389.
Wardour Castle, I. 37.
Warmsley, Bishop of London, I. 74.
Washington, Gen., I. 56, 58, 87, 187.
Wayne, Gen., I. 147.
Weld, Thomas, I. 74.
Wharton, Rev. C. H., I. 51.
Wheeling, Va., I. 269.
Whelan, Bishop, I. 516, 535, 541, II. 155.
Whitfield, Right Rev. A.: His Life, I. 456; At Lyons, 457; Archbishop, 460; His Labors, 449, 460, 497; Orphan Asylum, 461; Councils, 463-470; Jubilee, 466; Cathedral, 467; Episcopal residence, 468; Death, 471; Character, 472.
Williams, Bishop, II. 331.
Wilson, Rev. T., I. 329, 331.
Wood, Bishop, I. 516, II. 68.
Woodstock College, I. 92.

Y.

Young Catholic Friend Society, I. 211, 230.
Young, Rev. N. D., I. 334, 341, 343.
Young, Right Rev. J. M.: His Life, II. 514; Ancestors, 514-517; A Printer, 518; A Convert, 519; At Cincinnati, 520; A Priest, id.; Mission, id.; Bishop of Erie, 521-522; His Labors, 523-526; Death, id.

Z.

Zalvidia, Father, II. 139.

THE END.

www.ingramcontent.com/pod-product-compliance
Lightning Source LLC
Chambersburg PA
CBHW021225300426
44111CB00007B/427